T0374824

Also by Geoffrey Roberts

The Unholy Alliance: Stalin's Pact with Hitler
The Soviet Union and the Origins of the Second World War
The Soviet Union in World Politics, 1945–1991
Ireland and the Second World War (co-edited with Brian Girvin)
The History and Narrative Reader (editor)
Victory at Stalingrad: The Battle That Changed History
Stalin – His Times and Ours (editor)
Stalin's Wars: From World War to Cold War, 1939–1953
Molotov: Stalin's Cold Warrior
Stalin's General: The Life of Georgy Zhukov
Churchill and Stalin: Comrades-in-Arms during the Second World War
(with Martin Folly & Oleg Rzheshevsky)

STALIN'S LIBRARY

A DICTATOR AND HIS BOOKS

GEOFFREY ROBERTS

YALE UNIVERSITY PRESS
NEW HAVEN AND LONDON

For information about this and other Yale University Press publications, please contact:
U.S. Office: sales.press@yale.edu yalebooks.com
Europe Office: sales@yaleup.co.uk yalebooks.co.uk

Set in Minion Pro by IDSUK (DataConnection) Ltd
Printed in Great Britain by TJ Books, Padstow, Cornwall

Library of Congress Control Number: 2021946778

ISBN 978-0-300-17904-0

A catalogue record for this book is available from the British Library.

10 9 8 7 6 5 4 3 2 1

With thanks to Moscow friends

CONTENTS

List of Plates   *viii*

Introduction: The Kremlin Scholar   1

1. Bloody Tyrant and Bookworm   6
2. The Search for the Stalin Biographers' Stone   18
3. Reading, Writing and Revolution   36
4. The Life and Fate of a Dictator's Library   66
5. Bah Humbug! Stalin's *Pometki*   97
6. Reverse Engineering: Stalin and Soviet Literature   171
7. Editor-in-Chief of the USSR   190

Conclusion: The Dictator Who Loved Books   210

Notes   *213*
Further Reading   *244*
Acknowledgements   *246*
Index   *249*

PLATES

1. Stalin working in his Kremlin office, 1938.
2. Shushanika Manuchar'yants, 1960s.
3. Nadezhda Alliluyeva, 1917.
4. Stalin with his two youngest children, Vasily and Svetlana, 1935.
5. Stalin's handwritten library classification scheme, May 1925. Stalin Digital Archive, Yale University Press.
6. Title page of Nikolai Bukharin's *Revolutsionnyi Teoretik*. Stalin Digital Archive, Yale University Press.
7. Page from Lenin's *One Step Forward, Two Steps Back*. Stalin Digital Archive, Yale University Press.
8. Page from Karl Kautsky's *Terrorism and Communism*. Stalin Digital Archive, Yale University Press.
9. Front cover of *Lenin, Conspirationalism, and October*. Stalin Digital Archive, Yale University Press.
10. Front cover of Andrei Shestakov's *Short Course History of the USSR*. RGASPI.
11. Stalin's doodles on the back cover of Alexei Tolstoy's *Ivan Grozny*. RGASPI.
12. Page from an article on contemporary military art. Stalin Digital Archive, Yale University Press.
13. Pages from a draft of the *Short Course History of the CPSU*. Stalin Digital Archive, Yale University Press.
14. Page from a report on the discussion of the *Political Economy* textbook. Stalin Digital Archive, Yale University Press.

INTRODUCTION
The Kremlin Scholar

This book explores the intellectual life and biography of one of history's blood-iest dictators: Joseph Stalin. Uniquely, it does so through the prism of his personal library. A dedicated reader and self-improver, Stalin's accumulation of books was a lifelong passion. In the mid-1920s he acquired an identity for his library in the form of an ex-libris stamp – *Biblioteka I. V. Stalina* – the Library of J. V. Stalin. He also devised his own library classification scheme and engaged the services of a librarian. The centrepiece of his main Moscow dacha (country house) was a grand library room, though most of his vast collection was housed in an adjoining building with books delivered to him by staff. Dmitry Shepilov, who visited the dacha the day after the dictator died, recalled 'a large writing desk, with a second desk placed against it to form a T, both were piled high with books, manuscripts and papers, as were the little tables around the room'. Stalin himself lay dead on the couch in his library, where he had been struck down by a stroke a few days earlier.[1]

Shepilov, an economist by background, was editor-in-chief of *Pravda*. In 1956–7 he served as Soviet foreign minister, but lost office when he supported a failed attempt to oust from power Nikita Khrushchev, Stalin's successor as leader of the communist party. Shepilov was mainly an apparatchik and the title of the English edition of his memoirs, *The Kremlin's Scholar*, was something of a misnomer. But it was an appellation that could more justifiably have been applied to his dead boss.[2]

By the time of his death, Stalin's library contained some 25,000 books, peri-odicals and pamphlets. The collection might have been preserved intact but the plan to turn his dacha into a Stalin Museum was shelved following Khrushchev's denunciation of him and his personality cult at the 20th party congress in February 1956. Instead, the dictator's books were dispersed to other libraries, though important remnants and traces of his library survived in the communist party's archives, notably a collection of nearly 400 texts that he had marked and annotated. Rediscovered when Soviet communism disintegrated in the late 1980s, these *pometki* – or markings – revealed that Stalin was a serious intellectual who valued ideas as much as power. A true believer in the power of words, he read not only to learn but also to acquire a higher communist consciousness, seen as central to the utopian goals of Soviet socialism. An ideologue as well as an intellectual, Stalin's professed belief in Marxism-Leninism was wholly authentic, as can be seen from the library.

History was Stalin's favourite subject, followed closely by Marxist theory, and then fiction. Lenin was his favourite author but he also read, and sometimes appreciated, a great deal of writing by Leon Trotsky and other arch-enemies. As an internationalist, Stalin's interests were global, but he lacked command of any languages except Russian and his native Georgian, so his reading of foreign books was limited to those that had been translated.[3] He was very interested in ancient history and preoccupied with the lessons of Tsarist rule in Russia, especially the reigns of Ivan the Terrible and the Greats, Peter and Catherine. He read a good deal of military history and greatly admired Tsarist hero-generals such as Alexander Suvorov, the eighteenth-century strategist who never lost a battle, and Marshal Mikhail Kutuzov, who defeated Napoleon in 1812. More surprising, perhaps, was his fascination with Germany's 'Iron Chancellor', Otto von Bismarck. He also had high personal regard for other bourgeois statesmen, like fellow history buff Winston Churchill, and Franklin Delano Roosevelt, the US president whose country's constitution he studied.

While Stalin composed no memoirs and kept no diary he left a well-marked literary trail not only in the books he wrote and edited but in those he read as well. Through an examination of these books it is possible to build a composite, nuanced picture of the reading life of the twentieth century's most self-consciously intellectual dictator.

This book's first chapter, 'Bloody Tyrant and Bookworm', provides an overview of Stalin, the Bolshevik intellectual who revered written texts. Like all the Bolshevik leaders, he believed that reading could help transform not just people's ideas and consciousness but human nature itself.

'It is impossible to know somebody "inside out",' wrote Stalin to the poet Demyan Bedny in 1924,[4] but through his library we can get to know him from the outside in. In viewing the world through Stalin's eyes we can picture his personality as well as his most intimate thoughts.

Stalin was no psychopath but an emotionally intelligent and feeling intellectual. Indeed, it was the power of his emotional attachment to deeply held beliefs that enabled him to sustain decades of brutal rule.

INTRODUCTION

Chapter Two, 'The Search for the Stalin Biographers' Stone', broaches the issue of his biography by examining the dictator's own sparse accounts of his early life and his responses to official efforts to construct authorised versions of his personal story. Equally important is the chapter's treatment of Stalin's extensive involvement in the project to publish his collected works. Stalin viewed his many articles, speeches, lectures, pamphlets and booklets as a vital intellectual legacy. These were the works that he wanted to frame the writing of his biography. Incomplete at the time of his death in March 1953, the project was cancelled by Khrushchev, but the thirteen published volumes remain an essential source for understanding Stalin's life and thought, not least for those biographers who view Stalin as he saw himself – as an activist political intellectual.

Chapter Three, 'Reading, Writing and Revolution', is dedicated to the young Stalin. It examines Stalin's formation as an underground revolutionary, paying particular attention to his education, intellectual life and reading habits. Stalin's engagement with books began at an early age. He attended a church school and received his higher education in a seminary. He aspired to go to university to become a professor but in the face of Tsarist oppression opted for the life of a political activist.

The book the young Stalin read and studied most intensively was perforce the Christian Bible, but there is no evidence his religious upbringing had any profound, long-term effects. In becoming a Bolshevik, Stalin swapped a religious faith for a secular one but the absence of a deity in his new ideology meant that Marxism's claims to truth were rooted in science, not revelation. Stalin was as hostile to the church as any other Bolshevik and pursued a policy of harsh anti-religious repression when he gained power. For reasons of expediency there was a reconciliation with the Russian Orthodox Church and other faiths during the Second World War, but there is no evidence that Stalin retained any religious beliefs.

The chapter ends with Stalin's appointment as the party's general-secretary in 1922 and the ensuing controversy about 'Lenin's Testament' after the death of Bolshevism's founder in 1924. Stalin survived the criticisms levelled at him by Lenin in the so-called testament and emerged politically stronger and intellectually more confident. And his dedication to Lenin's memory was unabated.

Chapter Four, 'The Life and Fate of a Dictator's Library', begins in 1925 and tells the story of the creation, fragmentation and part resurrection of Stalin's personal library. It explores the dictator's reading interests and what he learned from books. It continues the treatment of Stalin's biography with a section on family life and his wife's suicide in 1932. It recounts what happened to the library after his death and summarises the scholarly reimagining of Stalin prompted by the rediscovery of the library's remnants.

Chapter Five, 'Bah Humbug! Stalin's *Pometki*', is a detailed, thematic exploration of Stalin's many marks and notes in the books he read. It begins by locating Stalin's markings within the venerable humanist tradition of writing in books as a means to assimilate new ideas and information. Stalin could be a highly active, engaged and methodical reader. The material traces of his reading reveal his interests, thoughts and emotional responses to the texts that he marked.

Stalin's life was one long performance in which he played many different parts. There was certainly an element of performance in his book markings, since he must have suspected that they would become an object of study. But they are the closest we will ever get to the spontaneous Stalin, an intellectual immersed in thinking.

Among the surprises of this chapter is that during the early post-revolutionary years, Stalin had a higher regard for Trotsky than most people think. After Marx, Engels and Lenin, Stalin learned more from Trotsky than anyone else.

Stalin's *pometki* are examined alongside the analysis of some key episodes in his biography: the intra-party power struggles of the 1920s, the Great Terror of 1937–8, the spymania of the 1930s and 1940s, the emergence of a Soviet patriotism, military affairs and the Great Patriotic War, and his interventions in postwar debates in philosophy, science, psychology and linguistics.

The title of Chapter Six, 'Reverse Engineering: Stalin and Soviet Literature', references Stalin's famous statement that the role of writers in a socialist society was to be 'engineers of the human soul'. Stalin read a lot of fiction and his library contained many thousands of novels, plays and volumes of poetry. Alas, because he didn't mark, stamp or autograph works of fiction, only a handful of these texts survived the dispersal of his library. However, from the late 1920s onwards, he had a lot to say about literature – not only poetry, novels and short stories, but plays and film scripts. From these remarks it is possible to infer what kind of literature he liked and how he read it.

Stalin was also an inveterate editor. Mostly, he edited documents, hundreds of which crossed his desk or passed through his office on a daily basis. But, as shown in Chapter Seven, 'Editor-in-Chief of the USSR', he was also involved in some notable book projects, including the revision of the postwar edition of his official *Short Biography*. In his 1956 denunciation, Khrushchev claimed Stalin embellished the biography to inflate his sense of self-importance. In reality, Stalin toned down the adulation. Even more striking was the way he reduced his personal presence in the notorious *Short Course History of the Communist Party of the Soviet Union* (1938) – a party textbook that denounced his enemies as degenerates, assassins and spies. Stalin's editing of these and other books was detailed enough for him to be considered a de facto co-author. Although there was nothing sophisticated about Stalin's editing, he was highly adept at marshalling material to convey simple and clear political messages.

Stalin retained considerable intellectual powers to the very end of his life. 'I'm seventy years old,' he told his errant son Vasily, pointing to the books he was reading on history, literature and military affairs. 'Yet I go on learning just the same.'⁵ By the early 1950s, however, with both his physical health and his intellect in decline, he was past his prime.

Anatoly Lunacharsky, Soviet commissar for enlightenment in the 1920s, described himself as an 'intellectual among Bolsheviks and a Bolshevik among intellectuals'.⁶ The same was true for Stalin, except that he was more Bolshevik than intellectual and lacked the scepticism that might have led him to moderate his deadly pursuit of socialist utopia.

CHAPTER 1

BLOODY TYRANT AND BOOKWORM

A bloody tyrant, a machine politician, a paranoid personality, a heartless bureaucrat, and an ideological fanatic. To a degree, Stalin was all those stereotypes. But he was also an intellectual who devoted himself to endless reading, writing and editing – solitary activities punctuated by the meetings he attended and the speeches he gave. Texts, written and spoken, were his world.

Given the scale of his misdeeds as Soviet ruler, it is natural to imagine Stalin as a monster, to see him in the mind's eye furiously denouncing opponents, betraying former comrades, poring over coerced confessions, ordering executions, turning a deaf ear to pleas of innocence and coldly ignoring the colossal human costs of his communist dystopia. Moral revulsion, however, is no substitute for explaining how and why Stalin was able to do what he did.

This book views Stalin through a different lens – as a dedicated idealist and as an activist intellectual who valued ideas as much as power, who was ceaseless in his own efforts at self-education, a restless mind, reading for the revolution to the very end of his life. It tells the story of the creation, fragmentation and part resurrection of his personal library. It explores the books Stalin read, how he read them and what they taught him.

Isaac Deutscher, one of Stalin's earliest and greatest biographers, thought that his 'socialism was cold, sober and rough'.[1] A key insight of this study of Stalin's life as a reader is the emotional power that imbued his ideas. In the marked books of Stalin's personal library we can glimpse his feelings as well as the ideas to which he attached so much significance. It was not psychosis but the vigour of Stalin's personal belief system that enabled him to initiate and sustain the barbarous methods he used to modernise and communise Soviet Russia. While Stalin hated his enemies – the bourgeoisie, kulaks, capitalists, imperialists, reactionaries, counter-revolutionaries, traitors – he detested their ideas even more.

As in Al Alvarez's definition of an intellectual, Stalin was someone to whom ideas were emotionally important.[2] This view of the nature of Stalin's intellectuality chimes with the idea that while he was an 'Enlightenment revolutionary' – a 'scientific socialist' who believed that socialism was a rational goal to be secured by reason – he was also a post-Enlightenment romantic who saw socialism as a human creation that could only be achieved through struggle, mobilisation and personal commitment.[3] Because he felt so strongly himself about what he was trying to achieve, it is not surprising that Stalin considered 'emotionally charged mobilization ... a vital instrument to accomplish ultra-rationalist goals' and 'was keenly aware of the mobilizational role of the emotions'.[4] For Stalin, striving to build socialism was a highly personal and voluntaristic project, and when the results of struggle disappointed, he invariably found the people, not the cause, to be wanting. He would surely have agreed with Fidel Castro's comment that while socialism had many defects and shortcomings, 'these deficiencies are not in the system, they are in the people'.[5]

It is sometimes said that Stalin was a psychopath who lacked empathy for the victims of his many crimes against humanity. 'One death is a tragedy, a million is a statistic' is an oft-cited apocryphal statement attributed to him. It encapsulates the idea that as an intellectual he could both rationalise and abstract himself from his terrible rule. Actually, Stalin had a high degree of emotional intelligence. What he lacked was compassion or sympathy for those he deemed enemies of the revolution. If anything, he had too much human empathy and used it to imagine the worst in people, inventing a mass of fictitious acts of betrayal and treachery – a critical ingredient of the Great Terror that swept through Soviet society in the 1930s, engulfing millions of innocent victims arrested, imprisoned, deported or shot for political crimes. Many lesser terrors followed, culminating with the grotesque 'Doctors' Plot' of the early 1950s, when scores of medics, many of them Jewish, were arrested for allegedly conspiring to murder Soviet leaders. Among those swept up in the last waves of unwarranted arrests were his long-time private secretary, Alexander Poskrebyshev, and the chief of his personal security detail, General Nikolai Vlasik, the former guardian of his young children.[6]

Like many politicians and public figures, Stalin was a subject constructed from the outside inwards; a politically driven personality, someone whose inner mental life was shaped by his public persona and by the ideological universe he chose to inhabit. Stalin was akin to a method actor who interiorised many roles in a performance that he sustained for a lifetime.

This interiorisation of his political selves began with a youthful flirtation with nationalism and populism that resulted in an enduring romantic streak in his personal make-up. Then, as a hardened Bolshevik agitator and propagandist, he reinvented himself as an *intelligent* and *praktik*, dedicated to enlightening and organising the masses.[7] His experience of the revolutionary upheavals of 1905 and 1917 habituated him to political violence. But it was the Russian Civil War, during which he implemented the harshest measures of Bolshevik repression, that inured him to large-scale loss of human life and marked his transition from romantic revolutionary to ruthless practitioner of realpolitik. Appointed the party's general-secretary in April 1922, he then positioned himself as the consummate administrator of a Soviet state apparatus that he helped create as well as serve.

The Soviet regime was nothing if not bureaucratic and what Stalin mostly read were the myriad of documents that crossed his desk every day. Yet he always found time for his personal collection of books, pamphlets and periodicals. On documents he scrawled decisions and directives for action. His innermost interests and feelings were reserved for the *pometki* – the annotations and markings he made in his library's many books. Stalin was quick to pass judgement on authors but he respected their books. This showed in the care with which he marked and annotated them, even those of his enemies. Stalin rarely read to confirm what he already knew or believed. He read to learn something new. Affairs of state abbreviated and disrupted his reading life but did not curtail it completely. In the midst of even the deepest national and international crises, he could be found reading, marking and often editing this or that book.

READING FOR THE REVOLUTION

Stalin learned to read and annotate at school and in a seminary but found his true métier in the radical bookshops of the Georgian capital, Tbilisi. Books converted him to socialism and guided him into the revolutionary underground of Tsarist Russia. Stalin believed in the transformative power of ideas for the simple reason that, if reading had radically changed his life, then so, too, could it change the lives of others.

Stalin was a voracious reader from an early age. As a young political activist and aspirant intellectual, his reading naturally focused on left-wing publications, especially the writings of Karl Marx and Friedrich Engels, and of Vladimir Lenin, the leader of Stalin's Bolshevik faction in the Russian Social Democratic Labour Party. But he also devoured the classics of Russian and western fiction – Tolstoy, Dostoevsky, Gogol, Chekhov, Shakespeare, Cervantes, Schiller, Heine, Hugo, Thackeray and Balzac.[8]

After Lenin's death in 1924, much of Stalin's reading concentrated on the writings of his rivals in the struggle to succeed the founder of the Soviet state, people like Leon Trotsky, Grigory Zinoviev, Lev Kamenev and Nikolai Bukharin. In the 1930s Stalin's attention switched to Soviet literature – to the post-revolutionary writings of Maxim Gorky, Alexander Fadeev, Alexei Tolstoy, Ilya Ehrenburg, Isaac Babel and Mikhail Sholokhov.

Another preoccupation of Stalin's was the history of revolutionary movements internationally. In 1919 the Bolsheviks established the Communist International to foment global revolution. Stalin was fond of giving strategic and tactical advice to visiting foreign communists and took pride in his knowledge of other countries, much of it gleaned from books.

Military strategy was an enduring interest. During the Russian Civil War he served at the front as a Bolshevik commissar, which meant that he controlled military as well as political decision-making in his spheres of operation. Later he collected and read the works of the foremost German, French, Russian and Soviet strategic theorists. Not surprisingly, this interest became paramount during the Second World War when he became the Soviet Union's supreme commander. He was particularly attentive to the experiences of his Tsarist predecessors as *generalissimo*, Alexander Suvorov and Mikhail Kutuzov, both of whose portraits hung in his office during the war. Other aspects of Russian history continued to fascinate Stalin, too, not least the comparisons between his rule and those of Ivan the Terrible and Peter the Great. Stalin was also attracted to the history of the ancient world, especially the rise and fall of the Roman Empire.

He devoted considerable time to reading about science, linguistics, philosophy and political economy. After the Second World War he made a number of notable interventions in debates about genetics, socialist economics and linguistic theory. The most notorious of these interventions was his support for Trofim Lysenko, a Soviet botanist who argued that genetic inheritance could be influenced by environmental controls. In private, however, Stalin ridiculed Lysenko's view that every science had a 'class character', writing on a report by Lysenko: 'Ha-ha-ha . . . And Mathematics? And Darwinism?'[9]

THE GIFT OF BOOKS

When Stalin's two younger sons, Vasily and an adopted son, Artem Sergeev, allowed the pages of an old and badly bound history textbook they were studying outdoors to blow apart in the wind, he collared the boys, telling them that it contained thousands of years of history – knowledge that people had shed blood to collect and store, material that scientists and historians then spent decades working on. Having insisted that Vasily and Artem glue the book back together, Stalin told them: 'You did good. Now you know how to treat books.'[10]

When Artem was seven, Stalin gave him a copy of Daniel Defoe's *Robinson Crusoe* and, when he was eight, Rudyard Kipling's *The Jungle Book*.[11] In the

Defoe book, Stalin wrote: 'To my little friend, Tomik, with the wish that he grows up to be a conscious, steadfast and fearless Bolshevik.'[12]

Vasily was destined to serve in the air force and on his thirteenth birthday, in March 1934, Stalin presented him with a Russian translation of *Air War 1936* – a fantasy about a future conflict between Britain and France by 'Major Helders', which was the pseudonym of the German aviator Robert Knauss.[13]

The young Vasily was not the most diligent of pupils, preferring sports to study. In June 1938 Stalin wrote a stinging letter to one of his teachers. Vasily was a 'spoilt youth of average abilities', wrote Stalin, who was 'not always truthful' and loved to 'blackmail' weak 'leaders', even though he was weak-willed himself. He also liked to remind people whose son he was. Stalin advised the teacher to take Vasily by the scruff of his neck and not to put up with any more nonsense from him.[14]

Stalin also gave Vasily a book whose composition he himself supervised, crafted and edited, the canonical *Short Course History of the Communist Party of the Soviet Union* (1938) – a book that was read and studied by tens of millions of Soviet citizens.[15] Vasily read this book quite thoroughly, underlining paragraphs on virtually every page with different coloured pencils.[16] His efforts paid off when he passed a state exam on the book with flying colours in 1939.[17]

Stalin's daughter, Svetlana, was more studious. In 1937 he gave the eleven-year-old a textbook history of the USSR and in 1938 her own a copy of the *Short Course*. Father 'commanded' me to read it, recalled Svetlana, because 'he wanted me to make a study of the party's history – his version of it'. Unlike her brother, she never did get around to reading it – 'it bored me so' – and when Stalin found out 'he grew very angry'.[18] But other books in her own personal collection that she did read included Lenin's *Materialism and Empirio-Criticism*, and Stalin's *Problems of Leninism*.[19]

BOLSHEVIK BOOK CULTURE

Stalin's presents to his children and his stricture to Vasily and Artem about taking care of their books were expressive of the Bolsheviks' print-based political culture and their valorisation of written texts. No book-burning dictator, Stalin would have sympathised with Victor Hugo's response to the Communards, who set fire to the Louvre library in 1871:

Have you forgotten that your liberator
Is the book? The book is there on the heights;
It gleams; because it shines and illuminates,
It destroys the scaffold, war and famine;
It speaks: No more slaves and no more pariahs.[20]

Stalin and the Soviets, to use Katerina Clark's words, had an *'extraordinary reverence for the book, which functioned as a cult object in a secular faith'.*[21] Under Stalin's tutelage, Moscow aspired to become a socialist 'Rome', a radical centre of world culture based primarily, though by no means exclusively, on the printed word.

After the Bolsheviks seized power in Russia in 1917, one of their first acts was to nationalise the publishing industry. For the Bolsheviks, words were the expressions of ideas that, allied to radical action, could become a material force capable of transforming not only societies but human nature itself. Under Stalin, Soviet writers were charged with helping to fashion the thoughts and feelings of the new Soviet men and women constructing socialism and communism. 'To build socialism we need civil, electrical and mechanical engineers,' Stalin was reported as saying in August 1934, as Soviet writers gathered for a national congress. 'We need them to build houses, automobiles and tractors. But no less important, we need engineers of the human soul, writer-engineers building the human spirit.'[22]

According to Lenin, communism was 'Soviet power plus the electrification of the whole country', i.e. people's democracy and advanced industrialisation. But there was also a third, critical element – mass literacy and cultural enlightenment. As Lenin said, 'an illiterate person stands outside of politics, and must first learn the alphabet. Without this there can be no politics.'[23]

Reading and writing were seen by the Soviet regime as a means of collective and individual self-emancipation from both bourgeois ideology and cultural backwardness and then the achievement of a higher, communist consciousness. Bolshevik leaders and activists were not exempted from this revolution of the mind. The creation of a new consciousness attuned to the collectivist culture of the Soviet socialist system was their personal mission, too. In power, the Bolsheviks remained committed to a permanent revolution of reading, learning and self-improvement. They believed that under socialism people should read a lot, and would read even more as society progressed to communism.[24]

Public libraries were to be central to the realisation of Lenin's vision. He envisaged a vast network of tens of thousands of libraries, reading rooms and mobile units that would bring books and revolutionary literature to within a ten-minute walk from every person's home. Decrees were issued to create a public library service on 'Swiss-American' lines – quick and free access to bookshelves, inter-library loans, long opening hours and easy borrowing facilities. Private libraries were nationalised, together with the expropriation of major book collections owned by individuals. During the Second World War, the Nazis destroyed or ransacked 4,000 Soviet libraries but by the war's end there were still 80,000 of them in the USSR, with 1,500 in Moscow alone. To satisfy demand, Soviet public libraries required the printing of at least 100,000 copies of any popular book.[25]

Among the booty extracted by the Red Army from Germany at the end of the war were thirteen railway wagons filled with books for Moscow University and 760,000 books for the state's main depository, the Lenin Library. By 1948, more than 2.5 million 'trophy books' had been claimed or put on display by 279 separate Moscow cultural institutions.[26]

Lenin preferred individuals to access and read books in the controlled, social environment of a public library rather than through accumulating a personal collection. However, that preference did not apply to Bolshevik party members who were encouraged to collect, read and retain the authorised writings of Lenin and other Soviet leaders.

The Bolsheviks were keenly aware that words could equally well be used to subvert the Soviet system as to buttress it. Censorship was abolished when they came to power but was reintroduced in 1922.[27] As the regime became progressively more authoritarian, an elaborate system of censorship was created to control the output of newspapers, magazines, publishing houses and printers. The communists could not easily control what Soviet citizens thought, said or wrote, but they could effectively control what they read. At its peak, Glavlit, the Soviet censorship organisation, had many thousands of employees located in offices all over the country. It is no coincidence that the communist system collapsed in the late 1980s, when Mikhail Gorbachev introduced glasnost and liberated Soviet political discourse from censorship. Gorbachev's intellectual revolution – the power of the words he unleashed – would have horrified but not surprised Stalin.

Public libraries were subject to censorship, too. From its earliest days the Bolshevik regime sent circulars (informally known as the *Talmud*) to librarians instructing them what books to remove from their shelves. In charge of the library purge during the early years was Lenin's wife, Nadezhda Krupskaya. One party directive instructed libraries to withdraw not only counter-revolutionary books, but also pro-Soviet material that articulated now out-of-date policy positions from the revolutionary and civil war period. 'Soviet Russia already in 1923 was disowning its utopian past,' observed Peter Kenez.[28] In 1925 the Leningrad region's censorship office banned 448 books for political and ideological reasons. Of these books, 255 had been issued by the private publishers then still in existence.[29]

Krupskaya prescribed as well as proscribed books, circulating to libraries lists of recommendations for mass consumption, especially children's literature. The Bolsheviks were particularly keen to get the masses reading the classics of fiction. In 1918 they set up a 'People's Library' of mass editions of books to be circulated free of charge. That same year they adopted the writer Maxim Gorky's proposal to translate the classics of world literature into Russian. Gorky envisaged thousands of such translations, an ambition prosaically stymied by paper shortages during the Russian Civil War.[30]

The 1930s saw successive purges of library book stocks. In 1938–9, '16,453 titles and 24,138,799 copies of printed works were removed from libraries and the book trade network'.[31] Sometimes local censorship was so extreme it had to be curbed. In 1933 the party leadership condemned 'the widespread practice of organising "closed stacks" in libraries' that had led to significant reserves of books being withdrawn from circulation. It decreed that books could only be removed from libraries upon special instruction of the central committee. In 1935 the central committee passed a resolution that curtailed the 'wholesale purge of libraries and the indiscriminate removal of books' that was 'plundering and damaging library resources'. It also directed that two copies of each withdrawn book were to be kept in the 'special library collections' of a number of central libraries, academic institutions and higher party bodies.[32]

STALIN'S LIBRARY

His peripatetic lifestyle as an underground revolutionary meant Stalin did not begin to collect books and build a permanent personal library until after the 1917 revolution. But his collection quickly grew to many thousands of volumes.

He had an ex-libris stamp that identified the books as belonging to him but the library was more a concept than a physical reality. It never became a specific building or had a single location as it could so easily have done. Stalin loved books for their ideas and information. He did not collect them for profit or aesthetics or as a monument to his cult image as a latter-day Renaissance man. His library was a living archive and its holdings were scattered across various domestic and work spaces. As Paul Lafargue said of Marx, books were tools of the mind for Stalin, not items of luxury.

Stalin was not alone in this endeavour. All the top Bolshevik leaders – Lenin, Trotsky, Kamenev, Zinoviev and Bukharin – collected books. Marshal Georgy Zhukov's library reportedly contained 20,000 books, while the extensive collection of Stalin's defence commissar, Kliment Voroshilov, was lost when his dacha (country house) burned down after the Second World War.[33]

There was little danger to Stalin's collection given the level of security and surveillance that surrounded him and his books. During the Second World War, as Hitler's armies approached Moscow, his library was boxed up and shipped to Kuibyshev (Samara) in south-east Russia, where many government departments were evacuated in anticipation of the capital's fall to the Wehrmacht.

Svetlana was also sent to Kuibyshev but returned to Moscow in summer 1942, recalling that Stalin's apartment was 'empty and depressing. My father's library was in Kuibyshev and the bookshelves in the dining room were empty.'[34]

In the 1990s the author Rachel Polonsky chanced upon the remnants of the library of Stalin's foremost deputy, his long-serving prime minister and foreign commissar, Vyacheslav Molotov. The books were stored in Molotov's old apartment, located just across the road from the Kremlin. In a story emblematic of post-communist Moscow, the upmarket apartment had been rented out by Molotov's grandson to an American investment banker who was a neighbour of Polonsky's.[35] There were only a few hundred books left of Molotov's collection but the library's surviving catalogue indicated to her there had once been ten thousand.

Polonsky was surprised by the eclecticism and cultural range of Molotov's books. There were, of course, various Marxist texts, together with Soviet war memoirs, books about economics and agriculture (a preoccupation of Molotov when he was Soviet premier), the *Great Soviet Encyclopaedia*, the *Short Course History of the Communist Party of the Soviet Union*, and a Russian translation of Winston Churchill's *History of the Second World War*. Books about Russian history and the correspondence of Tsar Nicholas II shared space on the shelves with a biography of Edgar Allan Poe and Oswald Spengler's *Decline of the West*. Alongside the classics of Russian literature and letters were works by Joseph Conrad, George Bernard Shaw, H. G. Wells and Anatole France, as well as Thomas Malory's *Morte d'Arthur* and an illustrated edition of Dante's *Divine Comedy*.[36] Stalin's library was equally diverse and more than twice the size of Molotov's.

While Molotov long outlived Stalin, dying aged ninety-six in 1986, he survived in office for little more than four years after his old boss's death. In 1957 he lost a bitter power struggle with Stalin's successor as party leader, Nikita Khrushchev. Ejected from the party leadership, Molotov was demoted to an ambassadorship in the People's Republic of Mongolia.[37]

One issue in contention between Molotov and Khrushchev was Stalin's historical legacy. While Molotov accepted that Stalin made many mistakes, he defended his constructive role in building socialism in the USSR. Khrushchev, on the other hand, wanted to denounce Stalin and the cult of his personality wholesale, and he did so at a closed session of the 20th congress of the Soviet communist party in February 1956.

Khrushchev's so-called secret speech sealed the fate of the dictator's personal library. A plan to turn Stalin's Moscow dacha into a museum celebrating his life was shelved and his books mostly dispersed to other libraries. However, Soviet archivists and librarians retrieved and retained some important remnants of the library, notably nearly 400 items that Stalin had read, marked and annotated. Preserved, too, were several thousand other books that identifiably belonged to his library. Rediscovered in post-Soviet times, these remnants came to be seen as a repository of the traces of Stalin's deepest and most intimate thoughts.

Jonathan Brent's encounter with the surviving books in Stalin's library in the early 2000s verged on the religious. A Yale University Press editor, Brent was in Moscow to negotiate the creation of Yale's Stalin Digital Archive (SDA), which was to contain images of all the documents in the dictator's personal file series, or *lichnyi fond*, as it is called in Russian. The annotated books were to be one segment of the series and he was shown some specimens:

> Nobody was prepared for what we found. . . . To see the works in his library is somehow to be brought face-to-face with Stalin. To see the words his eyes saw. To touch the pages he touched and smelled. The marks he made on them trace the marks he made on the Russian nation. . . . Not a single work I inspected was not read *by him*. Not a single work was not copiously annotated, underlined, argued with, appreciated, disdained, studied. . . . We see him thinking, reacting, imagining *in private*. [Original emphasis.][38]

By the time I started to examine Stalin's library books in the 2010s – the whole collection, not just a sample – I had travelled to Moscow every year since 1996 to do research in Russian archives. I had already seen hundreds of documents composed, edited or written on by Stalin. The novelty of trying to decipher the dictator's often unreadable scribblings had long worn off. I was interested in practicalities and particularities, not generalities. What did Stalin's *pometki* actually mean and what could they tell us about the modes and substance of his private thinking?

But Brent had a point. Apart from private photographs and some hastily written and often perfunctory letters to family members, Stalin's library books are among the best means we have of accessing the dictator's inner life.[39]

In Stalin's *lichnyi fond* there are many thousands of files containing tens of thousands of documents – memoranda, reports, drafts, records of conversations, and handwritten notes. Invaluable to historians though these files are, they constitute Stalin's official papers rather than his private ones. Only in his personal library, in the way he read, marked and wrote in his books, do we get really close to the spontaneous Stalin – the intellectual immersed in his own thoughts.

THE PARANOIA IS POLITICAL

Since the discovery in the archives of the residue of his personal library many people have searched its holdings hoping to glimpse Stalin's true nature – the key to the character that made his rule so monstrous. But while Stalin's books do indeed reveal his private thoughts and feelings, the key to understanding his capacity to countenance mass murder is hidden in plain sight: the politics and ideology of ruthless class war in defence of the revolution and the pursuit of communist utopia.

Stalin's oft-noted paranoia was political not personal; it reflected the fact that post-1917 popular support for the Bolsheviks was often flimsy, while internationally the Soviet state remained isolated and vulnerable to renewed attack by the grand coalition of capitalist powers that had already sought its overthrow during the Russian Civil War. As Stephen Kotkin put it, 'The problems of the revolution brought out the paranoia in Stalin and Stalin brought out the paranoia inherent in the revolution.'[40]

Apart from his writings on nationalism, Stalin's main contribution to the evolution of Marxist political theory was his propagation of the view that under socialism the class struggle intensified – an idea that derived from Lenin's writings during the civil war. The stronger the Soviet Union became, said Stalin, the more desperate the capitalists were to crush the socialist system through a combination of external force and internal subversion. Significantly, when this concept dropped out of the Soviet political lexicon after Stalin's death, the USSR rapidly transitioned to a softer and far less violent authoritarianism.

Stalin was too intelligent and self-aware to believe the panegyrics of his own personality cult. He famously chided Vasily for trading off the family name: 'You are not Stalin and I'm not Stalin. Stalin is Soviet power. Stalin is what he is in the newspapers and in the portraits, not you, not even me!'[41] Still, there is no doubt that he saw himself as a great intellectual and as Lenin's rightful heir as head of state, leader of the party and guardian of Marxist orthodoxy – 'the Lenin of today', as the cult slogan put it. There was no one whose books he read more assiduously and admiringly than those of Lenin. 'Lenin is our teacher,' Stalin proudly told the US Republican politician Harold Stassen in 1947.[42]

Stalin's personal library offers many fascinating insights into his private thinking but more than anything it reveals someone whose inner mental life was shaped by his public persona and by the ideological universe he inhabited. The view from his library is that from an inside window looking out. By following the way Stalin read books, we can glimpse the world through his eyes. We may not get to peer into his soul, but we do get to wear his spectacles.

Stalin was a fanatic who had no secret doubts. 'The most important thing is knowledge of Marxism,' he scribbled in the margin of an obscure military theory journal in the 1940s.[43] He meant it: in the thousands upon thousands of annotated pages in Stalin's library, there is not a single hint that he harboured any reservations about the communist cause. The energy and enthusiasm he applied to annotating arcane points of Marxist philosophy and economics is eloquent – and sometimes mind-numbing – testimony to his belief that communism was the way, the truth and the future.

While Stalin was undoubtedly a very dogmatic Marxist, he was not a blind prisoner of his ideology. He was capable of seeing and reaching outside the Marxian framework to engage with a diverse range of authors and perspectives. The vehemence with which he viewed his political opponents never prevented him from paying careful attention to what they wrote.

CHAPTER 2

THE SEARCH FOR THE STALIN BIOGRAPHERS' STONE

Stalin kept no diary, wrote no memoirs and evinced little interest in his personal history, yet he went to a great deal of trouble to shape both his biography and the documentary trail that would be followed by his biographers.[1]

'It is difficult to describe the process,' Stalin told an admiring American visitor, Jerome Davis, in 1926, when asked how he became a Bolshevik. 'First one becomes convinced that existing conditions are wrong and unjust. Then one resolves to do the best one can to remedy them. Under the Tsar's regime any attempt genuinely to help the people put one outside the pale of the law; one found himself hunted and hounded as a revolutionist.'[2]

Emil Ludwig, a German writer who had authored many biographies of famous people, asked Stalin a similar question in 1931, and received an equally terse and uninformative reply:

Ludwig: What drove you to become a rebel? Was it, perhaps, because your parents treated you badly?

Stalin: No. My parents were uneducated people, but they did not treat me badly by any means. It was different in the theological seminary of which I was then a student. In protest against the humiliating regime and the Jesuitical methods that prevailed in the seminary, I was ready to become, and eventually did become, a revolutionary, a believer in Marxism as the only genuinely revolutionary doctrine.[3]

In 1939 the Soviet dramatist Mikhail Bulgakov wanted to write a play about Stalin's youth, with the intention to stage it as part of the celebrations of Stalin's sixtieth birthday. But Stalin vetoed the project, saying that 'all young people are alike, why write a play about the young Stalin?'[4]

Stalin was occasionally more forthcoming about his early life, but not his childhood. It was the years he spent in the Bolshevik underground, a period that spanned his youth and early adulthood, that interested him. He loved to read and reflect on his writings from that time and to the end of his life remained engaged with the debates, splits, strategies, tactics and factional battles of Russia's revolutionary socialist movement. In the 1920s he marked copiously those volumes of the first edition of Lenin's collected works that dealt with the 1905 revolution. After the Second World War he reread with evident interest his own 1905 article on 'The Proletarian Class and the Proletarian Party', which had been republished in the first volume of his collected works. It was about the rules of the Russian Social-Democratic Labour Party and Stalin took the trouble to write out at the end of his article the three conditions of party membership: agreement with its programme, material support and participation in one of its organisations. Heavily marked, too, was his copy of Georgy Safarov's detailed 1923 study of the pre-1917 evolution of Bolshevik strategy and tactics.[5]

For Stalin, the party's history was not even past, let alone dead. His formative, life-changing experiences as an illegal political activist in Tsarist Russia remained eternally interesting and relevant. Speaking to visiting Indian communists in 1951, he was keen to share lessons he had learned decades earlier. He urged them to eschew the tactics of the peasant-based revolution that had recently brought the Chinese communists to power and instead to emulate the worker–peasant alliance that had secured victory for the Bolsheviks. He warned of the dangers of premature uprisings, pointing out that in July 1917 the Bolsheviks had restrained an insurrectionary workers' movement in Petrograd because it would have been defeated by counter-revolutionary forces. He argued against individual acts of terrorism, which had the effect of dividing the progressive movement into the heroes of such actions and the crowds who cheered them from the sidelines but did not themselves participate in revolutionary struggles. 'We are against the theory of the hero and the crowd,' he told them.[6]

Winston Churchill famously said in relation to Stalin's foreign policy: 'I cannot forecast to you the action of Russia. It is a riddle wrapped in a mystery inside an enigma.' Less often quoted is what he said next: 'But perhaps there is a key. That key is Russian national interest.'[7]

This was in October 1939 and Churchill was explaining to the listeners of his BBC radio broadcast why, on the eve of the Second World War, Stalin had concluded a non-aggression pact with Hitler and then joined in the German attack on Poland. Churchill's hope was that Soviet national interest and the Nazi threat would eventually lead Stalin to break with Hitler. In the event, the relationship was broken by Hitler when he launched his invasion of the USSR in June 1941.

The enigma of Stalin's pre-revolutionary years is that while quite a lot is known about his political views and activities, a great deal of uncertainty surrounds the details of his family life, education, personal relations and youthful character traits. Gaps in the evidence have typically been filled in by speculation, stereotyping and cherry-picking of partisan memoirs to suit the grinding of many different personal and political axes. 'When it comes to Stalin,' writes the foremost biographer of his early life, Ronald Suny, 'gossip is reported as fact; legend provides meaning; and scholarship gives way to sensationalist popular literature with tangential reference to reliable sources.'[8]

STALIN'S BIOGRAPHY: THE SEARCH BEGINS

In December 1920 Stalin handwrote his answers to a biographical question-naire, sent to him by the Swedish branch of ROSTA, the forerunner of the TASS news agency:

1. Name: *Joseph Vissarionovich Stalin (Dzhugashvili)*
2. Year and Place of Birth: *1878, Gori (Tbilisi Province)*
3. Origins: *Georgian. Father was a worker (shoemaker), died in 1909, Mother, a seamstress, is still alive*
4. Education: *Excluded from the sixth (final) class of the Tbilisi Orthodox Seminary in 1899*
5. How long have you been involved in the revolutionary movement? *Since 1897*
6. How long have you been in the RSDLP [Russian Social Democratic Labour Party] and in the Bolshevik faction? *Joined the RSDLP in 1898 and the Bolshevik faction in 1903 (when it was formed), 1898 – member of the Tbilisi committee of the party, 1903 – member of the Caucasus regional committee of the party, 1912 – member of the Central Committee of the Bolshevik Party*
7. Were you ever a member of any other revolutionary party? *No. Before 1898 I was an RSDLP sympathiser*
8. Penalties that you suffered under Tsarism – imprisonment, exile, emigration: *Arrested seven times, exiled six times (Irkutsk, Narym, Turukhansk etc.), escaped exile five times, served seven years in prison, lived illegally in Russia until 1917 (was in St Petersburg, not in emigration but did visit London, Berlin, Stockholm and Cracow on party business)*
9. What official posts have you occupied in Soviet Russia? *People's Commissar of the Workers and Peasants Inspectorate and People's*

Commissar for Nationalities, member of the Council of Labour and Defence and of the Revolutionary-Military Council of the Republic, member of the All-Russia Central Executive Committee

10. Literary activities. Books, pamphlets, major articles. What newspapers and journals have you edited? *Pamphlets: (1) About the Bolsheviks (in Georgian) 1904, (2) Anarchism or Socialism? (in Georgian) 1906, (3) Marxism and the National Question (in Russian) 1913. Edited the Georgian Bolshevik newspaper 'New Times' (1906), and Russian newspapers: 'The Baku Proletarian' (1908), 'The Star' in St Petersburg [at the time of the Lena massacre] (1912) and the central party organ 'The Worker's Way' during the days of Kerensky in 1917*

11. Personal Comments: *Currently a member of the party Central Committee and its Orgburo*
    J. Stalin[9]

One curiosity concerns Stalin's date of birth. According to church records he was born on 6 December 1878 (Old-Style Russian calendar) and that is the year he wrote in the ROSTA questionnaire. However, Stalin's publicly declared birthday was 21 December 1879 (New-Style Russian calendar) and that was the date extravagantly celebrated as his fiftieth in 1929, and again in 1939 and 1949 as his sixtieth and seventieth birthdays. The reason for this discrepancy remains a mystery but in October 1921 Stalin completed a party registration form in which he put down 1879 as the year of his birth.[10] A December 1922 biographical summary prepared by his staff stated that was the year of his birth, as did the opening line of a short biography prepared by Ivan P. Tovstukha, documents that Stalin would certainly have read and approved.[11]

Tovstukha's text was published as one of a series of portraits of Bolshevik leaders in the so-called *Granat* biographical dictionary, prepared to mark the tenth anniversary of the Russian Revolution. A trusted and valued assistant, Tovstukha was a long-time revolutionary activist who started working for the future dictator when Stalin was appointed people's commissar for nationalities. When Stalin became party general-secretary, Tovstukha followed him into the central party apparatus. Throughout the 1920s, he was one of Stalin's most important aides and performed a number of key functions, including a stint as director of the Lenin Institute, which was responsible for the publication of the first edition of Lenin's collected writings. In 1931 he was appointed deputy director of the newly created Institute of Marx, Engels and Lenin (IMEL), the party's archive-cum-research organisation. Tovstukha died of tuberculosis in 1935 but his memory was preserved by a plaque and by naming one of the archive's reading rooms after him.[12]

Tovstukha's 'biography' of his boss, which was little more than an extended chronology of Stalin's political career, was composed at the height of the internal party succession struggle following Lenin's death in 1924. It stressed Stalin's closeness to Lenin, before, during and after the revolution. It was also published as a fourteen-page pamphlet and an expanded version was published in *Pravda* in 1929 as one of several laudatory pieces marking Stalin's fiftieth birthday.[13]

Tovstukha's account was devoid of any really personal information about Stalin, and the same was true of the other Bolshevik biographies featured in the *Granat*. In theory, if not in always in practice, the Bolsheviks believed in self-effacement. They lived their lives in and through the collective that was the party. Their individual biographies were part and parcel of the history of the party. Their personalities and private lives were strictly subordinate to their political stories. The absence of interiority in the manner of *Bildungsroman* was a matter of pride.

In June 1926 Stalin went on a month-long trip to Georgia. In Tbilisi he gave a speech to railway workers in which he summarised his pre-revolutionary political journey. As befits a former seminarian, the speech was steeped in religious imagery. It was the closest he ever came to writing an autobiography.

Stalin was replying to the workers' greetings and he began by modestly denying he was the 'legendary warrior-knight' they thought him to be. The true story of his political life, said Stalin, was that he had been educated by the proletariat. His first teachers were those Tbilisi workers he came into contact with when he was placed in charge of a study circle of railwaymen in 1898. From them he received lessons in practical political work. This was his 'first baptism in the revolutionary struggle', when he served as an '*apprentice* in the art of revolution'. His 'second baptism in the revolutionary struggle' were the years (1907–9) he spent in Baku organising the oil workers. It was in Baku that he 'became a *journeyman* in the art of revolution'. After a period in the wilderness – 'wandering[s] from one prison or place of exile to another' – he was sent by the party to Petrograd where in 1917 he received his 'third baptism in the revolutionary struggle'. It was in Russia, under Lenin's guidance, that he became 'a *master workman* in the art of revolution'.[14]

Striking about Stalin's telling of this story was that he cast it entirely in class and political terms. His Georgian background was of no consequence except as an accidental matter of geography. His formative experiences of class struggle could have happened anywhere there were workers and the culminating episode took place in Petrograd – the radical heartland of the Russian proletariat. 'You know, Papa used to be a Georgian once,' the young Vasily Stalin told his six-year-old sister, Svetlana, who also recorded in her memoirs that when she was a child her family 'paid no special attention to anything Georgian – my father had become completely Russian'.[15]

THE SEARCH FOR THE STALIN BIOGRAPHERS' STONE

Tovstukha wanted to write a full biography of Stalin but he had rivals for that honour within the party. One of his competitors was the party official Yemel'yan Yaroslavsky (1878–1943), who fancied himself a historian. Among his later claims to fame was co-authorship with Stalin and others of the *Short Course History of the Communist Party of the Soviet Union* (1938) that served as the bible of the party's history until Stalin's death.

Yaroslavsky's ambition to publish a biography of Stalin was stymied by Tovstukha and others in IMEL. When he appealed to Stalin for help in August 1935, he was given short shrift. 'I am against the idea of a biography about me,' wrote Stalin on Yaroslavsky's letter. 'Gorky had a plan like yours, and he also asked me, but I have backed away from this issue. I don't think the time has come for a Stalin biography!'[16]

The problem was that the absence of a proper, official biography was a yawning gap in a vista that Stalin himself had opened up in 1931 when he published a letter on 'Some Questions Concerning the History of Bolshevism' in the journal *Proletarskaya Revolyutsiya*.[17] Stalin's missive was a long and boring diatribe against a young historian called Anatoly Slutsky who published an article that had the cheek to criticise aspects of Lenin's policy towards German social democracy before the First World War. Stalin denounced the article and its author as 'anti-party' and 'semi-Trotskyist'. Tedious and tendentious though it was, Stalin's denunciation of Slutsky was not a purely dogmatic assertion of the party line on Lenin: his criticisms were supported by a detailed textual and historical analysis of the issue.

As punishment for his temerity, Slutsky was expelled from the Society of Marxist Historians and lost his post at the Communist Academy's Institute of History. He was then expelled from the communist party.[18]

In his 'letter', Stalin took the opportunity to launch a broader attack on the work of party historians, including Yaroslavsky: 'Who, except hopeless bureaucrats, can rely on written documents alone? Who, except archive rats, does not understand that a party and its leaders must be tested primarily by their *deeds* . . . Lenin taught us to test revolutionary parties, trends and leaders not by their declarations and resolutions, but by their *deeds*.'[19]

In his interview with Emil Ludwig a couple of months later, Stalin reinforced the point that in the study of history, people and their actions mattered most. When the German writer commented that 'Marxism denies that the individual plays an outstanding role in history', Stalin responded that 'Marxism does not at all deny the role played by outstanding individuals or that history is made by people', though, of course, they do not make history under conditions of their own choosing: 'And great people are worth anything at all only to the extent that they are able to correctly understand these conditions, to understand how to change them.' When Ludwig persisted with his argument, saying that 'Marxism denies the role of heroes, the role of heroic personalities in history', Stalin replied that 'Marxism has never denied the role of heroes. On the contrary, it admits that they play a considerable role.'[20]

By suggesting that 'heroes' can by their actions fundamentally change the existing social order – the pre-eminent example being Lenin's determination to stage a socialist revolution in 1917 – Stalin gave a voluntaristic spin to the deterministic Marxist orthodoxy that individuals are only important insofar as they personify the historical process and act in accordance with the laws of social development.[21] But devotees of his personality cult yearned for an edifying account of their hero's epic life story.

BERIA AND BARBUSSE

The vacuum created by the absence of an authorised Stalin biography was filled by two publications. Firstly, a book-length lecture by Lavrenty Beria, *On the History of the Bolshevik Organisations in Transcaucasia*. Secondly, and more surprisingly, a semi-official popular biography of Stalin by the French communist intellectual Henri Barbusse (1873–1935).

Prior to becoming Stalin's security chief in 1938, Beria headed the Georgian communist party. The Tbilisi branch of IMEL was particularly dedicated to the study of Stalin's pre-1917 political activities in Transcaucasia and Beria published a (ghost-written) article on this topic in the party's theoretical journal *Bol'shevik* in 1934. In July 1935 he delivered a long lecture on the same subject to a party audience in Tbilisi. The text of his lecture was serialised in *Pravda* and then published as a book. Party members throughout the USSR were instructed to study it carefully. Beria sent an inscribed copy to his 'Dear, beloved, teacher, the Great Stalin', who read the book and marked a few of its pages, mainly underlining the dates of events that he had been involved in. As Judith Devlin writes, the book soon became a Stalin cult classic, was issued in eight separate editions and remained in print until Stalin's death in 1953.[22]

Beria's glowing account of the young Stalin's revolutionary activities was notable for the number of unsigned publications in Georgian that he attributed to Stalin and for his utilisation of unpublished memoirs by Stalin's old comrades and acquaintances. The limitation of Beria's rather turgid text was that, apart from Stalin, it was populated by personages that few people had ever heard of – or cared about – and dealt with equally obscure events.

Henri Barbusse was a famous pacifist and anti-war writer. A member of the French communist party from 1923, he helped organise the 1932 Amsterdam World Congress Against War and headed the World Committee Against War and Fascism founded in 1933. While Stalin conversed with a number of prominent western intellectuals in the 1930s, Barbusse was the only one he met in the 1920s as well. Stalin talked to Barbusse four times – in September 1927, October 1932, August 1933 and November 1934. 'I'm not so busy that I can't find time to talk to Comrade Barbusse,' Stalin remarked at their 1932 meeting.[23]

The idea of writing a biography of Stalin was prompted by conversations that Barbusse had with the communist propaganda impresario Willi Münzenberg, a German revolutionary who worked for the Moscow-based Communist International (Comintern), established by the Bolsheviks in March 1919 to spread the revolution.[24] In December 1932 the Soviet party's propaganda section wrote to Stalin recommending that Barbusse's proposal to write such a book should be accepted. Tovstukha was proposed as the overseer of the project but, in the event, that task was carried out by party propaganda chief Alexei Stetsky.[25]

Though published in the USSR, as well as France and other countries, Barbusse's biography was intended mainly for an international audience. It was this propagandistic purpose, together with Barbusse's fame as a writer and his reliability as a communist, that persuaded Stalin to back the project. No doubt Stalin was impressed, too, by the fact that Barbusse had already written a biography of one of his literary heroes, Emile Zola, a Russian translation of that book having been published in early 1933.

In September 1934 Stetsky sent Barbusse a long list of corrections and queries concerning the manuscript of his biography of Stalin. Stetsky's letter to Barbusse was in French but was translated into Russian for the benefit of Stalin and other party officials.

Stetsky's amendments had two main strands. Firstly, there were numerous corrections of factual mistakes about Stalin's life and the history of Bolshevism. Stalin's father was a shoemaker who worked in a factory, not a peasant. Stalin went to church school because it was free and accessible, not because his father was particularly religious. It was not Lenin but his brother who was a Narodnik (Populist). Neither Stalin nor Lenin lived in Berlin for several months. Barbusse had got wrong the dates of Stalin's many arrests, imprisonments, exiles and so on.

Secondly, Stetsky made a sustained effort to persuade Barbusse to endorse the Soviet party view that Trotsky and the Trotskyists were not only Stalin's political opponents but a malign and insidious influence, a counter-revolutionary force that must be rooted out of the communist movement by any means necessary.

In his covering note to Barbusse, Stetsky also expressed concern about his depiction of Stalin as a practical, commonsensical individual rather than as the greatest Marxist theoretician since Lenin. Stetsky also felt that Barbusse's portrayal of Stalin as a person was incomplete. The biography did not show Stalin's 'style of work, the way he talked or his multifaceted connections with the masses; it does not show the love that surrounds Stalin'. However, Stetsky was confident that Barbusse, with all his great talent, would be able to capture and convey Stalin in all his 'majesty'.[26]

The biography was published in French in 1935 (*Staline: Un monde nouveau vu à travers un homme* – a signed copy may be found in Stalin's library) and in Russian in 1936. In his preface to the Russian edition, Stetsky wrote that 'the book has been written with a tremendous amount of love for the Soviet land, its peoples and its leader'. Unfortunately, by this time Barbusse was dead, having passed away during a trip to Moscow in August 1935.

His memorial meeting in Moscow was packed with Soviet intellectuals and party officials and an honour guard escorted Barbusse's mortal remains to the railway station. An official delegation then accompanied them to Paris on the *Siberian Express*. Stalin himself issued a statement: 'I share pain with you, on this occasion of the passing of our friend, the friend of the French working class, the noble son of the French people, the friend of the workers of all countries'.[27]

Barbusse's biography of Stalin was a hagiography but it was a clever and interesting one. Rather than a conventional biography, it was a political portrait of Stalin as the personification of the Soviet socialist project. Barbusse's privately stated aim in writing the book was 'to provide a complete portrait of the man on whom this social transformation pivots so that the reader may get to know him well'.[28] To achieve that goal he wrote a potted history of revolutionary Russia in which Stalin, together with Lenin, is the key figure, while at the same time contrasting the personalities of Trotsky and Stalin. Trotsky is depicted as arrogant, self-important, fractious, impractical, flashy, obstinate and verbose, a man of despotic character, while Stalin

> relies with all his weight upon reason and practical common sense. He is impeccably and inexorably methodical. He knows. He thoroughly understands Leninism. . . . He does not try to show off and is not worried by a desire to be original. He merely tries to do everything that he can do. He does not believe in eloquence or sensationalism. When he speaks he merely tries to combine simplicity with clearness.[29]

As this quotation shows, Stetsky did not succeed in shifting Barbusse from his view that Stalin was primarily a *praktik* – a man of action. He was more successful in relation to Barbusse's treatment of Trotsky, though he would probably have wished that Stalin's rival did not loom so large in the book. Barbusse's conclusion was the orthodox one that by the time Leningrad party chief Sergei Kirov was assassinated in December 1934, Trotsky had become a counter-revolutionary. But Barbusse plotted Trotsky's alleged path to counter-revolution carefully and plausibly. His account of the disputes with Lenin and Stalin that led Trotsky to a counter-revolutionary position was highly effective compared to the hysterical denunciations and polemics of Soviet propagandists.

Barbusse's book, Andrew Sobanet suggests, may have provided a template for the plot of the official Soviet *Short Biography* of Stalin that was to be published in 1939:

> The *Short Biography*, like *Staline*, recounts Stalin's early family life and schooling, followed by a description of life in his native region and the rising importance of Marxism. Both texts elaborate on Stalin's affection for Lenin's work and writing, his work as a propagandist, his pre-1917 revolutionary activities, and his heroic work in the revolutionary and civil war eras. Just as in Barbusse's text, Stalin is described in the *Short Biography* as 'the worthy continuer of the cause of Lenin . . . Stalin is the Lenin of today'. References to Stalin's alleged omnipotence and omniscience are also found in both books. . . . Both books end with pages on Stalin that praise him in absurdly grandiose terms.[30]

The problem with Barbusse's book was that it was hostage to the fortunes of the people who populated its pages, some of whom would soon became 'unpersons' in the USSR after falling victim to Stalin's purges. Within a couple of years of its publication, the Russian edition had been withdrawn from circulation and a block put on further editions or translations.

The English edition of the book contained a photograph of Stalin and Marshal Alexander Yegorov, with whom he had served during the Russian Civil War. However, Yegorov was arrested in 1938 for participating in an anti-Soviet conspiracy, and shot in 1939. Tantalisingly, the English edition also carries a photo of some bookcases said to be 'Stalin's Secret Library, Now in Tiflis Museum', a secret stash, one assumes, from his underground days.

In general, Stalin remained resistant to biographies or hagiographies of himself, because he didn't want to give too much encouragement to his personality cult. In 1933 he opposed a proposal from the Society of Old Bolsheviks to stage an exhibition based on his biography, commenting that 'such undertakings lead to the strengthening of the "cult of personality", which is harmful and incompatible with the spirit of our party'. He also prohibited publication of a Ukrainian party brochure about his life to mark the fifteenth anniversary of the foundation of the Komsomol (Young Communist League). When, in 1935, a journal wanted to publish a military-related article about 'Stalin in the Sal'sk

Steppe', he objected that his role was exaggerated and there was little about other people. Stalin was particularly averse to the publication of accounts of his childhood.[31] Most dramatic was his intervention to stop publication in 1938 of a children's book by V. Smirnova called *Tales of Stalin's Childhood*:

> The little book is filled with a mass of factual errors, distortions, exaggerations and undeserved praise. The author has been misled by fairy tale enthusiasts, liars (perhaps 'honest' liars) and sycophants. A pity for the author, but facts are facts. . . . Most important is that the book has a tendency to inculcate in the consciousness of Soviet children (and people in general) a cult of personalities, great leaders and infallible heroes. That is dangerous and harmful. . . . I advise you to burn the book.[32]

He was similarly outraged by an article on 'J. V. Stalin at the Head of Baku Bolsheviks and Workers, 1907–1908'. Mikhail Moskalev (1902–1965) was its author and it was published in a historical journal in January 1940 and then summarised by a feature article in *Pravda*. Stalin read the *Pravda* piece and marked it with some angry-looking red-penned underlining and question marks. He also read the original article and marked it in a similar fashion. Stalin then wrote to the editor of the journal, who, as it happens, was Yaroslavsky. The letter was marked 'not for publication', but Stalin forwarded copies to the Politburo and to the editor of *Pravda* as well as to the author. Stalin complained to Yaroslavsky that the article distorted historical truth and contained factual errors. He criticised Moskalev's use of dubious memoir sources and concluded that 'the history of Bolshevism must not be distorted – that's intolerable, it contradicts the profession and dignity of Bolshevik historians'.[33]

Yaroslavsky wanted to meet Stalin to discuss the matter but ended up writing him a detailed letter setting out the sources on which Moskalev's article had been based. Stalin replied two days later, on 29 April, repeating and detailing his point that the sources were unreliable. 'An historian has no right', wrote Stalin, 'to just take on trust memoirs and articles based on them. They have a duty to examine them critically and to verify them on the basis of objective information.' The party's history, Stalin stated, had to be a scientific history, one based on the whole truth: 'Toadyism is incompatible with scientific history.'

One issue in dispute was Moskalev's statement that Stalin had been the editor of the Baku oil workers' newspaper *Gudok* (The Siren), which, as Yaroslavsky pointed out, was based on a number of different sources, including the recollections of the paper's editor-publisher. The publisher was 'confused', Stalin wrote in reply. 'I never visited the *Gudok* editorial offices. I was not a member of its editorial board. I was not the *de facto* editor of *Gudok* (I didn't have the time). That was Comrade Dzhaparidze.' However, Stalin did make numerous contributions to the paper in 1907–8, so a little confusion in the memories of his old comrades was not all that surprising.[34]

STALIN'S COLLECTED WORKS

Stalin's sixtieth birthday celebrations in December 1939 provided an opening for Yaroslavsky to revive his attempts to publish a Stalin biography. When a piece about Stalin that he wrote for a Soviet encyclopaedia was rejected by its editors as too long and dense, he appealed to Stalin to allow its publication as a short book, assuring him that it had been written in a 'simple style accessible to the masses'. His book was published at the end of 1939 but he had been upstaged by IMEL's publication of a *Short Biography* of Stalin, with a print run of more than 1.2 million copies. However, when Stalin was sent a copy of the book's proofs, he wrote on the covering note that he had 'no time to look at it'.[35] The signed copy of Yaroslavsky's book was unmarked by Stalin, and probably unread.

A project closer to Stalin's heart was the publication of his collected writings. Articles, leaflets, letters, speeches, statements, reports, interviews and contributions to Marxist theory – these were texts that charted his political life, marked its milestones and recorded his most important thoughts.

Publishing the collected works of Bolshevik leaders was a small industry in the prewar USSR. As early as 1923, a twenty-two-volume edition of Zinoviev's writings was in print. In 1929 Trotsky's collected works reached volume twenty. By the mid-1930s, there were already three editions of Lenin's collected works. By these standards, the publication of Stalin's works was slow off the mark.

The indefatigable Tovstukha started gathering material for Stalin's collected works in the early 1930s, and in 1931 Stalin himself sketched a plan for an eight-volume edition. In August 1935 – a fortnight after Tovstukha's death – the Politburo, spurred on by the unauthorised republication of his pre-revolutionary writings, passed a resolution decreeing the publication of Stalin's collected works. The job was given to IMEL, in conjunction with Stetsky and the party's propaganda department.[36]

By November, Stetsky had outlined to Stalin the plans for publication. There would be eight to ten volumes called *Sochineniya* (Works or Writings). The edition would contain Stalin's previously published writings plus unpublished items such as stenograms of speeches, letters, notes and telegrams. The documents would be published in chronological order and would be supported by detailed factual information on their content. The volumes would contain a chronology of Stalin's life and political activities and would be published in all the national languages of the USSR as well as various foreign languages.[37]

In later years, the intended number of volumes was increased to twelve and then to sixteen but the rest of the plan remained much the same and, indeed, was mostly delivered. However, it took a lot longer than expected. The intention was to publish the first volumes in 1936 and to complete the series by 1937 – in time for the twentieth anniversary of the Russian Revolution. But the first volume did not see the light of day for another decade, for reasons that were many and varied.

The technical challenge was that Stalin's earliest writings were in Georgian, many of them published anonymously or under pseudonyms. They had to be identified, authenticated as Stalin's and then translated into Russian. There was a bit of a turf war between IMEL and its Tbilisi affiliate, which was controlled by the Georgian communist party. Needless to say, the Georgian comrades were keen to assert custodianship of their native son's youthful writings. Then there was the disruptive impact of the Great Terror. In the mid-1930s many IMEL staff were arrested or dismissed from their posts as 'enemies of the people'. The terror also cut a swathe through the ranks of party historians. Among party officials, Stetsky was a prominent victim; he was arrested and shot in 1938. During the Great Patriotic War, many IMEL staffers served in the armed forces, often as political officers in charge of propaganda, education and morale. The section responsible for Stalin's works was reduced to three people and evacuated to Ufa. Among its additional responsibilities was the urgent preparation of special wartime collections of Stalin's writings, with stirring titles like 'Articles and Speeches about Ukraine' and 'The Military Correspondence of Lenin and Stalin'.[38]

There is no evidence that Stalin was unduly worried about the delays. This was a project for posterity; in the meantime there were millions upon millions of copies of Stalin's books already circulating in the USSR: *The Foundations of Leninism, Marxism and the National and Colonial Question, Problems of Leninism* and *Dialectical and Historical Materialism*. During the war these Stalinist classics were joined by a collection of Stalin's speeches, *On the Great Patriotic War of the Soviet Union*.

IMEL sent Stalin regular progress reports and consulted him about matters great and small, including the technicalities of translating his Georgian writings. He was often remiss or slow to reply to queries and not until the eve of the first volume's publication in 1946 did he become intensively involved in the process and take charge of curating his own intellectual legacy. Stalin was sent a 'dummy' (in Russian, *maket*) of each volume, from which he would make the final selection of documents to be published. He used the opportunity to correct and edit texts. Stalin's handwritten amendments were stylistic rather than substantive. It was a case of him glossing rather than rewriting his personal history.[39]

Besides, politically embarrassing or dubious statements had already been weeded out by the time the proofs arrived on Stalin's desk. More often than not, weeding took the form of omission and elision rather than the direct doctoring of documents. History was not so much altered by Stalin's underlings as distorted. The trickiest issue was how to deal with favourable mentions in his writings of people who were at the time Stalin's comrades-in-arms but later became political opponents or, worse still, 'enemies of the state'. Among them were the many former leaders of the party who had been accused of treason and arraigned at a series of gruesome show trials in the 1930s. Where possible, favourable references to them were excluded, and those texts that featured Stalin's polemics against them omitted 'comrade' when referring to them. One egregious example of such censorship was this omission from an article by Stalin on the Bolshevik seizure of power that was originally published by *Pravda* in November 1918:

All the practical work of organising the insurrection was conducted under the ingenious leadership of the Chairman of the Petrograd Soviet, Comrade Trotsky. It is safe to say that the rapid switching of the [Petrograd] garrison to the side of the Soviet was due to the work of the party's Military-Revolutionary Committee, above all Comrade Trotsky.[40]

A key figure in the preparation of Stalin's works was a young historian called Vasily Mochalov, who specialised in the history of the labour movement in the Caucasus. He knew Georgian very well and was appointed head of IMEL's Stalin section in 1940. Frustrated by the slow progress, he wrote to Stalin and the Politburo in August 1944 to urge the appointment of extra staff and the imposition of short deadlines for the publication of the first two or three volumes.[41]

While Stalin did not reply to Mochalov's letter, it provoked a flurry of Politburo decisions to speed up the project, which did not please Mochalov's superiors in IMEL.[42] His letter cast them in a bad light and added to the pressure to produce results. Mochalov was also in conflict with the Georgian comrades about translation issues and about which unsigned publications to attribute to Stalin. According to his Tbilisi colleagues, Mochalov's knowledge of the languages and history of the Caucasus was inadequate and had led to mistakes in the editing and translation of Stalin's early writings.

In October 1944 Mochalov was told by IMEL's newly appointed director, Vladimir Kruzhkov, that the Institute no longer required his services. When Mochalov asked why, he was told it was because of a personality clash between him and Kruzhkov.[43] In his correspondence with the Politburo, Kruzhkov blamed Mochalov, and former IMEL director M. B. Mitin, for the lack of progress in the publication of Stalin's collected works.[44] Undaunted, Mochalov continued to participate in the Institute's discussions about the preparation of the *Sochineniya* and to register his objections to IMEL's handling of the project. He also reached out to Stalin again, asking for a meeting to discuss the publication. His efforts were rewarded by a summons to meet Stalin on 28 December 1945. Also in attendance was Kruzhkov, and Pyotr Shariya, the Georgian communist party's propaganda chief and the former head of IMEL's Tbilisi office.

Mochalov wrote quite a detailed report of the meeting, which took place in Stalin's Kremlin office in the evening and lasted for ninety minutes.

Stalin began the meeting by asking about the disagreements between Kruzhkov and Mochalov. Kruzhkov claimed these had been resolved but Mochalov restated his objections to including in the first two volumes several articles whose authorship was uncertain, including two articles published in the Georgian newspaper *Brdzola* (Struggle), which he thought had a 'calm tone' compared to other articles attributed to Stalin.

When Stalin asked if his objections were the reason he had been kicked out of IMEL, Mochalov replied that it was for Kruzhkov to say, but, in his view, the director was obviously not happy about the letter he had written to the party leadership. Mochalov also mentioned his differences with Shariya, who favoured old-style translation as opposed to the 'new translation' that Mochalov advocated.

Stalin responded by saying that while some of the translation was poor, part of it was quite artistic and it seemed to be the work of a different translator. 'Translation', opined Stalin, 'is more difficult than writing.' He then mused on the need to amend his writings, taking as an example his articles on 'Anarchism or Socialism?', which he had written on the hoof in instalments for different newspapers.

About his articles in *Brdzola*, Stalin agreed their tones were different. The calm tone, he explained, was because he 'aspired to be a professor and wanted to go to university. . . . The Batumi shootings changed everything for me. I started to curse. . . . The tone changed.'[45]

Discussing the size of the print run, Stalin modestly suggested that 30,000–40,000 copies would be enough. When someone pointed out the print run for Lenin's collected works was half a million, Stalin said that he was no Lenin, but was eventually persuaded to accept a figure of 300,000. Stalin wanted each volume to be no more than 300–360 pages long. He preferred the small-scale format of Lenin's works but was indifferent as to whether the cover should be grey or claret (the colour actually chosen).[46]

According to Mochalov's wife, Raisa Konushaya (who also worked at IMEL), he returned home from the meeting 'ashen-faced but bright-eyed'. He told her that Stalin had supported his position and publications that were not his would be excluded from the first two volumes of the works.[47] However, Shariya's recollection was that Stalin let Mochalov have his say and then proceeded to claim the authorship of the disputed unsigned publications.[48]

Not long after the meeting in Stalin's office, the Politburo passed another resolution on the publication of his works. There would be sixteen volumes, each with a print run of 500,000, priced at six roubles a book. The first three volumes would be published in 1946, volumes four to ten in 1947 and the rest in 1948. Resolutions were also passed on the speedy translation of the series into various languages, with print runs in the tens and, in some cases, hundreds of thousands.[49] The edition was announced publicly in *Pravda* on 20 January 1946 and the first volume went on sale in July.

Stalin contributed a preface to the first volume in which he urged his readers to regard his early writings as the work 'of a young Marxist not yet moulded into a finished Marxist-Leninist'. He highlighted two youthful errors. He admitted to having been wrong to advocate the distribution of landlords' lands to the peasants as private property rather than taking them into state ownership, as Lenin favoured. This first mistake he linked to his failure to appreciate fully Lenin's view that the popular overthrow of Tsarist autocracy would be rapidly followed by a socialist revolution in Russia. Stalin also admitted he had been wrong to go along with the then prevailing view among Marxists that socialist revolutions required the majority of the population in any given state to be working class, whereas Lenin had shown that the victory of socialism was possible even in a predominantly peasant country like Russia.[50]

Thirteen volumes of the *Works* covering the period 1901–34 were published between 1946 and 1949. Publication then stalled and the project was cancelled after Khrushchev's denunciation of Stalin at the 20th party congress.

It is hard to understand why the final three volumes were not published while Stalin was alive. 'Dummies' of all the volumes were available to him from 1946 onwards. One possibility is that Stalin couldn't make up his mind about whether to update the 1938 *Short Course History of the Communist Party of the Soviet Union*, which was slated for publication as volume fifteen of his works (its authorship now having been attributed to him rather than an anonymous party commission). In October 1946 Kruzhkov sent him the dummy of that book, together with a note detailing what corrections had been made to the original. In January 1947 party propaganda chief Georgy Alexandrov (1908–1961) and Pyotr Fedoseev (1908–1990), editor of the party's journal, *Bol'shevik*, sent him drafts of two chapters that extended the CPSU's history to 1945, taking their cues from Stalin's February 1946 election speech in which he had characterised the war and analysed the reasons for the Soviet victory. In August 1948 another party official submitted a draft of two additional chapters of the *Short Course*, seemingly at Stalin's own request. In 1951 yet another dummy of volume fifteen, containing just the corrected 1938 text, was sent to Stalin but it, too, was never published.[51]

Volume fourteen, covering the period 1934–40, was also problematic, not least because of Stalin's effusive reply to sixtieth birthday greetings from Hitler's foreign minister, Joachim von Ribbentrop: 'The friendship between the peoples of Germany and of the Soviet Union, cemented by blood, has every basis for being lasting and firm.' Such embarrassments could be glossed over but publication of the volume would inevitably draw attention to the Nazi–Soviet pact of 1939–41.[52]

Far better for Stalin's public image was the proposed publication of an edition of his wartime correspondence with Winston Churchill and Franklin Roosevelt. His long-time deputy, Vyacheslav Molotov, was put in charge of this important project in the late 1940s and two volumes of correspondence were ready for printing by 1952. There was no tampering with these documents, since copies of his private messages to Churchill and Roosevelt were readily available in western archives. Again, publication was delayed for no obvious reason and the volumes did not appear until 1957. Most likely, this was because of the favourable treatment of Tito in the correspondence. Tito, the communist leader of a mass partisan movement in Yugoslavia, was then a Soviet hero and a Stalin favourite. The two men fell out after the war and Tito was excommunicated from the communist movement on grounds that he was, in fact, an imperialist agent bent on the restoration of capitalism in Yugoslavia. After Stalin's death, this impediment to the publication of the correspondence was removed by Khrushchev's disavowal of the Stalin–Tito split and the restoration of fraternal relations with socialist Yugoslavia.[53]

As the American historian Robert H. McNeal observed, 'Stalin's *Sochineniya* falls far short of the standards one would hope for in a definitive collection of a statesman's papers.'[54] The *Works*, as they are called in the English translation, claimed to contain 'nearly all' of Stalin's writings, yet McNeal identified 895 separate writings that had been signed by or identified as Stalin's for the period covered by the thirteen published volumes, only 480 of which appeared in the *Sochineniya*. McNeal's figure was inflated by an excessive number of unsigned pre-1917 publications attributed to Stalin by Beria and other Soviet authors, but there is no doubt that many documents that were verifiably his were omitted from the *Sochineniya*. In the Russian archives there are lists of nearly a hundred such items left out of the volumes.[55] While some documents may have been omitted because they were deemed trivial or repetitive, in many cases the motivation was plainly political. The analysis of these unpublished texts awaits their historian, but it is difficult to disagree with Olga Edel'man's comment that they do not reveal a Stalin substantially different from the one that presents himself in those that were published.[56]

Their limitations notwithstanding, the thirteen published volumes of Stalin's *Sochineniya* were destined to become the single most important source for his biography – 'fundamental' to 'the study of the man and his age', as McNeal put it.[57] They have been particularly important for those biographers who see Stalin as he saw himself – primarily a political activist and theorist, whose driving force was his unstinting commitment to the communist ideology that shaped his personality as well as his behaviour. But not everyone agrees that politics is the Stalin biographers' stone.

CHAPTER 3

READING, WRITING AND REVOLUTION

Among the best-known stories about Stalin's childhood is that he was beaten and brutalised by his drunken father, Vissarion Dzhugashvili (Beso). The source of this story is Joseph Iremashvili, a Georgian childhood friend of Stalin's. Like Stalin, Iremashvili became a member of the Russian Social-Democratic Labour Party, but he was allied with the Mensheviks, the opponents of Lenin's (and Stalin's) Bolshevik faction. By the time the memoir was published in 1932, he was living in exile in Germany. According to Iremashvili, 'undeserved beatings made the boy as hard and heartless as his father himself. Since all men who had authority over others either through power or age reminded him of his father there soon arose a feeling of revenge against all men who stood above him.'[1]

Another boyhood friend of Stalin's, Soso Davrishev, who had emigrated to France, also recalled that Beso beat his son, but his memoir was not published until many years after Iremashvili's. Stalin's daughter, Svetlana, recalled he'd told her that as a child he was beaten by his mother. Svetlana repeated this claim in a second memoir but also highlighted Beso's violent behaviour:

> Fights, crudeness were not a rare phenomenon in this poor, semi-literate family where the head of the family drank. The mother beat the little boy, the husband beat her. But the boy loved his mother and defended her, once he threw a knife at his father [who] then chased him.[2]

Based on these reports, innumerable pathological theories of Stalin's personality have been constructed. The most extreme is Roman Brackman's, who speculates it was Stalin's patricide that started him down the path of a mass-murderous political life. But medical records show Beso was not murdered but died in hospital of TB, colitis and chronic pneumonia in 1909 – the year of death stated by Stalin in the personal questionnaire for ROSTA that he completed in 1920.

Brackman is also a leading exponent of another conspiracy theory: that Stalin was, in fact, an agent of the Okhrana, the Tsarist security police. The point of departure for this hypothesis is the so-called 'Eremin letter' of July 1913, in which a Tsarist police colonel of that name recorded that Stalin was one of his agents. The source of the document, published in English by *Life* magazine in 1956, was Alexander Orlov, an officer in Stalin's security police who defected to the west in the 1930s. While Brackman, like most scholars, accepted that the Eremin letter was an obvious forgery, he argued that the document was, in fact, manufactured by Stalin himself as a means of discrediting the idea that he actually was a police agent. For Brackman, the Great Terror of the 1930s is above all a cover-up operation by Stalin, designed to kill anyone who had knowledge of his past treachery. All the evidence he adduces in support of this hypothesis is circumstantial and speculative but for Brackman the absence of direct evidence is in itself proof of cover-up and conspiracy.[3]

More credible, but no less speculative, is Robert Tucker's synthesis of political biography and insights gleaned from the German psychoanalyst Karen Horney's analysis of the neurotic personality. According to Tucker, Stalin was a neurotic who responded to childhood trauma by creating an idealised image of himself. Far from being merely a political device to manipulate and mobilise the masses, the Stalin personality cult reflected 'Stalin's own monstrously inflated vision of himself as the greatest genius of Russian and world history'. Stalin's lust for power and the purging of his political enemies was psychodynamic and reflected the striving for the fame and glory that would match his exalted self-image.

Tucker formulated this hypothesis in the early 1950s while serving as a diplomat in the US embassy in Moscow. As he admitted himself, there was no direct evidence to support his theory and the prevailing wisdom among his then colleagues was that neither Stalin nor other Soviet leaders took the personality cult too seriously. But Tucker took heart from Khrushchev's denunciation of Stalin at the 20th party congress. Included in Khrushchev's indictment was, to use Tucker's words, a depiction of Stalin 'as a man of colossal grandiosity' who had 'a profound insecurity that caused him to need constant affirmation of his imagined greatness'.[4]

Evidence cited by Khrushchev and highlighted by Tucker was Stalin's editing of his official Soviet biography, in which he marked passages containing insufficient praise. Like many of Khrushchev's claims about Stalin, this was way off the mark. Stalin did indeed edit the second, postwar edition of his *Short Biography* but he actually toned down the adulation and insisted that other revolutionaries should be accorded more prominence. The same was true of many other texts that Stalin edited. While Stalin had a high opinion of himself, it fell far short of the extremities of his personality cult.

Stalin's own view of his family history was much more relaxed than many of his biographers. In a March 1938 speech to a meeting of high-ranking air force officers, he used his own background to illustrate the point that class credentials were no guarantee of honesty. Workers could be scoundrels and non-proletarians could be good people:

> For example, I'm not the son of workers. My father was not born a worker. He was a master with apprentices, he was an exploiter. We didn't live badly. I was ten when he went bust and had to join the proletariat. I couldn't say that he was glad to join the workers. He cursed his bad luck all the time, but for me it turned out to be a good thing. For sure, that is funny [laughter]. When I was ten I was not happy that my father had lost everything. I didn't know that 40 years later it would be a plus for me. But in no way was it an advantage I had earned.[5]

SOSO THE STUDIOUS

Stalin's benign recollection chimes with the views of those historians who believe he had a relatively privileged childhood. While both his parents had been born serfs and his family was not well off, it was not among the poorest and it had the connections to secure Stalin entry into a church school in his home-town of Gori in Georgia and then into a prestigious seminary in the province's capital, Tbilisi. His father had a drink problem and his parents' marriage broke up, but he was the only surviving child of a doting and strong-willed mother who wanted him to become a priest. As a young child, Stalin, or Soso as he was then called, suffered from smallpox and was left with a permanently pockmarked face. He also had an abnormality which reduced the use of his left arm, a condition that may have been genetic or the result of an accident. Adding to Soso's woes was an accident he had aged eleven, when a runaway horse-drawn carriage ran over his legs, which left him with a permanently inhibited gait.

Stalin is said to have been the leader of a children's street-gang in Gori but, as Stephen Kotkin has pointed out, Soso was one of the town's best pupils. Far from being a street ruffian, he was a dedicated 'bookworm' and 'autodidact', which turned out to be a lifelong trait.[6] This fundamental fact about Stalin's early life was captured in a cult painting by the Georgian artist Apollon Kutateladze, *Comrade Stalin with Mother* (1930), which shows a well-dressed, studious boy reading a book, while being overlooked by an encouraging and supportive mother.

READING, WRITING AND REVOLUTION

Born in 1878, Stalin entered the church school in Gori in 1888, having passed the entrance exam with flying colours. According to his mother, Keke, Soso was a good boy who 'studied hard, was always reading and talking, trying to find out everything'.[7] He excelled at singing and was known among his teachers as *bulbuli* (the nightingale). Keke was a devout Christian, and so was her son. As one of his schoolmates recalled, Stalin 'was very believing, punctually attending all the divine services'. According to the same informant, 'Books were Joseph's inseparable friends; he would not part with them even at meal times.'[8]

Because he was such a good pupil, the church assembly waived tuition fees, gave him free textbooks and a stipend of three roubles a month. He was also awarded an inscribed Georgian version of the Psalms, the *davitni*, that praised him as an intelligent and successful pupil. Soso matriculated in May 1894 and on the basis of his results was recommended for entry into a seminary. His marks were (with five being the highest):

Conduct: 5

Sacred History and Catechism: 5

Liturgical Exegesis and Ecclesiastical Typikon: 5

Russian, Church Slavonic and Georgian: 5

Greek and Arithmetic: 4

Geography and Handwriting: 5

Liturgical Chant: 5[9]

That same year, Stalin took his first step on the road to his revolutionary conversion when he visited a recently opened radical bookshop in Gori. There, in its reading room, he encountered an alternative literature to that prescribed by the school, notably the classics of Georgian and Russian literature.

At fifteen, Stalin moved to the capital to enter the Tbilisi Spiritual Seminary which, like his school, was run by the Georgian branch of the Russian Orthodox Church. There were two such seminaries in Tbilisi, one for Georgians and the other for Armenians; both were reserved for bright boys destined for the priesthood. He did very well in the entrance exams, excelling across the board in Bible studies, church Slavonic, Russian, Greek, catechism, geography and penmanship (though not in arithmetic), and was awarded a state subsidy. As Robert Service has commented, Stalin's biographers have tended to underrate the high-quality education he received from the Orthodox Church.[10]

The Georgian seminary had only recently reopened after being shut for a year because of a protest strike about student conditions and restrictions. By the time Stalin arrived at the seminary, there was a well-established tradition of student protest and intellectual rebellion. Students especially resented the 'Russification' policies implemented by the church authorities, which included teaching only through the medium of Russian and suppressing any study of Georgia's language, history and culture.

In Soso's class were students who should have started the year before as well as nine other boys from his school in Gori. Stalin did well academically, scoring fours and fives in most of his subjects, even though the instruction was in Russian, a foreign language with which he was still grappling. Among the secular subjects studied by Stalin were Russian history and literature, logic, psychology, physics, geometry and algebra. Diligent and obedient, he still found the time and spirit to write some patriotic poetry (in Georgian) that he submitted to a nationalist newspaper called *Iveria*.

Five poems were published in 1895 under the pen-name of 'Soselo'. In the longest, 'To the Moon', which had six four-line stanzas, the boy Stalin wrote:

Know well, those who once
Fell to the oppressors
Will rise again with hope
Above the holy mountain

His life as a poet was short lived. Another poem was published in 1896 in a Georgian progressive newspaper, and that was it.[11] In Soviet times his poems were secretly translated into Russian, but there was no question of them being published or included in his collected works. They were far too nationalistic. For Stalin, the political utility of literature was always paramount and their publication would have served no purpose except to complicate his life story. Or, maybe, they no longer pleased him aesthetically and didn't translate well into Russian.

In 1896–7 Soso joined a secret study group organised by an older seminarian, Seit Devdariani. According to Devdariani, the plan was to study natural science, sociology, Georgian, Russian and European literature and the works of Marx and Engels. This subversive involvement impacted on Stalin's grades, which dropped to twos and threes.[12]

One source of forbidden secular books was the Georgian Literary Society's 'Cheap Library' run by *Iveria* editor Ilia Chavchavadze. In November 1896 the seminary inspector wrote in the conduct book: 'It appears that Dzhugashvili has a ticket to the Cheap Library, from which he borrows books. Today I confiscated Victor Hugo's *Toilers of the Sea* in which I found the said library ticket.' In response the principal confined Stalin to the punishment cell for a 'prolonged period', noting that he had already warned him about the possession of Hugo's book on the French Revolution, *Ninety-Three*. Another entry into the conduct book, dated March 1897, stated:

> At 11 p.m. I took away from Joseph Dzhugashvili Letourneau's *Literary Evolution of the Nations*, which he had borrowed from the Cheap Library ... Dzhugashvili was discovered reading the said book on the chapel stairs. This is the thirteenth time this student has been discovered reading books borrowed from the Cheap Library.[13]

One writer favoured by rebellious students like Soso was the Georgian Alexander Qazbegi, whose fictional hero Koba was an outlaw who resisted Russian rule in Georgia. That character provided Soso with his first pseudonym when he joined the illegal revolutionary underground. Not until 1913 did Koba become the more Bolshevik-sounding Stalin – the 'man of steel'.

According to his official Soviet *Short Biography* (1939), Stalin led Marxist study circles in his third and fourth years at the seminary and it was this subversive activity that led him to join the Russian Social-Democratic Labour Party (RSDLP) in 1898 and then to his expulsion from the seminary in May 1899. However, as Alfred J. Rieber has highlighted, the seminary's records show Soso was a troublesome student but not a radical activist.[14] He was not expelled from the seminary for political activity but dismissed for failing to appear at examinations.[15] When Soso dropped out, the seminary issued him with a document testifying to his good behaviour during his four years as a student priest. Four months later the seminary authorities, at Soso's own request, issued a final report card on him, which showed a marked improvement in his grades.[16]

Exegesis of the Holy Script: 4

History of the Bible: 4

Ecclesiastical history: 3

Homiletics: 3

Russian literature: 4

History of Russian literature: 4

Universal secular history: 4

Russian secular history: 4

Algebra: 4

Geometry: 4

Easter liturgy: 4

Physics: 4

Logic: 5

Psychology: 4

Greek: 4

Ecclesiastical singing (Slavic): 5

Ecclesiastical singing (Georgian): 4

Since he had failed to graduate, Stalin could neither go to university nor become a priest. He was qualified to teach in a church school but instead got himself a job at the Tbilisi Meteorological Observatory, where he lived on the premises and kept records of instrument readings. This was the first and last normal job he ever had.

Stalin continued his studies of radical thought and extended the scope of his political involvement. A key influence was Lado Ketskhoveli, whose younger brother Vano also worked at the Observatory. Lado, from Gori, had been expelled from the Tbilisi seminary for leading a student strike in 1893. In 1896 he was expelled from a seminary in Kiev and the next year he returned to Tbilisi where he joined a group of Georgian Marxists and contacted Stalin's cohort of seminarians. Lado became the young Stalin's mentor, and the conduit for his connection to both the illegal revolutionary movement and workers' study circles. An intellectual as well as an activist, Lado was Stalin's first political role model.

AN ORTHODOX STALIN?

By the time he dropped out of the seminary, Stalin had spent a decade being educated by the church. There was no book that he studied more intensively than the Bible. He was well versed on matters theological, had a detailed knowledge of church history and an intimate acquaintance with the rituals of Eastern Orthodoxy. While his education had a significant secular component, immersion in Christian thinking was at its core.

Many have wondered about the long-term impact on Stalin of his religious education, the most radical claim being that he remained a secret believer who continued to pray and read the Bible. Like the conspiracy theory that he was a secret police agent, the hypothesis of a hidden 'Orthodox Stalin' has no evidentiary basis. When it came to religion, Stalin was a model of Bolshevik orthodoxy.

Having left the seminary, he turned his back on all religion. As a Marxist socialist he was a self-proclaimed atheist and the movement to which he belonged made no bones about its anti-clericalism or that it wanted to destroy organised religion and eradicate supernatural thinking at all levels of society. The Bolsheviks saw the Russian Orthodox Church as integral to the capitalist status quo and a fundamental obstacle to their modernising project of socialist enlightenment.

The Bolsheviks espoused religious freedom but reserved the right to campaign against religion. As Stalin himself wrote in 1906:

> Social-Democrats will combat all forms of religious persecution ... will always protest against the persecution of Catholicism or Protestantism; they will always defend the right of nations to profess any religion they please; but at the same time ... they will carry on agitation against Catholicism, Protestantism and the religion of the Orthodox Church in order to achieve the triumph of the socialist world outlook.[17]

The Bolsheviks' leader, Lenin, was among the most implacable opponents of the church and was fond of quoting Marx's aphorisms that religion was the sigh of the oppressed, the opium of the people and so on. Opposed to Lenin on the religion question was Anatoly Lunacharsky, a socialist poet, philosopher and lover of the arts who described himself as intellectual among Bolsheviks and a Bolshevik among intellectuals. He was an exponent of what he called 'god-building' (*Bogostroitel'stvo*). Lunacharsky believed that socialism was a secular religion and that socialists should seek to build bridges to Christians. Christian doctrine was scientifically false and the church was indeed a reactionary institution, but the ethics, values and sentiments of Christianity were laudable and overlapped with those of socialist humanism. In Lunacharsky's version of Christian socialism there was no deity. Socialism was an anthropocentric religion whose God was humanity: 'It is not necessary to look for God. Let us give him to the world! There is no God in the world, but there might be. The road of struggle for socialism ... is what is meant by God-building.'[18]

Lunacharsky's views were set out in a two-volume work, *Religion and Socialism*, published in 1908 and 1911. Stalin possessed a number of Lunacharsky's books and pamphlets but *Religion and Socialism* is not recorded as being among them. Still, it seems likely that Stalin read or was at least familiar with the two books.[19]

God-building never did gain much traction among the Bolsheviks and Lunacharsky reconciled with Lenin in 1917. As the Bolsheviks' commissar of enlightenment from 1917 to 1929, he abandoned god-building but strove to moderate the Bolsheviks' anti-religious fervour. Even so, Bolshevik policy towards the church was highly repressive.[20] Soon after they seized power, they separated church from the state and schools from the church. While freedom of religious conscience was guaranteed by a constitution adopted in 1918, so too was the right to anti-religious propaganda. Priests, capitalists, criminals and other undesirables were categorised as second-class citizens with limited political rights. In 1922 the Bolsheviks expropriated church valuables and responded to popular opposition to their confiscation decrees with show trials and executions of priests and lay believers.[21]

Anti-religious propaganda and the promotion of Soviet atheism was a major Bolshevik priority from the early 1920s. It included sponsorship of an anti-religious newspaper, *Bezbozhnik* (Godless), and the creation of a League of the Godless, both of which were headed by that ubiquitous Stalin acolyte, Yemel'yan Yaroslavsky. Stalin was not enamoured of some of the propaganda, which he considered 'anti-religious trash', and in 1924 he decreed 'hooliganish escapades under the guise of so-called anti-religious propaganda – all this should be cast off and liquidated immediately'.[22]

In 1927 Stalin explained to a visiting American labour delegation that while the communist party stood for religious freedom, it 'cannot be neutral towards religion, and it conducts anti-religious propaganda against all religious prejudices because it stands for science . . . because all religion is the antithesis of science'. Referring to the recent Scopes trial in Tennessee about the illegality of teaching evolution theory, Stalin assured the delegation that Darwinists could not be prosecuted in the USSR because communists defended science. But he was unapologetic about the continuing persecution of priests: 'Have we repressed the clergy? Yes, we have. The only unfortunate thing is that they have not yet been completely eliminated.'[23]

The Bolsheviks' anti-religion campaign moderated in the mid-1920s in the context of 'NEP socialism'.[24] The New Economic Policy, introduced by Lenin after the end of the civil war, permitted a revival of private peasant agriculture and was accompanied by some social and cultural relaxation, although no independent political activity outside the communist party was permitted. The Bolsheviks sought to persuade believers by propaganda and education until the return to a more coercive approach at the end of the 1920s when Stalin launched the campaign to forcibly collectivise Soviet agriculture. Peasant adherence to religion was deemed as pernicious as their attachment to land ownership. In 1929 the party declared a 'merciless war' against counter-revolutionary religious organisations.[25]

Another ebb in the tide of anti-religious militancy came in the mid-1930s with the introduction of the so-called 'Stalin Constitution' of 1936, which guaranteed religious freedom and restored the voting rights of priests. But the church suffered again in the Great Terror of 1937–8, when 14,000 churches were closed and 35,000 'servants of religious cults' were arrested. By 1939 there were fewer than a thousand Orthodox churches in the USSR compared to 50,000 in Tsarist Russia.[26]

The great turning in Stalin's policy on religion was his famous meeting with the leaders of the Russian Orthodox Church in September 1943. The meeting took place in his Kremlin office and he began by noting with approval the church's patriotic support for the Soviet war effort. In the course of a meeting that lasted an hour and twenty minutes, Stalin readily agreed to the appointment of a new patriarch, the opening of more churches, the freeing of arrested priests and the organisation of courses, seminaries and academies to educate the clergy. He even offered state financial support for the church and promised to allow the creation of candle factories to mass-produce a religious prop that had hitherto been handmade.

The record of the meeting was drawn up by Georgy Karpov, a former NKVD officer, whom Stalin subsequently appointed head of a Council for the Affairs of the Russian Orthodox Church.[27] Reported in the press the next day, the meeting signalled peaceful co-existence between organised religion and the Soviet regime. In return for political fealty, the Orthodox Church and its followers were allowed to practise their religion, though without too much active proselytising.[28]

Had Stalin perhaps returned to the religious fold? That was certainly the impression given by the patriarchy, who henceforth referred to him as 'deeply revered' and 'beloved by all', and as a 'wise, divinely appointed leader' who had become so through 'God's Providence'.[29] However, there were plenty of pragmatic reasons for Stalin to invite the church into his tent. It played well with public opinion in Britain and the United States, allies in the struggle against Hitler. Stalin didn't need the church's support to win the war, which had decisively turned in his favour since the Soviet victory at Stalingrad in January 1943, but every little helped. There had been a popular religious revival in the Soviet Union since the German invasion of June 1941 and it was more expedient to recognise and channel the phenomenon into a mainstream church than to repress it. As Victoria Smolkin has pointed out, Stalin made similar moves in relation to Muslims and Baptists.[30] Above all, Russian Orthodoxy would be a powerful ally when the vast territories occupied by the Germans between 1941 and 1944 were recaptured and reintegrated into the Soviet system.[31]

Another way of viewing Stalin's relationship with his religious upbringing is to see communism as a 'political religion'. The idea that when Stalin became a communist he swapped one faith for another is intuitively appealing. Certainly, the parallel between communism and Christianity is compelling. Communism had its sacred texts and ritual practices, its heretics, martyrs, sinners and saints. It also had a secularised eschatology of progress to heaven on earth through predetermined stages of history – slavery, feudalism, capitalism, socialism and communism. Communism, like Christianity, rested on an emotive, faith-based commitment from its adherents.

Stalin's writings were 'sprinkled with biblical allusions, invocations and inflections', noted Roland Boer.[32] Trotsky was labelled a Judas in the *Short Course History of the Communist Party of the Soviet Union* and Stalin was prone to invoke God in his everyday speech: 'God bless', 'God only knows', 'it is for God to forgive' and so on. In a speech to the Baku Soviet in November 1920 on the third anniversary of the Bolshevik Revolution, Stalin alluded to Martin Luther's famous statement to the Diet of Worms in 1521:

> Here I stand on the border line between the old capitalist world and the new socialist world. Here, on this border line, I unite the efforts of the proletarians of the West and the peasants of the East in order to shatter the old world. May the god of history be my aid![33]

But the political religion analogy cannot be pushed too far. Communism had no deity, not even Stalin at the peak of his personality cult was deemed a god. The agent of humanity's fate was the party and the people, according to communist ideology. Communism had no churches or temples. Lenin's body was embalmed and put on public display in Red Square, as was Stalin's for a time, but their bodies were not deified like the remains of saints. For a conscious, committed Marxist like Stalin, communism was based on science and empirically verifiable laws of social development. To paraphrase Lenin, Marxism was not deemed true because it was omnipotent; it was omnipotent because it was true, or so Stalin believed.[34]

BOLSHEVIK INTELLECTUAL

According to Napoleon, understanding a person requires you to know something about their world when they were twenty years old.[35] Stalin's world at that age was the fringe of a vast land empire that stretched thousands of miles across ten time zones from Warsaw to Vladivostok, from the Arctic Ocean to the Caspian and Black Seas. According to the 1897 census, 125 million people lived in Russia, most of them peasants, although state-led industrialisation was creating a significant urban working class. Within Russia's borders were more than 100 nationalities and ethnic groups. Nearly half the population were ethnic

Russians, but there were also large numbers of Ukrainians, Belorussians and Jews, as well as various Turkic and central Asian groups. Stalin's Georgians, whose territory had been a Russian protectorate since 1783, numbered about a million. Nearly 70 per cent of Tsarist Russia's population were affiliated to the Eastern Orthodox Church, though there were many adherents of other Christian traditions, and of Islam and other faiths.

The Russian Tsarist Empire, ruled by the Romanov dynasty for nearly 300 years, was an autocracy in which there was no parliament and political parties were banned. Radical opponents of the Tsar were subject to surveillance, harassment, arrest, imprisonment and exile. Strikes were illegal, as were trade unions, and the nascent underground labour movement was riddled with spies and informers, and plagued by fake organisations set up by the Okhrana. Insidious misinformation was spread by Tsarist agents that named leftist activists as being in cahoots with the authorities, while labour unrest was met with violence and harsh repression. Stalin observed and experienced this first-hand as a political agitator in Tbilisi, Baku and Batumi. Indeed, his first arrest – in Batumi in 1902 – was the result of a strike and demonstration in which many protesters were killed or wounded. While Stalin was under arrest, his childhood friend and close comrade Lado Ketskhoveli was shot and killed by a prison guard.

The political movement Stalin joined believed the working masses were exploited and oppressed by a capitalist system that must be overthrown by a democratic revolution followed by a socialist one. While some radicals thought peasant revolts were the key to revolutionary change in Russia, Marxists like Stalin looked to the urban working class as agents of social transformation. The role of political activists like himself was to educate and recruit workers to the socialist cause and to encourage, support and guide their social, political and economic struggles.

Quite early on in Stalin's political life, the party that he had joined – the RSDLP – split into two main factions. Stalin sided with Lenin's Bolshevik faction, so called because it claimed a majority at the party's second congress in 1903 when the first split occurred. Opposed were the Mensheviks, the supposed minority headed by Julius Martov. In truth, support for each faction was quite evenly balanced and many party members, Leon Trotsky, for example, preferred not to choose between them.

Disagreement about the conditions of party membership was the initial reason for the split. Should the RSDLP be a relatively open party, broad-based and engaged in as much legal activity as possible, as the Mensheviks argued? Or should it be the disciplined, highly centralised and clandestine cadre party that Lenin favoured? In part, this was a dispute about tactics in conditions of illegality and Tsarist repression. But more important were underlying differences about the role of the party. While the Mensheviks envisaged socialist consciousness spreading and embedding spontaneously through the experience of popular struggles to improve conditions and rights, the Bolsheviks thought party members should transmit 'scientific socialism' to the masses. A related issue was assessment of the prospects for socialist revolution in Russia. Socialism was a distant goal for the Mensheviks, hence spreading socialist consciousness and recruiting advanced workers into the party was less important to them than day-to-day social and economic struggles and the agitation for political reform that would feed into a democratic revolution in Russia. Believing that socialist revolution could occur sooner than the Mensheviks thought, the Bolsheviks sought a higher level of socialist consciousness among the toiling masses. Lenin believed there were good prospects for an effective alliance between the working class and the poorer peasants. Stalin's spin on Lenin's position was expressed in a letter written in 1904: 'We must raise the proletariat to a consciousness of its true interests, to a consciousness of the socialist idea, and not break this idea up into small change, or adjust it to the spontaneous movement.'[36]

Stalin's support for Lenin was by no means obvious and automatic. In his neck of the woods – Georgia and Transcaucasia – the Mensheviks were the dominant faction. Much of Stalin's early political life was devoted to fighting and losing factional battles with the local Mensheviks. It was the Mensheviks who came to power in Georgia as result of the 1917 revolutions, where they remained in control until forced out of office by the Bolsheviks in 1921.

While Stalin could easily have found favour with Mensheviks as an authentic man of the people immersed in the daily class struggles of the toiling masses, he was highly educated and committed to proselytising socialism. Stalin saw himself as neither a worker nor a peasant but as, in effect, an intellectual whose task it was to spread enlightenment and socialist consciousness. It was this fundamental choice of an intellectual identity that motivated his fanatical, life-long commitment to reading and self-improvement. While Stalin respected ordinary workers, he did not revere them like some middle-class socialists. The good worker was someone like himself, an educated person who was able to grasp the truth proffered by the party. And it was through such workers that the larger population of the working class could be reached and educated.[37]

Stalin's biographers have tended to neglect the niceties of the politics, day-to-day struggles, factions and personalities of the Russian revolutionary underground. Yet this constituted nearly half his adult life. That was the political and social environment in which his character and personality was formed. As a young revolutionary, Stalin adopted beliefs, acquired attitudes, underwent experiences and made choices.

There is no shortage of evidence about the life of the young Stalin. The problem is that much of it consists of highly partisan and biased memoirs, very little of his primary personal documentation from this early period having survived. Typically, how memoirists recall Stalin correlates with how they see and judge his later life. Perceptions of Stalin, even by those who knew him personally, are overdetermined by later knowledge of his life and persona after the Bolsheviks seized power, and clung to it through civil war, terror and mass violence.

Historians are as divided as the memoirists in assessing the young Stalin's personality. Most agree that while many traits of the mature Stalin may be detected as nascent in his youth, he continued after the revolution to embrace new roles and identities.

As a young man, Stalin was confident and self-assured. He was a faithful member of Lenin's Bolshevik faction and an intriguer and conspirator in internal party battles with the Mensheviks. He was loyal to his comrades and contemptuous of political opponents. He was not shy coming forward but could be low key and reserved when the occasion demanded. Though well capable of anger, he mostly kept his cool. Not much of an orator, he was a skilled polemicist in print. Dogmatic in his political beliefs, he could change his mind in the light of experience, be pragmatic as well as intransigent. His personal life – there was one short-lived marriage and a few dalliances with other women – was strictly subordinate to his all-consuming political passions. Stalin saw little or nothing of his mother after 1904 and did not even write her a letter until 1922. Much of Stalin's youthful political style derived from that of his mentor and exemplar, Lenin. 'Conciliation was in Lenin's view a negative quality for a militant revolutionary,' writes Ronald Suny. 'Sharp ideological distinctions, principled divisions, and purity of position were turned into virtues. Accommodation, compromise and moderation were thrown aside in favour of impatient commitment to action.'[38]

The documentary record of Stalin's political activities is fairly detailed and the evolution of his political views reasonably clear. However, there remain some contentious issues. To what extent was Stalin involved in robberies and extortion to raise funds for the party? Was he the true author of his famous 1913 tract on *Marxism and the National Question*? Was he as loyal to Lenin as he later claimed to be? Was he a 'grey blur', 'the man who missed the revolution' in 1917,[39] notwithstanding cultic claims about his prominence in the Bolshevik seizure of power? Was he the most ruthless of Bolshevik leaders during the Russian Civil War? Did he undermine the Red Army's attempt to capture Warsaw in 1920 and thereby subvert the spread of Bolshevik revolution to Europe?

During the Russian revolutionary upheavals of 1905–7, Stalin was involved in the organisation of Bolshevik armed gangs who took violent actions on behalf of the party. The revolt against the Tsar had been sparked by the Bloody Sunday shooting of peaceful demonstrators in St Petersburg in January 1905. Political assassinations in Russia were nothing new and thousands of Tsarist officials were killed by leftist-led armed groups during the popular disturbances of this period.

In July 1905 Stalin published an unsigned newspaper article on 'Armed Insurrection and Our Tactics' in which he decried the Menshevik view that an insurrection would arise spontaneously from the actions of the masses. On the contrary, argued Stalin, an insurrection had to be prepared and implemented on a co-ordinated basis, including by the advance organisation of armed groups that would protect the people and stockpile arms.[40]

Stalin was peripheral to the Tbilisi coach robbery of June 1907 that features so prominently in Simon Sebag Montefiore's *Young Stalin*.[41] This violent robbery, which netted 250,000 roubles but resulted in a number of deaths, was controversial within the RSDLP because it took place after the party had voted to end such 'expropriations'. While Stalin was blamed by Menshevik opponents for his involvement in the robbery, he was not a direct participant in the heist and may not have even been in the town at all that day. In all probability, Stalin's involvement was limited to providing information and lending moral support to the operation.

Stalin never denied or admitted any connection to the so-called Tbilisi 'Ex' (expropriation). The German writer Emil Ludwig recalled that when he asked Stalin about his role in bank robberies, he 'began to laugh, in that heavy way of his, blinked several times and stood up for the first and only time in our three-hour interview. The question of the bank robbery was the only one he would not answer – except to the extent that he answered it by passing it over.'[42]

Stalin's silence was criticised by Trotsky, who complained that it was 'cowardly' to exclude this 'bold' action from his official biography. It was excluded not because there was anything wrong with robbing banks on behalf of the party, which, Trotsky said, testified to Stalin's 'revolutionary resoluteness', but to cover up a political miscalculation by Stalin – the fact that in 1907 the revolutionary tide was receding and such expropriations had 'degenerated into adventures'.[43]

Stalin's general attitude to political violence was the same as Lenin's: instrumental. Violence was generally abhorrent but acceptable if it furthered the revolutionary cause. Individual acts of terror were only permissible if part of a mass terror campaign underpinned by a popular movement. Moreover, individual assassinations and expropriations were less important than organised guerrilla warfare and preparations for armed insurrection.[44]

READING, WRITING AND REVOLUTION

When the 1905–7 revolutionary period passed, the Bolsheviks abjured armed struggle in favour of non-violent political agitation, notably during elections to the State Duma or parliament established by Tsar Nicholas II as concession to the popular revolt. Duma elections were indirect rather than based on universal suffrage and the institution itself was pretty powerless. Leftist parties boycotted elections to the first Duma, which sat in 1906, but participated in those for the second Duma in 1907. For the third Duma the franchise was rigged in favour of conservative parties, but social democrats, including the Bolsheviks, were able to contest the fourth Duma elections in 1912.

The Bolsheviks secured mandates for six deputies, while the Mensheviks won seven seats. Roman Malinovsky, the leader of the Bolshevik Duma faction, proved to be highly effective. Unfortunately, he was also an agent of the Okhrana. Among his many betrayals was one of his 'best friends', Joseph Stalin, who was arrested in St Petersburg in February 1913. Malinovsky resigned his Duma role in 1914 but was not definitively unmasked as a police spy until 1917, when documentary proof was discovered in Tsarist archives. A year later he was tried and executed by the Bolsheviks. Malinovsky was not the first police spy caught by the Bolsheviks, but his exposure was the most shocking, not least to Stalin.[45]

The idea that Lenin not Stalin was the true author of *Marxism and the National Question* derives from Trotsky's biography of his arch-enemy, which was published posthumously in 1941, a text that Isaac Deutscher, who wrote biographies of both men, described as 'a book of queer fascination, full of profound insight and blind passion'.[46]

The article was Lenin's idea and he edited Stalin's draft. Stalin also had some help with the translation of German-language sources; though Stalin studied English, French, German and Esperanto, he never mastered any foreign language except Russian. But there is no doubt that Stalin was the prime author of this Marxist classic, which set out the fundamentals of Bolshevik policy on the national question.[47]

As internationalists, the Bolsheviks opposed nationalism because they believed it was divisive and diverted from class struggle. But they acknowledged the appeal of nationalist sentiment and accepted the political utility of nationalist-motivated mobilisation against capitalist and imperialist oppression. Hence the Bolsheviks supported the right to national self-determination and would fight for it themselves if national independence ended oppression and, as Stalin put it, 'removed the grounds of strife between nations'.

Stalin's piece was published in three parts in the pro-Bolshevik journal *Prosveshchenie* (Enlightenment) in early 1913. It was signed 'K. Stalin' – a pseudonym he had just started to use but which became permanent and displaced Koba as his underground party name.

After seizing power in 1917, the Bolsheviks continued to uphold the right to national self-determination, and enshrined it in successive versions of the Soviet constitution. However, an important shift in Bolshevik discourse effectively ruled out secession by the nations that constituted the Soviet Union. As people's commissar for nationality affairs, Stalin was the chief articulator of the caveat that national self-determination would not be allowed to endanger the revolution or impede the development of socialism.[48]

While Stalin did not have any really major disagreements with Lenin before 1917, there were some important differences of emphasis and perspective.[49] Stalin spent a lot of time in prison and in internal exile; unlike Lenin and other Bolshevik leaders, he was never an émigré revolutionary living abroad. It was Stalin's presence on the ground in Russia and his work as a grassroots agitator, propagandist and journalist, that made him so valuable to Lenin and lubricated his rise to the top of the Bolshevik party. None was fiercer in their criticism of the Mensheviks, but for practical reasons Stalin often favoured party unity. He disdained internal splits within the Bolshevik faction and his attitude to schisms on matters of theory was much the same. Responding to a philosophical dispute about the nature of Marxist materialism, Stalin described it as 'a storm in a glass of water'. As Ronald Suny has noted, Stalin 'worked through these philosophical distinctions . . . and came to his own conclusions. But his paramount concern was that these disputes over materialism and perception not lead to further factional fractures.' Philosophical discussion was important, wrote Stalin in a 1908 letter from prison, 'but I think that if our party is not a sect – and it has not been a sect for a long time – it cannot break up into groups according to *philosophical* (gnoseological) tendencies'.[50]

Stalin spent several years in exile. Opportunities for political activity were limited, which meant there was plenty of time for reading and study. During his time in Vologda (northern Russia) between 1908 and 1912, the police observed him entering and spending time in local libraries on numerous occasions. Another witness to his activities in Vologda was Polina Onufrieva, the girlfriend of Petr Chizhikov, a political activist who worked closely with Stalin. According to her 1944 testimony, the three of them spent a lot of time together and talked at length about literature and art. Stalin, recalled Polina, was very well informed about both Russian and foreign literature. He became her intellectual mentor and gave her a copy of P. S. Kogan's *Ocherki po Istorii Zapadno-Evropeiskikh Literatur* (1909) (Essays on the History of West European Literature), which he inscribed: 'To intelligent, nasty Polia from oddball Joseph'.[51]

In February 1912 Stalin disappeared from his digs in Vologda. A few weeks later his landlady informed the police and enclosed a list of the things he had left behind in his room, which included quite a few books. Among them were books about accountancy, arithmetic, astronomy and hypnotism. The philosophy texts included works by or about Voltaire, Auguste Comte, Karl Kautsky and the Menshevik philosopher Pavel Yushkevich. Literature was represented by a Russian poets' collection and an unnamed work by Oscar Wilde.[52]

Stalin's longest exile was to Turukhansk in Siberia. He was deported there in July 1913 and stayed for nearly four years. A few of Stalin's letters from this period have survived, including some that he wrote to his great friend Roman Malinovsky. It was a harsh place of confinement and Stalin was often in bad health. As you might expect, he complained about his material conditions to his friends and comrades and pleaded for their financial support. But most of all he badgered them to send him books and journals, especially those necessary to continue his studies of the national question.[53]

As Stalin's landlady's list indicates, he had various interests and read many different kinds of books. But it was Marxist literature that preoccupied him, especially the classic works of Marx and Engels. His first major published work was a series of newspaper articles on *Anarchism or Socialism?* (1906–7) in which he deployed their views to counter the argument of anarchist philosophers that Marxism was too metaphysical. In *Marxism and the National Question* (1913), he criticised the so-called Austro-Marxist view that nations were a psychological construct rather than, as he believed, historical entities based on land, language and economic life. Apart from Lenin, his favourite Russian Marxist was Georgy Plekhanov, one of the founders of Russia's revolutionary socialist movement, who wrote a highly influential historical theory text that Stalin read again in later life – *The Monist View of History*.[54]

WAR AND REVOLUTION

The First World War broke out a year after Stalin was exiled to Turukhansk. It caused a split in the international socialist movement, with many parties rallying to their country's defence. As radical and intransigent as ever, Lenin not only opposed the war but called for socialists to work for the defeat of their own country. Lenin's idea was to turn the international war into a civil war and into a class war that would trigger revolution in Russia and in all the warring states.

Stalin's exile, scheduled to end in summer 1917, was cut short by a dramatic and unexpected event: the fall of the Tsar, Nicholas II. Forced to abdicate by a garrison mutiny and popular uprising in the Russian capital of Petrograd (formerly St Petersburg), the Tsar had also been under pressure from Duma politicians seeking democratic reform and from military leaders who hoped a dramatic gesture would stabilise the home front. The Tsarist administration was taken over by a Provisional Government intending to hold free elections to a constituent assembly charged with adopting a new, democratic constitution. Also vying for power were the Soviets, organs of popular mobilisation that had first appeared during the 1905 revolution and were rapidly revived in 1917. Dominated by socialists, they consisted of worker, peasant and soldier delegates and claimed to represent the population at large, unlike the elitist Duma, which, in any event, had not sat since December 1916.

When Stalin returned to Petrograd in March 1917, the most pressing political issue facing the Bolsheviks was their attitude to the Provisional Government: should they support it or not? Should they continue to oppose the war against Germany and its allies now that the Tsar was gone? Some Bolsheviks wanted to support the Provisional Government as the embodiment, together with the Soviets, of the ongoing democratic revolution in Russia and to moderate the party's anti-war position. Others wanted to have nothing to do with the new government and to continue with Lenin's 'defeatist' position. Initially, Stalin opted for a centrist stance that entailed supporting the Provisional Government as long as it fulfilled the demands of the Soviets while at the same time pressing the new regime to end Russia's participation in the war.

Lenin returned to Russia from exile in Switzerland in April to demand outright opposition to the war and to the Provisional Government. He wanted the Soviets to take power and effect a rapid transition to a socialist revolution. Stalin initially resisted Lenin's radical stance but was soon persuaded by him to change his position.

While Stalin did not go along with everything Lenin said or proposed in 1917, he sided with him at every major turning point. However, Stalin stood his ground on the question of land distribution to individual peasants as against the socialisation of agriculture.[55] Bolshevik support for peasant land seizures in 1917 was crucial to gaining a foothold of popular support in the countryside.

Like Lenin, Stalin thought the Russian Revolution could be the catalyst for European and world revolution: 'The possibility is not excluded that Russia will be the country that will lay the road to socialism. . . . We must discard the antiquated idea that only Europe can show us the way. There is dogmatic Marxism and creative Marxism. I stand by the latter.'[56]

Stalin did oppose Lenin on one important matter: the expulsion of Lev Kamenev and Grigory Zinoviev from the party because of their public opposition to Lenin's call for a Bolshevik insurrection in Petrograd in October 1917 – a proposal they believed was adventurist and would result in defeat and counter-revolution. Stalin was quite close to Kamenev before the revolution, having spent time in exile with him. On grounds of party unity, Stalin insisted that both men remain in the organisation and retain their membership of the Bolshevik central committee, as long as they agreed to abide by CC decisions.

That was another attitude of Stalin's that derived from his long experience in the revolutionary underground, one that was not shared by some 'émigré' Bolsheviks or many of the newer members of the rapidly expanding party – the importance of central control and member discipline in carrying out decisions: 'Once a decision of the Central Committee is made, it must be carried out without any discussion.'[57] This was the basis of the so-called 'democratic centralism' that governed the operation of the party.

The much-quoted observation that in 1917 Stalin was a 'grey blur, looming up now and then dimly and without leaving without any trace' comes from the 1922 memoirs of the Menshevik Nikolai Sukhanov. Often counterposed to Sukhanov's perception of Stalin as a drab and uninteresting individual is Trotsky's dramatic impact after he returned to Russia in May 1917. Elected to the Petrograd Soviet, he joined up with the Bolsheviks in July and in September was elected chairman of the Soviet's Executive Committee. He supported Lenin's call for a Bolshevik insurrection and established a Military-Revolutionary Committee as the armed wing of the Petrograd Soviet. It was this body that carried out the Bolshevik coup in Petrograd in November 1917 when it forcibly seized control of key buildings and communications infrastructure. The following day Trotsky told delegates to the Second Congress of Soviets that the Provisional Government had been overthrown, and jeered the moderate social-ists who opposed the seizure of power as belonging 'in the dustbin of history'.

Lenin's Soviet-based government was a coalition of the Bolsheviks and Left Socialist Revolutionaries, who represented militant peasants. Its ministers were called commissars because Lenin thought that sounded more revolutionary. Lenin was chair of the Council of Commissars, Trotsky was people's commissar for foreign affairs and Stalin filled the entirely new post of commissar for the nationalities. Upon taking office, Trotsky famously said: 'I will issue a few revo-lutionary proclamations to the peoples of the world and then shut up shop.'[58]

Though overshadowed by Trotsky in historical memory, there were few Bolsheviks more important than Stalin in 1917. One of the first Bolshevik leaders to reach Petrograd from exile, he was a member of the editorial board of the party's newspaper *Pravda*, contributing numerous articles to the Bolshevik press. When *Pravda* was supressed by the authorities, he edited the paper issued by the party as a substitute. When the Provisional Government clamped down on the Bolsheviks in summer 1917 and Trotsky was gaoled, while Lenin fled to Finland, Stalin remained at large. He spoke at all the party's major meetings and in Lenin's absence presented the main report to the 6th congress of the Bolshevik party in July–August 1917. This was a tough assignment, coming as it did in the wake of the party's setbacks following the radical demonstrations of the July days that had provoked the Provisional Government's crackdown. Stalin supported Lenin's proposal for an insurrection and was one of seven party leaders entrusted with overseeing its preparation. As Chris Read puts it, 'If Stalin was a blur it might seem to be a result of his constant activity rather than indistinctiveness!'[59]

Having grabbed power, Lenin, Stalin and Trotsky were determined to retain it at all costs. At stake, they believed, was not just the fate of the Russian Revolution but also the socialist future of all humanity. Scheduled elections to a Constituent Assembly were permitted at the end of November but when they produced an anti-Bolshevik majority the first democratically elected parliament in Russian history was not allowed to function. The Bolsheviks claimed the Soviets, which they and their allies controlled, were more representative of public opinion and better placed to protect the interests of the people.[60]

In March 1918 Lenin's government signed the Brest-Litovsk peace treaty with Germany, Austria-Hungary, Bulgaria and the Turkish Ottoman Empire. The treaty negotiations provoked a deep split in the Bolsheviks' ranks and broke up the alliance with the Left Socialist Revolutionaries.

One of the very first acts of Lenin's regime had been the proclamation of a Decree on Peace which called for a general armistice and negotiations for 'a just and democratic peace'. When the fighting continued, Lenin agreed a separate ceasefire with the Germans and started the negotiations at Brest-Litovsk. Foreign Commissar Trotsky, who led the Soviet negotiations, had no intention of actually concluding a peace treaty. Instead, he aimed to spin out the negotiations and to use them as a platform for propaganda, the hope being that the revolutionary situation in Europe would mature and the war could be stopped by mass action. The Germans played along with this charade for a while but in January 1918 issued an ultimatum that demanded the annexation of large chunks of the western areas of the former Tsarist Empire in return for a peace deal.

Lenin and Stalin wanted to accept the German terms on grounds that the alternative was losing the war and with it the revolution. Opposed were Nikolai Bukharin and 'Left Communist' supporters of a revolutionary war against Germany, who argued that the European proletariat would rise in support of Bolshevik Russia. The Left Socialist Revolutionaries also favoured a revolutionary war. Trotsky proposed a compromise formula of 'neither war nor peace' – a unilateral declaration of an end to hostilities. Trotsky's proposal was accepted and this is what he told the astonished German negotiators at Brest-Litovsk.

Trotsky's calculation that the Germans would acquiesce in such a peace because it would enable them to concentrate on defeating their western enemies proved to be disastrously wrong when Berlin launched an Eastern Front offensive that achieved rapid success. Faced with the prospect of military collapse, the Bolsheviks had little choice but to accept the Germans' terms, which had hardened considerably. Even so, it was only after a sharp debate at a specially convened party congress in March 1918 that the Bolsheviks voted in favour of the peace treaty. At the same gathering they changed their name to the All-Russian Communist Party (Bolsheviks).

CIVIL WAR COMMISSAR

The Brest peace paved the way for the Russian Civil War. Now Russia was no longer at war, the Bolsheviks' opponents did not hesitate to use force in an attempt to topple them from power. The deal also provided a pretext for foreign intervention as Russia's former allies moved to stop supplies they had sent to the Tsar and the Provisional Government from falling into German hands. More allied troops poured into Russia when the First World War ended in November 1918 and foreign military intervention became part of an anti-Bolshevik crusade aimed at regime change in Russia.

The civil war was a close-run thing. At its height in 1919, the Bolsheviks were corralled in central Russia, under attack from all sides by 'White Armies' led by former Tsarist generals and admirals. Having resigned from the Foreign Commissariat as a result of the Brest-Litovsk debacle, Trotsky played a central role in the Bolshevik victory over the Whites. As commissar for war, he raised a 5-million-strong Red Army, controversially recruiting to its ranks 50,000 former Tsarist officers and NCOs.

During the civil war, Stalin was Lenin's troubleshooter-in-chief on the front line. Stalin's contribution to the Red victory was, as Robert McNeal has observed,

> second only to Trotsky's. Stalin had played a smaller role in the overall organisation of the Red Army, but he had been more important in providing direction on crucial fronts. If his reputation as a hero was far below Trotsky's, this had less to do with objective merit than with Stalin's lack of flair, at this stage of his career, for self-advertisement.[61]

In June 1918 Stalin was sent to Tsaritsyn (renamed Stalingrad in 1924) to protect food supply lines from southern Russia. With the city about to fall to the enemy, Stalin responded with a wave of arrests and executions of those deemed disloyal and traitorous. He was outraged by the attempted assassination of Lenin in August 1918 by Fanny Kaplan, a member of the Socialist Revolutionary Party, which had been banned by the Bolsheviks. Stalin cabled to Moscow that he was responding to this 'vile' act by 'instituting open and systematic mass terror against the bourgeoisie and its agents'.[62]

While in Tsaritsyn, Stalin clashed with Trotsky over the role of the bourgeois military specialists who had sided with the Bolsheviks. Stalin was all in favour of using whatever expertise was available but he distrusted these specialists and preferred to rely on those with established political loyalties. When Stalin obstructed Trotsky's appointment of a former Tsarist general to command the Bolsheviks' Southern Front, the war commissar demanded his immediate recall to Moscow. Lenin, who agreed with Trotsky on the use of bourgeois military specialists, acceded to this but retained his confidence in Stalin.

In January 1919 Stalin was sent to the Urals to investigate why the Perm region had fallen to Admiral Kolchak's White Army. Stalin was accompanied by Felix Dzerzhinsky, the fearsome head of the Cheka – the agency of the Bolsheviks' 'Red Terror' during the civil war. Reporting back to Moscow, they highlighted the number of former Tsarist officers who had defected to the Whites.

Trotsky's recruitment of former Tsarist officers was debated at the Bolshevik party's 8th congress in March 1919. Since Trotsky was at the front, it fell to Lenin to defend his war commissar's position. Notwithstanding his own doubts, Stalin sided with Lenin against those who wanted to stop employing bourgeois military specialists.

In the spring Stalin was sent to bolster the defence of Petrograd, which was threatened by General Yudenich's White Army based in Estonia. For several months he was a highly visible figure of authority in the Petrograd area, touring the front line and inspecting military bases. In October 1919 Stalin went to the Southern Front to help with the defence of the southern approaches to Moscow, which were threatened by General Denikin's troops.

Stalin's next assignment was the South-West Front, whose forces were attacked by the armies of newly independent Poland in April 1920. Recreated in the aftermath of the First World War, the new Polish state was carved out of territory that belonged to Germany, the Austro-Hungarian Empire and Tsarist Russia. Its border with Russia was demarcated by an international commission headed by the British foreign secretary, Lord Curzon. This border, which became known as the 'Curzon Line', was unacceptable to the Poles, who decided to grab as much territory as they could while civil war raged in Russia.

Headed by Marshal Józef Piłsudski, the Poles' campaign went well at first, but the Red Army soon halted and then reversed their advances. The question arose of taking the fight into Polish territory, with the aim of defeating Piłsudski and inspiring a proletarian revolution in Poland that would then spread to Germany and the rest of Europe. Stalin was cautious as he had already experienced many rapid advances and reverses during the civil war. His front had to contend also with Baron Wrangel's White forces based in Crimea. In an interview with *Pravda* in mid-July, Stalin said:

our successes on the anti-Polish Front are unquestionable. .... But it would be unbecoming boastfulness to think that the Poles are as good as done with, that all that remains for us to do is to 'march on Warsaw'. .... It is ridiculous to talk of a 'march on Warsaw' ... as long as the Wrangel danger has not been eliminated.[63]

But when asked by Lenin how the government should respond to a ceasefire proposal from Curzon, Stalin cabled, on 13 July, that

the Polish armies are completely falling apart. .... I don't think imperialism has ever been as weak as it is now, at the moment of Poland's defeat, and we have never been as strong as we are now, so the more resolutely we behave ourselves, the better it will be for Russia and for international revolution.[64]

The party central committee duly decided to invade Poland. And on 23 July the Politburo established a Provisional Polish Revolutionary Committee.[65]

The Red Army's thrust into Poland was initially quite successful. As it approached Warsaw, delegates to the Second World Congress of the Communist International (Comintern) meeting in Moscow were thrilled by Lenin's charting of the Red Army's progress on a large-scale war map.[66]

Stalin got rather carried away, too. On 24 July he wrote to Lenin:

It would be a sin not to encourage revolution in Italy now that we have the Comintern, a beaten Poland and a reasonable Red Army while the Entente is trying to obtain a breathing space for the Polish army so it can be reorganised and rearmed. .... The Comintern should consider organising an uprising in Italy and in weak states such as Hungary and Czechoslovakia (Romania has to be smashed, too).[67]

Among the formations under Stalin's remit as the South West Front's Bolshevik commissar was Semen Budenny's First Cavalry Army. In mid-August Budenny was ordered by Moscow (the Bolshevik capital since March 1918) to support the Red Army's campaign to capture Warsaw. Amid continuing concerns about the threat from Wrangel, Stalin, who had his eye on taking Lvov not Warsaw, refused to counter-sign the order.[68] While the delay in Budenny's redeployment did not help matters, the Red Army's offensive was probably doomed anyway, not least because the anticipated proletarian insurrection in Poland failed to materialise. By the end of August the Poles had repulsed the attack on Warsaw and the Red Army was in full-scale retreat. Lenin was forced to sue for peace and then, in March 1921, to sign the Treaty of Riga, an agreement that imposed severe territorial losses on Soviet Russia, notably the incorporation into Poland of western Belorussia and western Ukraine, territories that were populated mainly by Belorussians, Ukrainians and Jews.

Stalin's actions during the Polish campaign became a cause of considerable controversy. An early contributor to the debate was Boris Shaposhnikov, who later served as Stalin's chief of the General Staff. In his 1924 book, *Na Visle: K Istorii Kampanii 1920* (On the Vistula: Towards a History of the 1920 Campaign), a copy of which may be found in Stalin's library, he concluded that while Budenny's delay did have a negative impact on the Red Army's march on Warsaw, his army would not, in any event, have arrived in time to save the Soviets' West Front from defeat by the Poles.[69] In his study of Stalin as a military commander, British military historian Albert Seaton arrived at a similar verdict:

> The extent to which Stalin's refusal or delay in carrying out orders was indirectly responsible for the defeat of the West Front and the consequent loss of the Russo-Polish war is a question which can only be examined by considering the . . . war as a whole. Many other factors contributed to the defeat: political misjudgement, military misdirection, poor training and organisation, indiscipline in the West as well as the South-West Front, over-confident and inexpert commanders and inadequate signals communications. It seems probable, however, that . . . [the West Front] might have been saved from so overwhelming a defeat.[70]

Stalin responded to the unfolding Polish debacle by submitting a memorandum to the Politburo that argued the defeat resulted from a 'lack of effective fighting reserves' (Trotsky thought that supplies were the main problem). Stalin also called for a high-level investigation of the reasons for the defeat in Poland.[71] This created tension with Lenin as well as Trotsky, both of whom had a vested interest in avoiding too deep a discussion of the failed Polish adventure. Together with Trotsky, Lenin successfully manoeuvred within the Politburo to stymie Stalin's proposed investigation.

At the Bolsheviks' 9th party conference in September 1920, Stalin was criticised by Lenin and Trotsky for his 'strategic errors' during the Polish campaign. He responded with a dignified statement which pointed to his publicly expressed doubts about the 'march on Warsaw' and reiterated the call for a commission to examine the reasons for the catastrophe.[72]

By this time Stalin had, at his own request, been relieved of military responsibilities. The civil war was nearly over and he had plenty of other work to do. Throughout the conflict he had remained nationalities commissar and in March 1919 was appointed head of the People's Commissariat of State Control, later renamed the Worker-Peasant Inspectorate, whose job it was to protect state property and to keep wayward officials in line.

Stalin played little direct role in the day-to-day operations of either commissariat, which he delegated to officials. But he kept his finger on the policy pulse in relation to the national question. Lenin's was still the dominant Bolshevik voice on this matter, and Stalin did not always agree with him. He favoured a future confederation of socialist states rather than the more tightly knit world federation proposed by Lenin. Stalin argued that advanced and well-established nations would want to have their own independent states for the foreseeable future. Their new socialist rulers would not accept Lenin's proposal to universalise the federal relations between nationalities that prevailed within Soviet Russia. Of more practical import, though, was Stalin's preference for a highly centralised Soviet state. When the Union of Soviet Socialist Republics was created in 1922 it reflected a compromise with Lenin in which behind a façade of the federalism there was the highly centralised state preferred by Stalin.

Georgia was the most serious source of tension between Stalin and Lenin. Stalin's native land was ruled by a Menshevik government headed by Noe Zhordania, an old adversary of his from the underground days. The Georgian Menshevik state was recognised by the Bolsheviks in May 1920, who pledged non-interference in its internal affairs in return for the legalisation of communist party activity. Lenin favoured a more conciliatory approach to Georgia than Stalin and Trotsky, who both wanted to occupy the country militarily. In February 1921 the Red Army marched in.

In the early weeks of the Bolshevik takeover in Georgia, Stalin was ill and he spent the summer recuperating at a spa in the North Caucasus. In July he crossed the mountains to support the Georgian Bolsheviks in rallying the masses to their new regime. Appalled by the nationalist fervour he encountered, he ordered the Cheka to quell resistance to Bolshevik rule. Among the more than 100 arrestees was Stalin's childhood friend Joseph Iremashvili.[73]

It was not only Georgian nationalism that worried Stalin. His solution was a Transcaucasian Socialist Federation as a container for all the region's nationalisms and ethnic differences. That federation, which consisted of Armenia, Azerbaijan and Georgia, was established at the end of 1921 and was a signatory of the treaty that established the USSR in 1922 (the other signatories being Russia, Ukraine and Belorussia).[74]

THE GENERAL-SECRETARY

Differences over the Polish war, the national question and the Georgian crisis did some damage to Stalin's personal relations with Lenin. But it was Lenin who pushed through Stalin's appointment as general-secretary of the communist party in April 1922, a post that involved oversight of the central committee apparatus, allocation of key personnel and agenda-setting for Politburo meetings. A *praktik* as well as an intellectual, Stalin's appointment to the post made a lot of sense, particularly since he had again proved himself to be Lenin's loyal lieutenant. At the 10th party congress in March 1921 he backed Lenin in a dispute about the role of Soviet trade unions. Trotsky wanted to subordinate unions to state commands, while the leftist Workers Opposition wanted proletarians to directly control their factories. Stalin agreed with Lenin that the role of trade unions was to protect workers' interests in accordance with the party's political directives. He also sided with Lenin on the introduction of the New Economic Policy – the party's retreat from the draconian 'war communism' of the civil war years. As a consistent advocate of party unity, Stalin supported the congress's ban on factions – groups within the party that operated with their own internal organisation and discipline. However, that ban did not prevent Lenin from asking Stalin to secure control of the central party apparatus for their group.[75]

Stalin's ascendancy to the general-secretaryship coincided with the culmination of the party's encroachment on state functions which had begun during the civil war. When Lenin seized power in 1917 he intended to govern through state institutions, i.e. the Council of People's Commissars (Sovnarkom) and its respective departments and subunits. But that did not work out too well. Within Sovnarkom there was too much talk and too little action. It was not well suited to rapid and decisive decision-making, especially during the civil war. Sovnarkom's democratic legitimacy rested on the Soviets, which it supposedly represented, but these had collapsed during the civil war. Gradually, the party took over many state functions. The Politburo took all the important decisions and the Soviet regime rapidly evolved into a hybrid 'party-state' in which the party's power predominated at every level of state and society. The party did not just control or occupy the state – its organisation and personnel were the most important arm of the state.[76]

Lenin had intended to counter-balance Stalin's power as general-secretary by appointing Trotsky one of his deputies in Sovnarkom, but in May 1922 he had the first of a series of debilitating strokes.[77]

The succession struggle began while Lenin was ailing and one of the early salvos was fired by his soon-to-be widow, Nadezhda Krupskaya, when she revealed the existence of what became known as 'Lenin's Testament' – a series of notes dictated by him from his sickbed in late 1922 and early 1923. Doubts have been expressed about the provenance of the testament and it may be that Krupskaya and the staff who wrote down Lenin's utterings put some words into his mouth but, crucially, no one questioned the authenticity of Lenin's notes at the time.[78]

About Stalin and Trotsky, Lenin supposedly said:

Comrade Stalin, having become General-Secretary, has concentrated enormous power in his hands, and I am not sure that he always knows how to use that power with sufficient caution. On the other hand, Comrade Trotsky . . . is distinguished not only by his exceptional ability – personally, he is, to be sure, the most able man in the present CC – but also by his too far-reaching self-confidence and a disposition to be far too much attracted by the purely administrative side of affairs. These two qualities of the two most able leaders of the present CC might, quite innocently, lead to a split, and if our Party does not take measures to prevent it, a split might arise unexpectedly.[79]

Even more damning was this addendum to Lenin's testament:

Stalin is too rude and this defect, although quite tolerable in our midst and in dealing among us Communists, becomes intolerable in a General-Secretary. That is why I suggest that the comrades think about a way of removing Stalin from that post and appointing another man . . . more tolerant, more loyal, more polite and more considerate to the comrades, less capricious, etc. This circumstance may appear to be a negligible detail. But I think that from the standpoint of safeguards against a split and from the standpoint of what I wrote about the relationship between Stalin and Trotsky . . . it is a detail which can assume decisive importance.[80]

Lenin's proposal to remove Stalin as general-secretary was not as drastic as it might appear in retrospect since the post was still predominantly administrative. Being relieved of such a burden might even have suited Stalin, as long as he remained one of the party's top leaders.

Lenin's testament provoked little more than a storm in a political teacup. Identifying Trotsky as the main danger to their own leadership ambitions, Stalin's Politburo comrades backed the nascent dictator and efforts to use the testament to whip up opposition to Stalin among party activists did not get very far. Stalin offered on more than one occasion to accede to Lenin's wishes and resign as the party's general-secretary, but there was never any question his resignation would be accepted.

Stephen Kotkin is convinced that Stalin found the Lenin Testament episode profoundly psychologically disturbing and harboured a deep sense of victimhood and self-pity.[81]

Stalin may have been peeved by the testament and irritated by Lenin's words, but there is no evidence the episode had any lasting impact on his psychological make-up. Stalin was not the self-pitying type, did not see himself as a victim and remained loyal to Lenin's memory. When he commented on Lenin's remarks about him at the central committee plenum in July 1927, he was unrepentant. Having quoted in full the testament's passage about his rudeness, Stalin said: 'Indeed, I am rude, Comrades, to those who rudely and perfidiously destroy and split the party. I have not hidden this, and still do not.'[82]

Stalin was well placed to emerge as Lenin's successor. After Lenin's death in January 1924 he gradually established himself as the pre-eminent party leader. He helped create a Lenin cult and projected himself as Lenin's most faithful pupil. He positioned himself as a centrist in the various policy disputes that beset the party. He used the patronage of official appointments to gather support. He paid attention to the needs and interests of regional party officials. Most importantly, he gave meaning to the lives of party officials and activists by prioritising the construction of socialism at home over the spread of revolution abroad.

When the Bolsheviks took power they expected their revolution to be bolstered by revolutions in more advanced countries. The failure of the revolution to spread abroad prompted Stalin to fashion a new doctrine – Socialism in one country – which proclaimed that Soviet Russia could build a socialist state that would safeguard both the Russian Revolution and the future world revolution. 'Internationalism' was reformulated to serve the interests of the one successful revolution. 'An internationalist', said Stalin in 1927, 'is one who is ready to defend the USSR without reservation, without wavering, unconditionally; for the USSR is the base of the world revolutionary movement, and this revolutionary movement cannot be defended and promoted unless the USSR is defended.'[83]

Stalin's own explanation for his success in the factional battles of the 1920s was that he had secured the support of middle-ranking party and state officials: 'Why did we prevail over Trotsky and the rest?' he asked in 1937. 'Trotsky, as we know, was the most popular man in our country after Lenin. Bukharin, Zinoviev, Rykov, Tomsky were all popular. We were little known. . . . But the middle cadres supported us, explained our positions to the masses. Meanwhile Trotsky completely ignored those cadres.'[84]

Stalin's workload as general-secretary was enormous and continued to grow as the party-state bureaucracy expanded. The paper trail of reports, resolutions and stenograms passing through his office was endless, as were the frequent visitors, and the numerous meetings he had to attend. But he proved a highly capable administrator, one measure of his success being the scale of the task he faced: 'The General-Secretary had to establish a system that tracked the skills and experience of hundreds of thousands of officials ... to organise 350,000 mostly poorly qualified ... "staff", who together had to bring the world's largest country, with a population of almost 140 million, out of an appalling economic crisis amidst serious political divisions.'[85]

As for many political leaders, the vast bulk of Stalin's reading life was taken up by reports, briefings and correspondence. When President Barack Obama left office, he complained that while such material was good for working the analytical side of the brain he sometimes lost track of 'not just the poetry of fiction, but also the depth of fiction. Fiction was useful as a reminder of the truths under the surface of what we argue about every day.' In a similar vein, President Vladimir Putin said that he kept a volume of Mikhail Lermontov's poetry on his desk in order 'to have something to think about, to take my mind off things and, generally speaking, to find myself in a different world – a worthwhile, beautiful and interesting one.'[86]

Stalin certainly shared Obama's liking for Shakespeare and, quite possibly, Putin's penchant for Lermontov. But armed with his Marxist outlook on life, he found the poetry of non-fiction equally appealing.

CHAPTER 4

THE LIFE AND FATE OF A DICTATOR'S LIBRARY

In May 1925 Stalin entrusted his staff with a highly important mission: the classification of his personal book collection:

My advice (and request):

1. Classify the books not by author but by subject-matter:
   a. Philosophy
   b. Psychology
   c. Sociology
   d. Political Economy
   e. Finance
   f. Industry
   g. Agriculture
   h. Co-operation
   i. Russian History
   j. History of Other Countries
   k. Diplomacy
   l. External and Internal Trade
   m. Military Affairs
   n. The National Question
   o. Congresses and Conferences
   p. The Position of the Workers

q. The Position of the Peasants

r. The Komsomol

s. The History of Revolutions in Other Countries

t. 1905

u. February Revolution 1917

v. October Revolution 1917

w. Lenin and Leninism

x. History of the RKP (B) and the International

y. Discussions in the RKP (articles, pamphlets)

z. Trade Unions

aa. Fiction

bb. Art Criticism

cc. Political Journals

dd. Science Journals

ee. Dictionaries

ff. Memoirs

2. Exclude from this classification and arrange separately books by

a. Lenin

b. Marx

c. Engels

d. Kautsky

e. Plekhanov

f. Trotsky

g. Bukharin

h. Zinoviev

i. Kamenev

j. Lafargue

k. Luxemburg

l. Radek

3. All the rest can be classified by author (putting to one side: textbooks, small journals, anti-religious trash, etc.).[1]

STALIN'S LIBRARY

Stalin evidently had in mind a rather grandiose personal library, one that would contain a vast and diverse store of human knowledge, not only the humanities and social science but aesthetics, fiction and the natural sciences. His proposed schema combined conventional library classification with categories that reflected his particular interests in the history, theory and leadership of revolutionary movements, including the works of anti-Bolshevik socialist critics such as Karl Kautsky and Rosa Luxemburg, as well as the writings of internal rivals such as Leon Trotsky, Lev Kamenev and Grigory Zinoviev. Naturally, pride of place went to the founders of Marxism – Karl Marx and Friedrich Engels – and to its pre-eminent modern exponent, Vladimir Lenin.

The inclusion of the French socialist Paul Lafargue in the list of revolutionary writers with a separate classification might seem odd to contemporary eyes but there were a number of his books in Stalin's library. Lafargue was famous among revolutionaries of Stalin's generation as the author of the radical tract *The Right to Be Lazy* (1880). He was also married to Marx's second daughter, Laura. Indeed, the couple committed suicide together in 1911. Shortly after, the Bolshevik journal *Prosveshchenie* (Enlightenment) published an obituary by Kautsky and in its next issue carried an analysis of Lafargue's contribution to the international socialist movement, articles that Stalin may well have read.[2] In his 1950 intervention in the Soviet linguistics debate about the monogenetic language theories of Georgia-born Nikolai Marr, Stalin quoted with approval Lafargue's pamphlet *Language and Revolution*.[3]

STALIN'S LIBRARIAN

Stalin's classification scheme is listed in the Russian archival register as intended for an unnamed 'librarian'. However, the document in question, which was handwritten by Stalin, contains no addressee. Stalin's secretary and aide, Ivan P. Tovstukha, was identified as the recipient by General Dmitry Volkogonov in his groundbreaking 1989 Soviet biography of Stalin, *Triumph and Tragedy*. Volkogonov, who served in the Soviet army's main political administration and headed the Defence Ministry's Institute of Military History from 1988 to 1991, was able to secure unprecedented access to confidential party and state archives. Although he started work on the biography in the 1970s, he was only able to publish it when the reforming Mikhail Gorbachev came to power in the USSR.

According to Volkogonov, Stalin called in Tovstukha and asked his trusted assistant to sort out a decent personal library for him. When Tovstukha wanted to know what books it should contain, Stalin started to dictate something but then decided to dash off the above-cited note.[4]

THE LIFE AND FATE OF A DICTATOR'S LIBRARY

Volkogonov often failed to cite the sources for his stories about Stalin, and this was one such example. But that didn't deter other historians from repeating this highly improbable story.[5] Stalin did habitually issue detailed on-the-spot instructions to his staff, usually in the form of dictation. When he handwrote such instructions they were invariably immediately edited and corrected by him. This note had no such corrections and has the air of careful not spontaneous composition by Stalin.

It is possible that Stalin did ask a high-level functionary to supervise if not carry out the classification of his books, but the actual recipient of his 'request' was probably a librarian called Shushanika Manuchar'yants. She was certainly one recipient of the note because, on 3 July 1925, she wrote to Stalin asking him if he wanted to expand his categories to include Transport, Education, Statistics, Popular Science and Law. Manuchar'yants also wanted to know if items such as reports, surveys and popular tracts were to be kept separate and whether to order some adjustable shelving that she thought would be ideal for his library.

As was his custom, Stalin replied by writing his answers in the margins of her typed memo. To the first question, he answered *nuzhno* (one should) but added in brackets after Law, *isklyuchaya dekrety* – 'excluding decrees'. The answer to the second and third questions was a simple *da* (yes).[6]

Manuchar'yants had been Lenin's librarian and after his death in 1924 continued to work for his sister Maria and his widow Nadezhda Krupskaya. It seems likely she served as Stalin's librarian as well, which would explain why he presented her with a signed copy of his book *Voprosy Leninizma* (Problems of Leninism) in 1926.[7] In all probability, it was Shushanika who prompted Stalin to devise his classification scheme and have created his ex-libris stamp – *Biblioteka I. V. Stalina* – which had the same simple design as the one she used when working as Lenin's librarian.

Lazar Kaganovich, Stalin's transport commissar in the 1930s, also had an ex-libris stamp. Like Stalin, Kaganovich was from a modest, non-intellectual background. He, too, numbered as well as stamped his books, indicating an intention to build up a substantial collection.[8]

When she went to work for Lenin in 1920, Manuchar'yants was surprised there were not more books in his office, but she soon learned that he kept to hand only those volumes he needed for current work or for reference purposes. Even so, there were about 2,000 books, many of them in foreign languages, and another 3,000 were kept in a room adjacent to Lenin's small Kremlin flat. The books were shelved in alphabetical order on six bookcases, one of which contained the classics of Marxism, while another was filled with counter-revolutionary 'White Guard' literature that had been published abroad. On other shelves were collections of encyclopaedias, dictionaries and journals,

69

military books and maps, Russian and foreign literature, texts on communism and Soviet foreign policy, and the writings of Russian revolutionary democrats.

Lenin was a fast reader and had a habit of writing in his books with a red or black pencil. Manuchar'yants's recollection of her daily routine as Lenin's librarian was as follows:

> Have a look at the newly received books and take the most essential to the table beside Lenin's desk. Register the new books and fill out the cards for the catalogue. Tidy up the bookshelves and bring to Lenin the books he has asked for. Order books that he needs from other libraries.[9]

Among Shushanika's co-workers in Lenin's office was Stalin's wife, Nadezhda Alliluyeva. According to Stalin's daughter Svetlana, hundreds of the history and art books in her father's library belonged to her mother, a sub-collection to which she (unsuccessfully) laid claim in a 1955 letter to the party leadership.[10] Maybe it was Nadezhda's idea to ask Shushanika to organise their books.

Manuchar'yants's memoir did not refer to working for Stalin, nor even mention his name, except once in passing. Such reminiscences were prohibited in the USSR after Khrushchev denounced the dictator; the only exceptions were military-related memoirs concerning Stalin's role as supreme commander during the Second World War.

In 1930 Manuchar'yants went to work at the Lenin Institute, which in 1931 became the core of the newly formed Institute of Marx, Engels and Lenin (IMEL). Initially, she worked on Lenin-related projects but in 1940 transferred to the section responsible for the publication of Stalin's collected writings and remained there until retirement in 1955. She died in 1969, just before publication of the second edition of her book in the Lenin centenary year of 1970.

Manuchar'yants's transfer to IMEL may have saved her life. In 1935 a great number of Kremlin support staff – cleaners, guards, administrators and librarians – were implicated in a (concocted) conspiracy to assassinate Stalin and other Soviet leaders. Among those arrested and shot was the librarian Nina Rozenfel'd, the former wife of Lev Kamenev's brother.

'You've heard what went on in the Kremlin,' Stalin told a meeting of the central committee's Orgburo in March 1935:

> A single person who has access to the apartments of our leaders – a cleaning woman who cleans the rooms, or a librarian who visits an apartment under the pretext of bringing the books in order. Who are they? Often, we don't know that. There exists a very great variety of poisons which are very easy to apply. The poison is put in a book – you take the book, you read and write.

Or the poison is put on a pillow – you go to bed and breathe. And a month later it's all over.[11]

Manuchar'yants's departure from the Kremlin coincided with a fateful development in the life of the dictator's library since after she left the system of stamping new acquisitions atrophied. As we shall see, after Stalin's death only those books bearing his *pometki* (markings or annotations) or other identifiers were retained in the archives. The rest were dispersed and disappeared into other libraries.

COLLECTING AND BORROWING BOOKS

Classification of a personal book collection often entails the creation of a catalogue but the only known catalogues of Stalin's books are those constructed after his death as part of the process of transferring the remnants of his library's holdings for archiving by IMEL. Classification also implies a central location or locations where the library's holdings may be accessed. Stalin's library, however, was a personal, working archive that was sprawled across his offices, apartments and dachas.

From the early 1920s Stalin had accommodation and an office in the Kremlin and another working space just a few minutes away in the party's central committee building on Staraya Ploshchad' (Old Square). These spaces certainly contained many of his books. Transport Commissar I. V. Kovalev noted that during meetings Stalin was fond of plucking a volume of Lenin's off the shelves, saying, 'Let's have a look at what Vladimir Ilyich has to say on this matter.'[12] A. P. Balashov, who worked in the central committee building, sometimes borrowed books from Stalin's collection: 'There were cupboards with a splendid library. Stalin was sent two copies of every book published by the central publishers, often signed copies. Many authors themselves sent their books. Stalin passed one copy on to us and we divided them among ourselves.'[13] Stalin's daughter Svetlana recalled that in his Kremlin apartment 'there was no room for pictures on the walls – they were lined with books',[14] while his adopted son Artem Sergeev remembered that 'Stalin read a lot. Every time we saw each other he would ask me what I was reading and what I thought about it. At the entrance to his office there was a mountain of books. He would look through them and set aside those which he would put in his library.'[15] Svetlana's first husband (from 1944 to 1947), Grigory Morozov, was allowed to use the library in Stalin's Kremlin flat:

As an avid and an inquisitive reader I spent a lot of happy times there. It has to be said that the collection was unique. Encyclopaedias, textbooks, volumes by well-known scholars, [literary] classics, the works of party leaders. Stalin read them all attentively, as evidenced by the numerous and sometimes detailed notes in the margins.[16]

During the Second World War, a British interpreter, Major A. H. Birse, had occasion to visit Stalin's Kremlin bedroom, where he observed a large bookcase: 'I had a look at the books. They were a collection of Marxist literature, with a good many historical works, but I could see no Russian classics. There were a few books in Georgian.'[17]

Sergo Beria, the son of Stalin's security commissar Lavrenty Beria, claimed that when Stalin visited someone from his inner circle,

> he went to the man's library and even opened his books to check whether they had been read. . . . Stalin liked to give advice on reading and was indignant at the gaps in my knowledge of literature. For example, I had not read *Germinal* (I had read only *Nana*) whereas he worshipped Zola.

Sergo also recalled that Stalin told him that he read 500 pages a day. This is a recurrent claim of memoirists and Stalin may well have said something like that to someone, but his enormous workload meant that it was highly unlikely to be true. Except on holiday or on days that he spent outside the office, he simply would not have had time for such extensive reading. According to another memoir account, Stalin said he read 'a set quota – about 300 pages of literary or other writing every day'.[18]

Beria junior also says Stalin used bookmarks and 'hated the practice of underlining or writing notes in books'.[19] Many of the surviving books from Stalin's library have paper tags tucked into their pages, so Beria is probably right, but to say he 'hated' to mark texts is demonstrably false since there are hundreds of texts that prove the contrary.[20]

According to Roy and Zhores Medvedev, in the 1920s Stalin ordered 500 books a year for his library.[21] That seems a lot of books for a busy politician but it was commensurate with his ambitions for the library and in his *lichnyi fond* (personal file series) are to be found many publishers' lists and catalogues.

The broader context of Stalin's extensive book acquisition was that the Bolsheviks had inherited a vast publishing industry when they seized power. In 1913 Tsarist Russia published 34,000 titles; only Germany printed more. Numbers declined drastically during the civil war but in 1925 the Soviet Union published 20,000 titles and had surpassed the Tsarist peak by 1928. That same year the Soviets printed 270 million copies of books – more than double the rate produced in Tsarist times.

The book trade was 'municipalised' by the Bolsheviks in 1918 (i.e. taken over by various city Soviets) but in 1921 a number of private publishers were allowed to resume operations as part of the New Economic Policy's revival of commercial activities.[22] They continued to operate throughout the 1920s. Although dwarfed by state publishers, private companies had a good market share of some categories of books such as belles-lettres titles, children's literature and foreign translations. There was also little or no control over the importation of books printed abroad, including those produced by Russian émigré publishers hostile to the Soviet regime.[23]

Other than his own orders, Stalin's most numerous source of books were the unsolicited copies sent to him by publishers and authors. Soviet publishers were expected to supply top Bolsheviks with copies of their books and authors needed little incentive to gift their works to the party's general-secretary, particularly after the Stalin cult took off at the end of the 1920s. In the 1930s the Kremlin was deluged with gifts for Stalin, including many hundreds, if not thousands, of books. Even in the 1920s, a steady stream of publications flowed his way, as shown by a surviving 'Register of Literature sent to Stalin in his Apartment, April–December 1926'.[24] Scores of books were sent to him during this nine-month period alone.

As you would expect, many of these books concerned Marxist philosophy, economics and politics but there were also texts on Russian history, the sociology of art, child psychology, sport and religion. Literature was represented by Turgenev, Dostoevsky and Pushkin, as well as Russian translations of Jack London, and of Mark Twain's *A Connecticut Yankee in King Arthur's Court*. Among the memoirs received by Stalin were those by Lenin's widow Krupskaya, and Anton Denikin, the Tsarist general who had fought the Bolsheviks during the civil war. Among the oddities that found their way to Stalin's flat were books on syphilis, the law of murder, Jewish ritual slaughter, and hypnosis. Many journals – scientific and cultural as well as political – were also routinely sent to him.

By far the most important tome that Stalin received in this particular batch of books was the first volume of Boris Shaposhnikov's *Mozg Armii* (Brain of the Army), a study of general staffs before the First World War. Widely read and discussed in Soviet military circles, it was a book that came to be seen as the template for the functioning of Stalin's high command during the Second World War. In 1929 Shaposhnikov reportedly sent Stalin an inscribed, specially bound copy of the three volumes of *Mozg Armii*.[25]

Stalin also liked to borrow books from other libraries, both personal and institutional. The Soviet poet Demyan Bedny, whose own library was said to contain 30,000 volumes, complained about Stalin leaving greasy fingermarks on books he borrowed from him.[26] A favourite source was the main state repository, the Lenin

Library; after Stalin's death, seventy-two unreturned books were found in his private collection. Borrowing but not returning books was an old habit of Stalin's. When he dropped out of the seminary in 1898, the authorities demanded a payment of 18 roubles and 15 kopeks for eighteen books he'd taken away from the seminary's main library.[27]

Most of the Lenin Library books Stalin borrowed were returned, fines unpaid, in 1956, three years after his death. But twenty-four texts, which had been marked by him, were retained by the Institute of Marxism-Leninism (the renamed IMEL), among them two volumes of Herodotus's classic *Histories*. However, like some other items noted on the retained list, they seem to have disappeared from the archive.[28]

UNHAPPY FAMILY

Grand though Stalin's Kremlin accommodations were by the standards of ordinary Soviet citizens, they were not big enough to house a large-scale personal library. At the height of his power Stalin could easily have carved out or had constructed a convenient space for his books but he showed no inclination to do so. Instead, the books were mainly kept at the places he spent most of his leisure and reading time from the 1920s through to the 1950s – his two Moscow dachas.

The first Moscow dacha, allocated to him by the state in the early 1920s, was not far from a village called Usovo, about 20 miles outside Moscow. It was called the Zubalovo dacha because before the 1917 revolution the house and its estate belonged to the Zubalov brothers, who were Armenian oil magnates. On the estate were three separate houses, each occupied by a high-ranking Bolshevik and their family. Stalin's dacha was a relatively modest two-storey house that contained a large room with floor-to-ceiling bookcases.

Stalin and his extended family (which consisted mostly of his in-laws) spent a lot of time there at the weekends and during the summer. By all accounts the 1920s were a fairly happy time for the Stalin family. As his daughter Svetlana fondly recalled:

> My father transformed Zubalovo from a dark country place that was densely overgrown, with a gloomy gabled house and a lot of old furniture, into a sunny, abundant estate with flower and vegetable gardens and all sorts of useful out-buildings. The house was rebuilt and the high Gothic gables removed; the rooms were remodelled and the musty old furniture carted away. . . . My mother and father lived upstairs, and the children and my grandmother, grandfather and anyone who happened to be staying with us downstairs.[29]

The Stalin family idyll ended abruptly in November 1932 when Svetlana's mother Nadezhda ('Nadya') Alliluyeva committed suicide. As Svetlana's biographer Rosemary Sullivan has remarked, 'Nadya is an elusive figure in the Stalin universe'[30] and the reasons and circumstances of her death remain unclear.

Stalin's romance with her began in 1917 when he returned to St Petersburg from exile. Aged sixteen, Nadya was the daughter of an Old Bolshevik family that Stalin had known for a long time. When the Bolsheviks made Moscow their capital in March 1918, she followed Stalin there and worked with him in the Nationalities Commissariat. She joined the Bolshevik party and when Stalin was despatched to the front during the civil war, she went with him. They registered their marriage in March 1919. Nadya was the forty-year-old Stalin's second wife. They had two children, Vasily (b.1921) and Svetlana (b.1926). Stalin also had a son, Yakov, from his marriage to Ekaterina (Kato) Svanidze (1885–1907), whose mother died of typhus a few months after he was born. Brought up by his mother's relatives, in the 1920s, Yakov went to live with his father. Stalin didn't get on with Yakov but relations improved when he became an artillery officer in the late 1930s. Like millions of other Soviet soldiers, Yakov was taken prisoner by the Germans in summer 1941. He died in captivity in 1943, possibly while trying to escape.

Soviet soldiers were not allowed to surrender unless severely wounded. To encourage soldiers to fight to the death, their families suffered if they were captured, and Stalin's son was no exception. While Yakov was a POW, his wife Yulia, a ballerina, was under arrest and their daughter Galina brought up by other members of the extended Stalin family.

After Vasily's birth, Nadya was expelled from the party for inactivity, but since she'd worked in Lenin's office, her membership was soon restored.[31] Nadya hired servants to look after her children and strove for a political and professional life independent of Stalin. In 1929 she enrolled in the textile production faculty of the Industrial Academy in Moscow.

It is claimed that Nadya had some health issues, physical and mental. There is also much talk about her political differences with Stalin, notably over the violent 'revolution from above' he unleashed at the end of the 1920s, but there is no probative evidence to support such speculation. The conspiracy theory that Stalin had her murdered because of these supposed differences may be safely dismissed.

Hard evidence about the Stalin marriage is sparse and the memoir literature overdetermined by post hoc speculation about what led to Nadya's suicide. Their surviving correspondence from the late 1920s and early 1930, conducted while Stalin was on holiday at his dacha in Sochi and Nadya was in Moscow studying, suggests theirs was a happy if not always smooth marriage.[32]

Their marriage breakdown appears to have been gradual rather than sudden, and gender inequality may have played a role. As radical socialists, the Bolsheviks were committed to female emancipation and sought to mobilise Soviet women in support of the communist project. But while there were many female activists and leaders throughout Soviet society, there were hardly any at the top levels of politics and power. One exception was Molotov's wife, Polina Zhemchuzhina – a good friend of Nadya's – who ran the fisheries industry in the 1930s and also looked after Soviet cosmetics.[33] Another was Bolshevik feminist Alexandra Kollontai, who later became ambassador to Sweden – the only female Soviet diplomat of that rank. An early diary of hers was part of Stalin's book collection. Among the very few other female authors that featured in his library were Lenin's widow Krupskaya, the German communist Clara Zetkin, and the Polish Marxist Rosa Luxemburg, whose book on the General Strike as a revolutionary tactic was copiously marked by him. He was particularly interested in her treatment of the experience of strikes in Russia, especially in the Caucasus, where he himself had been active.[34]

The early years of the Stalin marriage coincided with the most liberationist and egalitarian phase of Bolshevik policy and practice on gender issues. However, from the early 1930s there developed a more conservative approach towards 'the woman question' and a reversion to more traditional gender relations.[35]

Soviet political culture from the outset was heavily male-dominated and Bolshevik leaders, including Stalin, affected a tough, coarse macho style. 'Today I read the section of international affairs,' Stalin wrote to Soviet premier Vyacheslav Molotov in January 1933, congratulating him on a speech. 'It came out well. The confident, contemptuous tone with the respect to the "great" powers, the belief in our own strength, the delicate but plain spitting in the pot of the swaggering "great powers" – very good. Let them eat it.'[36] For a young and ambitious female activist like Nadya, this was an inhospitable climate, even with the privileges that came from being Stalin's wife. Matters came to a head at a private party in the Kremlin to celebrate the fifteenth anniversary of the Bolshevik Revolution. After a drunken row with Stalin, Nadya left the room and shot herself with a revolver that her brother had brought back from Berlin as a souvenir.

Her suicide was obfuscated but not her death, which was announced in *Pravda*: 'On the night of 9 of November, active and dedicated Party member Nadezhda Sergeevna Alliluyeva died'. The dedication that followed was signed by top Soviet leaders and their wives:

We have lost a dear, beloved comrade with a beautiful soul. A young Bolshevik filled with strength and boundlessly dedicated to the Party and the Revolution, is no more. . . . The memory of Nadezhda Sergeevna, dedicated Bolshevik, close friend and faithful helper to Comrade Stalin, will remain forever dear to us.[37]

Further tributes were paid when she was buried at the Novodevichy cemetery on 12 November and a few days later Stalin replied publicly to all the sympathy messages he had received: 'With heartfelt gratitude to all organisations, comrades, and individuals who have expressed their condolences on the occasion of the death of my close friend and comrade Nadezhda Sergeevna Alliluyeva-Stalina.'[38]

As Sheila Fitzpatrick has written, 'Stalin's reactions [to Nadya's suicide] are variously reported but grief, guilt and a sense of betrayal were all evidently present.'[39] After his wife's death, Stalin gradually withdrew from the family life that he had enjoyed in the 1920s. He moved into another apartment in the Kremlin, one that was located directly below his office. He stopped going to Zubalovo, although many of his books remained there.

STALIN'S MAPS

A grand, new Moscow dacha was constructed for Stalin in 1933–4.[40] The Kuntsevo mansion was only ten or so minutes' drive from the Kremlin using a fast highway reserved for government vehicles – hence the dacha's colloquial name 'Blizhnyaya' (Nearby). Post-Nadya, Stalin's daily life settled into a new pattern. Rarely staying overnight in his Kremlin apartment, he worked in his office until late and was then driven to Blizhnyaya. Not until the early hours of the morning did he go to bed.

The main house at Kuntsevo contained Stalin's study and work spaces, a bedroom for Svetlana, a billiard room, a bath house, extensive servants' quarters and a small dining room as well as a grand hall for large-scale banquets and events. The centrepiece of the dacha, however, was its library, a 30-square-metre room with four large bookcases whose shelves were deep enough to take two rows of books. But the bulk of Stalin's collection, including those books transferred from his Kremlin apartment and office, were stored in a separate building nearby.

The dacha's vestibule displayed three large multicoloured maps: a world map, a map of Europe and one of European Russia. As Molotov recalled: 'Stalin loved maps . . . all maps.'[41] The Yugoslav communist Milovan Djilas reported that when he visited the dacha in June 1944, Stalin stopped before the world map and pointed at the Soviet Union, which was coloured red, exclaiming that the capitalists would 'never accept the idea that so great a space should be red, never, never!' Djilas misremembered that Stalin had encircled Stalingrad in blue on the world map. Actually, the city was marked by Stalin on the map of European Russia as part of a line drawing showing the German invasion's deepest penetration into the USSR.[42]

In his attack on Stalin's war record at the 20th party congress, Khrushchev accused him of planning military operations on a globe. Stalin did have a big globe in or near his Kremlin office, but Khrushchev's calumny has been rejected by members of the Soviet high command who worked with him closely during the war. Moreover, Stalin's *lichnyi fond* contains nearly 200 maps with his *pometki*, including many large-scale maps used for planning and plotting military operations. There are also maps of many different countries and parts of the world, as well as numerous political, economic, administrative, road and physical geography maps of the USSR and its regions.[43]

The dacha maps were conventional political maps (Mercator projection) that divided the world into differently coloured nations, states and empires. That political cartography was his chief preoccupation.

As a native Georgian, Stalin was, to use Alfred J. Rieber's memorable phrase, a 'man of the borderlands'.[44] It was Stalin's Georgian origins and background and his early experience of political activity in the multi-ethnic borderlands of the Russian Empire that shaped his approach to the creation and protection of the Soviet system. The Bolsheviks seized power in 1917 with a strong sense that the durability of their revolution depended on its spread to other countries. Stalin shared that outlook but felt the political and economic interdependence of Russia and its borderlands was just as important.

The danger posed by the porous borders of its multi-ethnic periphery underpinned Stalin's commitment to a strong, centralised Soviet state. He was a centraliser who subordinated the periphery of the former Russian Empire to its advanced proletarian Russian core. National and ethnic minorities were allowed regional and cultural autonomy but denied the possibility of self-government. This practice chimed with the view he had expressed in *Marxism and the National Question* (1913) and other writings: the Bolsheviks supported national self-determination in theory but reserved the right to repress nationalist movements if they threatened the interests of the working class and endangered the socialist revolution.

As Rieber also showed, Stalin's borderlands policy was central to his domestic as well as his foreign policy. Forced collectivisation of agriculture and accelerated industrialisation were part of the struggle to secure the backward and underdeveloped borderlands. The Great Terror of the 1930s was in large part an ethnic purge of perceived nationalist elements in the borderlands.[45]

The sweep of Stalin's interests is captured by an anecdote about a map of the USSR's new borders that was brought to him just after the war:

The map was small – like those for school textbooks. Stalin pinned it to the wall: 'Let's see what we have here. . . . Everything is all right to the north. Finland has offended us, so we moved the border from Leningrad. Baltic States – that's age-old Russian land! – and they are ours again. All the Belorussians live together now, Ukrainians together, Moldovans together. It's OK to the west.' And he turned to the eastern borders. 'What do we have here? The Kuril Islands belong to us now, Sakhalin is completely ours – you see, good! And Port Arthur's ours, and Dairen is ours' – Stalin moved his pipe across China – 'and the Chinese Eastern Railway is ours. China, Mongolia – everything is in order. But I don't like our border right here!' Stalin said and pointed south of the Caucasus.[46]

Stalin was adamant that he would keep all these territories, not least because of his strategic goal of ethno-political stability along Soviet borders.

Stalin's ambitions south of the Caucasus centred on claims that Turkey should return the provinces of Kars and Ardahan to the USSR. These areas of eastern Turkey with Armenian and Georgian populations had been part of the Tsarist Empire from 1878 until 1921, when a Soviet–Turkish treaty transferred the two districts to Turkey. While there was communist-inspired nationalist agitation for the return of these territories to Georgia and Armenia, Stalin's main aim was to put pressure on Turkey to share control of the Black Sea straits with the USSR.

He also sponsored an Azerbaijani separatist movement in Iran, which threatened to split the country by linking up with Soviet Azerbaijan. In this case his motives were mostly economic – to secure a Soviet oil concession in northern Iran.

Stalin focused on the countries and territories that bordered the USSR, but his geopolitical outlook was global. As a Bolshevik internationalist he paid attention to revolutionary struggles across the world. Among the remnants of his library are many books on Britain, France, Germany, China and the United States and a good number of texts on Ireland, India, Indochina, Indonesia, Italy, Japan and Mexico (including a translation of John Reed's book on the Mexican Revolution) as well as volumes on imperialism, colonialism, slavery, and oil and world politics.

The USSR was primarily a land power but in the 1930s Stalin embraced the idea of building a powerful ocean-going navy and his collection contained a 1932 Russian translation of *Some Principles of Maritime Strategy* by Julian Stafford Corbett, a British sea-power theorist who emphasised the importance of wartime control of the seas, as opposed to large-scale fleet actions. In various conversations with Churchill during the war, Stalin lamented that while the

United States controlled the Panama Canal and Britain the Suez Canal, the Soviet Union had no control over the Black Sea straits.[47]

LIFE AND DEATH AT THE DACHA

Blizhnyaya served many purposes for Stalin. It was an extension of his Kremlin office, a playground for his children and a reception for visiting foreign communists. It was a place to party with his political cronies and listen to his extensive collection of gramophone records (he liked to watch his comrades dance, apparently).[48] It was a secure and secluded spot in which he could relax and do some gardening. But, above all, time spent at the dacha was a break from affairs of state and the opportunity to browse his books.

Never was downtime more necessary than during the war when Stalin worked twelve- to fifteen-hour shifts in the Kremlin. 'Many allied visitors who called at the Kremlin during the war were astonished to see on how many issues, great and small, military, political or diplomatic, Stalin took the final decision,' wrote Isaac Deutscher in his 1948 biography. 'He was in effect his own commander-in-chief, his own minister of defence, his own quartermaster, his own foreign minister, and even his own chef de protocole. . . . Thus he went on, day after day, throughout four years of hostilities – a prodigy of patience, tenacity, and vigilance, almost omnipresent, almost omniscient.'[49] Research in the Russian archives has amply borne out Deutscher's graphic picture of Stalin as the ever-busy warlord.[50]

By the end of the Second World War, Stalin was sixty-six years old. Four years of intense toil as supreme commander had exacted a personal toll and he began to take long vacations by the Black Sea. Aside from these vacations, the pattern of his working life was much the same as before, although he did step back from the day-to-day running of the country, leaving a little more time for leisure and reading when he was on holiday or at Blizhnyaya. Svetlana had long since left home and in 1951 the dacha's library was enlarged by the incorporation of what had been her bedroom.

Given how much time Stalin spent at Blizhnyaya, the chances were that he would die there, and so he did in March 1953 at the age of seventy-three. There are many conspiracy theories about his death but the truth is that he suffered a stroke on 1 March and died four days later.[51] On the day of his death Soviet leaders established a subgroup tasked with 'putting the documents and papers of Comrade Stalin, his archive as well as all current materials, in proper order'.[52] The group consisted of head of government Georgy Malenkov, security chief Lavrenty Beria and deputy party leader Nikita Khrushchev. Two days later Beria's security personnel removed all Stalin's belongings and furniture from the dacha.

THE LIFE AND FATE OF A DICTATOR'S LIBRARY

When Stalin fell ill, Svetlana was summoned to Blizhnyaya from a French class. 'Strange things happened at Kuntsevo after my father died,' she recalled:

> The very next day . . . Beria had the whole household, servants and body-guards, called together and told that my father's belongings were to be removed right away. . . . In 1955, when Beria himself had 'fallen', they started to restore the dacha. My father's things were brought back. The former servants and commandants were invited back and helped put everything where it belonged and make the house look as it had before. They were preparing to open a museum, like the one in Lenin's house in Leninskiye Gorki.[53]

The decision to establish a Stalin Museum at Blizhnyaya was taken by the Soviet leadership in September 1953 but the plan was dropped after Khrushchev's secret speech.[54] The dacha was then placed at the disposal of the central committee and used to accommodate vacationing party apparatchiks and visiting foreign communists. An intriguing coda to the Stalin museum project was that in 2014 an exhibition on 'The Myth of the Beloved Leader' was mounted in a Moscow museum adjacent to Red Square. Ostensibly about Lenin, the exhibition was devoted mainly to Stalin and included many of the personal artefacts that had been assembled for the aborted Stalin Museum.

Stalin remained popular in Georgia and in 1957 a museum in his honour was opened in his hometown of Gori. Among its exhibits was a reproduction of Stalin's childhood house and the railway carriage that transported him to the Potsdam Conference. The museum's main building was palatial but badly maintained in post-Soviet times (when I visited in December 2015 the power failed and it was freezing). Among its exhibits are Stalin's desk from his Kremlin office, a box made by his son Vasily, and, in a respectfully darkened space, the dictator's death mask. The latter was one of ten such plaster casts of Stalin's face (and hands) that were distributed to various museums and archives after his death.[55]

The museum's continued existence has been a matter of intermittent political controversy in independent Georgia but, so far, the locals' desire to attract tourists and celebrate their most famous son has trumped all political considerations.

Svetlana did not mention in her memoirs that while she relinquished any claim she may have had to Blizhnyaya, she tried to trade this off for some time and space in another of Stalin's dachas.[56] She also had an eye on her father's library and in March 1955 wrote to the party leadership:

> I would like to ask the government to consider the possibility of letting me have part of the library. It is huge and has many books of no interest to me

but I would be very grateful if I could be permitted to take some books. I'm interested in the history books and Russian and translated literature. I know this part of the library very well since in the past I used it a lot.[57]

Svetlana had quite an eventful personal life, including three husbands, two children by different fathers and an Indian communist lover, Brajesh Singh, who died in 1966. Svetlana was granted permission to take his ashes back to India, where, in Delhi, she sensationally defected to the United States. The following year Svetlana published a memoir of her life as Stalin's daughter called *20 Letters to a Friend*, which remains a unique, though not always reliable, source of information and insight about her father.

The loss of Stalin's library books rankled Svetlana so much that when she published a second memoir two years later, she complained bitterly that the Soviet government had 'decided to confiscate my father's [library], disposing of it at its discretion. . . . In the USSR the State twists the law whichever way it wants, including laws governing private property.'[58]

DISCOVERING STALIN'S LIBRARY

As part of the preparations for the short-lived Stalin Museum project, staff from the then Marx-Engels-Lenin-Stalin Institute (formerly IMEL, later IM-L) were allowed to examine Stalin's library books. Among them was the bibliographer Yevgenia Zolotukhina, who recalled that 'the atmosphere at the dacha was stiff and formal, the only agreeable room was the library, which had a cosy feel. . . . The books were housed in a neighbouring building and brought to Stalin according to his requirements.'

Zolotukhina described Stalin's Kremlin apartment as 'a suite of vaulted rooms', with a spiral staircase that led to his study:

The [apartment's] library was furnished with a large number of old-fashioned bookcases that were filled with books on a great variety of subjects. . . . Clearly Stalin was an educated person. He got extremely irritated whenever he came across grammar and spelling mistakes, which he would carefully correct with a red pencil. These books, therefore, all the ones he marked, were transferred to the Central Party Archive.

Zolotukhina was struck by 'the large assortment of books about Pushkin, all published during the Soviet period, as well as individual old editions – a number of books had slips from second-hand bookshops.'[59] Stalin was also 'interested in books about Peter the Great and Ivan the Terrible' and 'read all the emigre literature that appeared in Russian . . . including the celebrated biographies by

Raymond Gul of Voroshilov and others.[60] In the postwar years he became interested in books and magazines about architecture, which must have been related to the construction of tall buildings in Moscow. These books could be found on his bedside table.'[61]

In 1957 Stalin's apartment and dacha were visited by Yury Sharapov, head of IM-L's library.[62] Sharapov's mission was to sort through Stalin's books with a view to incorporating them into the Institute, a task which took several months to complete. In the Kremlin he found 'a tall Swedish bookcase with detachable shelves. It was crammed with books and booklets, many with bookmarks in them. Literature written by emigres and White Guards, works by the opposition – those whom Stalin regarded as ideological adversaries or simply enemies – I must give Stalin his due – he read them all with great attention.'

At Blizhnyaya, Sharapov found that the bulk of Stalin's books were kept in a separate wooden house with a large cellar. He started with the books on military matters, noting that Stalin was more interested in history than strategy and tactics: 'The pages of old books about the wars waged by the Assyrians, Ancient Greeks and Romans were covered with his notes.'

There was a special section for fiction in the library and Sharapov recalled with disdain what Stalin had written in a copy of Maxim Gorky's *Death and the Maiden* in 1931: 'This piece is stronger than Goethe's *Faust* (love conquers death).'[63] More happily, he noted that Stalin had studied the great nineteenth-century Russian satirist Mikhail Saltykov-Shchedrin in some depth.

The only Shchedrin book that remains in Stalin's library is a 1931 edition of previously unpublished writings, which he read and marked in some detail.[64] In 1936 Stalin put his knowledge of Shchedrin to good use in a mockery of foreign critics' claims that the new Soviet constitution was a façade with no substance, a fraud like the fake 'Potemkin Villages' built to impress Catherine the Great as she travelled through the Russian countryside:

In one of his tales the great Russian writer Shchedrin portrays a pig-headed official, very narrowminded and obtuse, but self-confident and zealous to the extreme. After this bureaucrat had established 'order and tranquillity' in the region 'under his charge,' having exterminated thousands of its inhabitants and burned down scores of towns in the process, he looked around him, and on the horizon espied America – a country little known, of course, where, it appears, there are liberties of some sort or other which serve to agitate the people, and where the state is administered in a different way. The bureaucrat espied America and became indignant:

What country is that, how did it get there, by what right does it exist? (*Laughter and applause.*) Of course, it was discovered accidentally several centuries ago, but couldn't it be shut up again so that not a ghost of it remains? (*General laughter.*) Thereupon he wrote an order: 'Shut America up again!' (*General laughter.*)[65]

Final decisions on what to do with Stalin's book collection were not taken until January 1963. Prompted perhaps by the renewal of the anti-Stalin campaign at the 22nd congress of the CPSU in 1961, IM-L's directorate resolved (1) to retain in the Institute's archive all those texts containing Stalin's *pometki*; (2) to house in IM-L's own library, as a separate collection, books inscribed to Stalin and those with his library's stamp; and (3) to disperse the remaining unmarked and unstamped books (those in good condition anyway) into the Institute's own library and to other scientific and specialist libraries. It was also decided to place in a special file any letters or notes from authors and publishers found inside Stalin's books.[66]

Work began on cataloguing the books but it does not seem to have included listing which books were dispersed to libraries. In the absence of such a register it is impossible to know precisely which books were in Stalin's library when he died or how many of them there were. But an idea of the numbers involved may be gleaned from a 1993 newspaper article by the historian Leonid Spirin, who had worked in IM-L for a number of years.[67]

According to Spirin, the bulk of Stalin's library consisted of the classics of Russian, Soviet and world literature – Pushkin, Gogol, Tolstoy, Chekhov, Gorky, Mayakovsky, Hugo, Shakespeare, France. These and other unstamped books, about 11,000 in all, were transferred to the Lenin Library in the 1960s. Another 3,000 unstamped non-fiction books – socialist writings mostly – were added to IM-L's library or given to other libraries, leaving a non-fiction remnant of 5,500. So, according to Spirin's figures, there were about 19,500 books in Stalin's personal library.

Spirin's number of 5,500 non-fiction titles correlates with the catalogue of Stalin's stamped books prepared by IM-L's library. After the collapse of the USSR in 1991, the library separated from IM-L and became the Gosudarstvennaya Obshchestvenno-Politicheskaya Biblioteka – the State Socio-Political Library (SSPL). Located on Wilhelm Pieck Street in Moscow, this is where the only extant catalogue of Stalin's library may be found, together with the books themselves.

The handwritten SSPL card indexes divide Stalin's books into seven categories:

1. Books with the Library of J. V. Stalin stamp (3,747)
2. Books with the author's autograph (with and without stamp) (587)

3. Books inscribed to Stalin (with and without stamp) (189)
4. Books with an identifiable subject classification (without stamp or autograph) (102)
5. Books with no identifiers (347)
6. Books belonging to members of Stalin's family (34)
7. Books bearing the stamps of other libraries (49)

All but a few of the books listed in this catalogue were published before the early 1930s, which strongly suggests that rather being the non-fiction remnant of the library as a whole they are a subset of it and were retrieved from a particular location – Stalin's apartment, perhaps, or his first dacha at Zubalovo. Spirin's 5,500 figure needs to be revised significantly upwards to take account of the many books that Stalin acquired in subsequent years. While Spirin's 11,000 figure for fiction etc. seems about right, his estimate of 3,000 non-fiction books in addition to those in those in the SSPL is far too low. Stalin must have acquired as least as many non-fiction books in the 1930s and 1940s as he did in the 1920s, and probably a lot more. Hence a better estimate of the size of Stalin's library may be that it contained some 25,000 books, pamphlets and periodicals.[68]

The one cataloguing exercise undertaken by the IM-L archive itself was listing all texts with Stalin's *pometki*. In the version of the *pometki* list finalised in July 1963, there were 300 such titles.[69] However, a handwritten amendment of unknown date changed this number to 397 whereas the *opis'* (inventory) made available to researchers in the 1990s lists 391 such items.[70] To be added to this total are upwards of a hundred books in other sections of Stalin's *lichnyi fond*, many of which also contain his markings and annotations.

STALIN'S BOOKS

Despite its limitations, the SSPL catalogue is the best guide we have to the contents and character of Stalin's library.[71] What it shows is that it was over-whelmingly a Soviet library – a collection of post-1917 texts published in Soviet Russia. Most of the texts are books but there are also a large number of short, pamphlet-type publications. Nearly all the texts are in Russian and the great majority are written by Bolsheviks or other varieties of Marxists and Socialists. In the first section of the catalogue, which lists books with Stalin's library stamp, the most heavily featured author is Lenin (243 publications) and there are also numerous works about Lenin and Leninism. The most favoured authors after Lenin are Stalin (95), Zinoviev (55), Bukharin (50), Marx (50), Kamenev (37),

Molotov (33), Trotsky (28), Kautsky (28), Engels (25), Rykov (24), Plekhanov (23), Lozovsky (22), Rosa Luxemburg (14) and Radek (14). Five of these authors (Zinoviev, Bukharin, Kamenev, Rykov and Lozovsky) were purged and executed by Stalin, while Radek died in the Gulag and Trotsky was assassinated by a Soviet agent in Mexico in 1940. But their books remained part of Stalin's collection. The catalogue also lists hundreds of reports of communist party congresses and conferences, as well organisations such as the Comintern and Soviet trade unions.

Apart from the works of Marx, Engels, Kautsky and Luxemburg, there are very few foreign translations in Stalin's collection. Notable exceptions include Russian translations of Winston Churchill's book about the First World War, *The World Crisis*; three books by the German revisionist social democrat Eduard Bernstein; two books by Keynes, including *The Economic Consequences of the Peace*; Jean Jaurès's *History of the Great French Revolution*; Tomáš Masaryk's *World Revolution*; the German economist Karl Wilhelm Bucher's *Work and Rhythm*; an early work by Karl Wittfogel on the 'awakening' of China; John Hobson's *Imperialism*; Werner Sombart's book about modern capitalism; some works of the founder of modern Turkey, Kemal Atatürk; the Italian Marxist Antonio Labriola on historical materialism; John Reed's *Insurgent Mexico*; several works by the American writer Upton Sinclair, and the letters of executed US anarchists Sacco and Vanzetti. Among the many works on economics in the collection is a translation of Adam Smith's *The Wealth of Nations*: in his heavily marked copies of David Rozenberg's three volumes of commentary on Marx's *Capital*, Stalin displayed a particular interest in the sections on trade and Adam Smith.[72]

There is very little fiction listed in the catalogue but Stalin's interest in the history of the ancient world is reflected in the presence of a translation of Flaubert's *Salammbô*, a novel set in Carthage at the time of the First Punic War.

Three slightly off-beat authors who feature in the collection are L. N. Voitolovsky, an early Soviet theorist of the social psychology of crowd behaviour; Moisey Ostrogorsky, the author of one of the founding texts of western political sociology, *Democracy and the Organization of Political Parties*; and Victor Vinogradov, a Soviet literary theorist, who wrote a book about the evolution of naturalism in Russian literature.

Among Stalin's philosophy books was Moris G. Leiteizen's *Nietzsche and Finance Capital* (1928).[73] Nietzsche was one of those 'petty-bourgeois' 'idealist' philosophers whose works the Bolsheviks banned from public libraries. Because of his appropriation by fascist and Nazi thinkers, he was totally rejected by official Soviet culture after Hitler came to power, and there is no evidence that he was read by Stalin.

As the title of his book indicates, Leiteizen was highly critical of Nietzsche but also detected a certain affinity between Bolshevism and the nihilist German philosopher, a point endorsed by enlightenment commissar Anatoly Lunacharsky in his introduction to the volume. Leiteizen expressed this idea and sentiment in terms that Stalin might well have appreciated:

> Nietzsche is the most distant thinker for us but at the same time he is close to us. Reading his works, one breathes pure and sharp mountain air. There is clarity and lucidity of concept, there is nothing hiding behind a beautiful sentence. There is the same nakedness and unambiguity of class relations, the same struggle against all illusions and ideals, the Nietzschean struggle against petty gods and first of all against the most haughty and deceptive one of them – democracy. ... What brings us together is Nietzsche's struggle against the individualism and anarchy of capitalist society, his passionate dream of world unification, his struggle against nationalism ...[74]

The unstamped books listed in the SSPL catalogue are much the same as those that were stamped but do include c.150 foreign-language books, mostly in French, German or English. These include John Reed's *Ten Days that Shook the World* (1919); Alfred Kurella's *Mussolini: Ohne Maske* (1931); a book about the Spanish civil war, *Garibaldini in Spagna* (1937); a signed copy of the 1935 edition of Sidney and Beatrice Webb's *Soviet Communism: A New Civilisation*; and various translations of works by Lenin, Stalin, Trotsky, Bukharin and Radek. We know from other sources that Stalin was sent many other books in foreign languages, which have since disappeared from his collection. But there is no sign he read any of them.

Marxist and Bolshevik writings predominate among the 391 marked books, periodicals and pamphlets retained by the IM-L archive, especially the works of Marx, Engels, Lenin and Stalin himself. Erik van Ree estimated that about three-quarters of these titles are concerned with communist ideology and tactics.[75] The other major categories are history (36), economics (27) and military affairs (23).

Unlike the SSPL collection, the marked collection in the party archive contains a number of pre-1917 publications, including several works by the classical historian Robert Vipper (1859–1954) and the Tsarist military strategist Genrikh Leer (1829–1904).

If revolutionary history and military history are included, then historical works are by far the largest category of books in the marked collection, apart from the Marxist classics.

One marked book that combined various of Stalin's interests is a 1923 text on the history of revolutionary armies by Nikolai Lukin (1885–1940), based on his lectures to the Red Army's General Staff Academy. A former pupil of Vipper's, Lukin was active in the revolutionary movement from 1905 onwards. He had personal connections to Nikolai Bukharin and joined his Left Communist group after the 1917 revolution. Lukin had quite a distinguished career as a Soviet historian, but it was not without controversy, and in 1938 he was arrested and sentenced to ten years hard labour. He died in captivity.

His book dealt with the French Revolution and the Paris Commune but it was the chapter on Oliver Cromwell and his New Model Army that most interested Stalin. He noted Lukin's point that the peculiarity of the English Revolution was the participation of part of the regime's army on the side of the rebellious population. Cromwell's task was to create a new army based on those soldiers and officers who had the courage to side with the revolution. He did this by establishing a unified command backed by a representative military council. Among Cromwell's most ardent supporters were the New Model Army's chaplains, who mobilised the troops' religious enthusiasm for the Puritan revolt against the monarchy. Beside this passage Stalin wrote 'politotdel' (the political department) and later noted the use of the term commissar to denote representatives of rank-and-file soldiers.[76]

Stalin made good use of his knowledge of English history in an interview with H. G. Wells in July 1934: 'Recall the history of England in the seventeenth century. Did not many say that the old social system had decayed? But did it not, nevertheless, require a Cromwell to crush it by force?' When Wells objected that Cromwell acted constitutionally, Stalin retorted: 'In the name of the constitution he resorted to violence, beheaded the king, dispersed Parliament, arrested some and beheaded others!' In that same interview he lectured Wells about nineteenth-century British history and the role of the radical Chartist movement in the democratic political reforms of that era.[77]

Boris Ilizarov, a scholar who has done more work on Stalin's library than any other Russian historian, believes that Stalin wasn't much interested in history before 1917 and didn't become seriously interested in reading history books until the 1930s, when he became involved in discussions about the production of new textbooks for Soviet schools.[78]

Ilizarov may be right that the young Stalin was more immediately preoccupied with Marxist politics and philosophy. However, the study of history featured in both his school and seminary education and it was a branch of knowledge foundational to Marxism, a theory of human affairs that combined an account of social change with a teleological vision of humanity's progression from ancient slavery to communism. All revolutionary socialists of Stalin's generation were interested in seismic events like the French Revolution and in past popular struggles from which they could derive lessons for their own day. His first significant piece of writing, *Anarchism or Socialism?* (1907), cited both Arthur Arnould's and Olivier Lissagaray's histories of the Paris Commune.[79] His tract on *Marxism and the National Question* (1913) had a big historical content and in the 1920s he made many references to history. In a 1926 speech he observed that neither Ivan the Terrible nor Peter the Great were true industrial-isers because they didn't develop the heavy industry necessary for economic growth and national independence. In 1928 he alluded to a parallel between Peter's efforts to modernise Russia and those of the Bolsheviks, although in his discussion with Emil Ludwig in 1931 he denied the comparison, pointing out that Peter had striven to strengthen the upper-class character of the Russian state whereas he served the workers.[80] Stalin's most dramatic pronouncement on Russian history was his February 1931 speech on the urgency of the drive for modernisation and industrialisation:

> The history of old Russia consisted, among other things, in her being beaten for her backwardness. She was beaten by the Mongol khans. She was beaten by the Turkish beys. She was beaten by the Swedish feudal rulers. She was beaten by the Polish-Lithuanian lords. She was beaten by the Japanese barons. Everyone gave her a beating for her backwardness. For military backwardness, for cultural backwardness, for state backwardness, for indus-trial backwardness, for agricultural backwardness. They beat her because it was profitable and could be done with impunity. . . . Such is the law of the exploiters: beat the backward because you are weak – so you are in the wrong and therefore can be beaten and enslaved. . . . We have fallen behind the advanced countries by 50 to 100 years. We must close that gap in 10 years. Either we do this or we will be crushed.[81]

Memoirs and diaries were another category of books that interested Stalin. Among the books he read and annotated are the memoirs of the British intelli-gence agent R. H. Bruce Lockhart, the First World War German General Erich Ludendorff, and Annabelle Bucar, who defected to the Soviet Union from the American embassy in Moscow in 1948 and then became a star of Radio Moscow's English-language broadcasting service.

Perhaps the quirkiest author in Stalin's library was 'Professor Taid O'Conroy', whose book *The Menace of Japan* (1933) was published in Russian in 1934.[82] Born Timothy Conroy in Ballincollig, County Cork, Ireland in 1883, he ran away to sea at the age of fifteen and joined the Royal Navy. Having served in South Africa, Somaliland and the Persian Gulf, he then spent a year teaching

English at a Berlitz school in Copenhagen before moving to Russia in 1909 to teach at the Imperial Court in St Petersburg. After the First World War he ended up in Japan, where he married a waitress, described by the publisher of his book as descended from a venerable Japanese aristocratic family. He and his wife left Japan in 1932. In London, O'Conroy contacted the Foreign Office and submitted a briefing document on Japan that eventually became his book. He died in 1935 from liver failure.[83]

As the title of his book indicates, O'Conroy's main message concerned the danger of Japanese militarism now that Japan had invaded and occupied Manchuria (in 1931). Stalin had no need of his counsel in that regard. There were two Soviet-authored books in his library dating from 1933 that detailed the militarisation of Japanese society and the build-up of Japan's armed forces. Both books he read and marked heavily.[84] Stalin also had at his disposal numerous news reports from TASS's Tokyo office. TASS bulletins from various countries were one of Stalin's most important sources of international information and in the early 1930s he paid particular attention to reporting from and about Japan.[85] During the Second World War, Stalin's staff produced an information bulletin for him that contained translated and summarised material from the foreign press, particularly reports on the Soviet Union.[86]

REIMAGINING STALIN

Sharapov's 1988 memoir was the first public inkling that Stalin had an extensive private library. It was published in English in *Moscow News* under the headline 'Stalin's Personal Library'.

The idea that Stalin was a bit of an intellectual who read and collected a lot of books was not uncommon, Trotsky's caricature of him as a mediocrity notwithstanding. He was, after all, a published author whose pretensions as a Marxist theorist were well known. The Stalin cult proclaimed him to be a genius and a succession of bedazzled western intellectuals, diplomats and politicians had publicly hailed his knowledge and erudition. Cult images often depicted him reading, writing or standing by books. But the discovery of his personal library focused attention on the intellectual aspect of Stalin's persona and identity. Crucially, his biographers now had a source they could use to explore the workings of his mind alongside their studies of his exercise of power.

In a chapter in his 1989 biography entitled 'Stalin's Mind', Dmitry Volkogonov counterposed Stalin as an 'exceptional intellect' to Trotsky's disparaging characterisation. It was Volkogonov who first published Stalin's 1925 library classification schema, revealed the existence of the ex-libris label and noted his habit of writing in books: 'Lenin's *Collected Works*, for instance, are covered with underlinings, ticks and exclamation marks in the margins'. Stalin, wrote Volkogonov, sought ammunition against his rivals from wherever he could, including their own writings. He kept a special collection of hostile émigré literature and insisted on maintaining subscriptions to White émigré publications.[87]

Volkogonov's claim that Stalin read and underlined key passages in Hitler's *Mein Kampf* cannot be verified, since there is no copy of the book in what remains of Stalin's collection, but it rings true.[88] Not that he needed to read *Mein Kampf* to find out what Hitler had said about 'Lebensraum' and German expansion into Russia, since these words of the Führer were cited widely in the Soviet press. He was also very well briefed about internal developments in Nazi Germany. In 1936, for example, he was sent detailed documentation about that year's Nuremberg Rally.[89] An avid reader of confidential TASS bulletins from around the world, Stalin scrawled 'ha ha' across the report of an October 1939 Turkish news story that he had been invited by Hitler to visit Berlin. Reportedly, Stalin had declined the invitation but the possibility remained that Hitler might visit him in Moscow.[90]

Subsequent Stalin biographies featured themes similar to those of Volkogonov. In a chapter on 'Vozhd and Intellectual', Robert Service considered Stalin to be a thoughtful man who had studied a lot: 'his learning, though, had led to only a few basic changes in his ideas. Stalin's mind was an accumulator and regurgitator. He was not an original thinker nor even an outstanding writer. Yet he was an intellectual until the end of his days.'[91] According to Donald Rayfield, author of *Stalin and His Hangmen*, 'the most common mistake of Stalin's opponents was to underestimate how exceptionally well read he was'.[92] In a section called 'A World of Reading and Contemplation', the Russian historian Oleg Khlevniuk's post-Soviet biography explored Stalin's *pometki*, noting that 'he liked books. Reading played a major role in shaping his ideas. . . . Stalin loved history and constantly used historical example and analogies in his articles, speeches and conversation.' But while Stalin loved history, 'he was not particularly interested in scholarly discussions and actual historical evidence, choosing instead to adapt the facts to his preferred narrative. . . . In the end Stalin's self-education, political experience, and character formed a mind that was in many ways repellent but ideally suited to holding onto power'.[93] Stephen Kotkin's multi-volume biography of the dictator is replete with references to Stalin as intellectual and reader, beginning with his observation that the young Stalin 'devoured books, which, as a Marxist, he did so in order to change the world'.[94]

Nikolai Simonov, a senior IM-L researcher, was the first scholar to explore some of Stalin's *pometki* in depth. His article 'Reflections on Stalin's Markings in the Margins of Marxist Literature' appeared in the party's theoretical journal *Kommunist* in December 1990.[95] Published at the tail end of the Gorbachev era,

Simonov's analysis echoed the late Soviet orthodoxy that Stalin was not a Leninist. His focus was Stalin's views on the theory of the state under socialism and he used the marginalia in his library books to show that the dictator disagreed with Marx, Engels and Lenin on this question.

According to classical Marxist doctrine, the capitalist state (the government, civil service, judiciary, police and armed forces) was a bourgeois instrument of class oppression that would wither away under socialism when antagonistic classes were abolished. Stalin's view was that socialism needed a strong state to ensure the proletariat could hold onto power.

Simonov cited Stalin's detailed annotations of Trotsky's *Terrorism and Communism* (1920) to show that while he approved of his future rival's staunch defence of revolutionary violence during the civil war, it didn't go far enough. According to Trotsky, the dictatorship of the proletariat was exercised by the communist party. Stalin considered Trotsky's reasoning 'inexact' and preferred the idea of the party as a political apparatus that dominated the state and other public organisations such as the trade unions. According to Simonov, classical Marxism viewed the state 'mechanistically' as a temporary, artificial instrument of capitalist class power, whereas Stalin's 'organicist' view of state saw it as a long-term entity whose continued existence as a coercive force was essential to the protection of the Soviet socialist system. Classical Marxism pointed towards a process of democratisation and a reduction of the state's power over citizens, while Stalin's theory of the state provided a rationalisation for his repressive rule under the guise of defending socialism against its enemies.

Stalin's deviation from the traditional Marxist theory of the state under socialism was no secret. At the 18th party congress in March 1939, he mounted a spirited public defence of his revision of the views of Marx, Engels and Lenin. What the three great teachers had not anticipated, Stalin told the delegates, was that socialism would triumph in a single state that would then have to co-exist with powerful capitalist states. Under conditions of capitalist encirclement, the Soviet Union needed a strong state apparatus to defend itself against external threats and internal subversion. Only when capitalism was liquidated globally would the state, in accordance with Marxist theory, wither away.[96]

In December 1994 another former IM-L staffer, the journalist and politician Boris Slavin, published an article in *Pravda* that examined some of the comments Stalin had written in his library books. Slavin was particularly interested in his reading of Lenin's *Materialism and Empirio-Criticism*, noting Stalin's adherence to the classical Marxist definition of freedom as the recognition of necessity. Slavin also noted Stalin's favourite philosophical aphorisms: 'Lots of learning does not teach understanding' (Heraclitus); 'Marxism is a guide to action, not a dogma' (Lenin); and 'Freedom lies beyond the realm of material necessity' (Marx).[97]

Dutch historian Erik van Ree, who was interested in Stalin's political thought, was the first western scholar to extensively research his library books. His presumption before he set out for Moscow in 1994 was that the key to understanding the evolution of Stalin's thinking was the impact of Russian political traditions on his Marxism. That belief was 'shaken' by his encounter with the contents of Stalin's private library, which were overwhelmingly Marxist and betrayed little or no sign of non-Marxist influences. Van Ree's conclusion, after studying every single one of Stalin's annotations, was that Stalin was primarily a creature of the rationalist and utopian west European revolutionary tradition that began with the Enlightenment. While the dictator did absorb some Russian traditions – autocracy and the strong state, for example – he fitted them into a Marxist framework. Stalin admired some of the Tsars – Ivan the Terrible, Peter the Great, Catherine the Great – but thought that, armed with Marxist theory, he could do a better job of creating a powerful, protective Soviet state. The end result in Stalin's thinking was what van Ree termed 'revolutionary patriotism' – the primacy of the defence of the socialist fatherland. Revolution abroad remained a key goal but its pursuit was adapted to the reality of Soviet co-existence with a hostile capitalist world composed of competing nation states.[98]

Among the first Russian scholars to explore Stalin's library books were Boris Ilizarov and Yevgeny Gromov. Ilizarov started working on the library in the late 1990s, when the books still contained what he imagined to be the detritus of Stalin's pipe![99] Suitably inspired, he went on to publish a series of groundbreaking articles and books, both on Stalin's reading life and, most importantly, on the history of the library.[100]

In 2003 Gromov published a wide-ranging study of Stalin's relations with Soviet writers and artists that drew extensively on the holdings of his *lichnyi fond*. Among the documents referenced by Gromov was Stalin's marking of Gorky's novel *Mother*, which is a propagandistic story of revolutionary factory workers in early twentieth-century Russia. Running through the novel is the role of radical books and subversive literature in fomenting revolution. The chapter that attracted Stalin relates how an elderly peasant-turned-factory worker, Mikhail Rybin, having been won over to the revolutionary cause, went to a comrade's house to pick up some illegal books for distribution among the people. Stalin side-marked several pages of this chapter, but what really excited him was Rybin's peroration:

> Give me your help! Let me have books – such books that when a man has read them he will not be able to rest. Put a prickly hedgehog to his brains. Tell those city folks who write for you to write for the villagers also. Let them

write such hot truth that it will scald the village, that the people will even rush to their death.[101]

Another Russian historian who took a great interest in Stalin's library was Roy Medvedev. It was Medvedev who interviewed the bibliographer Zolotukhina about her knowledge of the library and in 2005 he published a book entitled *Chto Chital Stalin?* (What Did Stalin Read?)

Medvedev and his twin brother Zhores were famous Soviet-era dissidents. Roy was expelled from the Soviet communist party in 1969 and Zhores, a plant biologist, was exiled to the west in the 1970s. Both were 'loyal oppositionists' who believed in the Soviet system but wanted to reform and democratise it. Of critical importance for the Medvedevs was the 'destalinisation' process begun by Khrushchev at the 20th party congress, not least the need to tell the whole truth about the massive Stalinist repressions of the 1930s. To this end Roy wrote a long book about Stalinist repression, *Let History Judge*. He was unable to publish the book in the USSR but it was translated and published in the west in the early 1970s. Medvedev's verdict on the dictator, much influenced by Khrushchev's 1956 denunciation of Stalin, was damning: 'boorishness and self-importance, pathological conceit and callousness, mistrust and stealth, an inability to take the criticism of his comrades and a craving for influence and power.'[102] His assessment of Stalin's theoretical legacy was that it was poor: what was of interest in his writings was unoriginal and what was original was wrong. 'He did not derive theoretical positions from concrete reality; he forced theory to fit his wishes, subordinated it to transient situations – in a word he politicised theory.'[103]

As a dissident, Medvedev had no access to Soviet archives. Instead, he utilised documentation from the public sphere together with a great number of unpublished memoir sources. One memoir that he cited was E. P. Frolov's story about his friend Jan Sten, a party philosopher who in the 1920s was recruited by Stalin to teach him Hegelian dialectics. Sten 'often told me in confidence about these lessons', recalled Frolov, 'about the difficulties he, as a teacher, was having because of his student's inability to master the material.'[104]

During the post-Lenin succession struggles Sten backed Stalin against the Trotsky-Zinoviev United Opposition. A pamphlet he wrote on 'The Question of the Stabilisation of Capitalism' (1926) is preserved in Stalin's library. Stalin read the text attentively and evidently agreed with Sten's critique of the United Opposition. Contrary to Trotsky and Zinoviev, Sten argued that capitalism had successfully stabilised itself economically and politically following the intense crisis it experienced immediately after the First World War. Such stabilisation would not last, said Sten, but it could endure for some time yet, something the United Opposition had failed to grasp.[105]

Sten's critique of Trotsky and Zinoviev echoed the views of Nikolai Bukharin, a former 'Left Communist', who came to favour a more moderate course than the one canvassed by the United Opposition, which favoured more radical foreign and domestic policies because it believed the crisis of capitalism was ongoing. Stalin was allied to Bukharin in the mid-1920s but changed his mind at the end of the decade in response to crises in town–country trade relations that threatened to cut food supplies to the cities. Stalin also believed the world economic depression of the late 1920s and early 1930s signalled a return of the revolutionary wave. Hence his abandonment of the New Economic Policy and his embrace of more militant policies. This policy turn meant Stalin fell out with Bukharin and his supporters, including Sten. Like so many opponents and critics of Stalin, Sten was expelled from the party in the 1930s, accused of counter-revolutionary activities, arrested and shot. He was exonerated and posthumously readmitted to the party in 1988.

While Frolov's tale is reminiscent of the legend that Ivan the Terrible was educated by a philosopher known as Maximus the Greek, the story is not implausible. Hegel's philosophy is notoriously difficult to understand and Stalin habitually consulted experts. The story is usually told against him, as a way of puncturing his intellectual pretensions, but his apparent willingness to be tutored in philosophy shows how serious the middle-aged Stalin was about developing intellectually.

STALIN REVIVIFIED

Roy Medvedev continued his studies of Stalin and Stalinism after the USSR's collapse but his views of the dictator changed markedly. The critique of Stalinist terror remained in his writings but was balanced by greater appreciation of the more positive aspects of Stalin's political leadership and intellectual endeavours:

Stalin was a ruler, a dictator and a tyrant. But under the mantle of the despot's 'cult of personality' there was also a real person. He certainly was cruel and vindictive but he had other qualities as well: Stalin was a thinking, calculating, hard-working man possessed of an iron will and a considerable intellect; undoubtedly he was a patriot, concerned to uphold historic Russian statehood.[106]

Medvedev's changed view reflected the post-Soviet rehabilitation of Stalin's historical reputation in Russia. By the early twenty-first century, most Russians believed that Stalin had done more good than harm to their country, not the least of his achievements being the defeat of Hitler. When Russia's main TV channel staged a competition and viewers' poll in 2008 to name the greatest figure in Russian history, Stalin came third (519,071 votes), after Alexander Nevsky (524,575) and Peter Stolypin (523,766), but rumours were rife that the ballot had been rigged to stop him coming first. According to a March 2018 opinion poll, Stalin was voted the greatest leader of all time for Russians: 38 per cent of 1,600 respondents granted him the number one rank – an amazing jump since 1989, when he received just 12 per cent of the vote.[107]

To paraphrase Walter Benjamin, personal book collections are often beset by the disorder that springs from the haphazard way that books are bought, borrowed or otherwise acquired. Cataloguing may mask the confusion but the underlying disorder remains. In the 1920s a degree of order was imposed on Stalin's library by stamping, numbering and classifying the books. At Blizhnyaya he had a library room that housed part of his collection, while other books resided on the many shelves and bookcases of various other homes and workspaces. The shelving of these books was far from random but his library ended up as chaotically organised as many of our own. While Soviet archivists could have centralised, catalogued and preserved the library intact after his death, post-1956 political developments prompted its disassembly. But as Walter Benjamin also said, it is not books that come alive by being collected, it is the collector.[108] Among the remnants of his library, in the pages of its surviving books, Stalin lived on.

CHAPTER 5

BAH HUMBUG! STALIN'S *POMETKI*

Stalin read books in diverse ways – selectively or comprehensively, cursorily or with avid attention. Some he read cover to cover, others he merely skimmed. Sometimes he would begin reading a book, lose interest after a few pages and jump from the introduction to the conclusion. Some books he read in a single sitting, others he dipped in and out of.

Most of the books in what remains of his collection are unmarked by him except for an autograph or the imprint of his library stamp, so it is impossible to know for sure how much of it he actually read. Erik van Ree suggests that Stalin habitually marked the books he did read.[1] But even the most inveterate of annotators do not write in all their books. Only those books or parts of books whose pages remained 'uncut' can be safely eliminated from his reading life, assuming he didn't read another copy of the same text.

It is rare for readers (unless they are educators) to mark fiction books, and Stalin was no exception. The texts he marked were nearly all non-fiction. *Pometki*, the Russian word for such markings, encompasses both the verbal and non-verbal signs that appear on the pages. The closest English word is marginalia, but Stalin's marks are to be found between the lines and on the front, inside and back covers as well as in the margins. Marginalia also implies annotation – the use of words – but 80 per cent of Stalin's surviving *pometki* consist of what H. J. Jackson has called 'signs of attention'.[2]

Stalin marked the text of the pages, paragraphs and phrases that interested him by underlining them or by vertical lines in the side margin. To add emphasis, he double-lined or enclosed the passages in round brackets. To provide structure he numbered the points that interested him – numbering that could reach into the high double-digits and be spread over hundreds of pages of a single text. As an alternative or supplement to these signs of attention, Stalin wrote subheadings or rubrics in the margin. Indeed, much of his marginalia consists of repetition of words and phrases from the text itself.

His style of *pometki* is both normal and conventional, as anyone who marks their books will attest. As Jackson pointed out, readers marking books is a venerable tradition that stretches back to the dawn of the print era. For Erasmus, it was the essential study skill of a humanist education:

> Carefully observe when reading writers whether any striking word occurs, if diction is archaic or novel, if some argument shows brilliant invention or has been skilfully adapted from elsewhere, if there is any brilliance in the style, if there is any adage, historical parallel, or maxim worth committing to memory. Such a passage should be indicated by some appropriate mark. For not only must a variety of marks be employed but appropriate ones at that, so that they will immediately indicate their purpose.[3]

Virginia Woolf was not alone in complaining that marking books was an abomination, an intrusion designed to impose one's own interpretation on other readers. In his classic riposte to this accusation, Mortimer J. Adler insisted that 'marking up a book is not an act of mutilation but of love'. As an active process of reading, marking means that 'your marks and notes become an integral part of the book and stay there forever'. But he was clear that the reader should only mark their own books, not those that belonged to others or were borrowed from public libraries.[4] Stalin recognised no such distinction and freely marked any book that came into his possession, including those he borrowed from the Lenin Library and other state institutions.

As well as marking nearly 900 texts in his personal library Lenin filled notebooks with quotations, summaries and commentaries on the books he read. Stalin's research notes were solely marked in the texts themselves. To aid retrieval of the most important or useful material, he sometimes inserted thin strips of paper between the relevant pages. Some of these now yellowing and disintegrating bookmarks can still be found in the Russian archival collection of Stalin's library books.[5]

As Jackson also points out, the next step up from non-verbal signs is to enter into a one-way conversation with the text in the form of a brief word or phrase. When so moved, Stalin could be highly expressive.

Charles Dickens may well have been among the writers read by Stalin. Dickens was studied in Soviet schools and his writings used to teach English. The Bolsheviks didn't like all his novels (the anti-revolutionary *A Tale of Two Cities*, for example) but they relished his bleak descriptions of nineteenth-century industrial capitalism. Appealing to puritanical Bolsheviks like Stalin would have been the complete absence in Dickens of any mention of physical sexuality.[6] As far as we know, Stalin never wrote Scrooge's famous expletive 'bah humbug' in the margin of any of his books, but he used plenty of Russian equivalents. Among his choice expressions of disdain were 'ha ha', 'gibberish', 'nonsense', 'rubbish', 'fool', 'scumbag', 'scoundrel' and 'piss off'.

But he could also be effusive – 'yes-yes', 'agreed', 'good', 'spot on', 'that's right' – and pensive, which he sometimes signalled by writing *m-da* in the margin, a difficult to translate expression which indicates a combination of puzzlement and pondering what is being said. A free translation would be a polite 'really?' or 'are you sure?' Like Lenin, his most frequent annotation was NB (in Latin script) or its Russian equivalent Vn (*vnimanie* – attention).

Stalin's *pometki* varied according to his mood and purpose. They were usually informational and highly structured and disciplined. Typically, he used coloured pencils – blue, green, red – to make his marks. Occasionally, for no discernible reason, he would mark a book with two or three colours. Sometimes he used abbreviations but mostly he wrote out words in full, though not always legibly. Stalin's style of annotation did not change much over the years, except that as he got older he became less wordy.

While Stalin read mainly to learn something new, he also reread many of his own writings. One example is his February 1946 election speech, delivered in the theatre of the Bolshoi Ballet in Moscow. Stalin gave the speech not long after the great Soviet victory over Nazi Germany but his theme was that, *contra* Catherine the Great, victors should be judged and criticised.

In a pamphlet that reproduced the text of his speech, Stalin marked the opening paragraphs in which he had said the war was not an accident or a function of personalities, it had been the inevitable result of a fundamental crisis of the capitalist system. He also marked the paragraphs in which he stated that the war had demonstrated the superiority of the Soviet social system and the viability of its multinational character. He went on to highlight the role of the communist party in securing victory and how crucial it had been to industrialise the country before the war. The final paragraph that he marked was one at the very end of the speech in which he pointed out that the communists were contesting the elections to the Supreme Soviet as part of a bloc with non-party members.[7]

Stalin did not use speechwriters. He composed his own speeches and often edited those of his colleagues. But he had a habit of recycling elements of his speeches. His reports to the 17th and 18th party congresses in 1934 and 1939 look and feel so similar because he took a copy of his 1934 speech and used it as a template for the one he delivered in 1939.[8] It may be that he reread his 1946 election speech thinking he could use parts of it at the forthcoming party congress, preparations for which were already under way by 1947–8.

The same reason might explain why he read and marked a pamphlet containing Andrei Zhdanov's September 1947 speech 'On the International Situation'. Delivered at the inaugural conference of the Cominform, it was, in effect, the Soviet declaration of the cold war. The postwar world, Zhdanov told delegates from European communist parties, had split into two polarised camps – a camp of imperialism, reaction and war, and a camp of socialism, democracy and peace. Stalin knew this speech very well, since Zhdanov had extensively consulted him about its contents. Yet he made quite a few marks in the pamphlet. One theme was past and present imperialist efforts to destroy or weaken the Soviet Union. Another was the growing power and influence of the United States as a result of the war. A key marked paragraph was that, since its abandonment of President Franklin Roosevelt's policy of co-operation with the Soviet Union, the United States was heading towards a policy of military adventurism.[9]

In the event, the 19th party congress did not take place until October 1952 and Stalin chose not to deliver the main report. Instead, he edited – in great detail – the speech that was given by his deputy, Georgy Malenkov.[10]

In tracking Stalin's *pometki*, it is tempting to be always on the lookout for deeper meanings and significant connections, both political and psychological. Yet, sometimes, Stalin just read for pleasure and interest, his markings signalling little more than his level of engagement with the text.

Librarian-archivist Yury Sharapov was one of the last people to view the bulk of Stalin's book collection intact. It was his 1988 memoir that revealed the existence of the dictator's library and Stalin's habit of marking books. As he astutely observed, 'notes made in the margins of books, periodicals or any text . . . form quite a dangerous genre. They betray the author completely – his emotional nature, his intellect, leanings and habits.'[11] As the foremost interpretor of Lenin's *pometki*, he knew what he was talking about.

It has also proved to be a dangerous genre for scholars searching the library for smoking-gun marginalia that would substantiate their various theories of Stalin's psychology and motivation. One example is the graphic annotation of a couple of pages of a Russian edition of Anatole France's *Under the Rose*, a series of humanist dialogues about the existence and meaning of God. But it turned out that these were made by Svetlana, not Stalin.[12] Svetlana's style of annotation was similar to her father's but more florid and irreverent, and harder to make sense of. Examining these markings, a perplexed Yevgeny Gromov concluded that 'it's hard to understand what Stalin wanted to express'.[13]

Another example of the perils of over-interpreting Stalin's *pometki* is his multiple scribbling of the word *uchitel'* (teacher) on the back cover of Alexei Tolstoy's 1942 play, *Ivan Grozny*. Stalin could be a bit of a doodler and the word 'teacher' features among several other, unrelated and barely legible words and phrases on the back cover.[14] Yet some have chosen to take this as prima facie evidence that Stalin considered Ivan the Terrible his teacher and exemplar.[15] As we see below, Stalin did have a lot of time for the Terrible, but he looked down on all the Tsars, even the Greats such as Peter and Catherine. His one and only true hero and role model was Lenin.

Another mountain made out of a molehill is Stalin's underlining of this quotation in a 1916 Russian history textbook: 'The death of the defeated is necessary for the tranquillity of the victors' – attributed to Genghis Khan.[16] Is that why Stalin killed all those Old Bolsheviks, asked two Russian historians.[17] That Stalin might have been interested in Genghis Khan's motivation for what the book's author terms the 'Tatar Pogroms' does not seem to have occurred to them.

Another apparently smoking gun spotted by some is the text written at the back of Stalin's heavily marked 1939 edition of Lenin's *Materialism and Empirio-Criticism*:

1) Weakness, 2) Idleness, 3) Stupidity. These are the only things that can be called vices. Everything else, in the absence of the aforementioned, is undoubtedly virtue. NB! If a man is (1) strong (spiritually), 2) active, 3) clever (or capable), then he is good, regardless of any other 'vices'![18]

According to Donald Rayfield, this was 'the most significant statement' Stalin ever made: 'Stalin's comment gives a Machiavellian gloss to the credo of a Dostoevskian satanic anti-hero and is an epigraph to his whole career.'[19] Robert Service saw the inscription as 'intriguing' and thinks that Stalin, in 'communing with himself' and in using 'the religious language of the spirit and of sin and vice', was 'reverting to the discourse of the Tbilisi Spiritual Seminary', his early schooling having 'left an indelible imprint'.[20] Slavoj Žižek considered it 'as concise as ever a formulation of immoral ethics'.[21]

All very interesting, except the handwriting is not Stalin's. Who wrote those words and how they came to be inscribed in a book in his library remains mysterious, as does their intended meaning.

In truth, no smoking guns are to be found anywhere in the remains of Stalin's library. His *pometki* reveal preoccupations not secrets, and the way he engaged with ideas, arguments and facts.

JOINED AT THE HIP: STALIN, LENIN AND TROTSKY

Stalin revered Lenin. He first met him in December 1905 at a party conference in Tampere, Finland, then an autonomous province of Tsarist Russia. In January

1924, at a memorial meeting for the recently deceased founder of the Soviet state, Stalin recalled that what captivated him about Lenin was the 'irresistible force of logic' in his speeches. Other features of Lenin's political practice that so impressed Stalin were 'no whining over defeat'; 'no boasting in victory'; 'fidelity to principle'; 'faith in the masses'; and 'the insight of genius, the ability to rapidly grasp and divine the inner meaning of impending events'.[22]

There were hundreds of works by Lenin in Stalin's book collection, dozens of them marked and annotated. Lenin was Stalin's most-read author. In Stalin's own collected writings there are many more references to Lenin than any other person.[23] Stalin was renowned as the master of the Lenin quote. He didn't just pore over Lenin's original writings, he read summaries and condensations by other authors, being particularly fond of publications that provided excerpts of Lenin's writings on the 'Dictatorship of the Proletariat' and other vital issues of the day.[24] Another useful crib were collections containing notes and plans for his major speeches, which gave Stalin insight into how Lenin constructed and presented arguments.[25] In a book about the reasons for Bolshevik victory in the civil war, Stalin simply highlighted all the quotes from Lenin: the Bolsheviks had won because of international working-class solidarity, because they were united whereas their opponents were divided, and because soldiers had refused to fight against the Soviet government. Lenin's reference to the failure of Winston Churchill's prediction that the allies would take Petrograd in September 1919 and Moscow by December was double-lined in the margin.[26]

In his comprehensive study of Stalin's political thought, Erik van Ree concluded that his 'notes in Lenin's writings are remarkable for their lack of criticism. In the most intensively read books by his predecessor there is no hint of it all.' The same was true of Marx: 'I did not find a single critical remark by Stalin.' While Stalin's reading of Engels was more critical, his markings of Engels's books was always attentive and respectful. 'Only idiots can doubt that Engels was and remains our teacher,' he wrote to the Politburo in August 1934. 'But it does not follow from this at all, that we must cover up Engel's short-comings.' As van Ree also pointed out, the marked books in his library show that Stalin kept on reading Marx, Engels and Lenin until the very end of his life.[27]

Stalin's toast to scientists at a reception for higher education workers in May 1938 is one of his many fulsome tributes to Lenin:

> In the course of its development science has known not a few courageous men who were able to break down the old and create the new. . . . Such scientists as Galileo, Darwin . . . I should like to dwell on one of these eminent men of science, one who at the same time was the greatest man of modern times. I am referring to Lenin, our teacher, our tutor. (*Applause.*) Remember

1917. A scientific analysis of the social development of Russia and of the international situation brought Lenin to the conclusion that the only way out of the situation lay in the victory of socialism in Russia. This conclusion came as a complete surprise to many men of science. . . . Scientists of all kinds set up a howl that Lenin was destroying science. But Lenin was not afraid to go against the current, against the force of routine. And Lenin won (*Applause*).[28]

When Stalin devised his library classification schema in May 1925, Trotsky had already emerged as his fiercest rival and a leading opponent in the post-Lenin succession power struggles. Yet Stalin placed Trotsky sixth in the list of Marxist authors whose books were to be separated from the general, subject-based classification scheme. Apart from Marx, Engels and Lenin, only Kautsky (the chief theoretician of German social democracy) and Plekhanov (the founding father of Russian Marxism) were listed ahead of Trotsky. After Trotsky's name came those of Stalin's then close allies – Bukharin, Kamenev and Zinoviev.

More than forty of Trotsky's books and pamphlets, including some quite hefty tomes, may be found among the remnants of Stalin's library, but he was particularly interested in his rival's 'factional' polemics – *The New Course* (1923) and *The Lessons of October* (1924). Stalin combed through these and other writings seeking ammunition for his critique of Trotsky and Trotskyism. His withering attacks on Trotsky's views made his name as a top-class polemicist and consolidated his authority as the party's general-secretary. At the 15th party conference in November 1926, he was scathing in his criticism of Trotsky's statement in *The New Course* that 'Leninism, as a system of revolutionary action, presumes a revolutionary instinct trained by reflection and experience which, in the social sphere, is equivalent to muscular sensation in physical labour.' Stalin's commented: 'Leninism as "muscular sensation in physical labour". New and original and very profound, is it not? Can you make head or tail of it? (*Laughter*).'[29]

Trotsky, for all his undoubted brilliance as a Marxist intellectual and orator, was an easy target for Stalin. He had a history of criticising Lenin and the Bolsheviks and only joined up with the group in summer 1917. Trotsky tried to airbrush these criticisms but Stalin insisted on reminding the party of his past errors.

He was particularly fond of quoting Trotsky's 1915 attack on Lenin's view that proletarian revolution and socialism were possible in a single country, even in culturally backward and economically underdeveloped peasant Russia. At stake was the belief that it would be possible to build socialism in Soviet Russia,

Trotsky's view being that the Russian Revolution needed successful revolutions in more advanced countries if it was not going to be crushed by imperialism and capitalism. Stalin accepted the socialist revolution in Russia would not be 'finally' victorious until there was a world revolution, but also believed that Soviet socialism would survive and thrive on its own. The great majority of the Bolshevik party agreed with Stalin, preferring his doctrine of socialism in one country to Trotsky's advocacy of world revolution as the primary goal.

Like all the leading Bolsheviks, Stalin quoted Lenin selectively to suit his argument. In 1915, for example, Lenin was speculating on the possibility of an *advanced* country adopting socialism without the support of revolutions in other countries. But Lenin's views on this matter did evolve post-1917 in response to the reality of a revolution in 'backward' Russia that had brought the Bolsheviks to power.[30] For Stalin and his supporters within the party, the fact of their successful revolution was all-important, and they did not take kindly to Trotsky's suggestion in *Tasks in the East* (1924) that the centre of world revolution could shift to Asia in the absence of European revolutions: 'Fool!' wrote Stalin in the margin. 'With the existence of the Soviet Union the centre cannot be in the East.'[31]

Another favourite target of Stalin's was *The Lessons of October*, in which Trotsky dredged up the Kamenev–Zinoviev conflicts with Lenin in 1917. The party was split in 1917, argued Trotsky, and the same rightist Old Bolsheviks were holding it back after the revolution. Only Lenin's incessant pressure for an insurrection to seize power had saved the day.[32]

Kamenev and Zinoviev were old friends and comrades of Stalin's and his allies in the struggle against Trotsky, so he rose to their defence, even though he personally was not targeted in *The Lessons of October*. In a 1924 speech on 'Trotskyism or Leninism?' he accepted there were disagreements in the party in 1917 and admitted that Lenin had correctly steered the Bolsheviks towards a more radical policy of opposing and then overthrowing the Provisional Government. But he denied the party was split and pointed out that when the central committee endorsed Lenin's proposal for an insurrection it established a political oversight group that included Kamenev and Zinoviev, even though they had voted against the proposed putsch. Stalin also decried what he called the 'legend' of Trotsky's special role in 1917:

I am far from denying Trotsky's undoubtedly important role in the uprising. I must say, however, that Trotsky did not play any special role. . . . Trotsky did, indeed, fight well in October; but Trotsky was not the only one . . . when the enemy is isolated and uprising is growing, it is not difficult to fight well. At such moments even backward people become heroes.[33]

The Lessons of October was not Trotsky's first attempt to write the history of the Russian Revolution. During the 1918 Brest-Litovsk peace negotiations he spent time drafting a short book called *Oktyabr'skaya Revolyutsiya*, published later that year and then translated into many languages, appearing in English as *History of the Russian Revolution to Brest-Litovsk*.[34] It was a pro-Bolshevik propaganda effort by Trotsky so he played down differences within the party. This account of the revolution was much to Stalin's liking. He read and marked the text in detail and with evident satisfaction at its contents. He was particularly interested in Trotsky's treatment of the 'July Days', when the Bolsheviks had drawn back from a premature uprising – an episode that had embedded itself in the party's historical memory as an object lesson that sometimes political retreats were necessary in order to live and fight another day.[35] And, as we have already seen, in his November 1918 *Pravda* article on the first anniversary of the revolution, Stalin was fulsome in his praise of Trotsky's role in organising the insurrection.

A 1921 pamphlet on Trotsky by an M. Smolensky, published in Berlin, was part of a series designed to explain Bolshevik ideas to the workers of the world. According to its author, 'Trotsky was, perhaps, both the most brilliant and the most paradoxical figure in the Bolshevik leadership'. Stalin did not mark that particular comment but he did underline the author's next observation – that while Lenin was a socialist 'bible scholar' devoted to the sacred texts of Marxism, Trotsky saw it as a method of analysis: 'if Lenin's Marxism was dogmatically orthodox, Trotsky's was methodological'. There followed a series of faint ticks in the margin by Stalin which seemingly expressed approval of a variety of Trotsky's quoted views. He also margin-lined Trotsky's contention that there were currently two socialist ideologies in contention with each other – that of the Second (socialist) International and that of the Third (communist) International.[36]

Trotsky's *Terrorism and Communism* (1920) was a reply to a publication of the same name by Karl Kautsky, the 'renegade' the Bolsheviks had once much admired, not least for his staunch defence of revolutionary Marxism against the 'revisionism' of Eduard Bernstein, who favoured a more moderate and reformist socialist movement. In his pamphlet, Kautsky criticised the violence and dictatorial methods that the Bolsheviks used to gain and hold power, particularly during the ongoing Russian Civil War. In his reply to Kautsky, Trotsky laid out in stark terms the rationale for the Bolsheviks' violent seizure of power, their subsequent suppression of Russian constitutional democracy, and their use of 'Red Terror' in the civil war. Stalin needed no lessons in realpolitik from Machiavelli, or even Lenin, when he had Trotsky's text to hand.

We can be fairly sure that Stalin read Trotsky's book quite close to the time of its publication. The Bolsheviks, including Lenin, were keen to refute Kautsky's critique, not least because it had undermined their standing in the international socialist movement.

Stalin's heavily underlined copy of the book was peppered throughout by expressions of approval such as NB and *tak* (in this context, yes).[37] 'The problem', wrote Trotsky, 'is to make a civil war a short one; and this is attained only by resoluteness in action. But it is just against revolutionary resoluteness that Kautsky's whole book is directed.' NB, wrote Stalin in the margin. He made the same annotation at the head of Chapter Two on the 'Dictatorship of the Proletariat' and wrote out Trotsky's statement in the first paragraph that 'the political autocracy of the proletariat is the "sole form" in which it can realise its control of the state'. In the same chapter, Stalin underlined, double margin-lined and wrote NB alongside Trotsky's barb that 'the man who repudiates terrorism in principle i.e. repudiates measures of suppression and intimidation towards determined and armed counter-revolution, must reject all idea of the political supremacy of the working class and its revolutionary dictatorship. The man who repudiates the dictatorship of the proletariat repudiates the socialist revolution and digs the grave of socialism.'

Trotsky next mounted a prolonged defence of the argument that the interests of socialist revolution trumped the democratic process because the latter was merely a façade behind which the bourgeoisie hid its power. Stalin agreed wholeheartedly and was particularly taken by Trotsky's quotation of Paul Lafargue's view that parliamentary democracy constituted little more than an illusion of popular self-government. 'When the proletariat of Europe and America seizes the State, it will have to organise a revolutionary government and govern society as a dictatorship, until the bourgeoisie has disappeared as a class' is among the Lafargue quotes underlined by Stalin.

Trotsky justified the Bolsheviks' dissolution of the Constituent Assembly in January 1918, saying they signed the decree authorising elections to that body, expecting it to vote to dissolve itself in favour of the more representative Soviets. But 'the Constituent Assembly placed itself across the path of the revolutionary movement, and was swept aside' (underlined by Stalin).

Stalin liked to number points made by authors and did this to Trotsky's list of three previous revolutions that had experienced violence, terror and civil war – the sixteenth-century religious Reformation that split the Catholic Church, the English revolutions of the seventeenth century and the French Revolution in the eighteenth century. Trotsky concluded from his historical analysis that 'the degree of ferocity of the struggle depends on a series of internal and international circumstances. The more ferocious and dangerous is the resistance of the class enemy who has been overthrown, the more inevitably does the system of repression take the form of a system of terror.' The underlining of the last subclause is Stalin's.

Beside the following underlined paragraph, Stalin wrote two expressions of approval, NB and *tak*:

The Red Terror is not distinguishable from the armed insurrection, the direct continuation of which it represents. The State terror of a revolutionary class can be condemned 'morally' only by a man who, as a principle, rejects (in words) every form of violence whatsoever – consequently, every war and every rising. For this one has to be merely and simply a hypocritical Quaker.

When Trotsky wrote that 'Kautsky has not the least idea of what a revolution is in practice. He thinks that theoretically to reconcile is the same as practically to accomplish', Stalin underlined the two sentences, and in the margin wrote another of his favourite exclamations of approval – *metko* (spot on).

According to Trotsky, Kautsky believed the Russian working class had seized power prematurely. To which Trotsky responded: 'No one gives the proletariat the opportunity of choosing whether it will or will not . . . take power immediately or postpone the moment. Under certain conditions the working class is bound to take power, under the threat of political self-annihilation for a whole historical period.' This was underlined by Stalin, too, and in the margin he wrote *tak!*

Trotsky's clinching argument in favour of the Bolshevik dictatorship was underlined, bracketed *and* crossed through by Stalin:

We have more than once been accused of having substituted for the dictatorship of the Soviets the dictatorship of our party. Yet it can be said with complete justice that the dictatorship of the Soviets became possible only by means of the dictatorship of the party. It is thanks to the clarity of its theoretical vision and its strong revolutionary organisation that the party has afforded to the Soviets the possibility of becoming transformed from shapeless parliaments of labour into the apparatus of the supremacy of labour. In this 'substitution' of the power of the party for the power of the working class there is nothing accidental, and in reality there is no substitution at all. The Communists express the fundamental interests of the working class.

Actually, Stalin was not convinced by Trotsky's wording here. In the margin he wrote: 'dictatorship of the party – not exact', his preferred formulation being that the proletariat ruled *through* the party. He also expressed doubts about Trotsky's view that under socialism compulsory labour service was the natural concomitant of the socialisation of the means of production. Stalin signalled scepticism by writing *m-da* in the margin several times.[38] By the time of the

10th party congress in March 1921, Stalin's questioning of Trotsky's position had hardened into outright opposition to his proposals for the militarisation of labour.

Stalin had his own copy of the Russian translation of Kautsky's original text, which he read as attentively as Trotsky's rejoinder.[39] The margins of the Kautsky book were liberally sprinkled with the ridiculing 'ha ha' and 'hee hee' as well as choice insults such as *svoloch'* (swine) and *lzhets* (liar). When Kautsky argued that Bolshevik intransigence was based on their claim to a monopoly of truth, Stalin responded that he was a *durak* (fool) for believing that all knowledge was provisional and limited. The same kind of invective may be found written in other Kautsky books that Stalin read. 'Only he can mix up the dictatorship of the proletariat with the dictatorship of a clique', he wrote in a 1922 copy of Kautsky's *The Proletarian Revolution and Its Programme*.[40] 'Rubbish', 'nonsense', wrote Stalin, when Kautsky claimed that another revolutionary crisis in nineteenth-century Austria-Hungary would have doomed the Czechs to Germanisation.[41] Yet he read and marked many sections of Kautsky's *Terrorism and Communism* without further comment. There were even a few NBs and one or two *m-das* in the margin. The same indicators of positive interest in the substantive detail of Kautsky's many writings may be found in Stalin's reading and marking of other works, particularly those that dealt with economic affairs and the 'Agrarian Question', Kautsky being an acknowledged Marxist expert on these topics.[42] Always on the lookout for useful information and arguments, Stalin was willing to learn from even the most despised opponents.

At the central committee plenum in July 1926, Stalin claimed that hitherto he had 'held a moderate, not openly inimical stand against Trotsky' and 'had kept to a moderate policy towards him'.[43] His close reading of Trotsky's technical-economic writings of the mid-1920s – *Towards Socialism or Capitalism?* (1925); *8 Years: Results and Perspectives* (1926); and *Our New Tasks* (1926) – suggests this might have been true. These works date from the period when Trotsky, having been forced to step down as war commissar in January 1925, was a member of the Supreme Council of the National Economy, which controlled Soviet industry.

Trotsky was sceptical about the New Economic Policy as a strategy for socialism but was a moderate critic compared to some hard-line leftists within the Bolshevik party. He believed that NEP's revival of the market in agriculture had over-empowered the so-called kulaks or rich peasants. He also saw the danger of a capitalist restoration across the economy and thought that socialist industrialisation was being neglected. Stalin's marking without comment of many passages in Trotsky's writings indicates that he shared these concerns to some extent but he was more optimistic about NEP's capacity to generate the resources necessary to pay for socialist industrialisation. He was also confident the party and the proletariat could continue to dominate the peasants, their much larger numbers notwithstanding.[44] However, when food supplies to the cities were threatened by peasant hoarding at the end of the 1920s, Stalin did not hesitate to abandon NEP and force through, at great human cost, accelerated industrialisation and the forced collectivisation of Soviet agriculture. Many of Trotsky's supporters hailed Stalin's 'left turn' and supported his struggle against the so-called Right Opposition led by Nikolai Bukharin, who resisted the abandonment of NEP. Trotsky himself thought Stalin had gone too far too fast. He even began to think that 'market socialism' – the underpinning model of NEP – had some merits after all.[45]

The biggest differences between Stalin and Trotsky concerned the doctrine of 'socialism in one country', which was a dispute about whether or not socialist construction at home should take priority over spreading the revolution abroad. Yet Trotsky was as committed as Stalin to building socialism in the USSR, and while Stalin de-prioritised world revolution, he didn't abandon it. This was an important strategic difference but it did not constitute an unbridgeable ideological gulf. It was factional battles and the narcissism of small differences that escalated such disagreements into an existential struggle for the soul of the Bolshevik party.

Trotsky was expelled from the party and sent into exile at the end of the 1920s. To an extent, he was the author of his own misfortune.[46] It was Trotsky who launched the 'history wars' about who had done what during the revolution. In 1923 it was Trotsky who broke the unity of the Politburo leadership collective that had assumed control when Lenin was stricken by a series of strokes. As head of the Commission on State Industry, he proposed acceleration of socialist industrialisation and modification of NEP's strategy of gradual economic growth based on peasant capitalism and small-scale private production. Piling the pressure onto his leadership colleagues, Trotsky organised a campaign within the party that accused the Politburo majority, headed by a triumvirate of Stalin, Zinoviev and Kamenev, of constituting a 'factional dictatorship'. It was this same campaign that led to the publication of *The New Course* by *Pravda* in December 1923. However, the matter was settled by a resounding victory for the triumvirate at the 13th party conference in January 1924.[47]

Trotsky's next move was an opportunistic and ill-advised alliance with Kamenev and Zinoviev, who, now much more left-wing than they were in 1917, had fallen out with Stalin over NEP and socialism in one country and wanted the party to adopt a more militant approach. Like Trotsky's Left Opposition of 1923, the United Opposition of Kamenev, Trotsky and Zinoviev attempted to rally support within the party but was overwhelmed by the power and popularity of Stalin, at this time closely allied to Bukharin, a former Left Communist who had moved rightwards and emerged as the leading theorist of NEP as a gradualist political and economic strategy for socialism.[48]

In October 1926 Trotsky was removed from the Politburo and a year later from the central committee, as were Kamenev and Zinoviev. In November 1927 Trotsky and Zinoviev were expelled from the party and the rout was completed by the 15th party congress in December 1927, which excluded seventy-five oppositionists, including Kamenev, from its ranks. Those expulsions triggered a purge of the United Opposition's grassroots activists.

Kamenev and Zinoviev, together with many of their supporters, quickly recanted their opposition to the majority line and were soon readmitted to the party. Trotsky stood his ground, declaring that the party, like the French Revolution in 1794, had been captured by counter-revolutionary 'Thermidorian forces'. In January 1928 he was exiled to Alma-Ata in Kazakhstan.

A philosophical as well as a political logic underlay what Igal Halfin has called the 'demonization' of the Bolshevik opposition to Stalin's majority faction in the party.[49] Kautsky was right. The Bolsheviks believed their movement was armed with a scientific theory of society and history that gave them – and only them – access to absolute truth. Their party and its leaders had proven themselves in the crucible of revolution and civil war and were now building the world's first socialist society – an endeavour that would lead all of humanity to a classless and oppression-free utopia. Within this Weltanschauung, opposition to the party majority was inconceivable except as a deviation expressive of the insidious influence of class enemies.

As Trotsky put it at the 13th party congress in May 1924:

Comrades, none of us wishes to be or can be right when against the Party. In the last instance the Party is always right because it is the only historical instrument in the hands of the working class. . . . The English have a saying: 'My country, right or wrong.' We may say, and with much greater justice: 'My party, right or wrong.'[50]

Demonisation of dissent within the party was a gradual process that took place over several years. Initially, dissenters were deemed a 'petty-bourgeois deviation' that was objectively but not knowingly counter-revolutionary. Then the opposition came to be characterised as anti-party and actively counter-revolutionary.

One widely distributed critique of Trotskyism in the mid-1920s was Semen Kanatchikov's *History of One Deviation*, which portrayed Trotsky as an isolated individualist who had rejected party discipline and gathered around himself 'loners' prone to hysterical panic. We don't know if Stalin read the book but there was certainly a copy in his library, together with several other Kanatchikov publications.[51]

Trotsky was exiled to Alma-Ata in 1928 for 'counter-revolutionary activities', but was allowed to continue his factionalising by post. Accused of being involved in 'anti-Soviet' activities, he was exiled to Turkey in 1929 and deprived of his Soviet citizenship in 1932.

Trotsky published a number of notable books after he was expelled from the Soviet Union: *The History of the Russian Revolution* (1930); *My Life* (1930); *The Permanent Revolution* (1931); *The Revolution Betrayed* (1936); and *The Stalin School of Falsification* (1937). Apart from a 1931 German-language book on fascism, no post-expulsion works by Trotsky are to be found among the remnants of Stalin's library. Dmitry Volkogonov claimed that 'Stalin read the translation of *The Revolution Betrayed* in a single night, seething with bile', but, typically, cites no source.[52] Stephen Kotkin reports that 'the omnipotent dictator … maintained a collection of everything written by and about Trotsky in a special cupboard in his study at the Near Dacha', but he provides no evidence either.[53] Certainly, Stalin was kept well informed about Trotsky's activities abroad and about his efforts to stay in touch with oppositionists who remained in the USSR. He also received a stream of reports from his security services about their repression of so-called 'Trotskyist groups'.[54]

STALIN'S TERROR

At the beginning of the 1930s Stalin was seemingly sanguine about the threat posed by Trotsky and Trotskyism. 'The gentlemen in the Trotsky camp chattered about the "degeneration" of the Soviet regime, about "Thermidor", about the "inevitable victory" of Trotskyism,' Stalin told delegates to the 16th party congress in June 1930. 'But, actually, what happened? What happened was the collapse, the end of Trotskyism.'[55] In his 1931 letter to *Proletarskaya Revolyutsiya*, Stalin expressed concern not about the strength of Trotskyism but about its misidentification as a faction of communism, when, 'as a matter of fact, Trotskyism is the advanced detachment of the counter-revolutionary bourgeoisie'.[56] Talking to Emil Ludwig in December 1931, Stalin insisted that Trotsky had been largely forgotten by Soviet workers and if they did remember him it was 'with bitterness, with exasperation, with hatred'.[57] At the 17th party congress in January 1934 – the so-called 'Congress of Victors' – Stalin said nothing about Trotsky except that 'the anti-Leninist group of Trotskyists has been smashed and scattered. Its organisers are now to be found in the backyards of bourgeois parties abroad.'[58]

Stalin was shaken from his complacency by the shooting dead in December 1934 of Leningrad party secretary Sergei M. Kirov. He rushed to Leningrad to personally interrogate the perpetrator, Leonid Nikolaev. On the way he drafted a draconian decree that abrogated the rights of those accused of terrorism and streamlined their prosecution, conviction and execution. This became the legal basis for thousands of summary shootings during the ensuing campaign of state-sponsored terror against Stalin's political opponents.[59]

Nikolaev was, in fact, a lone assassin who gunned down Kirov outside his office because of a personal grudge. But suspicions still linger that Stalin was the architect of Kirov's killing. Like most conspiracy theories about Stalin, there is no hard evidence for such a claim.[60] Not even Trotsky thought Stalin guilty of this particular crime, although he rightly feared it would be used as a pretext for a further crackdown on the anti-Stalinist opposition.[61]

Stalin had his own conspiracy theory: Kirov was a victim of the Zinovievites. On 16 December, Kamenev and Zinoviev were arrested. On 29 December, Nikolaev and thirteen alleged associates were executed, while Kamenev and Zinoviev were imprisoned for abetting the murder. In 1935 hundreds of former Zinovievites were rounded up and the scope of the investigation was broadened to include former Trotskyists.

In his coerced confession, Zinoviev said: 'Because we were unable to properly submit to the party, merge with it completely but instead continued to look backward and to live our separate, stifling lives – because of all that, we were doomed to the kind of political dualism that produces double-dealing'.[62]

In June 1935 Stalin's deputy security chief, Nikolai Yezhov, presented a report to the central committee claiming that Kamenev, Zinoviev and Trotsky were 'the active organisers of the murder of comrade Kirov, as well as of the attempt on the life of Comrade Stalin that was being prepared within the Kremlin'.[63]

The latter charge was a reference to the so-called 'Kremlin Affair', which began when three cleaners confessed to spreading slander about the state and its leaders. Among those implicated in anti-Soviet activities were three librarians working in the Kremlin's government library. Of the 110 Kremlin staff arrested, 108 were imprisoned or exiled and two shot.[64]

Stalin was fond of giving lessons in realpolitik to soft-hearted western intellectuals and in June 1935 he told the well-known French writer Romain Rolland that a hundred armed agents from Germany, Poland and Finland had been shot for plotting terrorist attacks on Kirov and other Soviet leaders:

Such is the logic of power. In these conditions power must be strong, hard and fearless. Otherwise it's not power and won't be recognised as such. The

French Communards didn't understand this, they were too soft and indecisive. Consequently, they lost, and the French bourgeoisie was merciless. That's the lesson for us. . . . It is very unpleasant for us to kill. This is a dirty business. Better to be out of politics and keep one's hands clean, but we don't have the right to stay out of politics if we want to liberate enslaved people. When you agree to engage in politics, then you do everything not for yourself but only for the state. The state demands that we are pitiless.[65]

He also told Rolland about the Kremlin Affair:

We have a government library, which has female librarians who can enter the apartments of responsible comrades in the Kremlin in order to tidy up their libraries. It turns out that some of these librarians had been recruited by our enemies for the purposes of terrorism. It has to be said that these librarians are remnants of the old, defeated ruling classes – the bourgeoisie and the aristocracy. We found out that these women had poison and intended to poison some of our officials.[66]

Egged on by Yezhov, Stalin decided to stage a public trial of Kamenev, Zinoviev and fourteen others accused of being the leaders of a 'United Trotskyite-Zinovievite Centre' that had organised the network that killed Kirov and plotted to assassinate other Soviet leaders. Stalin, together with Chief State Prosecutor Andrei Vyshinsky, drafted the detailed indictment and the trial took place in Moscow in August 1936. Having confessed to their crimes, all sixteen defendants were found guilty and executed. Trotsky and his son, Lev Sedov, were sentenced to death *in absentia*.

As Wendy Goldman so aptly summarises events so far: 'The case, which began in December 1934 with a domestic murder and a lone gunman, now involved sixteen defendants, multiple murder plots, foreign spies, fascist contacts, and terrorist conspiracies. The initial objective, to find and punish Kirov's assassin, had expanded into a nationwide attack on the former left opposition.'[67]

The arraignment of Zinoviev and Kamenev was in line with an established and well-rehearsed Soviet tradition, inspired in part by the political trials of radicals staged by Tsarist Russia in the late nineteenth century.[68] The first trial was of the leaders of the Socialist Revolutionary party in 1922, accused of being involved in armed struggle and subversive activities against the state. That same year priests and lay believers who had resisted the Bolsheviks' expropriation of church valuables were tried. In 1928 a large group of engineers and managers in the North Caucasus town of Shakhty were tried for conspiracy to sabotage the town's coal mines. At the 'Industrial Party' trial of 1930, Soviet scientists and engineers were accused of conspiring with foreign powers to wreck the USSR's economy. In 1931 a group of 'Menshevik' economists was tried for using disinformation to undermine the first five-year plan. In 1933 six British employees of Metro-Vickers, a company contracted to install electrical equipment, were prosecuted for economic wrecking and espionage.

But the charges levelled against Zinoviev and Kamenev in 1936 were far more serious, since those indicted were Old Bolshevik leaders who had once been among Stalin's closest comrades-in-arms. It was a piece of crude political theatre whose none-too-subtle message was that even top leaders could turn out to be traitors and that no enemy of the system could hide from state security.

In January 1937 Stalin staged a trial of members of an 'Anti-Soviet Parallel Trotskyist Centre' – said to be a reserve network in the event the Trotskyist-Zinovievite Centre was exposed. The main defendants were the former deputy commissar for heavy industry, Georgy Pyatakov, former *Izvestiya* editor Karl Radek, and Grigory Sokolnikov, the former deputy commissar for foreign affairs. They and fourteen others were accused of treason, espionage and wrecking, their ultimate aim being to take power and restore capitalism in the USSR after it had been militarily defeated by Germany and Japan. Mostly former Trotskyists, the great majority of the accused were sentenced to death following their confession-based trial. The defendants implicated the leaders of the so-called Right Opposition – Bukharin and the former prime minister Alexei Rykov. These two were expelled from the party in March 1937, paving the way for their arrest, and the staging a year later of the third and last of the great Moscow show trials – the trial of the 'Bloc of Rightists and Trotskyites'. At this trial Bukharin and Rykov duly confessed to conspiring with foreign powers to overthrow Soviet power and, together with most of their co-defendants, were sentenced to death and executed.[69] The third leader of the so-called Right Opposition, the former head of the Soviet trade unions Mikhail Tomsky, escaped that gruesome fate by shooting himself in August 1936.

It is hard to credit that Stalin actually believed the absurd charges levelled against these former members of the Soviet political elite or that he gave any credence to the fantastical confessions upon which they rested. But, to paraphrase that adage about supporters of President Donald J. Trump, while Stalin took the confessions seriously he did not take them literally. Arguably, while his general belief in the existence of an anti-Soviet conspiracy was unshakeable, the detailed veracity of the specific confessions was another matter entirely.

In their analysis of the Great Terror, J. Arch Getty and Oleg Naumov distinguish between Yezhov, who truly believed in the existence of the enemies he hunted down on Stalin's behalf, and Bukharin, who chose to serve Stalin by falsely confessing to being one. Yezhov, who was appointed head of the NKVD in September 1936, embraced official discourse as a description of reality; to Bukharin it was an invention, a drama in which he was prepared to play his prescribed role in order to safeguard the Soviet system.[70] Stalin seems to have been a hybrid case. For him the conspiracy against Soviet power was as real as it was for Yezhov but he knew the truth was more complex and contradictory than the story framed for the show trials.

It was the February–March 1937 plenum of the party's central committee that set the scene for a general purge of Soviet polity and society. In 1937–8 alone there were a million and a half political arrests and hundreds of thousands of executions. Stalin told the plenum that the 'wrecking and diversionist-espionage' activities of foreign agents had impacted on nearly all party and state bodies, which had been infiltrated by Trotskyists.

The party had underestimated the dangers facing the Soviet state in conditions of 'capitalist encirclement', said Stalin, notably the penetration of the USSR by numerous imperialist wreckers, spies, diversionists and killers. Pretending to be loyal communists, the Trotskyists had 'deceived our people politically, abused confidence, wrecked on the sly, and revealed our state secrets to the enemies of the Soviet Union'.

The strength of the party, said Stalin, lay in its connection to the masses. By way of illustration he cited the ancient Greek myth of Antaeus, the son of Poseidon, god of the seas, and of Gaea, goddess of the earth. In battle, Antaeus was invincible because of the strength he drew from his mother via the earth. But one day an enemy appeared who vanquished him. It was Hercules, who held him aloft and prevented him from touching the ground:

I think that the Bolsheviks remind us of the hero of Greek mythology, Antaeus. They, like Antaeus, are strong because they maintain connection with their mother, the masses who gave birth to them, suckled them and reared them. And as long as they maintain connection with their mother, with the people, they have every chance of remaining invincible.[71]

The military purge began in May 1937 with the arrest of Marshal M. N. Tukhachevsky and seven other Soviet generals, who were accused of a fascist plot to overthrow the government.

Stalin's doubts about the loyalty of the Red Army dated back to the civil war debate about the recruitment of bourgeois military specialists. In the 1920s White émigré circles fantasised about Tukhachevsky as a 'Red Napoleon' and there were fears the armed forces would be infiltrated by former Tsarist officers. There were many Trotsky supporters in the highly politicised armed forces and in 1927 the head of Stalin's political police warned him they were plotting a military coup. During the forced collectivisation campaign, elements of the Red Army wavered when faced with orders to seize peasant lands and produce.

None of this stopped Tukhachevsky from rising to the rank of deputy defence commissar or from being promoted to marshal in 1935. But Stalin's attitude towards him changed drastically during the feverish atmosphere that developed after Kirov's assassination. The trigger for his arrest seems to have been a report from Voroshilov in early May 1937 that the armed forces had been infiltrated by foreign agents and that sabotage and espionage were rife.[72] After a summary trial, Tukhachevsky and his colleagues were executed, as were several thousand other officers, in an extensive purge that lasted until the end of 1938. Among those who perished were three marshals, sixteen generals, fifteen admirals, 264 colonels, 107 majors and seventy-one lieutenants. By the time the purge had run its course, 34,000 officers had been dismissed from service, although 11,500 of them were later reinstated.

On 2 June 1937, Stalin addressed the country's Military Council about the existence of a military-political conspiracy against Soviet power. Its political leaders were Trotsky, Rykov and Bukharin; its military core, the High Command group led by Tukhachevsky. The chief organiser of this conspiracy was Trotsky, who dealt directly with the Germans, while Tukhachevsky's group acted as agents of the Reichswehr, which controlled them like 'marionettes and puppets'.

Stalin cautioned against persecuting people just because they had a dubious political background but bemoaned the weakness of Soviet intelligence services, which were 'childlike' compared to those of bourgeois states. Intelligence was the Soviet state's eyes and ears and, for the first time in twenty years, it had suffered a severe defeat, he said.[73]

Stalin was also perturbed by the subversive activities of so-called kulaks, allegedly rich peasants who had been deprived of their property during the forced collectivisation drive. In early July 1937, the Politburo directed local and regional party leaders to draw up lists of anti-Soviet 'kulaks and criminals' who had returned home from deportation exile in Siberia, 'so that the most dangerous of them can be arrested and shot'.[74] At the end of that month the Politburo approved a proposal from the NKVD to repress nearly 300,000 kulaks and criminals, including more than 72,000 summary executions. The stated rationale for this 'mass operation' was that anti-Soviet elements were involved in extensive crime, sabotage and subversion, not only in the countryside but in urban areas, too. By the end of the operation, the NKVD had exceeded its target for arrests by 150 per cent and for executions by over 400 per cent.[75]

The outbreak of the Spanish Civil War in July 1936 had reinforced Stalin's fears concerning the interaction of foreign and domestic threats. General Francisco Franco's military mutiny against the country's leftist government was supported by troops and munitions from Fascist Italy and Nazi Germany. Stalin backed the Republic's democratically elected government and some 2,000 Soviet military personnel served in Spain alongside the Comintern's 40,000 volunteers in the International Brigades. He was convinced that Franco's military successes were the result of sabotage and subversion behind the front lines.[76]

Spanish communists were in the vanguard of the anti-fascist struggle but there was also a strong anarchist movement and a small but vocal semi-Trotskyist party called POUM (Workers' Party of Marxist Unification). In the context of the unfolding Great Terror in the USSR, the POUM leftists, who sought a more radical revolution in Spain than the communists, were categorised as Nazi and fascist *agents provocateurs*. In May 1937 a POUM revolt in Barcelona was put down viciously, including the abduction and execution by Soviet agents of their leader, Andrés Nin.

Stalin became obsessed with the damage that 'wreckers and spies' could do if the Soviet Union was attacked by foreign powers and considered Spain an object lesson in that regard. 'They want to turn the USSR into another Spain,' he told the Military Council in June 1937.[77]

In November 1937 Stalin received into his Kremlin office the head of the Communist International, Georgi Dimitrov, a Bulgarian who was in Berlin in 1933 when Hitler came to power and was arrested by the Nazis for complicity in the burning down of the Reichstag. Deported to the Soviet Union in February 1934, it was Dimitrov who, with Stalin's support, steered the Comintern towards the politics of anti-fascist unity. He delivered the main report at the Comintern's 7th World Congress in Moscow in August 1935 and was elected its general-secretary, a position he retained until the organisation was dissolved in 1943. Dimitrov developed a close working relationship with Stalin and his notes on their confidential conversations in his personal diary are highly revealing.

Stalin told Dimitrov that the Comintern's policy on the struggle against Trotskyism did not go far enough: 'Trotskyites must be hunted down, shot, destroyed. These are international provocateurs, fascism's most vicious agents.'[78]

After several attempts, the NKVD did finally manage to assassinate Trotsky, in Mexico in August 1940. Stalin himself edited the *Pravda* article about his death. He changed the headline from 'Inglorious Death of Trotsky' to 'Death of an International Spy' and added this sentence to the end of the unsigned article: 'Trotsky was a victim of his own intrigues, treachery and treason. Thus ended ingloriously the life of this despicable person, who went to his grave with "international spy" stamped on his forehead.'[79]

Stalin's orchestration of the Great Terror was an awesome demonstration of his power within the Soviet system. Equally, only he had the power to end the purge. In summer 1938, the Politburo took steps to curb arrests and executions and curtail the activities of the NKVD. In November 1938 Yezhov resigned, confessing that he had failed to root out traitors within the NKVD who had conspired to target innocent people. Arrested in April 1939, he was shot in February 1940. His successor as security chief was Lavrenty Beria, the head of the Georgian communist party.[80]

At the 18th party congress in March 1939, Stalin declared victory over the enemies of the people and an end to mass purges. The party had 'blundered' in not unmasking sooner top-level foreign intelligence agents like Trotsky and Bukharin, he admitted. This resulted from an underestimation of the dangers posed by the capitalist encirclement of the Soviet Union. He linked this deficiency to the Marxist theory of the withering away of the state under socialism, a doctrine that needed to be updated in the light of historical experience. A strong Soviet state was necessary to protect the socialist system from internal and external enemies.[81]

SPYMANIA

Stalin disdained spies, even the ones who spied for him. A spy, he once said, 'should be full of poison and gall; he must not believe anyone'. Intensely suspicious, he didn't even trust his own spies, fearful they might have been 'turned' by the enemy. Famously – and disastrously – he discounted numerous warnings from Soviet spies that the Germans would attack the USSR in summer 1941, thinking he had a better grasp of Hitler's intentions than did they. On one report from a high-level informant in the German air force, Stalin told his intelligence chief that he should tell him 'to go fuck his mother. This is a disinformer, not a "source"' – a comment written in green rather than his usual red or blue.[82]

He had more time for intelligence officers, as opposed to spies, and valued mundane intelligence-gathering activities such as compiling press cuttings from bourgeois newspapers. At a reception for Winston Churchill in Moscow in August 1942, he proposed a toast to military intelligence officers: 'They were the eyes and ears of their country . . . honourably and tirelessly serving their people . . . good people who selflessly served their state.'[83]

R. H. Bruce Lockhart, who served as vice-consul in Russia before the First World War, was the most famous British spy of the early twentieth century. He returned to Russia after the outbreak of war and was there in 1917 when the Tsar fell, remaining until just before the Bolshevik takeover. He went back to Russia again in January 1918, ostensibly as British consul-general, but his true mission was to organise a spy network. He became involved in a plot to overthrow the Bolshevik government but was arrested after a failed attempt to assassinate Lenin in August 1918. He evaded trial and a possible death sentence by being exchanged for Maxim Litvinov, the Bolshevik diplomatic representative in London, who had been arrested by the British.

Bruce Lockhart's 1932 *Memoirs of a British Agent* was a huge hit across the world and his publishers, with an eye to the White émigré market, also had them translated into Russian, an edition that came into Stalin's possession. He had no interest in Lockhart's stories of derring-do but underlined his observation that 'Trotsky was a great organiser and a man of immense physical courage. Morally, however, he was no more able to stand up to Lenin than a flea to an elephant.'[84]

In September 1937 Yezhov sent Stalin a translation of Major Charles Rossel's *Intelligence and Counter-Intelligence*. He may have been prompted to do so by Stalin's great interest in a big *Pravda* article of May 1937 on the recruitment of spies by foreign intelligence agents.[85] Stalin edited that article and contributed to it a story about how Japanese intelligence had recruited a Soviet citizen working in Japan by using an aristocratic Japanese woman as bait.[86]

Stalin's copy of the Rossel book was no. 743 of a restricted-circulation print run of 750 aimed at Soviet intelligence officers. Rossel, an American, based the book on his lectures to military audiences in New York. Its Soviet editor was Nikolai Rubinstein, who headed a special NKVD unit dedicated to gathering information on the modus operandi of western intelligence agencies. Rossel's book, wrote Rubinstein in his introduction, would inform Soviet readers about the structure of the US system of intelligence and counter-intelligence as well as provide a lot of useful practical advice on how to conduct such work.

The lectures focused on the experience of military intelligence during the First World War. Rossel noted how the Germans had infiltrated spies into other countries long before the war began. He identified three categories of spy: the permanent, the once-off and the accidental. His concluding advice to intelligence officers operating abroad was that they should stay away from women, read the local newspapers and talk to ordinary people.

Soviet fears of foreign intelligence operations were a constant but there were two really intense bouts of 'spymania': the 'Yezhovshchina' (the Yezhov thing) or Great Terror of 1937–8, and the 'Zhdanovshchina' (the Zhdanov thing) of the mid- to late 1940s. Named after Stalin's ideology chief Andrei Zhdanov, the latter was a cultural campaign to reverse the penetration of Soviet society by western influences that occurred because of the USSR's wartime coalition with Britain and the United States. It coincided with the outbreak of the cold war and heralded a return to the atmosphere of fear, suspicion and anxiety of the Great Terror years. In Leningrad, a purge of the party leadership involved accusations of spying and espionage. The Soviet Jewish Anti-Fascist Committee was disbanded amid arrests of its members for being Zionists and Jewish nationalists. One arrestee was Molotov's Jewish wife, Polina Zhemchuzhina, who was expelled from the party and exiled to Kazakhstan. Molotov remained a member of the party leadership but was replaced as foreign minister by one of his deputies, none other than the former state prosecutor Andrei Vyshinsky. A minor casualty was the left-wing journalist and long-time supporter of the Soviet Union Anna Louise Strong, who was deported from the USSR on the foot of allegations that she was an American spy.

The cultural cold war was as intense as the east–west political struggle and in 1949 the Soviets published a book called *The Truth about American Diplomats*. Its nominal author was Annabelle Bucar, an American citizen employed by the United States Information Service in the US embassy in Moscow until she left her post in February 1948, ostensibly because she had fallen in love with an opera star, Konstantin Lapshin, said by some to be the nearest Soviet equivalent to Frank Sinatra. Walter Bedell Smith, the US ambassador at that time, claimed in his memoirs that she defected because Soviet citizens were not allowed to marry foreigners.[87]

Concocted to counter western propaganda about Soviet spies, minister for state security Victor Abakumov sent Stalin a dummy of the Russian translation and asked permission to publish it with a big print run.[88] Stalin made one or two minor factual corrections and wrote on the book's front cover, 'And will it be published in English, French and Spanish?'[89]

The book caused a sensation.[90] The initial 10,000 copies of the Russian edition were snapped up, as were the 100,000 copies of a second printing. In March 1949 the Politburo decreed 200,000 more copies should be printed. It was also published in many other languages, including those requested by Stalin. A film based on the book, *Proshchai, Amerika!* (Farewell, America), was to be made by a well-known Soviet filmmaker, Alexander Dovzhenko, a Stalin favourite.[91]

Bucar's book detailed how the American embassy in Moscow was a nest of spies: 'The American diplomatic service is an intelligence organisation', a sentence that Stalin underlined in his copy of the published book. Stalin's reading and marking of the book as if it was a briefing document from his intelligence officials was not unreasonable, since they were the main source of its information and analyses, not Bucar, who had been a low-level member of the embassy's staff. The chapter to which Stalin paid most attention was entitled 'The Leadership of the Anti-Soviet Clique in the State Department'.

Duly noted by Stalin was the main culprit, George F. Kennan, the former chargé d'affaires in the Moscow embassy who had recently found fame as the outed anonymous author of the 'X' article on 'The Sources of Soviet Conduct'. Published by the influential American journal *Foreign Affairs* in July 1947, the article argued that the Soviet Union was a messianic, expansionist state that should be contained by the adroit deployment of countervailing power. It was widely seen as a key influence on the American turn towards confrontation with the Soviet Union in the late 1940s.

Kennan was characterised by Bucar as the representative of aggressive anti-Soviet circles in the United States and as a key figure in efforts to reverse President Roosevelt's policy of co-operation with the USSR. Another sentence underlined by Stalin was Kennan's supposed statement that 'war between the USA and the Soviet Union was inevitable' and that the United States could not tolerate the continued existence of a successful socialist system. The policy of containing communism that Kennan favoured was, wrote Bucar, being used by him to justify America's domination of the whole world.[92]

Kennan, who spoke fluent Russian, met Stalin on at least two occasions and penned this memorable portrait of the Soviet dictator:

> His words were few. They generally sounded reasonable and sensible; indeed they often were. . . . Stalin's greatness as a dissimulator was an integral part of his greatness as a statesman. So was his gift for simple, plausible, ostensibly innocuous utterance. Wholly unoriginal in every creative sense, he had always been the aptest of pupils. He possessed unbelievably acute powers of observation. . . . I was never in doubt, when visiting him, that I was in the presence of one of the world's most remarkable men – a man great, if you will, primarily in his iniquity: ruthless, cynical, cunning, endlessly dangerous; but for all of this – one of the truly great men of the age.[93]

Kennan returned to Moscow in May 1952 as the US ambassador but on a stopover in Berlin in September he complained to reporters about his personal isolation in Moscow, comparing it to how the Germans had treated him in Berlin after Hitler declared war on the United States in December 1941. *Pravda* attacked his 'slanderous' remarks and he was declared *persona non grata* as a diplomat – the only US ambassador ever expelled from the Soviet Union. Such an extreme sanction could only have been imposed (though not necessarily proposed) by Stalin himself. It was an unfortunate move, since Kennan had abrogated his hard-line views on Stalin and the Soviets. As a Russophile, the expulsion hurt Kennan deeply, but that did not stop him becoming the foremost western advocate of détente with the USSR in the 1950s and 1960s.[94]

BISMARCK, NOT MACHIAVELLI

Among the books Stalin borrowed and failed to return to the Lenin Library was a Russian edition of the memoirs of Otto von Bismarck.[95] When he was sent a list of books on foreign policy earmarked for reissue or translation into Russian, the item that caught his eye was a new, three-volume translation of Bismarck's memoirs, the first volume of which was ready and with the publisher. Stalin wrote in the margin: 'Definitely translate the second volume as well and publish it together with the first.'[96]

Appealing to Stalin would have been Bismarck's political realism, pragmatism and tactical flexibility. Another trait the two men had in common was the ability to combine strategic vision with successful short-term manoeuvring in complex situations. Their politics may have been polar opposites but, like Stalin, the 'Iron Chancellor' was a concentrator and centraliser of state power. As a devotee of Marxist teleology, Stalin may well have appreciated Bismarck's aphorism that 'political judgement is the ability to hear the distant hoofbeats of the horse of history'.[97]

The introduction to the first volume of Bismarck's translated memoirs was written by the historian Arkady Yerusalimsky (1901–1965), a specialist on German foreign policy, who was summoned to Stalin's Kremlin office for a discussion about his piece. Stalin had a pre-publication 'dummy' of the book, which he had marked, including entitling Yerusalimsky's introductory article 'Bismarck as Diplomat'. To make the changes required by Stalin, Yerusalimsky took the dummy away with him and it eventually ended up in the hands of the Soviet historian and dissident Mikhail Gefter (1918–1995). According to Gefter, Yerusalimsky told him that Stalin didn't like his emphasis on Bismarck's warning that Germany should not go to war with Russia. 'Why are you scaring them?' asked Stalin. 'Let them try.'[98]

Fellow dissident Roy Medvedev reports that Gefter showed him Stalin's copy of the first volume of a 1940 edition of Bismarck's 'collected works' in the 1960s. In that book, recalled Medvedev, Stalin had marked the editor's observation that Bismarck had always warned against Germany becoming involved in a two-front war against Russia and western powers. In the margin Stalin wrote, 'Don't frighten Hitler'. It seems likely that the book in question was, in fact, this first volume of Bismarck's memoirs.[99]

Yerusalimsky's meeting with Stalin, on 23 September 1940, lasted thirty-five minutes and was recorded in Stalin's appointments diary. The next day deputy foreign commissar Solomon Lozovsky wrote to Stalin that the requested changes to Yerusalimsky's introduction would be completed by the end of the day. However, the proposal to move the explanatory notes from the end of the book to the end of each chapter would necessitate pulping the 50,000 copies that had already been printed. He proposed instead – and Stalin agreed – that those copies should be published as they stood but the notes would be shifted in time for the next print run.

All three volumes were published in 1940–41.[100] After Stalin's death, volumes 1 and 2 were listed by IMEL as marked books in his personal library.[101] But, like the Bismarck book he borrowed from the Lenin Library, they are no longer listed as part of the archive's holdings. There are various reports of items from Stalin's book collection ending up in private hands and that may have been the fate of these Bismarck volumes.

Nikolai Ryzhkov, prime minister of the USSR from 1985 to 1991, wrote in his 1992 memoir that he came into possession of Stalin's copy of an 1869 Russian edition of Machiavelli's *The Prince*. Heavily marked by Stalin, wrote Ryzhkov, the book was the 'dictator's textbook': 'Sometimes I think about gathering together all Stalin's underlinings, putting them in order and publishing them as his digest of Machiavelli. Then there would be no need for Medvedev, Volkogonov, Cohen . . . or any of the other biographies and interpretations of Stalin.'[102]

Another story about Stalin and Machiavelli is that during his final exile in Siberia, when his then good friend and comrade Lev Kamenev was researching the Italian philosopher's writings, Stalin apparently found a copy of *The Prince* in the local library and plied Kamenev with questions about the history and politics of Machiavelli's era.

This story's source was Boris Nikolaevsky, a Menshevik historian and activist who was exiled abroad by the Bolsheviks in the early 1920s.[103]

In the 1930s Kamenev contributed a preface to a Russian translation of *The Prince*. At Kamenev's show trial in August 1936, prosecutor Andrei Vyshinsky quoted his laudatory words about Machiavelli as 'a master of political aphorism and a brilliant dialectician'. Machiavelli, said Vyshinsky, was Kamenev's and Zinoviev's 'spiritual predecessor', though he 'was a puppy and a yokel compared to them'. We don't know if Stalin read Kamenev's Machiavelli piece, but he did read his 1933 biography of the nineteenth-century revolutionary Nikolai Chernyshevsky and marked this sentence: 'A politician is always dealing with power – challenging, exercising or implementing it'.[104]

Another Stalin and Machiavelli story was related by Fedor Burlatsky, who worked in the Soviet Academy of Sciences during the 1950s. His source was Stalin's private secretary, Alexander Poskrebyshev, who told him that Stalin periodically borrowed *The Prince* from the central committee library and then returned it after a few days.[105]

While none of these claims has been verified, it is possible, likely even, that Stalin did read Machiavelli, but it was history that informed Stalin's knowledge and understanding of the exercise of power, not philosophy or political theory.

Another book about the 'Iron Chancellor' that attracted Stalin's attention was Wolfgang Windelband's *Bismarck and the European Great Powers, 1879–1885*. Information about the issue of a German edition was recorded in a TASS bulletin from Berlin in December 1940. Stalin wrote on the bulletin that it should be translated into Russian.[106] And so it was. In February 1941 Beria sent Stalin a three-volume translation of Windelband's book.[107] This was for private use by Stalin but, again, there is no discernible trace of the volumes in the Russian archives.

Stalin was interested in Bismarck's domestic as well as his foreign policy. His copy of volume 16 of the first edition of the *Bol'shaya sovetskaya entsiklopediya* (Great Soviet Encyclopaedia), published in 1929, contains a heavily underlined section on the periodisation of the Bismarck era, which the editors divided into the struggle for German unification (1871–96), social reforms and the conflict between socialists and conservatives (1878–86) and Bismarck's 'Iron Chancellorship' (1887–90).[108]

Stalin's interest in diplomacy was longstanding; it was one of the headings of the classification scheme that he devised for his library in 1925. In the Soviet system, foreign policy-making was a function of the Politburo and, as general-secretary, Stalin was involved in foreign policy decisions great and small. In September 1935, for example, he reacted strongly against a suggestion from his Foreign Commissariat that Soviet exports to Italy should be banned because of the growing Italo-Abyssinian crisis, which culminated with Mussolini's attack on Abyssinia a month later. According to Stalin:

> The conflict is not only between Italy and Abyssinia, but also between Italy and France on one side, and England on the other. The old entente is no more. Instead, two ententes have emerged: the entente of Italy and France, on one side, and the entente of England and Germany, on the other. The more intense the tussle between them, the better for the USSR. We can sell bread to both so that they can fight. We don't profit if one of them beats the other just now. We benefit if the fight is lengthier, without a quick victory for one or the other.[109]

Books on international relations in Stalin's library included a 1931 Russian translation of the diary of the British diplomat Viscount D'Abernon, who served in the Berlin embassy in the 1920s. Stalin does not appear to have read the diary itself but he did pay close attention to the book's introduction, written by a leading Soviet diplomat and historian, Boris Shtein, and noted Shtein's analysis of Britain's policy of juggling support for France against Germany without driving the Germans into an alliance with Russia.[110] In December 1940 Stalin was sent the 'dummy' of a Russian edition of Harold Nicolson's classic *Diplomacy*, together with a note from the publisher seeking permission for a print run of 50,000 copies.[111] What caught Stalin's eye in his copy of the published book was the preface by A. A. Troyanovsky, a former ambassador who taught at the Soviets' Higher Diplomatic School. Stalin evidently did not like what Troyanovsky had to say about contemporary British foreign policy – basically, that it was anti-Soviet. This suggests that he read the book after the German invasion of the USSR in June 1941 when there was an anti-Hitler coalition with Britain's Winston Churchill. Stalin crossed through pages 20–25 of the book, with a view, perhaps, to its reissue with a more politically expedient preface.[112]

Stalin's only extensive public statement on an aspect of diplomatic history was his 1934 critique of Engels's 'The Foreign Policy of Russian Tsardom' (1890), prompted by the proposed inclusion of the article in a special issue of the party's journal, *Bol'shevik*. Stalin was against republication because he thought it would confuse people's thinking about the origins of the First World War, though he wasn't against the article appearing in a future number of the same journal.

Engels thought Tsarist Russia's predatory foreign policy was a function of its diplomacy, whereas Stalin believed it was driven by class interests and domestic pressures. Engels had exaggerated the importance of Russia's striving to control Constantinople and the Black Sea straits and omitted the role of Anglo-German rivalries in precipitating the First World War. Politically, Stalin worried that Engels's article lent credence to claims that the war with reactionary Tsarist Russia was not an imperialist war but a war of liberation and a struggle against Russian barbarism. In Stalin's view, Tsarist Russia was no better or worse than any of the other great capitalist powers.[113] Interestingly, Stalin's article was reprinted by *Bol'shevik* in May 1941.

With the advent of the Second World War, Stalin became directly and heavily involved in the conduct of diplomacy. His interest in the writing of a Soviet history of diplomacy was one sign of his growing engagement with diplomatic affairs. Put in charge of that project was Vladimir Potemkin (1874–1946), a prominent Soviet diplomat of the 1920s and 1930s. Potemkin had an hour-long meeting with Stalin in May 1940, the same day the Politburo passed a resolution mandating production of the history.[114] Potemkin sent Stalin a progress report in October which listed the names and topics of the historians who had been recruited to the project. It would be a two-volume Marxist history of diplomacy, wrote Potemkin, one based on original research and written for a broad popular audience. It would be adorned by maps and other illustrations.[115]

When the first volume of *Istoriya Diplomatii* was published in early 1941 – half a million copies of it – Stalin phoned Potemkin to personally congratulate him and his team.[116] Publication of the second volume was disrupted by the outbreak of war in June 1941 and by the time publication resumed in 1945, the work had expanded into three volumes. Potemkin sent Stalin a copy of volume 3 in December 1945 but the second volume of the trilogy, subtitled 'Diplomacy in New Times (1872–1919)', is the only one now to be found in Stalin's library.[117] Stalin's markings of the book, which were mostly informational, suggest that he read a good deal of it, though he didn't pay much attention to the section on Bismarck's foreign policy from 1885 to 1890, perhaps because the master of realpolitik was past his best by this time. Or maybe Stalin felt he knew enough about Bismarck already.[118]

In 1913 Stalin had declared that 'a diplomat's words must contradict his deeds – otherwise what sort of a diplomat is he? Words are one thing – deeds something entirely different. Fine words are a mask to cover shady deeds. A sincere diplomat is like dry water or wooden iron.'[119] Three decades later he had changed his tune. In an April 1941 meeting with the Japanese foreign minister, with whom he had just agreed a neutrality pact, Stalin said that he appreciated his visitor's plain speaking: 'It is well known that Napoleon's Talleyrand said that speech was given to diplomats so that they could conceal their thoughts. We Russian Bolsheviks see things differently and think that in the diplomatic arena one should be sincere and honest.'[120] In a similar vein, Stalin told British foreign minister Anthony Eden, in December 1941, that he preferred 'agreements' to 'declarations' because 'a declaration is algebra' while 'agreements are simple, practical arithmetic'. When Eden laughed, Stalin hastened to reassure him that he meant no disrespect for algebra, which he considered to be a fine science.[121]

In May 1942 Stalin sent Molotov to London to meet British premier Winston Churchill, as a follow-up to the discussions with Eden about the conclusion of an Anglo-Soviet wartime treaty of alliance. Stalin wanted to include a clause that committed the British to recognise the USSR's borders at the time of the German attack in June 1941. The British baulked at such a proposal since a lot of this territory had been gained as a result of the Nazi-Soviet pact. Molotov counselled rejection of the draft treaty as an 'empty declaration'. Stalin disagreed: 'We do not consider it an empty declaration. . . . It lacks the question of the security of frontiers, but this is not too bad perhaps, for it gives us a free hand. The question of frontiers . . . will be decided by force.'[122]

'The Pope,' asked Stalin. 'How many divisions has he got?' The quote is apocryphal, but he reportedly said – with a smile on his face – something similar to Pierre Laval in May 1935, when the visiting French foreign minister suggested he should build some diplomatic bridges to the Catholic Church by signing a pact with the Vatican: 'A pact? A pact with the Pope? No, not a chance! We only conclude pacts with those who have armies, and the Roman Pope, in so far as I know, doesn't have an army.'[123]

BAH HUMBUG! STALIN'S *POMETKI*

CAESARS AND TSARS

Stalin was aghast when Svetlana told him she wanted to study literature at university.

> So you want to be one of those literary types! You want to be one of those Bohemians! They're uneducated, the whole lot, and you want to be just like them. No, you'd better get a decent education – let it be history. Writers need social history, too. Study history. Then you can do what you want.

She took her father's advice, and did not regret it, but later switched to literary studies.[124]

Exhausted by the war, in October 1945 Stalin retreated to his dacha near Sochi on the Black Sea – the first of a series of long holidays he took in the postwar years. One of the first things he did was to invite two Georgian historians, Nikolai Berdzenishvili and Simon Dzhanshiya, to his dacha at Gagra to discuss their textbook history of Georgia.[125] When they arrived, Stalin was ready and waiting for them with a copy of their book in front of him. Incredibly, the conversation lasted four days and ranged far and wide: the origins of Georgia and its connections with the peoples of the Ancient East; the feudal era in Georgian history; the formation of Georgian society during the struggle against Tsarism; and the eighteenth-century monarchy of Heraclius II, who Stalin considered was a moderniser and state-builder.

Berdzenishvili wrote a near contemporary account of his encounter with the man he considered a genius.[126] He was bowled over by Stalin's knowledge and erudition, wondering how he found the time to read so much about the Ancient East. He waxed lyrical about Stalin as both a Georgian and a Soviet patriot, and dutifully noted his preferences when it came to historians: 'He likes Turaev and Pavlov and does not like Struve and Orbeli.'[127]

Stalin had plenty of queries about the book but the discussion was respectful throughout. Indeed, both authors were awarded Stalin Prizes for History in 1947.

According to Berdzenishvili, Stalin said that while the history of Georgia should be a patriotic history, it ought to feature the strivings of Georgians for connections with the Russian people and it had to acknowledge the progressive historical role of Russia: Georgia was a European country that had returned to the European path of development only when it became part of Russia.

These comments of Stalin's exemplified the Soviet concept of the 'Friendship of the Peoples', which originated in the mid-1930s but had developed strongly during the war – the idea that even in Tsarist times the Russian state and its core population of Russians had been staunch allies of non-Russian nationalities in their struggles for liberation, progress and modernity.[128]

Among Stalin's more general comments was that the study of history was a search for the truth about the past, a science based on evidence. He deplored those communists who liked to spout on about dialectical materialism and big-picture issues but made no reference to documentation. When Stalin came across Berdzenishvili in the corridor reading a newspaper, he asked him about the situation in the country. 'Peaceful and calm,' replied Berdzenishvili. 'I don't believe you,' said Stalin, before smiling and walking way. 'Where is the evidence?'[129]

The discussion was not limited to Georgian history. Stalin reminisced about his years in the Bolshevik underground and also spoke about the war. Prone to national stereotyping, Stalin told his audience that Russians were sturdy, the English well nourished, Americans crude, Italians short in stature and the Germans weak from eating too much ersatz food. About Soviet Jews during the war, Stalin had this to say:

> Among them there are proportionally fewer Heroes of the Soviet Union [the equivalent of the Victoria Cross or the Congressional Medal of Honor – GR]. They are more drawn to economic organisations, gathering around them and leaving military matters to others. No one will beat them to a warm and safe place. It has to be said that there are among them fearless warriors, but not many.[130]

Stalin's remark echoed the popular wartime prejudice that 'the Jews are fighting the war from Tashkent'. In fact, Soviet Jews were as courageous and committed as any other section of the country's population.[131]

Svetlana was convinced that he didn't like her first husband, Grigory Morozov, because he was Jewish, and claimed he wasn't happy that her eldest brother Yakov's wife, Yulia, was also Jewish.[132]

The extent to which Stalin was anti-Semitic remains contentious. Zhores Medvedev judged that Stalin was not so much personally anti-Semitic as politically hostile to Jewish nationalism, which he saw as a threat to the Soviet system, hence his purging of the Soviet Jewish Anti-Fascist Committee after the war.[133] Officially the Soviet state was opposed to all forms of racism, including anti-Semitism, and Stalin made many public statements to that effect. In 1947 the Soviet Union voted in favour of partitioning Palestine into Jewish and Arab states and in 1948 established diplomatic relations with newly created Israel. In Georgia anti-Semitism was not as widespread as elsewhere in Tsarist Russia. Stalin was surrounded by Jewish officials or officials with Jewish wives and he continued to fete Jewish writers and artists such as Ilya Ehrenburg. Lazar Kaganovich, Stalin's transport commissar and the highest-ranking Jew in his entourage, did not think he was anti-Semitic and recalled that Stalin proposed a toast to him at a reception for the Nazi foreign minister, Joachim von Ribbentrop, in September 1939.[134] On the other hand, there is little doubt that Stalin used or acquiesced in anti-Semitism in order to promote his anti-cosmopolitan campaign of the late 1940s and early 1950s.[135] Among Stalin's other prejudices was anti-homosexuality and in 1934 sex between men was outlawed.

Witness to Stalin's discussions with the Georgian historians was the first secretary of Georgia's communist party, Kandid Charkviani. It was he who sent Stalin a copy of the textbook. In an interview many years later, Charkviani was asked if Stalin's contributions to the discussion were 'categorical'. No, he replied, it was a discussion, not a polemic. While Stalin considered his own views to be the most plausible, he did not insist on having the final word.

Charkviani recalled that as well as Georgian history, they talked about the history of Rome, especially General Sulla, who seized power in the first century BC but was renowned as much for his reforms as his repressions. Indeed, Sulla, quipped Stalin, had been able to rule Rome from his villa.[136]

Stalin's interest in the Roman Empire was no passing whim. He possessed a number of books on the classical history of Greece and Rome. As we know, among the books Stalin borrowed from but did not return to the Lenin Library were two volumes of Herodotus's *Histories*.[137] In his copy of Alexander Svechin's history of military strategy it is the Roman section that is the most marked.[138] Reading a translation of Viscount D'Abernon's diary, he picked out from the book's introduction Edward Gibbon's aphorism that the Romans believed troops should fear their own officers more than the enemy.[139] At the 17th party congress in January 1934, Stalin used Roman history to mock Nazi racism:

It is well-known that ancient Rome looked upon the ancestors of the present-day Germans and French in the same way as the representatives of the 'superior race' now look upon the Slavonic tribes. It is well-known that ancient Rome treated them as an 'inferior race', as 'barbarians', destined to live in eternal subordination to the 'superior race'. . . . Ancient Rome had some grounds for this, which cannot be said of the representatives of the 'superior race' today. . . . The upshot was that the non-Romans . . . united against the common enemy, hurled themselves against Rome, and bore her down with a crash. . . . What guarantee is there that the fascist literary politicians in Berlin will be more fortunate than the old and experienced conquerors in Rome?[140]

Among Stalin's ancient history books were three by Robert Vipper: *Drevnyaya Evropa i Vostok* (Ancient Europe and the East, 1923), *Istoriya Gretsii v Klassicheskuyu Epokhu* (Greece in the Classical Epoch, 1908) and *Ocherki Istorii Rimskoi Imperii* (Essays on the History of the Roman Empire, 1908).

Stalin liked Vipper's book on ancient Europe so much that he wanted its first chapter on the Stone Age to be retitled 'Prehistorical Times' and added to a school textbook on ancient history.[141] The chapter in Vipper's book on Greece that captured Stalin's attention was the one on Sparta and Athens. It was Sparta that interested Stalin: its mythical and historical origins; its strategic position and military power; the 'spartan' life of its citizens; the city-state's authoritarian political structure; and its diplomatic manoeuvres during the various wars that it fought.[142]

Vipper's book on the Roman Empire was, as far as we know, the most heavily marked text in Stalin's whole collection, nearly every one of its 389 pages having words and paragraphs underlined or margin-lined. Alas, these *pometki* are probably not Stalin's. The markings are similar to but not quite the same as his. Absent are the brackets, numbered points and rubrics in the margin that would be expected if this detailed set of markings was Stalin's. The few scattered words in the margins do not appear to be in his writing.[143] The best guess is that the book belonged originally to a student or a teacher or, even, a historian marking up an important secondary source. This doesn't mean that Stalin didn't read the book. Given his evident regard for Vipper's work and his interest in the subject-matter, it is highly likely he did and may even have added some marks of his own.

Over what lines might Stalin's eyes have lingered? The markings of the unknown reader focused on military and political history: Rome's near defeat in the Second Punic War; the difference between Greek and Roman democracy; the structure of Roman political and military power; the fall of the Roman Republic; the seizures of power by Sulla and Julius Caesar; the overseas expansion of the empire; and the imperial slogan 'better Caesar's power than a free people'.[144]

Roman history has been a rich repository of lessons for rulers throughout the ages, but, as a Marxist, Stalin would also have appreciated Vipper's effort to tell the deeper story. Based on Vipper's lectures at Moscow University in 1899, the book's aim was to describe Roman polity and society and explain the class forces that drove the imperial expansion and the political crises that led to the Republic's downfall. Economic and financial issues are addressed as much as the power plays and political manoeuvres of Rome's rulers. Combining theme and chronology, events and processes, the general and the particular, was a feature of Vipper's historical writings, as was his exploration of the material basis of politics and ideologies.[145]

Vipper's type of historical writing may well have been behind a seminal outburst by Stalin at a meeting of the Politburo in March 1934, occasioned by a discussion of the poor state of history teaching in Soviet schools. No formal record of Stalin's remarks was kept but his sentiments were conveyed in a speech a few days later by the head of the party's education and propaganda department, Alexei Stetsky. In school textbooks, Stalin complained, history was replaced by sociology and class struggle by periodisation and the classification of economic systems. Also unacceptable to him was that Russia's history was reduced to that of revolutionary movements:

We cannot write such history! Peter was Peter, Catherine was Catherine. They rested on certain classes, expressed their moods and interests, but they acted, they were historical figures. While they were not our people, it is necessary to present the historical epoch, what happened, who ruled, what sort of government there was, the policies that were conducted and how events transpired.[146]

A couple of weeks later, at a special Politburo session attended by a number of historians, people's commissar for enlightenment Andrei Bubnov gave a report on the preparation of new textbooks. There is no stenographic record of the ensuing discussion but there are reliable eyewitness accounts of what Stalin said.

As he often did, Stalin strode around the meeting smoking his pipe, at one point picking up a textbook on the history of feudalism, saying: 'I was asked by my son to explain what was written in this book. I had a look and I also couldn't understand it.' Soviet school history textbooks, said Stalin, were not fit for purpose:

They talk about the 'epoch of feudalism', the 'epoch of industrial capitalism', the 'epoch of formations' – all epochs and no facts, no events, no people, no concrete information, no names, no titles, no content. . . . We need text-books with facts, events and names. History must be history. We need text-books about the ancient world, the middle ages, modern times, the history of the USSR, the history of colonised and enslaved people.

Stalin also attacked the late Mikhail Pokrovsky (1868–1932), dean of Soviet historians in the 1920s, who favoured broad-themed sociological history and downplayed the role of personalities in shaping the course of events. He decried Russian oppression of the non-Russian peoples and criticised the work of Vipper, deriding Latin and Greek as 'dead languages of no practical use whatsoever'.

'Tsars, ministers, reformers, etc. . . . will never be taught again', he predicted in 1927.[147] Ivan IV he vilified as a 'hysterical despot' and Peter the Great as 'a cruel, egotistical, syphilitic tyrant'.[148]

Stalin blamed Pokrovsky's 'un-Marxist' approach to history for the sorry state of Soviet historiography. As an antidote, he proposed the translation and adaptation of French and German texts such as the works of Max Weber and Friedrich Schlosser on the ancient world. He also suggested the assembled historians should make use of a textbook by Vipper.[149] Stalin didn't say which of Vipper's many textbooks he had in mind but they might have included his 1902 textbook on ancient history, which was another of those books he borrowed from the Lenin Library but failed to return.[150]

By the end of March the Politburo had resolved to establish groups of historians to work on new textbooks.[151] Stalin's preferred outcome to that process was signalled by the publication in May 1934 of a state decree 'On the Teaching of Civic History in the Schools of the USSR':

> Instead of civic history being taught in a lively and engaging way, with an account of the most important events and facts in chronological order, and with sketches of historical figures, pupils are given abstract definitions of socio-economic formations that replace consecutive exposition with abstract sociological schemas.
>
> The decisive condition for the lasting assimilation of a course of history is the maintenance of chronological sequence in the exposition of historical events, with due emphasis on memorisation by pupils of important facts, names and dates. Only such a course of history can provide pupils with the accessible, clear and concrete historical materials that will enable them to correctly analyse and summarise historical events and lead them to a Marxist understanding of history.[152]

The history of the USSR was of most interest to Stalin, although the title of the proposed textbook was something of a misnomer since much of it would be devoted to the pre-revolutionary history of Tsarist Russia. Progress on the project was so slow and unsatisfactory that in January 1936 the party leadership decided to organise a public competition and invited submissions of various textbooks, in the first instance those on modern history and the history of the Soviet Union. To guide contestants, *Pravda* republished two sets of notes, jointly authored by Stalin, the late Kirov and party ideology chief Andrei Zhdanov, which commented on previously submitted outlines of proposed books. The main criticisms of the outline for a book on the history of the USSR were, first, that it was not a history of the Soviet Union and all its peoples but of 'Great

Russia' and the Russians; second, it had not emphasised enough that internally Tsarism was a 'prison of people' and externally a reactionary 'international gendarme'; and, third, the authors had 'forgotten that Russian revolutionaries regarded themselves as disciples and followers of the noted leaders of bourgeois-revolutionary and Marxist thought in the West'.[153]

It took a year to whittle down the many submissions on Soviet history to a shortlist of seven, none of which were adjudged popular and accessible enough. Eventually, a twelve-strong group headed by Andrei Shestakov (1877–1941), a Moscow-based agrarian historian, was awarded a second-class prize (worth 75,000 roubles). The result of the competition was announced in August 1937, just in time for the twentieth anniversary of the October Revolution.[154] It meant that Shestakov's book would become a designated secondary school text on the history of Russia and the USSR.[155]

Millions of copies of the 223-page *Kratkii Kurs Istorii SSSR* (Short Course History of the USSR) were printed. Among its first recipients was Stalin's eleven-year-old daughter, who was given an inscribed copy: 'To Svetlana Stalina from J. Stalin 30/8/1937'. She appears to have read it attentively, paying particular attention to its many coloured maps, such as the one on the USSR that she used to trace the events of the Russian Civil War, including the role played by her father in the defence of Tsaritsyn.[156]

Shestakov's book was aimed at third- and fourth-grade pupils. Textbooks with similar approaches and themes were then produced for use by older pupils and university students.[157]

Stalin was so heavily involved in the preparation of the Shestakov book that Russian historian Alexander Dubrovsky considers him not merely an editor but one of the book's de facto authors.[158]

When editing a *maket* (dummy) of the book, Stalin paid much attention to the sections on revolutionary Russia and the Soviet period.[159] As he habitually did, Stalin toned down and reduced the coverage and adulation of him and his life. Finding his date of birth in the book's chronology of important historical events, he crossed it out and wrote beside it 'Bastards!'[160] Left in by Stalin was this entry: '1870–1924 Life of the Genius Leader of the Proletariat – Vladimir Ilyich Lenin'. The chronology ended with entries on the Kirov assassination of December 1934 and adoption of a new Soviet constitution in 1936.

Stalin's most important changes were to the book's treatment of Ivan IV (the Terrible) (1530–1584). He struck out a statement that Ivan had ordered the execution of all those living in Kazan following a siege of the city by his forces. Allowed to stand, however, was the sentence 'Kazan was plundered and burnt'. Nor did he like the implications of the authors' claim that Ivan wanted to expand

Russia to the Baltic Sea to establish contact with the *educated* peoples of western Europe, so he excised the word 'educated'. Stalin did approve of their view that Ivan had established the autonomous power of Tsarism by destroying the aristocratic boyars, but added that in so doing he had completed the task of forging a scattered collection of principalities into a single strong state that had been initiated by Ivan I in the fourteenth century.[161] The chapter's concluding verdict on Ivan IV was that under his rule the domain of Russia expanded exponentially and his 'kingdom became one of the strongest states in the world'.[162]

The dummy contained many illustrations, some of which Stalin didn't like. A notable excision was Ilya Repin's famous painting of Ivan the Terrible and his dying son – which alluded to the claim that he had been killed by his father following a family row. Instead, the book carried a photograph of Victor Vasnetsov's 1897 painting of Ivan, which depicted a stern-looking but majestic Tsar.[163]

After publication Shestakov was at pains to point out the book had been prepared with the direct participation of the central committee of the communist party.[164] Among the party leadership's many contributions was a directive from Zhdanov that its authors needed to revise the manuscript in order to 'strengthen throughout elements of Soviet patriotism and love for the socialist motherland'.[165] The end result was a stirring story of a thousand-year struggle by Russia and its Soviet successor to build a strong state to defend its population from outside incursions.

The dissemination of this new narrative of continuity in Russian and Soviet history was part of Stalin's efforts to imbue the USSR with a patriotic as well as a communist identity. David Brandenberger labels this repositioning by Stalin 'national bolshevism', while for Erik van Ree it was a form of 'revolutionary patriotism'. Stalin preferred the idea of 'Soviet patriotism' – the dual loyalty of citizens to the socialist system, which looked after their welfare, and to the state that protected them.

Stalin's patriotism was far from being merely a political device to mobilise the population and strengthen support for the Soviet system: it was integral to his changing views of the Tsars and Russian history.

Decidedly negative was the view of Tsarism expounded in Stalin's 1924 lecture on *The Foundations of Leninism*, where he characterised the Tsarist state as 'the home of every kind of oppression – capitalist, colonial, militarist – in its most inhumane and barbarous form'. Tsarism was the 'watchdog of imperialism' in eastern Europe and the 'agent of Western imperialism' in Russia itself. Russian nationalism was aggressive and oppressive and Tsarist Russia was 'the most faithful ally of Western imperialism in the partition of Turkey, Persia, China, etc.'[166]

BAH HUMBUG! STALIN'S *POMETKI*

While Stalin never ceased criticising the Tsars, his view of the state they had created shifted radically in the 1930s. During the course of a toast to the twentieth anniversary of the Bolshevik seizure of power, he said:

> The Russian Tsars did a great deal that was bad. They robbed and enslaved the people. They waged wars and seized territories in the interests of landowners. But they did one thing that was good – they amassed an enormous state, all the way to Kamchatka. We have inherited that state. And, for the first time, we, the Bolsheviks, have consolidated and strengthened that state as a united and indivisible state, not in the interests of the landowners and the capitalists, but for the benefit of the workers, of all the peoples that make up that state. We have united the state in such a way that if any part were isolated from the common socialist state, it would not only inflict harm on the latter but would be unable to exist independently and would inevitably fall under foreign subjugation.[167]

In that anniversary year there was a broad shift in Soviet discourse about Russia's past. The revolution was celebrated as a radical historical break and its heroes lionised, but so, too, was Alexander Pushkin. That year was the centenary of the poet's death and it provided an opportunity to appropriate him and his works for the Soviet project. He was deemed a revolutionary writer both aesthetically and politically, a man of the people whose poems were accessible to all. 'Only our time entirely and completely accepts Pushkin and Pushkin's heritage', editorialised *Literaturnyi Sovremennik* (Contemporary Literature). 'Only now has Pushkin become truly close to millions of hearts. For the new masses conquering the heights of culture, Pushkin is an "eternal companion".' A 1931 piece by the former commissar for enlightenment, Anatoly Lunacharsky, was reprinted: 'It is Pushkin who, among others, must become a teacher of the proletarians and peasants in the construction of their inner world. . . . Every grain that is contained in Pushkin's treasury will yield a socialist rose or a socialist bunch of grapes in the life of every citizen.'[168] Also revived was the heroic reputation of Peter the Great in a biopic based on Alexei Tolstoy's 1934 novel. Peter was lauded as 'a strong national figure who won territory through war and defended it through diplomacy' and praised for 'the achievement of raising Russia to the status of a great power in the European arena'.[169]

REHABILITATING IVAN THE TERRIBLE

Although Robert Vipper was primarily a historian of the ancient world and of early Christianity, his most influential book was about Russian history – *Ivan*

135

Grozny (Ivan the Terrible). First published in 1922, Vipper's book challenged the widely accepted view – in Russia and elsewhere – that Ivan IV was a blood-thirsty tyrant. Vipper's Ivan was fearsome and menacing towards the Russian state's domestic and foreign foes. Strengthening the monarchy was necessary to empower the Russian state and external threats and pressures motivated his harsh internal regime. His struggle for power against Russia's barons was just, and his security apparatus – the much-maligned *Oprichnina* – as honourable as it was effective. He was also a great warlord and diplomat who had built Russia into one of the greatest states in the world.[170]

Vipper was not alone in his rehabilitation of Ivan's reputation. S. F. Platonov (1860–1933) mounted a similar defence in his 1923 book on Ivan the Terrible.[171] We don't know for certain if Stalin read either of these books, since neither is to be found among the remnants of his personal library, although it does contain a copy of Platonov's 1924 history of Russia's north and the colonisation of its coastal lands.[172] It is not unreasonable to assume that Stalin read Vipper's book and that it influenced his conversion to a positive view of Ivan the Terrible's role in Russian history. The earliest hint that this was Stalin's direction of travel was his editing the first volume of *Istoriya Grazhdanskoi Voiny v SSSR* (History of the Civil War in the USSR) in 1934. He deleted a reference to Ivan IV as the initiator of the Tsarist policy of aggressive, land-grabbing conquests. The Tsars remained repressive as a group but Ivan was nothing special in that regard.[173]

This civil war history was Maxim Gorky's project, the writer with whom Stalin maintained close relations. At the first All-Union Congress of Soviet Writers in August 1934, Gorky made this somewhat ambiguous point which, depending on the folklore in question, could be construed as either anti-Vipper or anti-Pokrovsky:

> Since olden times folklore has been in constant and quaint attendance on history. It has its own opinion regarding the actions of Louis XI and Ivan the Terrible and this opinion sharply diverges from the appraisal of history, written by specialists who were not greatly interested in the question as to what the combat between monarchs and feudal lords meant to the life of the toiling people.[174]

Vipper was not a Marxist, or even a Bolshevik sympathiser, and neither he nor his views on Ivan the Terrible were welcomed by the Pokrovsky-led Soviet historical establishment. In an article on Ivan IV for the *Great Soviet Encyclopaedia* in 1933, Pokrovsky's pupil M. V. Nechkina attacked Vipper's book as a product of the counter-revolutionary intelligentsia and a veiled appeal for a fight against Bolshevism.[175] But the tide was already turning in Vipper's favour. Following Stalin's favourable reference to him during the history-teaching discussion and the publication of Shestakov's book, Vipper's textbook on the *History of the Middle Ages* was reprinted and placed on the syllabus of the higher party school for propagandists. In a 1938 article about Soviet historical writing on the ancient world, A. V. Mishulin commented that Vipper 'unquestionably represented the peak of bourgeois science in ancient history. It would be utterly unjust if we failed to take his contributions to ancient history into consideration as we proceed to reconstruct the teaching of world history.'[176] In a 1939 volume of the *Great Soviet Encyclopaedia* that dealt with the *Oprichnina*, both Vipper and Platonov received favourable mentions.[177] That same year saw the publication of the USSR history textbook for university students. Its section on the sixteenth century was written by S. V. Bakhrushin:

> No-one denies the great and strong intellect of Ivan IV. . . . He was well-educated for his day . . . and possessed literary talent. . . . He was an outstanding strategist and a capable leader of military action. Ivan the Terrible correctly understood the requirements of domestic and foreign policy. . . . In many cases his cruel actions were provoked by the stubborn opposition of the great feudal lords to his endeavours and by outright treason on their part. . . . Ivan the Terrible recognised the necessity of creating a strong state and did not hesitate to take harsh measures.[178]

A campaign to 'restore the true image of Ivan IV in Russian history, which has been distorted by aristocratic and bourgeois historiography', was launched by the party at the end of 1940.[179] As Kevin Platt points out, with the outbreak of war in June 1941, 'the campaign to rehabilitate Ivan took on an overtly mobilizational character'.[180]

The renowned cinematographer Sergei Eisenstein (1898–1948) was commissioned to direct a film about Ivan IV, and Alexei Tolstoy (1883–1945) to write a play.

The director of *Battleship Potemkin* (1925) and *October: 10 Days that Shook the World* (1928), Eisenstein's most recent film had been *Alexander Nevsky* (1938), a patriotic biopic of the thirteenth-century Russian prince who had defeated the Teutonic Knights at the Battle on the Ice on Lake Chudskoe. Tolstoy, whose origins were aristocratic, was distantly related to both Ivan Turgenev and Leo Tolstoy. Primarily a science fiction writer and historical novelist, his Peter the Great book was awarded a Stalin Prize in 1941.[181]

This was the propitious background against which Vipper, who had emigrated to Latvia in the early 1920s, returned to Moscow in May 1941. Upon arrival he sent Stalin a telegram expressing fulsome thanks for helping him and his family's joyful return to the land of socialism and pledging eternal loyalty to the country's 'great leader'.[182] He was given a post at the Moscow Institute of Philosophy, Literature and History but was then evacuated to Tashkent, where he joined Bakhrushin and other historians. In 1942 he published a second edition of his *Ivan Grozny*. By Soviet standards it was a very small print run (15,000), possibly because of wartime paper shortages, but the book was well received. A third edition (5,000 copies) was published in 1944 and in 1947 it was issued in English.[183]

Apart from the mandatory quotation of Lenin and Stalin, the main addition to the book's wartime editions was a new chapter called 'The Struggle Against Treason', in which Vipper clarified that the traitors Ivan had put to death were real, not imagined, enemies of the state.[184]

Bakhrushin developed his textbook chapter into a book and I. I. Smirnov published a short 'scholarly-popular' study of Ivan Groznyi in 1944.[185] In 1947 Bakhrushin wrote, 'In the light of new research, Ivan the Terrible appears as a majestic and powerful figure, as one of the greatest statesmen in Russian history.'[186]

While there are no signs of these books in Stalin's archive, he would certainly have been sent copies and he would surely have read *Pravda*'s report of Vipper's lecture to an audience in Moscow's Kolonnyi Zal (Hall of Columns) in September 1943.

TASS reported that Vipper's lecture on one of the most significant figures in Russian history had been a great success, noting that Ivan IV had created a powerful Muscovy state that played a crucial role in the gathering of the Russian lands and in developing close cultural, political and economic links with western Europe. The cause closest to Ivan's heart, however, was the Livonian War (1558–83), which, according to Vipper, was a war for the restoration of ancient Russian rights. Vipper also dealt with the common complaint that Ivan was a cruel tyrant. To understand his harsh actions, people needed to appreciate the depth of domestic opposition to his efforts to create a centralised state – opponents who had allied themselves with foreign enemies.

The comparisons with Stalin's time were self-evident and Vipper had no need to spell them out. He did, however, conclude with one explicit parallel between the sixteenth and twentieth centuries: then, as now, there were Germans who believed the Russians were incapable of defending themselves and underestimated the deep patriotism of the Russian people.[187]

A fortnight later, Vipper was elected a member of the Soviet Academy of Sciences and appointed to its Institute of History. In 1944 he was awarded the Order of the Red Banner of Labour and in 1945 the Order of Lenin.

The aesthetic rehabilitation of Ivan the Terrible proved to be more problematic than the historical. There were three parts to Tolstoy's projected play, the first of which dealt with the formation of Ivan's character, the second with affairs of state and the third with his 'inglorious end'.[188] He started work in autumn 1941 and had finished part one by the following spring. Printed copies of the script for the first part started to circulate, including one that found its way to Stalin's desk. It was quite short and Stalin made a few inconsequential marks, indicating that he had read it.[189] There was talk of Tolstoy being awarded a second Stalin Prize but the party leadership didn't like the portrayal of Ivan. At the end of April 1942 the Moscow party boss, Alexander Shcherbakov, who was also chief of the Soviet Information Buro, wrote to Stalin recommending prohibition of the play in its current form.[190] Shcherbakov also composed a longer version of his note, laying out detailed criticism of Tolstoy's work. Stalin's direct input into this critique remains unknown but it can be taken as read that it reflected his views as well.

'Ivan IV was an outstanding political figure of sixteenth-century Russia,' wrote Shcherbakov. 'He completed the establishment of a centralised Russian state . . . successfully crushing the resistance of representatives of the feudal order.' Tolstoy's 'confused play' had numerous historical inaccuracies and had failed 'to rehabilitate the image of Ivan IV'. The main flaw was not showing Ivan as a major, talented political actor, the gatherer of the Russian state and an implacable foe of the feudal fragmentation of Rus' and of the reactionary boyars.[191]

Undeterred by this criticism, Tolstoy rewrote part one and continued working on part two, utilising Vipper's book, among others. He sent both parts to Stalin for review but does not seem to have received any response, though they were published in the November–December 1943 issue of the magazine *Oktyabr'*.[192] Part one premiered in Moscow's Malyi Teatr (Little Theatre) in October 1944 but the production was not considered a success so it was restaged, to great acclaim, in May 1945.[193] Part two was performed by the Moscow Arts Theatre in June 1946. The final part of the trilogy – on Ivan's last years – remained unwritten, it seems.

Part one made it into print again in November 1944, when Stalin took a more active interest and marked a few passages from Ivan's longer lines of dialogue, the most interesting being this:

> They want to live in the old way, each sitting in a fiefdom with their own army, just like under the Tatar yoke. . . . They have no thought or responsibility for the Russian land. . . . Enemies of our state is what they are, and if we agreed to live the old way, Lithuania, Poland, Germans, Crimean Tatars and the Sultan would rush across the frontier and tear apart our bodies and souls. That is what the princes and boyars want – to destroy the Russian kingdom.[194]

Tolstoy, who died in February 1945, did not live to see part two of his play performed or to collect his second, posthumously awarded, Stalin Prize in 1946.

Averell Harriman, the US ambassador to the Soviet Union during the Second World War, said Tolstoy once told him that to understand Stalin's Kremlin you had to understand Ivan's reign. Harriman clarified that Tolstoy did not mean Stalin was like Ivan the Terrible, rather that to appreciate Stalin's Russia you needed to know something about Russia's past. Harriman, who spent a lot of time with Stalin during the war, saw no traces of a court like that of Ivan IV. In his view, Stalin was a popular war leader; he was the one who held the country together: 'So I'd like to emphasise my great admiration for Stalin the national leader in an emergency – one of the historic occasions where one man made so much difference. This in no sense minimises my revulsion against his cruelties; but I have to give you the constructive side as well as the other.'[195]

Sergei Eisenstein's film commission also ran into political trouble. At first, all went well. Stalin approved Eisenstein's screenplay, commenting that 'it did not work out badly. Com. Eisenstein has coped with his assignment. Ivan the Terrible, as a progressive force for his era, and the *Oprichnina* as his logical instrument, did not come out badly. The screenplay should be put into production as quickly as possible.'[196] Part one of Eisenstein's *Ivan the Terrible* premiered in January 1945, and in 1946 he, too, was awarded a Stalin Prize.[197]

Unfortunately, Stalin did not like Eisenstein's part two film and in March 1946 its screening was prohibited on grounds that it was historically and artistically flawed.[198] Stalin considered the film 'a vile thing', and explained why at a meeting of the central committee's Orgburo in August 1946:

> The man got completely distracted from the history. He depicted the *Oprichniki* as rotten scoundrels, degenerates, something like the American Ku Klux Klan. Eisenstein didn't realise that the troops of the *Oprichnina* were progressive troops. Ivan the Terrible relied on them to gather Russia into a single centralised state, against the feudal princes, who wanted to fragment and weaken it. Eisenstein has an old attitude toward the *Oprichnina*. The attitude of old historians towards the *Oprichnina* was crudely negative because they equated the repressions of Ivan the Terrible with the repressions of Nicholas II. . . . In our era there is a different view. . . . Eisenstein can't help but know this because there is a literature to this effect, whereas he depicted degenerates of some kind. Ivan the Terrible was a man with a will and character, but in Eisenstein he's a weak-willed Hamlet.[199]

As leading Soviet artists, writers and scientists often did when they came under such attack, Eisenstein petitioned for a meeting to plead his case. Because

Stalin was on a prolonged holiday by the Black Sea, a meeting with Eisenstein did not take place until February 1947. Also present in Stalin's Kremlin office were Molotov, Zhdanov and N. K. Cherkasov, the film's lead actor.[200] After the meeting, Eisenstein and Cherkasov reported the conversation to the writer Boris Agapov, and it is his notes that constitute the only known record of their conversation with Stalin.

Stalin's opening gambit was to ask Eisenstein if he had studied history. More or less, was the reply. 'More or less? I also know a bit about history,' said Stalin. 'You have misrepresented the *Oprichnina*. The *Oprichnina* was a King's army . . . a regular army, a progressive army. You have depicted the *Oprichniki* as the Ku Klux Klan. Your Tsar comes across as indecisive like Hamlet. Everybody tells him what to do and he doesn't take any decision himself.' Ivan, Stalin continued,

> was a great and wise ruler. . . . His wisdom was to take a national point of view and not allow foreigners into the country, protecting it from foreign influences. . . . Peter I was also a great ruler but he was too liberal towards foreigners, he opened the gates to foreign influences and permitted the Germanisation of Russia. Catherine allowed it even more. . . . Was the court of Alexander I a Russian court? Was the court of Nicholas I a Russian court? They were German courts.

Stalin made the same point again later in the conversation: 'Ivan Groznyi was a more nationalist Tsar, more far-sighted. He did not allow foreign influence into the country. Unlike Peter, who opened the gate to Europe and allowed in too many foreigners.'

On Ivan's cruelty, Stalin had this to say:

> Ivan the Terrible was very cruel. One can show this cruelty but it is also necessary to show why he had to be so cruel. One of his mistakes was not to finish off the five big feudal families. If he had destroyed these five boyar families there would not have even been a Time of Troubles. . . . But when Ivan Groznyi executed someone he felt sorry and prayed for a long time. God hindered him in this matter. . . . It was necessary to be decisive.

At this point Molotov interjected that historical events needed to be shown in their correct light, using the negative example of Demyan Bedny's comic operetta, *The Bogatyrs* (1936), which had made fun of Russia's conversion to Christianity. Stalin agreed: 'Of course, we aren't very good Christians, but we can't deny the progressive role of Christianity at a certain stage. This event had a major significance because it meant the Russian state turning around to close ranks with the West, instead of orienting itself towards the East. . . . We can't just toss out history.'[201]

Eisenstein and Cherkasov were keen to get as much guidance as they could about how they should rework the film. They were given a few pointers but basically Stalin was happy to leave the matter in their artistic hands, insisting only that they be as historically accurate as possible. There was general agreement when Eisenstein suggested that it would be better not to hurry production of the film.[202] In the event, Eisenstein, who had been ill for some time, died of a heart attack in February 1948. The film remained unrevised and was not released until five years after Stalin's death.

Do his remarks to Eisenstein and Cherkasov reveal, as Robert Tucker argued, that Stalin saw himself as a latter-day Tsar and modelled his terror on that of Ivan's? Hardly. Stalin had plenty of reasons of his own for conducting the purges. More plausible is Maureen Perrie's suggestion that rather than driving the Great Terror, the historical parallel with Ivan the Terrible's regime provided retrospective justification for the brutal repressions of the 1930s.[203] For Stalin, history was a guide, not a straitjacket. More often than not, it was the present that framed his view of the past and determined the use-value of history.

SCIENCE & SOCIETY

The immediate context for Stalin's stance on Ivan the Terrible was the Zhdanovshchina – the campaign against western capitalist cultural influences launched in summer 1946. Primarily a domestic campaign, it was prompted in part by Stalin's disquiet at the postwar deterioration of diplomatic relations with the west and his growing frustration with what he saw as western obstruction of his efforts to secure the just rewards of that costly Soviet victory over Nazi Germany. Stalin was determined to expand Soviet and communist influence in Europe, aiming to create a reliable bulwark of communist-controlled or influenced governments in central and eastern Europe to act as a barrier to future German aggression against the Soviet Union. Stalin thought he could achieve this while continuing to collaborate with Britain and the United States. Western political leaders had other ideas. In March 1946 Churchill declared that an 'iron curtain' had descended across Europe from the Baltic to the Adriatic. Behind that screen, all the 'ancient states' of central and eastern Europe were succumbing to communist totalitarian control. A year later, US President Harry Truman called for a global defence of the 'free world' by the United States and requested funding from Congress 'to support free peoples who are resisting attempted subjugation by armed minorities or by outside pressures'.

Party ideology chief Zhdanov fronted the anti-western cultural campaign but Stalin vetted and edited all his major statements on the matter, including this version of an August 1946 speech:

> Some of our literary people have come to see themselves not as teachers but as pupils [and] . . . have slipped into a tone of servility and cringing before philistine foreign literature. Is such servility becoming of us Soviet patriots, who are building the Soviet system, which is a hundred times higher and better than any bourgeois system? Is it becoming of our vanguard Soviet literature . . . to cringe before the narrow-minded and philistine bourgeois literature of the west?[204]

When officials from the Soviet Writers' Union went to see Stalin about some practical matters in May 1947, they found him preoccupied with the intelligentsia's inadequate patriotic education: 'if you take our middle intelligentsia – the scientific intelligentsia, professors and doctors – they don't exactly have developed feelings of Soviet patriotism. They engage in an unjustified admiration of foreign culture. . . . This backward tradition began with Peter . . . there was much grovelling before foreigners, before shits.'[205]

It was not only artists who came under attack for servility to the west. In 1947 there was a public discussion of a book on the history of western philosophy by Georgy Alexandrov, who was head of the party's propaganda department. That position did not save him from criticism and nor did the fact that his book had been awarded a Stalin Prize in 1946. He was accused of underestimating the Russian contribution to philosophy and of failing to emphasise Marxism's ideological break with the western tradition. While Stalin was not involved in the public discussion he had voiced his views in private meetings and Zhdanov made it clear that it was the *vozhd'* himself who had drawn attention to the book's flaws. As a result of this controversy, Alexandrov lost his party post, though he was given an only somewhat less important new job as director of an Institute of Philosophy.[206]

Alexandrov's 1940 book on the philosophical forerunners of Marxism features in Stalin's library but the markings in it are not his.[207] A piece by Alexandrov that Stalin did read was a co-authored article by him on the same topic that appeared in a 1939 volume of essays on dialectical and historical materialism. Marked by Stalin was the section on Feuerbach, including the citation of Marx's famous thesis that 'Philosophers have hitherto only interpreted the world in various ways; the point is to change it.'[208]

In the natural sciences, the campaign against pernicious western influences took the form of so-called 'honour courts'. The first victims were a biologist,

Grigory Roskin, and a microbiologist, Nina Klyueva, who had developed a new method of cancer therapy using a single-celled microorganism, *Trypanosoma cruzi*. Their sin was to give a copy of the manuscript of their book on treatment methods to American medical colleagues. On Stalin's initiative the government passed a resolution on the formation of honour courts to assess whether such actions were anti-patriotic. No criminal sanctions were imposed on the two scientists but their 'trial' in June 1947 was attended by the cream of the Soviet medical establishment as well as hundreds of other onlookers. A year later the central committee sent a secret circular to party members that recounted the affair and criticised 'slavishness and servility before things foreign' and warned against 'kowtowing and servility before the bourgeois culture of the west'.[209]

The patriotic imperative was also evident in the so-called Lysenko affair. Trofim Lysenko, a Soviet biologist who specialised in plant science, believed acquired characteristics could be inherited and were hence influenced by environmental changes. This was contrary to Soviet geneticists who contended inheritance was strictly a function of genes and nothing to do with environmental influences or the scientific manipulation of nature. This longstanding debate between the two factions took a new turn in April 1948, when Andrei Zhdanov's son Yury, who was in charge of the science section of the central committee, gave a lecture criticising Lysenko's views. Lysenko complained to Stalin and the result was a public apology by Yury Zhdanov and official endorsement of his position via the publication in *Pravda* of proceedings from a conference of July–August 1948 that expounded Lysenko's views and trounced those of his geneticist critics.

Politically astute, Lysenko couched his position in terms of 'Soviet' versus 'western' science, and of 'materialist, progressive and patriotic' biology versus 'reactionary, scholastic and foreign' biology. It was Lysenko's patriotism that appealed to Stalin more than anything.[210]

Stalin also supported Lysenko's position because it chimed with his own voluntaristic brand of Marxism, notably the belief that the natural world could be radically transformed by active human intervention. In line with this modernist vision, the Soviet press announced in October 1948 'The Great Stalinist Plan to Transform Nature', a project for the mass planting of trees and grasslands and the creation of 44,000 new ponds and reservoirs. 'Capitalism', editorialised *Pravda*, 'is incapable not only of the planned transformation of nature but of preventing the predatory use of its riches.'[211]

There was a strong element of Russocentrism in Stalin's postwar patriotic campaign, a trend that had begun to emerge during the war. When the Soviet leadership decided to adopt a new national anthem (to replace the communist

'Internationale'), they organised a public competition. One submission deemed worthy of Stalin's attention contained this pithy verse:

Since the Terrible Tsar, our state has been glorious
It bears the potent might of Peter.
The glory of Suvorov shines behind us
And the winds of Kutuzov's glory blow.
As our forebears loved the Russian land,
So we, too, love the Soviet land.[212]

It didn't make the cut but the winning anthem did contain this key verse:

The unbreakable union of free republics
Has been joined for ever by Great Russia
Long live the united and mighty Soviet Union
Created by the will of the peoples

At a military reception in the Kremlin in May 1945, Stalin proposed a toast to the health of the Soviet people but 'above all to the Russian people':

I drink above all to the health of the Russian people because they are the most prominent of the nations that make up the Soviet Union ... I drink to the health of the Russian people not only because they are the leading people but because they have common sense, social and political common sense, and endurance. Our government made not a few mistakes, we were in a desperate position in 1941–1942 ... Another people would have said: go to hell, you have betrayed our hopes, we are organising another government. ... But the Russian people didn't do that ... they showed unconditional trust in our government. ... For the trust in our government shown by the Russian people we say a big thank you.[213]

The 110th anniversary of Pushkin's death was commemorated with as much fanfare as his centenary a decade earlier.[214] In September 1947 Stalin issued greetings to Moscow on the 800th anniversary of the city's foundation:

The services which Moscow has rendered are not only that it thrice in the history of our country liberated her from foreign oppression – from the Mongol yoke, from the Polish–Lithuanian invasion, and from French incursion. The service Moscow rendered is primarily that it became the basis for uniting disunited Russia into a single state, with single government and a single leadership.[215]

Stalin's Russocentrism should not be overstated. As Jonathan Brunstedt has pointed out, in his February 1946 election speech, Stalin made no special mention of the wartime role of the Russian people. Instead, he emphasised that the war had demonstrated the strength of Soviet multinationalism and the unity of the peoples of the USSR. In 1947 he rejected a reference to the leading role of the Russian people in the draft of a newly proposed party programme. In his greetings to Moscow the city's historical contribution to Russian statehood was counter-balanced by celebration of its role in Soviet socialist construction. The Russians most lauded by Stalin were the post-revolutionary generations. As Zhdanov put it in August 1946: 'We are no longer the Russians we were before 1917. Our Russia (*Rus'*) is no longer the same . . . We have changed and have grown along with the great transformations that have radically altered the face of our country.'[216]

The international status of Russian science was very much on Stalin's mind after the war. In a 1946 book about the role of Russian scientists in the development of world science, he marked their contributions to fields such as electronic communications, atomic physics, seismology and magnetism.[217] In a 1948 journal article he highlighted claims concerning the Russian contribution to medical science.[218]

Responding to a session of the Soviet Academy of Sciences devoted to the history of Russian science, a *Pravda* columnist claimed in January 1948 that 'throughout its history, the Great Russian People have enriched national and world technology with outstanding discoveries and inventions'. A headline in *Komsomol'skaya Pravda* that same month proclaimed, 'The Aeroplane Is a Russian Invention'. According to the author of this article:

It is impossible to find one area in which the Russian people have not blazed new paths. A. S. Popov invented radio. A. N. Lodygin created the incandescent bulb. I. I. Pozunov built the world's first steam engine. The first locomotive, invented by the Cherepanovs, moved on Russian land. The serf Fedor Blinov flew over Russian land in a plane heavier than air, created by the genius Aleksandr Fedorovich Mozhaiskii, twenty-one years before the Wright Brothers.[219]

When the centenary of Ivan Pavlov's birth was celebrated in September 1949, the headline of *Pravda*'s front-page editorial was a 'A Great Son of the Russian People'.[220] Immortalised by his research on conditioned reflexes that gave rise to the concept of a Pavlovian response, the physiologist-cum-psychologist Ivan P. Pavlov (1849–1936) was in his time the Soviet Union's most famous scientist. He was the first Russian awarded a Nobel Prize – for Medicine in 1904 – and, unlike many other eminent Tsarist-era scientists, he opted to stay in the country after the 1917 revolution. Although not a Bolshevik, his materialist scientific research methods were deemed compatible with Marxism and seen as far preferable to the introspection and subjectivism of Freudianism. While his approach was dominant among Soviet physiologists, and remained so after his death, there were sceptics and doubters who questioned some of Pavlov's more mechanistic and reductionist research.

It's not clear how much Stalin knew about Pavlov or his work. His library contained a copy of the Russian edition of Pavlov's *Twenty Years of Experience of the Objective Study of the Higher Nervous Activities of Animals*, but it is unmarked.[221] What we do know is that he agreed wholeheartedly with a long memo sent to him by Yury Zhdanov in September 1949 that criticised 'anti-Pavlovian revisionism' among Soviet physiologists and psychologists. Zhdanov, the chastened former critic of Lysenko, was by this time married to Stalin's daughter Svetlana (though not for very much longer). He wanted to 'unmask' the revisionists and restructure research and teaching institutes to ensure orthodox, patriotic scientists were in charge. To that end, he proposed to convene a scientific discussion meeting that would smoke out the western-influenced anti-Pavlov elements. Stalin agreed with this strategy and kindly offered some tactical advice:

> It is necessary first of all to quietly gather together the supporters of Pavlov, to organise them, allocate roles and then convene the conference of physiologists ... where you should engage the opposition in a general battle. Without this the cause may collapse. Remember: for complete success you need to beat the enemy for sure.[222]

A joint Academy of Sciences and Academy of Medical Sciences 'Scientific Session on the Physiological Teachings of Academician I. P. Pavlov' duly took place in June 1950. With more than a thousand people in attendance, the leading doubters were criticised and subsequently demoted and a true believer placed in charge of a new Pavlov Institute of Physiology. This proved to be a temporary victory since within a couple of years of Stalin's death the status quo ante had been restored. Zhdanov's central committee Science Council was abolished and party interference in strictly scientific matters became frowned upon. Pavlovianism remained dominant but its critics recovered their place and status within the Academy.

Stalin believed himself to be a master of dialectical materialism – the Marxist methodology for understanding all aspects of human existence, including the natural world. He knew his limits, however, and generally stuck to subjects such as history, politics, economics and philosophy. However, in 1950 he intervened in a debate about linguistics focused on the views of the Anglo-Georgian language historian and theorist Nikolai Marr (1865–1934).

Marr specialised in the languages of the Caucasus but believed all the world's languages were related and had a common root in four basic syllables – SAL, BER, ROSH, YON. After the revolution he adapted his theories to Marxist categories. All languages were class-based, he argued, and changed in accordance with transformations of the economic bases of societies. In compliance with the Marxist base–superstructure metaphor, language was categorised as an aspect of the cultural-ideological superstructure of a society which in turn rested on a class-based socio-economic mode of production. All aspects of the superstructure, including language, were shaped and determined by class relations and the dynamics of the economic base. Different classes spoke different languages and the language of homologous classes in different countries had more in common with each other than with their compatriots who belonged to a different class. Language, Marr insisted, was a class question, not an national or ethnic one.

In the 1920s Marr was centrally involved in discussions about the Latinisation of the Cyrillic alphabet and was consulted by Stalin's staff about this matter.[223] Latinisation was a project promoted by enlightenment commissar Anatoly Lunacharsky, as part of the Bolsheviks' modernisation ethos. Cyrillic was deemed backward, bourgeois and chauvinistic, while the Latin alphabet was deemed modern and the core of a future world language. A number of minority, non-Cyrillic Soviet languages were Latinised in the 1920s but Stalin and the Politburo baulked when it came to Russian and vetoed the idea in a resolution passed in January 1930. Such a policy would have been hugely disruptive and ran counter to the emerging trend of resuscitating Russian history and culture as the foundation of a Soviet patriotism.[224]

Marr was selected to represent Soviet scientists at the 16th party congress in June 1930, telling delegates that he was dedicated to using all his 'revolutionary creativity to be a warrior on the scientific front for the unequivocal general line of proletarian scientific theory'. He joined the party immediately after the congress and within a year had become a member of the Central Executive Committee of the All-Union Congress of Soviets.[225] When Marr sought an audience with the dictator in 1932, he was politely turned down but Stalin said that he might be able to spare forty to fifty minutes at some point in the future.[226] That meeting never took place because in October 1933 Marr had a debilitating stroke and in December 1934 he died.[227]

The Marrites were strongly entrenched in the Soviet linguistics establishment but had critics such as Victor Vinogradov (1894–1969) and Arnold Chikobava (1898–1985). Vinogradov was a Russianist literary and grammar scholar who believed languages were best studied as members of family groups such as the Indo-European – a traditionalist approach despised by Marr's supporters. Chikobava, a Georgian linguist and philologist, also valorised the national-cultural character of different languages. Vinogradov's study of the evolution of Russian literary naturalism was part of Stalin's book collection, as was Chikobava's Georgian text on ancient nominal stems in the Kartvelian language of the South Caucasus.[228]

Among Marr's books in Stalin's library was the edited volume *Tristan and Isolde: From the Heroic Love of Feudal Europe to the Goddess of Matriarchal AfroEurAsia* (1932), his Svan-Russian dictionary (1922) and a collection of essays about the language and the history of Abkhazia (1938).[229]

Like the Pavlovites, the Marrites tried to use the Lysenko affair to promote themselves and their theories as the epitome of patriotic Soviet linguistics. Meetings were held, articles were published and there were orchestrated attacks on Marr's critics. Stalin's involvement was precipitated by a December 1949 letter from Georgian communist leader Kandid Charkviani.[230] Prompted, and probably drafted by Chikobava, it contained a detailed critique of Marr's views, which Stalin read carefully. Marr was a vulgar not a dialectical materialist, wrote Charkviani. His theories were not and should not be the basis for a proper Marxist-Leninist analysis of the origins, relations and roles of language and languages. Marr was wrong to believe that all languages were class-based from their inception and that there was no such thing as a non-class language. During the Latinisation debates Marr had adopted a 'cosmopolitan' position that disrespected local languages. He thought the main goal of Soviet linguistics was to work towards a single world language, whereas Stalin had stated that during the transition to world socialism national languages would persist.

Included with Charkviani's letter were writings by Chikobava containing further criticism of Marr's views. Also in Stalin's possession was a long Chikobava article about various theories of language, which concluded that while Marr had played a positive role in combatting idealist western language theorists (for example Ferdinand de Saussure), he had not provided a Marxist-Leninist resolution of the fundamental questions involved in the study of languages. Ironically, this 1941 article was published (in Russian) in the journal of the Georgian Academy of Sciences' 'N. Ya. Marr Institute for Language, History and Material Culture'.

Charkviani and Chikobava travelled to Moscow in April 1950, where they met Stalin at his dacha and had a long conversation about Marr. Stalin asked

Chikobava to write an article for *Pravda* on Soviet linguistics. His article, 'Some Problems of Soviet Linguistics', published on 9 May, was extensively edited by Stalin. Stalin did his usual editorial job of sharpening and polishing the prose and inserted a few sentences of his own. In a section on the origins of language, Stalin added that Marr had rejected the idea that language

> originated as means of communication by people, as an implement which arose from a persistent need for communication. Academician Marr forgets that people in the most ancient times lived and supported themselves in hordes, in groups and not individually. Academician Marr does not take into consideration the fact that it was just this circumstance that brought about their need for communicating, their need to have a common means of communication such as language.

Inserted into a section criticising Marr's advocacy of artificial methods to quicken the formation of a world language, were these lines by Stalin:

> Marxists understand this matter differently. They hold that the process of withering away of national languages and the formation of a single common world language will take place gradually, without any 'artificial means' invoked to 'accelerate' this process. The application of such 'artificial means' would mean the use of coercion against nations, and this Marxism cannot permit.

At the end of the article Stalin added this paragraph: 'Marr's theoretical formulation of a general linguistics contains serious mistakes. Without overcoming these mistakes, the growth and strengthening of a materialist linguistics is impossible. If ever criticism and self-criticism were needed, it is in just this area.'[231]

Stalin's interpolations presaged his own contribution to the linguistics debate, which proved to be a master class in clear thinking and common sense.

The arcane debate about linguistics staged by *Pravda* in May–June 1950 was an incredible spectacle, even by Soviet standards. Chikobava's 7,000-word article was published as a double-page centre spread that spilled over onto another page. It contained plenty of familiar ideological rhetoric but it was also highly specialised, technical and supported by footnotes. Defenders of Marr responded in kind, as did other critics such as Vinogradov. *Pravda* published twelve contributions to the discussion before Stalin intervened.[232]

Before he weighed into the debate, Stalin reportedly read a lot of books about linguistics. 'Stalin was such a quick reader, almost daily there was a new pile of books on linguistics in his study at Kuntsevo.'[233] Among the materials he did consult were the entries on *Yazyk* (language), *Yazykovedenie* (linguistics), *Yafet* and *Yafeticheskaya Teoriya* (Japhetic theory) in volume 65 of the *Great Soviet Encyclopaedia* (1931). Named after one of Noah's sons, Marr's Japhetic theory postulated common origins for Caucasian languages and the Semitic languages of the Middle East. It was the cornerstone of his contention that all languages had a common root. Sections of these entries were quite extensively marked by Stalin and included the intriguing marginal comment 'Yazyk – materiya dukha' – language is a matter of spirit.[234]

Stalin's intervention utilised one of his favourite devices: answering questions posed by *Pravda*.[235] He began by undercutting Marr's assumption – one shared by his critics – that language was part of the superstructure. Language, Stalin argued, was the product of the whole of society and its history. It was created by society and developed by hundreds of generations of people: 'Language exists, language has been created precisely in order to serve society as a whole, as a means of intercourse between people . . . serving members of society equally irrespective of their class status.'

Next, he attacked the idea that languages were class-based. Languages were based on tribes and nationalities, not classes: 'History shows that national languages are not class, but common languages, common to the members of each nation and constituting the single language of that nation. . . . Culture may be bourgeois or socialist, but language, as means of intercourse, is always a language common to the whole people and can serve both bourgeois and socialist culture.' The mistake that some people made, said Stalin, was to assume that class struggle leads to the collapse of societies. But that would be self-destructive: 'However sharp the class struggle may be, it cannot lead to the disintegration of society.' The characteristic feature of languages, Stalin pointed out, was that they derive their use and power from grammar as well as a shared vocabulary: 'Grammar is the outcome of a process of abstraction performed by the human mind over a long period of time; it is an indication of the tremendous achievement of thought.'

Marr was 'a simplifier and vulgariser of Marxism' who had 'introduced into linguistics an immodest, boastful and arrogant tone' and dismissed the comparative-historical study of language as 'idealistic'. Yet it was clear that peoples such as the Slavs had a linguistic affinity that was nothing to do with his 'ancestor' language theory.

In a subsequent interview with *Pravda*, Stalin also criticised Marr's view that thinking could be divorced from language: 'Whatever thoughts that may arise in the mind of a man, they can arise and exist only on the basis of the language material, on the basis of language terminology and phrases.'

Stalin published five contributions on this matter in *Pravda*. In his final pronouncement he reiterated his view that eventually all languages would merge into a common world language. But that process would only take place after the global victory of socialism. In the meantime, hundreds of languages would continue to co-exist and there was no question of suppressing any of them or of asserting the superiority of any one language.

Boris Piotrovsky was among many Marr disciples who sensibly kept their heads down during the linguistics discussion. Doubtless that helped save his job as a deputy director of the Hermitage Museum. It didn't save him from Stalin's scorn. He ridiculed Piotrovsky's contribution to a 1951 book on the history of ancient cultures and wrote 'ha ha' beside the editor's claim that Piotrovsky had provided the first scientific account of the rise and fall of Armenia's Urartu civilisation.[236]

Stalin's articles on Marxism and linguistics were republished in all Soviet newspapers. They were read over the radio and reprinted as pamphlets with print runs in the millions. Linguistic programmes were revamped to include new courses on 'Stalin's Teaching about Language'. A wave of anti-Marrite discussions swept the country. Critical books and articles multiplied. One beneficiary of this counter-revolution, Vinogradov, was appointed head of a new Institute of Linguistics.

Worth quoting is Evgeny Dobrenko's multi-metaphoric summary of these developments:

> Stalin's text is a discursive black hole that sucks in entire scholarly/scientific disciplines; they disintegrate at ever-increasing speed and produce more and more textual fragments. Put another way, one might compare this ever-expanding discourse originating from Stalin's text to a progressive tumour that continually metastasizes to new organs and tissues. As a sacred object that gives birth to text and procreates discourse, this short text truly engenders oceans of literature.[237]

STALIN THE PLAGIARISER?

Various bets have been staked on which of Stalin's writings were plagiarised from other authors. Trotsky's claim that Lenin, not Stalin, was the author of *Marxism and the National Question* has already been dealt with. Stephen Kotkin writes that Stalin 'plagiarized whole cloth' his first major work, *Anarchism or Socialism?*, from a deceased Georgian railway worker-intellectual called Giorgi Teliya.[238] The only cited evidence for this assertion is that in his 1907 obituary for Teliya, which was republished in his collected works, Stalin mentioned that

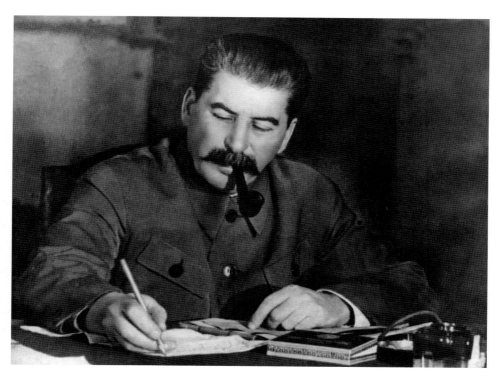

1. Stalin working in his Kremlin office in 1938.

2. Shushanika Manuchar'yants, Lenin's and Stalin's librarian (photo dating from the 1960s).

3. An early photo of Stalin's second wife, Nadezhda Alliluyeva, in 1917.

his dead comrade had written a piece called 'Anarchism and Social Democracy'.[239] As Kotkin himself admits, 'We shall never know how much of Teliya's work Stalin borrowed or how much he may have sharpened it.'[240] Or, indeed, if he made any use of it at all, except, perhaps, as an idea for his own series of articles.

Kotkin also repeats Roy Medvedev's claim that Stalin's 1924 lectures on *The Foundations of Leninism* – one of the key texts in the Stalinist canon – were heavily based on a manuscript by F. A. Ksenofontov on *Lenin's Doctrine of Revolution*.[241] Again, this was a hare set running by Stalin himself when he allowed a private letter he had written to Ksenofontov in 1926 to be published in the ninth volume of his collected works.[242] Stalin's purpose was to assert his authorship of the definition of Leninism as 'the Marxism of the era of imperialism and of proletarian revolution'. Medvedev maintained that Stalin derived that definition from Ksenofontov, and he may be right. But Stalin's elaboration of the definition in *The Foundations of Leninism* differs markedly from that of Ksenofontov. It is the broad strokes of the theory and practice of Bolshevism under Lenin's leadership that interests Stalin, not the close textual analysis and careful formulations favoured by Ksenofontov.

Of several works by Ksenofontov that remain in Stalin's book collection, the only text that he marked was *On the Ideological and Tactical Foundations of Bolshevism* (1928).[243] Stalin seems to have skipped the first section of the book in which the author reprised his analysis of the nature of Leninism and nor did he show any interest in Ksenofontov's history of Bolshevik strategy and tactics. Instead, Stalin homed in on his detailed reconstruction of Lenin's thinking on the New Economic Policy and its relationship to socialist construction – a subject that was very much on his mind at the end of the 1920s, when NEP was in crisis and he was on the verge of breaking with that policy. As so often, Stalin's reading interests reflected immediate and pressing political concerns.

Admittedly, complexity, depth and subtlety were not strengths of Stalin's, nor was he an original thinker. His lifelong practice was to utilise other people's ideas, formulations and information – that was why he read such a lot. His intellectual hallmark was that of a brilliant simplifier, clarifier and populariser. As Dobrenko put it: 'Stalin never strove for novelty in his thinking but rather aimed at political expediency. In every case, the forcefulness of his thought is in its efficacy, not originality.'[244]

Ernst Fischer, the Austrian communist art historian who worked for the Comintern and lived in exile in Moscow from the mid-1930s to the mid-1940s, was among the many intellectuals smitten by Stalin. He 'was the master of simplistic argument', recalled Fischer, and intellectuals 'succumbed' to this *simplisme* because of his ability to reconcile 'the critical reason of the thinker with the *élan*, the all or nothing, of the man of action'.[245]

MASTERS OF WAR

The interwar Red Army had at its disposal a talented and innovative group of military strategists: Mikhail Frunze (1885–1925), Boris Shaposhnikov (1882–1945), Alexander Svechin (1878–1938), Vladimir Triandafillov (1894–1931) and Mikhail Tukhachevsky (1893–1937).[246] Together they fostered a sophisticated discourse about the changing nature of modern warfare, the use of advanced military technology and the development of operational art. Especially important were the doctrines of 'deep battle' and 'deep operations', which entailed successive and sustained waves of combined arms forces (infantry, armour, airborne) penetrating the full depth of enemy defences and then the envelopment of enemy forces from the rear. These doctrines were similar to the contemporaneous German concept of *Blitzkrieg* but the Soviets were less tank centric and more inclined to use infantry and artillery for breakthrough operations. From 1936 these ideas were incorporated into successive editions of the Red Army's Field Service Regulations, which guided the organisation and deployment of military forces and the conduct of combat operations. During the Second World War, Stalin was a diligent reader of these manuals and made numerous textual corrections to draft versions.[247]

Stalin's interest in the details of military affairs was longstanding. His library included a copy of a Russian artillery journal dating from 1866, a 1911 history of the Russian army and fleet, and a photocopy of a description of the Madsen 20mm machine gun.[248] Heavily marked by Stalin was a 1925 work on artillery – a translation of a book by the French general Frédéric-Georges Herr (1855–1932). Stalin was interested in the extent and organisation of artillery in modern armies, with the types and calibre of artillery and its potential range (up to 200km, according to Herr). He noted Herr's comment that Germany was continuing to develop its armaments and had the lead when it came to chemical weapons. His attention was also drawn to the importance of technical education and the post-First World War British decision to establish a number of specialist military training schools.[249] Ambassador Averell Harriman recalled that Stalin

> had an enormous ability to absorb detail. . . . In our negotiations with him [about wartime military supplies from the US] we usually found him extremely well-informed. He had a masterly knowledge of the sort of equipment that was important to him. He knew the calibre of the guns he wanted, the weight of the tanks his roads and bridges would take, and the details of the type of metal he needed to build aircraft.[250]

Stalin was fond of talking about the impact on warfare of new technology and of hectoring his top commanders to break with their fixation on experiences during the Russian Civil War. Yet, judging by the books in his library, a favourite strategist was a nineteenth-century Tsarist General Staff officer called Genrikh Leer (1829–1904).

Leer was the closest Russian equivalent of Carl von Clausewitz (1780–1831), the great Prussian strategic theorist. Leer taught at the Tsarist General Staff Academy from 1858 to 1898, the last ten years as its chief. He published a number of books on strategy, tactics and military history. Leer believed that military strategy should be taught as a science based on historical experience and as one that could derive from empirical data enduring rules and precepts about the conduct of war.[251]

Stalin possessed four of Leer's works: *The Experience of Critical-Historical Research on the Laws of the Art of the Conduct of War* (1869); *Strategy (Part One: Main Operations)* (1885); *Combined Operations* (1892); and *The Method of Military Science* (1894).[252]

All these books were stamped as belonging to the office library of the Defence Commissariat, which dates their earliest acquisition by Stalin to the mid-1930s, which was a period in which he read a number of military-related books, including the memoirs of Helmuth von Moltke (1800–1891), who was chief of the Prussian General Staff, and General Erich Ludendorff, Germany's military supremo during the First World War. In Moltke's memoirs he was drawn to the chapter on preparations for war, while in Ludendorff's it was the stress on importance of popular support during wartime.[253]

An obscure figure in the twentieth century, Leer was quite well known in nineteenth-century Russia. His name came up in Soviet military theory debates in the 1920s, often coupled with that of Clausewitz. Stalin might have picked up on Leer from Svechin's writings. Stalin read and marked the latter's two-volume history of military art (from the Defence Commissariat library, too) and also had a copy of Svechin's own book on strategy. Svechin disagreed with Leer's scientific approach but agreed with him about the importance of the study of history. And it was military history that interested Stalin most.[254]

Apart from Svechin's strategy book, which approached the subject conceptually rather than historically, the alternative to Leer's writings would have been Clausewitz's *On War*. Although Stalin also 'borrowed' a copy of a 1932 Russian translation of this classic text from the Defence Commissariat, he does not appear to have paid it much attention, except to read the publisher's preface, which praised Clausewitz as a fine student of history and a master of the dialectical study of war. Stalin also marked the comment that lumped Leer and Svechin together as logicians and metaphysicians, compared to Clausewitz, who had liberated the theory of war from such 'bourgeois' methods.[255]

All four Leer books are heavily marked, three of them by the same hand, but it is not Stalin's. The fourth book, *Strategiya*, was marked by multiple readers, one of whom might have been Stalin. According to Leer, the chief tasks of military art were twofold: to prepare the means of war and then to rationally deploy them. That required close attention to the economic, political and geographical character of the theatre of war as well as to its strictly military aspects. In the conduct of war the choice of strategic direction was all-important, as was the safeguarding of the forces and supplies tasked to carry out operations.

An underlined Leer passage that might well have stuck in his Stalin's mind was that after his defeat by Napoleon at the battle of Borodino in 1812, Kutuzov faced a choice between saving his army and saving Moscow.[256] Kutuzov chose the former and then conducted a harassing campaign against Napoleon's forces when they retreated from Moscow. A similar dilemma confronted Stalin as Hitler's armies approached Moscow in October 1941. In the event, he decided that to save his army he had to save Moscow so he remained in the capital and organised its defence. On 7 November 1941, he addressed troops parading through Red Square on their way to the front:

> Remember the year 1918, when we celebrated the first anniversary of the October Revolution. Three-quarters of our country was . . . in the hands of foreign interventionists. The Ukraine, the Caucasus, Central Asia, the Urals, Siberia and the Far East were temporarily lost to us. We had no allies, we had no Red Army . . . there was a shortage of food, of armaments. . . . Fourteen states were pressing against our country. But we did not become despondent, we did not lose heart. In the fire of war we forged the Red Army and converted our country into a military camp. The spirit of the great Lenin animated us. . . . And what happened? We routed the interventionists, recovered our lost territory, and achieved victory.

Stalin returned to the patriotic theme in his peroration:

> A great liberation mission has fallen to your lot. Be worthy of this mission. . . . Let the manly images of our great ancestors – Alexander Nevsky [who defeated the Swedes], Dimitry Donskoy [who beat the Tartars], Kuz'ma Minin and Dimitry Pozharsky [who drove the Poles out of Moscow], Alexander Suvorov and Mikhail Kutuzov [the Russian hero generals of the Napoleonic Wars] – inspire you in this war. May the victorious banner of the great Lenin be your lodestar.[257]

Stalin's favourite among Soviet strategic theorists was Boris Shaposhnikov, a former Tsarist officer who had joined the Red Army in 1918. During the civil war he helped plan Red Army operations and then served in various capacities, including as head of the Red Army Staff, commandant of the Frunze Military Academy and chief of the General Staff (1937–40, 1941–3). He got on well with Stalin personally and is said to be the only Soviet general the dictator addressed using the familiar second person singular, *ty*, as opposed to the more formal second person plural, *vy* (like 'tu' and 'vous' in French).[258]

Like Stalin, Shaposhnikov was an intellectual as a well as a practical man of action. Before the First World War he attended the Tsarist General Staff Academy. A keen student of history, he was conversant with several foreign languages, including French, German and Polish. His *Mozg Armii* (Brain of the Army) was a study of strategic lessons from the First World War focusing on the role of General Staffs. Shaposhnikov's combination of grand strategy and critical organisational detail were also the hallmarks of Stalin's military and political leadership. Systematic and admirably lucid, Shaposhnikov's exposition in *Mozg Armii* was also a paragon of political orthodoxy, with many citations from the writings of Marx, Engels and Lenin, as well as western and Russian strategic theorists.[259]

The fundamental military lesson of the First World War, argued Shaposhnikov, was that General Staffs had prepared for a short, sharp war of annihilation but found themselves fighting a prolonged war of attrition. The lesson for future warfare was the necessity for prolonged economic and industrial mobilisation to fight protracted wars. Soviet preparations for the Second World War began even before Shaposhnikov had completed publication of *Mozg Armii* at the end of the 1920s. During the 1930s, defence's share of the national budget increased from 10 per cent to 25 per cent. The Red Army grew from under a million to more than 4 million. By 1939, the Soviet Union had the largest and most extensively equipped army in the world and was annually producing 10,000 planes, 3,000 tanks, 17,000 artillery pieces and 114,000 machine guns.

In *Mozg Armii*, Shaposhnikov rehearsed at length the Clausewitzian commonplace that since war was a continuation of politics, war's goals and overall direction were the prerogative of political leadership. On the one hand, General Staffs needed to understand the interrelations of domestic, foreign and military affairs while, on the other, political leaders required a good grasp of military matters. 'In our times', wrote Shaposhnikov, 'the study and knowledge of war is essential for all state leaders.'[260]

One idea that *Mozg Armii* helped to popularise was that 'mobilisation meant war'. Because of how modern armies must operate, mobilisation was, in effect, a declaration of war. When Russia's armed forces were mobilised to support Serbia against Austria-Hungary during the July Crisis of 1914, it also meant war with the Hapsburg Empire's German ally, whose Kaiser felt compelled to mobilise and attack not only Russia, but its ally, France.

When Germany attacked Poland in September 1939, Stalin kept the USSR out of the war by signing the Nazi–Soviet non-aggression pact. Indeed, the pact contained a secret protocol in which the Germans agreed that eastern Poland (i.e. western Belorussia and western Ukraine) and the Baltic States were in the Soviet sphere of influence. The quid pro quo was a guarantee of Soviet neutrality while Germany fought Poland's British and French allies. Stalin's deal with Hitler worked well for a while, but by June 1941 it was clear Hitler would soon attack the USSR. The question was: should the Red Army mobilise in anticipation of that attack? Stalin feared premature mobilisation would act as a catalyst for war, bringing forward the outbreak of hostilities. When Defence Commissar Semen Timoshenko and General Staff Chief Georgy Zhukov proposed precautionary mobilisation, Stalin reputedly responded: 'So, you want to mobilise the country, raise our armies and send them to the western border? That means war! Do you not understand this?'[261]

Stalin overruled his generals and forbade full mobilisation until German forces actually invaded the USSR. He was confident Soviet frontier defences would hold long enough for the Red Army to complete its counter-mobilisation. That proved to be a disastrous miscalculation when, on 22 June 1941, powerful German forces punched straight through Soviet frontier fortifications. By the end of 1941, the Wehrmacht had surrounded Leningrad, reached the outskirts of Moscow and penetrated deep into Ukraine and southern Russia. In these six months alone, the Red Army suffered a stunning 4 million casualties. Stalin sent Zhukov back to the front line and recalled Shaposhnikov as chief of the General Staff, giving him the opportunity to test the ideas of *Mozg Armii* in the crucible of total war.

One of the best-known war stories about Stalin, related by Khrushchev in his damning secret speech to the 20th party congress, is that he suffered a nervous collapse when the Germans invaded, and retreated to his dacha. It is a story reminiscent of pejorative tales about Ivan the Terrible skulking in his tent when confronted with military failure.

One oft-repeated version of this myth is that the shock and initial success of the German surprise attack on 22 June caused Stalin's mental anguish. Another version claims that what disturbed Stalin was the collapse of the Red Army's Western Front and the fall of the Belorussian capital, Minsk, at the end of June. There is no contemporaneous evidence to support either story. All the documentary evidence, notably Stalin's Kremlin appointments diary, shows he remained in command of both himself and the situation.[262] Post hoc witness testimony claims otherwise but the hostile memoirs of Khrushchev's supporters are contradicted by other witnesses. Stalin did, it is true, disappear to Blizhnyaya (not called 'nearby' for nothing) for thirty-six hours or so in early July, but he emerged to deliver a masterly radio broadcast. If Stalin did have a breakdown it was short-lived and he staged a miraculous recovery.

The common-sense explanation for Stalin's brief absence from the Kremlin is that he went there to think things over and to compose his speech – his first public statement on the war and his first-ever radio broadcast.

Stalin was doubtless perturbed by what had happened – which was completely unexpected, given the enormous strength of the Red Army. He may well have wondered whether his generals were conspiring against him. On 1 July 1941, he removed General G. D. Pavlov as commander of the Western Front and had him arrested along with his chief of staff, his chief of communications and other senior members of his team. Like Tukhachevsky in 1937, Pavlov was falsely accused of being involved in an anti-Soviet conspiracy (both men were rehabilitated after Stalin's death). But when Pavlov was sentenced to death it was not for treason but for cowardice, panic-mongering, criminal negligence and unauthorised retreats – a change in the charge sheet that signalled Stalin had chosen to discount the anti-Soviet conspiracy theory.

Another possibility is that when Stalin retreated to his dacha he did what he habitually did when he was there: he read a book. Not just any book, but Mikhail Bragin's *Polkovodets [Commander] Kutuzov*, sent for printing on 14 June 1941 with a run of 50,000 (normal by Soviet standards). Its price was 2.5 roubles, plus 50 kopeks extra for a bound copy.[263] The author was a young historian (b.1906) with a military background who had studied at the Frunze Military Academy. Major-General Levitsky's preface to the book was written before Hitler's attack but included an addendum that cited Molotov's national radio address announcing the invasion on 22 June 1941: 'When Napoleon invaded Russia our people responded with a patriotic war and he was defeated. Now Hitler has declared a new march on our country. The Red Army and the whole people will once again wage a patriotic war for the motherland, for honour and for freedom.'

Levitsky did not mention Stalin's broadcast, which dates publication to the last week of June or thereabouts. Stalin would certainly have been sent a copy of the book straight away and it may have grabbed his attention. In his broadcast, Stalin made the same Hitler and Napoleon comparison: Napoleon's army had been considered invincible but it had been smashed and so, too, would be Hitler's.[264]

Kutuzov's biography and the drama of his 1812 defeat of Napoleon's Grande Armée was, of course, well known to Stalin. The restoration of Kutuzov's status as a patriotic war hero began in the mid-1930s. By 1941, students at the higher party school were being taught a glowing account of Kutuzov's role in the 'people's war' of 1812. Stalin read the text of this lecture with avid interest, underlining lecturer E. N. Burdzhalov's conclusion that 'for Kutuzov, the overthrow of Napoleon was not important, it was his ejection from Russia.'

In 1942 the Red Army created two new medals for higher-ranking officers – the Orders of Kutuzov and Suvorov. At a meeting with the editors of *Voennaya Mysl'* (Military Thought) and *Voennyi Vestnik* (Military Herald) three years later, Stalin complained about the Soviet officer corps' narrow horizons, urging them to study the exploits of Russian military commanders such as Peter the Great, Kutuzov and Suvorov. He also criticised civilian historians who placed Kutuzov below Suvorov in the pantheon of military greats: 'Kutuzov commanded bigger armies than Suvorov, dealt with more difficult political and strategic problems and successfully fought against stronger opponents.'[265]

Stalin certainly read Bragin's book. His marks – underlinings and marginlinings – are scattered throughout its 270 pages.[266] The marks were made with different coloured pencils, indicating that he dipped in and out of its pages. Two themes of Bragin's were of particular interest to him. Firstly, what Kutuzov had learned from Suvorov: the maxim that the harder troops trained, the easier it would go for them in battle; the importance of the performance of ordinary front-line soldiers; and the need to avoid pointless offensives. Secondly, the parallels between 1812 and 1941. When Bragin quoted Napoleon – 'I cannot rest on my success in Europe when half a million children are being born in Russia every year' – Stalin underlined it. He noted, too, that when Napoleon invaded in June 1812 he did so without declaring war and had most of Europe at his disposal while Russia stood alone. Stalin also marked the section which noted how everyone expected Napoleon to win the initial battles. Kutuzov's own account of his defeat of Napoleon, how he had drawn the French emperor into capturing Moscow and then worn Napoleon's army down after it withdrew from the city, were double margin-lined by Stalin.

Bragin concluded by asserting Russia's military prowess. After 1812 the victorious Russian army penetrated deep into Europe: 'It entered Germany and seized Berlin, it entered France and took Paris and demonstrated the power of Russian arms to the whole world.' When, at the end of the Second World War, Harriman said to Stalin, 'Generalissimo, this must be a great satisfaction to you to be here in Berlin,' he replied, 'Tsar Alexander got to Paris.'[267]

Another book published just as Hitler invaded Russia was a biography of Suvorov by 'K. Osipov' – the pseudonym of the Soviet writer and literary critic Joseph Kuperman.[268] Stalin's copy has been lost but we can presume he read it, since in January 1942 he edited the draft of a review by the military historian

Colonel Nikolai Podorozhny.[269] Stalin changed the review's title, 'The Unsurpassed Master of War', to 'Suvorov', but retained the phrase in the first paragraph. As might be expected, Stalin edited the piece with an eye to current events. He inserted a paragraph attributing to Suvorov the idea that if you can frighten the enemy and make them panic, you have won the battle without even setting eyes on them. Another addition cited Suvorov's belief that victory was not won by capturing territory but by destroying enemy forces.

Given the stupendous defeats and retreats of the Red Army during the first six months of the war, it is, perhaps, understandable that Stalin would want to delete a paragraph describing Suvorov as the 'Marshal of the Advance' – a reference to Suvorov's slogan during the second Russo-Turkish war of 1789: 'Only forward! Not a step back. Else death. Forward!' He also deleted these stirring words of Podorozhny's: 'Not a step back! – demand the Soviet people of the Red Army. Beat the enemy on the spot, overrun them and smash their forces, chase them "day and night until they are destroyed" – this Suvorov maxim is as apt today as it was 150 years ago.' But the words may have stuck in his mind because, a few months later, as the Germans advanced on Stalingrad, Stalin issued his most famous of wartime decrees – *Ni shagu nazad!* (Not a Step Back): 'This must now be our chief slogan. It is necessary to defend to the last drop of blood every position, every metre of Soviet territory.'

The bulk of the review remained untouched by Stalin, including the colonel's recommendation for the book to be read by every Soviet commander. It may even have inspired Stalin to ask Osipov to author a version for 'command staff'. In August 1942 Osipov submitted an 189-page typescript to Stalin, who edited it but only to tone down Osipov's enthusiasm for Suvorov.[270]

Stalin had involved himself in Suvorov-related matters before. In June 1940 he reviewed a film script about Suvorov. The script was inadequate, wrote Stalin. It was tedious and insubstantial and depicted Suvorov as a 'kindly old man who occasionally crows "Cock-a-doodle-do" and keeps repeating "Russian", "Russian".' What the film should to do was show what was special about Suvorov's military leadership: the identification and exploitation of enemy weaknesses; well-thought-out offensives; the ability to select and direct experienced but bold commanders; the willingness to promote by merit not seniority; the maintenance of iron discipline among the ranks of the armed forces.[271]

Stalin's criticisms did not impede production of the film, which premiered in January 1941. Its two directors – Mikhail Doller and Vsevolod Pudovkin – were awarded Stalin Prizes, as was the actor who played Suvorov, Nikolai Cherkasov.

In the 1940s Stalin made a number of notable general statements about war that distilled his reading of strategy and military history books and synthesised it with the practical experience of supreme command. At an April 1940 conference on the lessons of the recently concluded 'Winter War' with Finland, Stalin delivered a long speech in which he explained to his generals why the Red Army had suffered such high casualties. First, the Red Army had expected an easy war and had not been prepared for hard battles with the Finns. Second, the war showed the Red Army was not a 'contemporary' army. In contemporary warfare, artillery was the main thing, followed by masses of airplanes, tanks and mortars. A contemporary army was an attacking, mechanised army. It also needed an educated command staff as well as trained and disciplined soldiers capable of themselves taking the initiative.[272]

At the back of Stalin's mind when making this speech might have been a recently read Tsarist-era history of Russia's armed forces in which he noted the problems Peter the Great experienced when unsuccessfully trying to capture Finland during the Great Northern War against Sweden (1700–1721). Stalin loved statistics: Peter's Finnish war had lasted twenty-one years and required the mobilisation of 1.7 million troops, 120,000 of whom had perished, while another 500,000 had deserted.[273] The Red Army's campaign in Finland in 1939–40 was equally disastrous, but it lasted only a few months and Stalin did defeat the Finns and capture territory deemed vital to the security of Leningrad, albeit at the cost of a quarter of a million Soviet casualties, including 70,000 dead.

Stalin returned to the theme of the Red Army as a contemporary army in a speech to 2,000 graduates of its staff academies on 5 May 1941. But this time Stalin stated that the Red Army had been transformed into a contemporary army – a mechanised and well-equipped army with the requisite amount of artillery, armour and air power. He also probed the reasons for Germany's victory over France in summer 1940, arguing the Germans had reconstructed their armed forces and had avoided fighting a war on two fronts. The Germans had been victorious because they fought to liberate their country from the shackles of the Versailles Peace Treaty imposed on Germany by Britain and France in 1919. That success would falter if they transitioned to wars of conquest, which is what happened to Napoleon when he stopped fighting wars of liberation. Many people believed the German army was invincible, said Stalin. It wasn't. There never was and never could be such an army.[274]

At the accompanying reception he proposed several toasts, including one recorded by Comintern leader Georgi Dimitrov: 'Our policy of peace and security is at the same time a policy of preparation for war. There is no defence without offence. The army must be trained in a spirit of offensive action. We must prepare for war.'[275]

In his Red Army day order of February 1942, Stalin identified five 'permanently operating factors' that would determine the outcome of the war now that the advantage the Germans had gained from their surprise attack had passed: (1) stability of the rear; (2) morale of the army; (3) number and quality of divisions; (4) armaments; and (5) organisational ability of army leaders.[276]

Estimating the relative significance of the Red Army's victory at Stalingrad and the great Soviet–German armoured clash at Kursk, Stalin reflected in November 1943 that 'while the battle of Stalingrad heralded the decline of the German-Fascist army', he said, 'The battle of Kursk confronted it with disaster.'[277]

In the annals of Soviet history 1944 became known as the year of the 'ten great victories' and in his November 1944 speech Stalin gave a masterly display of the narrative technique of military history when he structured an account of that year's events around a sequential series of battles and operations that pushed the Germans out of the USSR.[278]

He returned to the theme of the role of objective factors in war in his election speech to Moscow's voters in February 1946:

It would be wrong to think that such a historical victory could have been achieved without preliminary preparation by the whole country for active defence. It would be no less wrong to assume that such preparation could have been made in a short space of time, in a matter of three or four years. It would be still more wrong to assert that our victory was entirely due to the bravery of our troops. Without bravery it is, of course, impossible to achieve victory. But bravery alone is not enough to overpower an enemy who possesses a vast army . . . it was necessary to have fully up-to-date armaments.[279]

And at a private meeting in April 1947 Stalin distinguished 'military science' from 'military art':

To understand military science means to understand not only how to conduct war i.e. military art, but also to know the economy of a country, its potential, its weak and strong sides, and also how it is developing. To know the material and human resources, both your own and those of the enemy. Only by knowing . . . military science is it possible to count on the achievement of victory in war. . . . The former leaders of fascist Germany did not understand military science and were unable to administer the economy of their country.[280]

Before the Second World War, Clausewitz had been a figure of high esteem in Soviet military discourse, principally because Lenin viewed him favourably. In 1923 *Pravda* published Lenin's 'Notebook on Clausewitz', which was reprinted in a 1931 collection of Lenin's writings owned by Stalin.[281]

Then, in 1945, *Voennaya Mysl'* (Military Thought) – a journal published by the People's Commissariat of Defence – carried an article by a Colonel G. Meshcheryakov on 'Clausewitz and German Military Ideology'. Stalin read the article, noting three points. First, that Clausewitz's 'reactionary ideas' had been popularised in Germany after the Franco-Prussian war of 1870–71. Second, that Clausewitz had borrowed from Hegel his reactionary philosophical system as well as his dialectical method. In Clausewitz's writings, Hegel's concept of the absolute spirit, wrote Meshcheryakov, was transformed into that of absolute war. Third, Clausewitz favoured short, decisive wars because that was the only way that a small country like Prussia could win the total wars of the contemporary era.[282]

Colonel Yevgeny Razin, a lecturer at the Frunze Academy and the author of a four-volume textbook history of operational art, took exception to Meshcheryakov's article and wrote to Stalin. Meshcheryakov, complained Razin, had revised the positive view of Clausewitz held not only by Lenin but by Engels, too. Attached to his letter was his own short thesis on war and the art of war. Stalin replied almost immediately but his response was not published until March 1947.

Unfortunately for Razin, Stalin agreed with Meshcheryakov's critique of Clausewitz. Indeed, in a private meeting with the journal's editors in March 1945, Stalin himself had spoken of German military ideology as an ideology of attack, plunder and the struggle for world domination.[283]

'In the interests of our cause and the modern science of war, we are obliged not only to criticise Clausewitz,' wrote Stalin to Razin, 'but also Moltke, Schlieffen, Ludendorff, Keitel and other exponents of German military ideology. During the last thirty years Germany has twice forced a bloody war on the rest of the world and twice has suffered defeat.' Clausewitz was out of date, said Stalin; he 'was a representative of the time of manufacture in war, but now we are in the machine age of war'. As to Razin's own ideas, Stalin was scathing:

> The thesis contains too much philosophy and abstract statements. The terminology taken from Clausewitz, talking of the grammar and logic of war hurts one's ears. . . . The hymns of praise to Stalin also pain the ears, it hurts to read them. Also, the chapter on counter-offensive (not to be confused with counter-attack) is missing. I am talking of the counter-offensive after a successful but indecisive enemy offensive, during which the defenders assemble their forces to turn to a counter-offensive and strike a decisive blow to the enemy and inflict defeat upon him. . . . Our brilliant Commander, Kutuzov, executed this when he destroyed Napoleon and his army by a well-prepared counter-offensive.[284]

According to Roy Medvedev, the publication of Stalin's letter led to the colonel's arrest, but Stalin relented when he came across Razin's military art textbook while doing some homework in preparation for a meeting with China's communist leader, Mao Tse Tung, who was considered an expert on 'people's war'. Stalin was so impressed by Razin's book that he was released from prison, promoted to major-general and restored to his position at the Frunze Academy.[285] A different version of Razin's fate is that he was already under arrest for some wartime misdemeanours when he wrote to Stalin and Stalin's letter actually led to his release. Either story could be true, such were the vagaries of the Soviet system, especially when Stalin was involved. What is certain is that Razin did return to teaching and to publishing books about military affairs. He died in 1964. As far as we know, he kept his own counsel, and never wrote or spoke about his famous exchange with Stalin.

IMAGINING *AMERIKA*

Stalin was fascinated by *SShA* (*Soedinennye Shtaty Ameriki*). From the First World War onwards, the United States was the world's most advanced and powerful capitalist country. Soviet socialism aimed to catch up with and then surpass the USA. Stalin was confident the rationally planned and socially controlled Soviet economy would prevail in competition with American free enterprise capitalism but he was still keen to import superior US technology, mass production techniques and work organisation methods. 'Do it the Ford way' and 'create Russian Americans' were among the more surprising Bolshevik slogans of the 1920s.[286] In his 1924 lectures on *The Foundations of Leninism*, Stalin talked about the ideal 'style of work' being a combination of 'Russian revolutionary sweep and American efficiency'. American efficiency, said Stalin, was the 'indomitable force which neither knows nor recognises obstacles' and 'with business-like perseverance brushes aside all obstacles'.[287] In correspondence with the poet Demyan Bedny that same year, he explained Bolshevik 'philosophy' with a quote from Walt Whitman: 'We are alive. Our scarlet blood boils with the fire of unused strength.'[288]

When Emil Ludwig commented that in the Soviet Union 'everything American is held in very high esteem', Stalin demurred, but said he respected 'the efficiency that Americans display in everything – in industry, in technology, in literature and in life'. Compared with the old European capitalist countries, remarked Stalin, there was an element of democracy in American industrial practices, which he attributed to the absence of feudal remnants in a young country like the United States.

Keen not only to import but to make the best use of western technology, the Bolsheviks launched a campaign to bring 'Foreign Languages to the Masses'.

Soviet workers were exhorted and supported to learn key foreign languages, such as English and German, that would enable them to understand and use scientific and technical knowledge and products from the United States and western Europe. The Politburo also ensured that foreign languages were taught in Soviet schools and instructed party members to regard foreign language study as a fundamental duty.[289]

Stalin didn't exempt himself from this duty. Holidaying by the Black Sea in September 1930, he wrote home to his wife Nadya, who was in Moscow, and asked her to search for his copy of a self-study English-language book by A. A. Meskovsky, a text that was based on the methods of the American educator Richard S. Rosenthal. Nadya couldn't find it and, fearing Stalin would be annoyed, she sent him another textbook instead.[290] Stalin never attended classes or employed language tutors: home study was his preferred method of learning foreign languages, though he never got very far with any of them except Russian.

Stalin was confident that in time Soviet workers would be able to emulate the efficiency and technical expertise of their American counterparts. 'I consider it impossible to assume that the workers of any particular nation are incapable of mastering new technique,' he told visiting American progressive Raymond Robins in May 1933, noting that in the United States, 'negroes' were considered 'bottom category men' yet could master technique just as well as whites.[291]

By no means were all Soviet images of America positive. In August 1917 Stalin published an editorial in the party press on 'American Billions', in which he accused US capitalists of financing counter-revolution in Russia. 'It used to be said in Russia that the light of socialism came from the West,' he wrote. 'And it was true . . . it was there . . . that we learned revolution and socialism.' But now it was not 'socialism and emancipation that the West is exporting to Russia so much as subjection and counter-revolution.'[292]

Thousands of American troops fought on Soviet soil on the anti-Bolshevik side during the Russian Civil War. President Woodrow Wilson may have been a liberal hero in the west; to the Bolsheviks he was the ringleader of a global counter-revolutionary coalition.

During the 1930s Stalin was keen to import American know-how and expertise in many different spheres. In 1935 he sponsored a trip by a group of film professionals to Hollywood, the intent being to industrialise Soviet movie-making along American lines. In 1936 Stalin's trade commissar, Anastas Mikoyan, spent two months in America studying its food industry. When it was decided to build a gigantic Palace of the Soviets in the centre of Moscow, the project's engineers and architects were sent on fact-finding tours of the United States and American consultants were hired to provide further input. While the palace was never built, the project did pave the way for the series of skyscrapers (called 'tall buildings' by the Soviets) that were erected in Moscow after the war.[293]

Of enduring interest to Stalin was the US Constitution. In March 1917 he published an article in *Pravda* entitled 'Against Federalism', a response to proposals that post-Tsarist Russia should become a federal state. Stalin pointed out that the US was federal only in theory. Originally, the United States was a confederation and became a federation as a result of the American civil war. That federal structure did not last long, however, and the US soon became, in effect, a unitary state. Indeed, Stalin favoured a similar set-up in Russia – not a federal state but a strong, centralised one that would allow regions degrees of autonomy.

Following two years of public consultation and discussion, the USSR adopted a new constitution in December 1936.[294] Stalin's speech on the draft showed he'd done some comparative research on the constitutions of other states.[295] One of his sources was a section on the United States in a 1935 book, *Konstitutsii Burzhuaznykh Stran* (Constitutions of the Bourgeois Countries), in which he noted the US Constitution was based on the principle of balance between the Executive, the Judiciary and the Legislature. When the Soviet author of this piece, M. Tanin, commented that America's entry into the First World War had resulted in a presidency that amounted to a 'democratic Caesarism', Stalin circled the phrase and wrote NB in the margin. Then he marked passages describing the role of the different branches of government and the fact that American women had not been able to vote until the ratification of the 19th amendment to the Constitution in 1920. In relation to American 'Negroes' he marked a paragraph which stated that, while they had the formal right to vote, it was exceedingly difficult for them to do so in many southern states.

The book reproduced (in Russian translation) the full text of the American Constitution. What caught Stalin's eye was its first paragraph: 'We the People of the United States . . .'[296]

A year after the 1936 constitution was adopted, there were elections to the newly created Supreme Soviet of the Soviet Union. In his election speech, Stalin highlighted the differences between Soviet and bourgeois-democratic elections:

Universal elections exist and are held in some capitalist countries, too, so-called democratic countries. But in what atmosphere are elections held there? In an atmosphere of class conflicts, in an atmosphere of class enmity, in an atmosphere of pressure brought to bear on the electors by the capitalists, landlords, bankers and other capitalist sharks. Such elections, even if they are universal, equal, secret and direct, cannot be called altogether free and altogether democratic elections.

Here, in our country, on the contrary, elections are held in an entirely different atmosphere. Here there are no capitalists and no landlords and, consequently, no pressure is exerted by propertied classes on non-propertied classes. Here elections are held in an atmosphere of collaboration between the workers, the peasants and the intelligentsia, in an atmosphere of mutual confidence between them, in an atmosphere, I would say, of mutual friendship; because there are no capitalists in our country, no landlords, no exploitation and nobody, in fact, to bring pressure to bear on people in order to distort their will.

That is why our elections are the only really free and really democratic elections in the whole world.[297]

Implicit here was the theoretical rationale of the one-party Soviet system: competitive party elections in capitalist democracies reflected the existence of antagonistic classes, whereas in the Soviet Union class relations were non-antagonistic, so there was no need for more than one political party. Hence Soviet electors could only vote for candidates pre-selected by the communist party. They could vote against candidates (who required a majority to get elected) but in practice it was difficult to do so without identifying yourself as a dissident. Unsurprisingly, 98 per cent of the 90 million votes in the 1937 election were cast in favour of the party's candidates.

A decade or so later, Stalin read with evident interest a 1945 book, *Osnovy Inostrannogo Gosudarstvennogo Prava* (Fundamentals of Foreign State Law). Written by N. P. Farberov, it was based on the author's lectures to the Higher Intelligence School of the Red Army. Stalin followed closely Farberov's discussion of different federal and confederal systems and the nature and basis of state sovereignty. He also noted sections on the role of parliaments, cabinet government and the difference between constitutional referendums and 'factual' referendums. On the US, Stalin was drawn to details of eligibility to vote and to stand in congressional elections. He showed no particular interest in the role of the Supreme Court but marked the fact that the US Constitution had only been amended twenty-one times in its 157-year history.[298]

Soviet–American economic relations were hampered by the US's refusal to recognise the USSR diplomatically because of a dispute about the Soviets' refusal to pay Tsarist-era debts. When diplomatic relations were established in 1933, Stalin was enthusiastic, especially about newly elected US President Franklin Delano Roosevelt, whom he described as a realist and 'a determined and courageous politician'.[299] He repeated this characterisation in his interview with H. G. Wells in July 1934, adding that 'Roosevelt stands out as one of the strongest figures among all the captains of the contemporary capitalist world'.[300]

These remarks presaged the close working relationship that Roosevelt and Stalin enjoyed during the Second World War. Stalin was impressed by Roosevelt's policy of unconditional support for the Soviet war effort and by his determination to send as much American aid to the USSR as possible. Roosevelt's motive was transparent. 'Nothing could be worse', he said in March 1942, 'than to have the Russians collapse.' Better to 'lose New Zealand, Australia or anything else'. Why? Because 'the Russians are today killing more Germans and destroying more equipment than you and I put together', he wrote to Winston Churchill later that year.[301]

Stalin was genuinely upset when Roosevelt died unexpectedly in April 1945, shortly after the two men had met, along with Winston Churchill, at the Yalta conference. 'When I entered Marshal Stalin's office I noticed that he was deeply distressed at the news', reported American ambassador Averell Harriman. 'He greeted me in silence and stood holding my hand for about 30 seconds before asking me to sit down.' 'President Roosevelt has died but his cause must live on', Stalin told Harriman.[302]

Stalin's enthusiasm for the United States knew no bounds during the war, when the awesome power of American industrial capitalism flooded the USSR with billions of dollars' worth of Lend-Lease supplies. For a while after the war he hoped for an American loan that would help pay for the reconstruction of the ravaged Soviet economy. 'Had I been born and brought up in America', Stalin told the head of the American Chamber of Commerce in June 1944, 'I would probably have been a businessman.' Stalin's fervour cooled considerably when the cold war broke out in the mid-1940s, but as late as April 1947 he told the visiting US Republican politician Harold Stassen, 'I am not a propagandist, I am a man of business', pointing out that he and Roosevelt had never indulged in the name-calling game of 'totalitarians' v. 'monopoly capitalists'.[303]

Stalin was puzzled as well as impressed by the United States, finding it difficult to understand why the working class movement in the world's leading capitalist country was so weak politically. When asked why he thought this was the case by a visiting American labour delegation in 1927, Stalin had no answer except to blame reactionary trade union leaders for not forming an independent proletarian party to compete with the Democrats and Republicans.[304]

One of the last articles Stalin ever read was A. A. Poletaev's 'V. I. Lenin and the American Workers Movement', published in a 1952 issue of *Voprosy Istorii* (Questions of History) devoted to Lenin.

Poletaev's article seems to have been the only one that Stalin read in that issue of the journal and the first passage he marked was a 1907 citation from Lenin on the characteristics of the 'Anglo-American workers' movement'. There were four, and Stalin, as he often did, went to the trouble of numbering them: the fact that the proletariats of these two countries had no important social-national democratic tasks to fulfil; the complete subordination of the proletariat to bourgeois policy; the sectarianism and isolation of the socialist movement; and the lack of support for the left in elections.

Stalin picked up on the sectarianism point later in the article, noting the 'dogmatism' of both De Leon's American Socialist Party and the British Social Democratic Federation. He also underlined Lenin's point that what was needed in the United States was a mass Marxist party that would form an alliance between workers, farmers and 'toiling negroes'.

Always on the lookout for points with contemporary resonance, Stalin noted this graphic passage in Poletaev's article:

> The American bourgeoisie have more than once warmed their hands with the flames of war in Europe, thereby profiting from the blood and suffering of millions of people. US monopolies have rapidly developed into a mighty fortress of capital with a vice-like grip not only on the American people but the peoples of Europe and Asia.[305]

Another *Voprosy Istorii* article that Stalin read during these early cold war years was an article on American intervention in Siberia during the civil war. Beside the paragraph citing the official US claim that the intervention was prompted by 'love' for the Russian people, Stalin wrote 'ha ha'.[306]

A country that had once been a beacon of hope for Stalin, then a business partner and wartime ally, had reverted to being 'Enemy Number One'.[307]

CHAPTER 6

REVERSE ENGINEERING
Stalin and Soviet Literature

Stalin read literature for leisure, pleasure and edification. As a young man his first love was poetry, and patriotic poems were his earliest published writing. Radical fiction guided the young Stalin to the revolutionary cause. Like Marx and Lenin, he valued the enlightening role of literary classics, and quickly grasped the mobilisational power of theatre and film. Famously, he described writers in a socialist society as 'engineers of the human soul'. For Stalin, literature was the means to win hearts as well as minds.

Tragically, his vast collection of novels, plays and poems was dispersed after his death: it is the gaping hole among the archival remnants of Stalin's library. Yet we know quite a lot about how he read and appreciated literature because from the late 1920s he was highly active in this realm of Soviet cultural policy. His various interventions reveal how he felt about fiction as well as what he saw as its political function. From his policy pronouncements and detailed criticisms of particular texts we can identify his preferences as a reader.[1]

Andrei Gromyko was Soviet ambassador to the United States during the Second World War. He attended the Yalta and Potsdam summits in 1945 and served as deputy foreign minister after the war. He recollected of Stalin:

As to his taste in literature, I can state that he read a great deal. This came out in his speeches: he had a good knowledge of the Russian classics, especially Gogol and Saltykov-Shchedrin. Also, to my own knowledge, he had read Shakespeare, Heine, Balzac, Hugo, Guy de Maupassant – whom he particularly liked – and many other western European writers.[2]

A letter from Trotsky prompted Stalin's first foray in the field of cultural politics. Trotsky wrote to the Politburo in June 1922 that the party needed to foster relations with young writers. Trotsky proposed a register of writers, and the preparation of dossiers to guide party relations with specific individuals, the aim being to give material support and provide an alternative to bourgeois role models and publishing houses. Trotsky also suggested the creation of a non-party literary journal that would allow scope for 'individual deviations'.[3]

In response, Stalin asked deputy party agitprop chief Ya. A. Yakovlev to report on the situation among writers. Yakovlev's report highlighted the political struggle between the Bolsheviks and counter-revolutionary elements in relation to young writers. He also identified a number of writers who were close to the Bolsheviks politically and suggested organising a non-party association to gather them together, perhaps as a 'Society for the Development of Russian Culture'. Yakovlev emphasised it would be necessary for the party writers in such a society to avoid 'unjustifiable communist arrogance'.[4]

In forwarding the report to the Politburo on 3 July 1922, Stalin endorsed Trotsky's approach, as well as Yakovlev's 'Society' idea. Such a society, wrote Stalin, would contribute to the development of a 'Soviet culture' by bringing together 'Soviet-inclined' writers.[5] The resultant Politburo resolution combined Trotsky's and Stalin's proposals, i.e. various supports for young writers were to be put in place, including a non-party literary publishing house (rather than a journal), and the possibility of establishing a suitable society for sympathetic writers would be investigated.[6]

This relatively liberal approach to literary affairs was typical of the moderate politics of the NEP era and represented pushback against militants who wanted to impose a uniform 'proletarian' culture on all writers. A wide-ranging Politburo resolution 'On Party Policy in the Sphere of Literature', dated June 1925, pointed out that it would take the proletariat time to develop its own literature. In the meantime, there had to be an alliance with pro-Soviet 'fellow traveller' writers. The party would combat counter-revolutionary manifestations in literature but also be on guard against 'communist conceit'. It would steer writers' political preferences but not insist on any particular literary form; it would, indeed, stand for 'free competition among the various groups and trends in this sphere'.[7]

At the end of the 1920s Stalin executed a sharp left turn in pursuit of accelerated industrialisation and the forced collectivisation of agriculture. He attacked Bukharin and the so-called Right Opposition, who wanted to continue the moderate economics and politics of the NEP years. Internationally, the

Comintern declared world revolution imminent. In the cultural field, the militant campaign was spearheaded by the Russian Association of Proletarian Writers (Russian acronym: RAPP). Formed in 1928, the association aimed to achieve 'proletarian hegemony' over Soviet literature. In practice that meant pushing for a class-struggle line in creative works and attacking as politically deviant anyone who disagreed with RAPP's approach.

RAPP's importance and influence should not be exaggerated. As John Barber pointed out, it 'never enjoyed anything like complete control over the literary world. It was never acknowledged by the party as its spokesman on literary affairs, never achieved hegemony over other literary groups, and never even succeeded suppressing dissident voices within its own ranks.'[8]

Certainly, Stalin responded cautiously to the 'cultural revolution' he had unleashed. In December 1928 a group of proletarian playwrights wrote warning him of the 'right-wing' danger in literature. Their main target was Mikhail Bulgakov (1891–1940) and his plays about the counter-revolutionary White movement of the civil war years, *Days of the Turbins* and *Flight*.

Stalin replied on 1 February 1929, writing that he didn't think it appropriate to talk about a 'right-wing' and 'left-wing' in literature. Better to use descriptive concepts such as 'Soviet', 'anti-Soviet', 'revolutionary', 'anti-revolutionary'. While he thought that *Flight* was anti-Soviet, he wasn't against staging the play if Bulgakov 'were to add to his eight dreams, one or two more dreams depicting the internal social springs of the civil war in the USSR'.

Why are Bulgakov's plays produced so often, asked Stalin?

> Probably because we don't have enough of our own plays good enough for staging. In a land without fish, even *Days of the Turbins* is a fish. It is easy to 'criticise' and demand a ban on non-proletarian literature. But easiest is not always best. It is not a matter of ban but of . . . competition . . . only in a situation of competition can we achieve the formation and crystallization of our proletarian literature. As to *Days of the Turbins* itself, it's not all that bad, it yields more good than harm. Don't forget that the main impression the viewer takes away from this play is an impression favourable for the Bolsheviks.

Stalin sprang to Bulgakov's defence again a couple of weeks later, this time at a meeting with Ukrainian writers. As Leonid Maximenkov has commented, the document recording this meeting has a unique feature: 'we witness Stalin engaged in a spontaneous dialogue'.[9] Stalin spoke a set-piece at the start but most of the meeting consisted of a no-holds-barred discussion in which he was shown little or no deference by his audience.

During the course of this sometimes-raucous exchange, Stalin displayed knowledge of the work of quite a few Russian and Ukrainian writers: Vsevolod Ivanov, Boris Lavrenev, Fedor Panferov, Yakov Korobov, Nikolai Ostrovsky, Vladimir Bill-Belotserkovsky and Anton Chekhov. But a lot of what he had to say concerned the national question, not literature itself. The way to unite different national cultures, he argued, was to intensify their separate development. This formula – 'disunite in order to unite' – he attributed to Lenin, the idea being that once nations stopped being suspicious of one another they would voluntarily coalesce and culturally unify on a socialist basis.

Bulgakov's work came up because some of those present didn't like the way *Days of the Turbins* depicted the civil war in Ukraine. Again, Stalin defended the play (one he was rumoured to have seen fifteen times) on grounds that overall it gave a good impression of the Bolsheviks. He also made some more general points:

> I cannot demand of a literary author that he must be a communist and that he must follow the party point of view. For belletristic literature other standards are needed – non-revolutionary and revolutionary, Soviet and non-Soviet, proletarian and non-proletarian. But to demand that literature be Communist – this is impossible. . . . To demand that belletristic literature and the author follow the party line – then all non-party people would have to be driven out.

Stalin also invoked what would later be called reader-reception theory in support of Bulgakov:

> Workers go to see that play and they see . . . there's no power that can beat the Bolsheviks! There you have it – the general impression left by the play, which can in no way be called Soviet. There are negative sides to that play. Those Turbins are, in their own way, honourable people. . . . But Bulgakov . . . doesn't want to show . . . how these people . . . are sitting on the neck of other people and that's why they are being driven out. . . . But even from Bulgakov certain useful things can be taken.

In a June 1929 letter to Maxim Gorky, Stalin wrote that a play about the 1918 Baku Commune was 'generally speaking . . . weak'. The short-lived commune had ended in tragedy when it was overthrown by counter-revolutionaries and its Bolshevik leaders captured and executed. Stalin thought the play sinned against historical truth because it didn't deal with how and why the Baku Bolsheviks had '*abandoned* power'. Nor did Stalin like the dramatist's depiction of Caspian sailors as 'mercenary drunks' or the absence in the play of Baku's oil workers 'as subject'. Stalin, who had been a Bolshevik agitator in Baku before the revolution, concluded that while the play contained a few 'juicy pages' that spoke to the author's talent, its characters were mostly 'vague and lacklustre'.[10]

In 1930 the poet and satirist Demyan Bedny – a Bolshevik favourite – upset the authorities by publishing poems that caricatured Russian people as inherently lazy. Having been publicly censured by the central committee, he protested to Stalin, who rejected his pleas for artistic respect and berated him for slandering the USSR. He reminded Bedny that revolutionaries all over the world now looked to the Russian working class for leadership, something that filled 'the hearts of Russian workers with a feeling of revolutionary national pride. ... And you? Instead of grasping the meaning of this process ... retired to a quiet spot in the country and ... began to shout from the house-tops that Russia was an abomination of desolation ... that "laziness" and [lying on the couch] are well-nigh national traits of the Russian. ... And this you call Bolshevik criticism!'[11]

Stalin's strictures were mild by Bolshevik standards of robust debate and rudeness. Not until 1932 was Bedny ejected from his Kremlin apartment, ostensibly because of building works, allegedly because he had complained that 'he didn't like to lend books to Stalin because of the dirty marks left on the white pages by his greasy fingers'.[12]

The thrust of the RAPP-led campaign for a strictly proletarian literature was summed up by playwright V. M. Kirshon's belligerent speech to the 16th party congress:

> We must pass over to a decisive offensive, mercilessly liquidating bourgeois ideology. ... The class enemy on the literary front is becoming active. At a time of sharpened class struggle any liberalism, any respect for aesthetic language ... is direct aid to the class enemy. ... The whole purpose of our activity and our work lies in the fight for the building of socialism.[13]

This was too radical for Stalin, especially since the literature produced by the RAPPers was not particularly good. In April 1932 the Politburo resolved to abolish RAPP on the grounds that it had become an impediment to artistic creativity. Together with all the other writer organisations, it would be replaced by a single union of writers that would unite party members with all those who supported Soviet power and the construction of socialism.[14] Further insight into the rationale behind this move may be gleaned from Stalin's remarks at two informal meetings of writers held in Maxim Gorky's place in October 1932.

Gorky (1868–1936), a long-time ally of the Bolsheviks, was their most famous and prestigious literary associate. He was critical of the Bolsheviks' post-revolutionary repressive measures but never an outright opponent. In the 1920s he lived abroad, mostly in Italy, where he had resided before the First World War. In 1928 he returned to Soviet Russia for a countrywide tour and in 1929 published a travelogue, *Around the Union of Soviets*, that was highly favourable to the regime. Stalin was keen to entice him home permanently and showered him with honours and flattery. He was awarded the Order of Lenin and Moscow's main street, Tverskaya, was renamed after him, as was his birth-place, Nizhny Novgorod (both street and city reverted to their original names after the collapse of communism). Upon his return to Moscow, Gorky was allo-cated a grand mansion in the city centre.[15]

SOCIALIST REALISM

That first meeting at Gorky's house, on 20 October, was a gathering of commu-nist writers. Stalin told them there had been too many writers' groupings and too much internal squabbling, at the forefront of which had been RAPP. Non-party writers had been neglected and the task on the literary front was to unite them with party writers. The shared aim of building socialism did not mean destruction of the diversity of literary forms and creative approaches.

Stalin urged communist writers to write plays because staged drama was a very popular form. Poems, novels and short stories remained important but they weren't going to be discussed by millions of people. Asked about non-party writers and the mastery of Marxist dialectics, he responded:

> Tolstoy, Cervantes and Shakespeare were not dialecticians but that did not stop them being great artists. They were great artists and their works reflected their epochs quite well. Those who argue that writers should learn dialectics do not understand that writers have to study the classics of litera-ture as well as those of Marxism. [Lenin] taught us that without the knowl-edge and preserved experience of past human culture we won't be able to build a new socialist culture.[16]

Romanticism, Stalin said, was 'the idealisation, the embellishment of reality' but Shakespeare's romanticism was different from Schiller's, and Gorky's radical version had been that of a rising class, struggling for power and humanity's future. 'Revolutionary socialist realism must be the main current in the litera-ture of our epoch. But that doesn't exclude making use of the writers and methods of the romantic school.'[17]

Non-party as well as party writers were present during the second meeting at Gorky's place a few days later. As he often did when he addressed two different audiences on the same topic, Stalin recycled the points and formulations he had used a week earlier, including the importance of writing plays. Then he said:

> I forgot to talk about what you are 'producing'. There are different products: artillery, automobiles, machines. You also produce 'commodities', 'works', 'products'. Very important things. Interesting things. People's souls. . . . You are engineers of human souls. . . . Production of souls is more important than the production of tanks. . . . Man is remade by life itself. But you, too, will assist in remaking his soul. This is important, the production of human souls, That is why I propose a toast to writers, to the engineers of human souls.

When someone asked about dialectics, Stalin responded that an artist might well be a dialectical materialist:

> But I want to say that he will not then want to write poetry (*general laughter*). I'm joking, of course. But, seriously, you mustn't stuff an artist's head with abstract theses. He must know the theories of Marx and Lenin. But he must know life. An artist must above all portray life truthfully. And if he shows our life truthfully, he cannot but show it as leading to socialism. That will be socialist art. That will be socialist realism.[18]

It seems Stalin came to regret his engineering metaphor, since the statement attributed to him published by *Literaturnaya Gazeta* in August 1934 was deliberately omitted from publication in his collected works.[19] Be that as it may, it featured front and centre at the first All-Union Congress of Soviet Writers, as did the concept of socialist realism.

Stalin didn't attend the congress; he was on holiday. It opened on 8 August 1934 with a statement by the party's ideology chief, Andrei Zhdanov:

> Comrade Stalin has called our writers engineers of human souls. What does that mean? In the first place, it means knowing life so as to be able to depict it truthfully in works of art. The truthfulness and historical concreteness of the artistic portrayal should be combined with the ideological remoulding and education of the toiling people in the spirit of socialism. This method is what we call socialist realism. To be an engineer of human souls means standing with both feet planted on the basis of real life. And this in turn denotes a rupture with romanticism of the old type. Our literature cannot be hostile to romanticism, but it must be a romanticism of a new type, revolutionary romanticism. Soviet literature should be able to portray our heroes; it should be able to glimpse our tomorrow.

One cannot be an engineer of the human soul without knowing the technique of literary work. You have many different types of weapons (genres, styles, forms and method of literary creation). The mastery of the technique of writing, the critical assimilation of the literary heritage of all epochs, represents a task which you must fulfil without fail, if you wish to become engineers of human souls.[20]

Another prominent participant was Nikolai Bukharin, at that time back in favour and serving as editor of *Pravda*, who gave a report on poetry and socialist realism. Nothing that Stalin ever said about literature matched Bukharin's depth, breadth, subtlety and rhetorical power. Socialist realism was not naturalism, Bukharin told the congress, because it 'dares to dream' about the new world and about the new men and women being created by socialism. Socialism was anti-individualistic but not anti-lyrical because it entailed the flourishing of personality and a growth of individuality that united rather than divided people.

Vladimir Mayakovsky, the avant-garde poet who had committed suicide in 1930, was described by Bukharin as a 'Soviet classic': 'The poetry of Mayakovsky is poetry in action. It is poles asunder from the "contemplative" and "disinterested" concepts contained in the aesthetics of idealist philosophers. It is a hailstorm of sharp arrows shot against the enemy. It is devastating, fire-belching lava. It is a trumpet call that summons to battle.'[21]

Among Mayakovsky's works was the 3,000-line epic poem *Vladimir Ilyich Lenin*. A copy of the 1925 edition was part of Stalin's library and he was present in January 1930 when the poet recited the poem at a Lenin memorial meeting in the Bolshoi Theatre.

In November 1935 Mayakovsky's muse, Lilya Brik, wrote to Stalin appealing for help to save the poet's revolutionary legacy. Mayakovsky's memory, works, archive and artefacts were being neglected by the Soviet literary establishment, Brik complained, and his Lenin poem had been 'thrown out of the modern literature textbook' by the Enlightenment Commissariat. In response, Stalin instructed that Brik's complaints be looked into because 'Mayakovsky was and is the best and most talented poet of our Soviet era. Indifference to his memory and works is a crime.'[22] Stalin's laudatory comment soon surfaced publicly and the poet's reputation and place in the Soviet canon were rapidly restored.

Stalin's literary tastes were, like Lenin's, conservative and conventional. From the 1930s onwards that attitude prevailed in Soviet culture as a whole, not only in literature but in architecture, music, film and the fine arts. Some historians describe this retreat from the avant-gardism of the 1920s as a cultural counter-revolution. Its self-conscious political aim, however, was to connect more effectively Soviet culture to the masses. That was also the point of socialist realism, intended to be both popular and accessible as well as politically acceptable.

When anti-fascist German writer Lion Feuchtwanger (1884–1958) met Stalin in January 1937 he asked him about the function of writers, noting that he had called them engineers of the human soul. 'If he is in touch with the present needs of the masses, a writer can play an important role in the development of society,' replied Stalin. 'He captures the vague feelings and unconscious moods of the advanced sectors of society and makes explicit the instinctive actions of the masses. He shapes the epoch's public opinion. He helps society's vanguard realise its tasks.'

Asked by Feuchtwanger to differentiate scientific writers from artistic ones, Stalin said the former were concerned with concepts and analysis of the concrete and the latter were more interested in images and expressiveness. Scientific writers catered to a select audience, whereas artists aimed their works at the masses. Artistic writers were also less calculating and more spontaneous than their scientific counterparts.

Except for the ban on fascist and chauvinist works, said Stalin, Soviet writers were the freest in the world. But he agreed with Feuchtwanger you could learn from reactionaries and emphasised that a writer's Weltanschauung should not be confused with their artistic works, one example being Gogol's novel *Dead Souls*, whose title alluded to the status of serfs in Tsarist society, as well as to the characters that peopled his book: 'Gogol was undoubtedly a reactionary. He was a mystic. He was against the abolition of serfdom. . . . Yet . . . the artistic truth of Gogol's *Dead Souls* had a huge impact on generations of the revolutionary intelligentsia. . . . The world views of writers should not be confused with the impact of their works on readers.'[23]

Stalin also quoted to Feuchtwanger Hegel's well-known aphorism that 'the Owl of Minerva flies out at dusk'. He was fond of this metaphor, and in his 1938 edition of Plekhanov's *The Development of the Monist View of History*, he underlined this passage:

The owl of Minerva begins to fly only at night. When philosophy begins tracing its grey patterns on a grey background, when men begin to study their own social order, you may say with certainty that that order has outlived its day and is preparing to yield place to a new order, the true character of which will again become clear to mankind only after it has played its historical part: Minerva's owl will once again fly out only at night. It is hardly necessary to say that the periodical aerial travels of the bird of wisdom are very useful, and are even quite essential. But they explain absolutely nothing; they themselves require explanation.[24]

STALIN'S LIBRARY

Shakespeare was a ubiquitous figure in Soviet culture in the 1930s. The 1934 writers' congress was adorned by a huge portrait of Shakespeare, and Gorky urged those present to emulate the great Bard. Writers should 'Shakespeare-ise more', demanded the party. There was a project to translate Shakespeare into all the languages of the USSR. 'Stalin Learning English. Wants to Read Shakespeare', claimed the headline of a Tasmanian newspaper in September 1936.[25]

STALIN AT THE MOVIES

In the mid-1930s Stalin began to review film scripts and view and preview films in the Kremlin's new cinema. The transition to 'talkies' had made the medium more attractive to the text-obsessed Stalin, a particular influence being *Chapaev* (1934), the story of a Red Army commander who died a heroic death during the Russian Civil War – one of the most popular Soviet films of all time, which he is said to have watched thirty-eight times.

His general take on the scripts he read was that films should be historically accurate and aesthetically true to life, as well as politically progressive.

Stalin's response to Fridrikh Ermler's script *The Great Citizen* – a fictionalised account of the Kirov assassination – was that the politics that had led to murder should be at the centre of the screenplay, i.e. the struggle for the victory of socialism in the USSR versus the restoration of capitalism.[26]

Asked to choose between two screenplays about Giorgi Saakadze, a military commander who battled for Georgia's unity and independence in the early seventeenth century, Stalin opted for the one he thought was a better piece of history. However, he complained that even this version ended with an inaccuracy – with Saakadze's victory when, in fact, he had ultimately suffered defeat at the hands of the country's feudal princes. 'I think that this historical truth should be restored in the screenplay,' wrote Stalin. 'And if it is restored, the screenplay . . . could be characterised as one of the best works of Soviet cinematography.'[27]

In September 1940 Stalin was drawn into a controversy about a film called *Zakon Zhizni* (The Law of Life), based on a novel by Alexander Avdeenko, who also wrote the screenplay. Since the story concerned a morally corrupt Komsomol official, it went through quite an extensive process of censorship before being released, whereupon it was reviewed positively in *Izvestiya* and other publications. However, a *Pravda* review objected that such corruption was not typical of Soviet society and complained about the film's main protagonist being too richly drawn while other Komsomol members were depicted as his dupes.[28]

Stalin was among Avdeenko's critics at a specially convened meeting of the central committee but he also told the comrades that 'you have to give freedom of art. You have to let people express themselves. . . . There is one artistic line, but it can be reflected in different ways, various methods, approaches and ways of writing.'[29] Towards the end of the meeting, he made some general remarks about truthfulness and objectivity in literature.[30] He was all in favour of both but that didn't mean fiction should be impartial:

> Literature cannot be a camera. That's not how truthfulness should be understood. There cannot be literature without passion, it sympathises with someone, despises someone. . . . There are different ways of writing – the way of Gogol or of Shakespeare. They have outstanding heroes – negative and positive. When you read Shakespeare or Gogol, or Griboedov, you find one hero with negative features. All the negative features are concentrated in one individual. I would prefer a different manner of writing – the manner of Chekhov, who has no heroes but rather grey people . . .
>
> I would prefer we were given enemies not as monsters but as people hostile to our society but not lacking all human traits. . . . I would prefer it if enemies were shown to be strong. . . . Trotsky was an enemy but he was a capable person, undoubtedly he should be depicted as an enemy with negative features, but as one who also has positive qualities. . . . We need truthfulness depicting the enemy in a full-fledged way. . . . It's not that comrade Avdeenko presents enemies in a good light but that the victors, who beat them, are sidelined and lack colour. That's the problem. That's the fundamental inobjectivity and untruthfulness.[31]

Stalin's remark about the recently assassinated Trotsky was macabre, to say the least. There was no mention of his good points in the *Pravda* obituary that Stalin had personally edited and entitled 'Death of an International Spy'.

Stalin didn't have much time to read film scripts during the war. One exception was Alexander Dovzhenko's *Ukraine in Flames*. Dovzhenko was an important Soviet filmmaker, considered by some to be on a par with Eisenstein and Pudovkin. In 1943 he made the documentary *Battle for Our Soviet Ukraine*. His follow-up fictional treatment of the war in Ukraine was not so welcome and in January 1944 he was summoned to a meeting with Stalin in the Kremlin, who accused him of 'revising Leninism', of prioritising national pride above the class struggle, and of blackening the party's name.[32]

Ukraine in Flames never saw the light of day but in 1945 Dovzhenko redeemed himself with another documentary, *Victory in Right-Bank Ukraine*. And, as we have seen, he was the director selected to make the film about Annabelle Bucar's book, *The Truth about American Diplomats*.

In an August 1946 speech to the central committee's Orgburo, Stalin criticised three films: Vsevolod Pudovkin's biopic of the nineteenth-century Russian *Admiral Nakhimov*; part two of Leonid Lukov's *A Grand Life*, which dealt with postwar reconstruction in Ukraine; and Sergei Eisenstein's *Ivan the Terrible Part Two* (see p. 140 above).

Stalin's general gripe was that these filmmakers did not do enough research. He compared them unfavourably to Charlie Chaplin, who worked on projects for several years. 'You can't make good films without details,' said Stalin. 'Goethe, he worked on *Faust* for thirty years, that's how honestly and conscientiously he regarded what he was doing.'

Stalin praised Pudovkin as a capable producer and director, but he detected 'elements of an unconscientious' attitude, which had resulted in a film full of trivia and not enough history. The film had been sent back to Pudovkin but Stalin wasn't confident the filmmaker would make the requisite changes. In the event, Pudovkin was able to rework the film enough to secure its release in 1947.

Part one of *A Grand Life*, set in the 1930s, had been awarded a Stalin Prize in 1941, but the award's namesake was scathing about part two, complaining that it was aimed at 'the undemanding viewer'. Very little of the film was devoted to reconstruction, said Stalin.

It's simply painful when you look, can it really be that our producers, who live among golden men, among heroes, can't depict them as they should but must necessarily dirty them? We have good workers, damn it! They showed themselves in the war. . . . What kind of reconstruction is shown in the film where not a single machine figures? They've confused what took place after the Civil War, in 1918–1919, with what is taking place, say, in 1945–1946.[33]

This film was shelved until 1958.

Stalin was later to level similar complaints against a 1950 documentary, *Fishermen of the Caspian*. The director, Yakov Bliokh, was accused of using dramatisations that had the effect of 'distorting real life by showing faked episodes'. Most importantly, 'Instead of a truthful display of the organisation of labour among Caspian Sea fishermen, as well as advanced methods of fishing and fish processing, the film reproduces the old backward fishing technology based on manual labour.'[34]

It was not all work and no play on the film front. Stalin's daughter Svetlana remembered being thrilled by the many films she saw in the Kremlin as a child: 'The next day at school I could think of nothing but the heroes I'd seen on film the night before.'[35] While visiting the United States in 1959, Nikita Khrushchev told President Eisenhower, 'When Stalin was alive, we used to watch Westerns all the time. When the movie ended, Stalin always denounced it for its ideological content. But the very next day we'd be back in the movie theatre watching another Western.'[36] Stalin's trade minister, Anastas Mikoyan, recalled that Stalin was particularly fond of an English film about a marauding pirate who returned home with a fortune after raids on India and other countries. But the pirate did not want to share the glory (or the loot) with his erstwhile comrades-in-arms so got rid of them by destroying figurines of them.[37]

ZHDANOVSHCHINA

Having served as Leningrad party secretary, after the Second World War Zhdanov returned to his duties as the party's ideology chief. At Stalin's behest he initiated a campaign for a more ideologically orthodox, politically correct and patriotically inclined Soviet literature. A gathering of party propaganda officials in April 1946 was told by Zhdanov that Stalin was dissatisfied with Soviet literary journals. They published 'weak works' and there was a lamentable lack of proper criticism. To rectify this situation, the party's propaganda section would recruit some capable people and involve itself in literary criticism.

In August 1946 Zhdanov received a report from his officials on the 'unsatisfactory state' of the literary-artistic journals *Leningrad* and *Star* – both published in Leningrad. 'Over the last two years, these journals have published a number of ideologically harmful and artistically very weak works,' they informed Zhdanov. Among those singled out for criticism were Anna Akhmatova's poem 'A Kind of Monologue', and the satirist Mikhail Zoshchenko's children's story 'Adventures of a Monkey'.[38]

The next day, during the same Orgburo meeting at which Stalin lambasted the cinematographers for their lack of professionalism, the editors of the two journals were hauled over the coals. Stalin emphasised the political responsibilities of the two journals and their role in the patriotic education of Soviet youth.[39] He wanted to know why Zoshchenko's story had been published in the *Star* rather than in a children's journal: 'This is the silliest piece, it has nothing for the mind or the heart. It's a puppet-show anecdote.' Another concern was the two journals' deference to foreigners: 'You walk on tiptoe in front of foreign writers. . . . This is how you cultivate servile feelings, this is a great sin.' But Stalin's harshest words were reserved for Zoshchenko: 'A whole war went by, all the peoples were soaked in blood, and he didn't give us a single line. He writes some nonsense, it's an absolute mockery. The war is in full swing and he doesn't have a single word for or against, but he writes all kinds of cock-and-bull stories, nonsense that offers nothing for the mind or heart.'

When *Leningrad*'s editor pleaded for his journal because it was dear to the city's heart, Stalin responded: 'If the journal goes, Leningrad will remain.'

Zoshchenko had been a bad boy before. His 1943 novella *Before Sunrise* was banned for being too satirical. He pleaded with Stalin to allow publication of his book on grounds that it demonstrated 'the might of reason and its triumph over the basest of forces', but received no reply to his entreaties.[40]

In accordance with Stalin's wishes, *Leningrad* was banned, while the editorial board of *Star* was replaced.[41] The Orgburo passed a resolution on the two journals in which Zoshchenko and Akhmatova once again came under fierce fire. Zoshchenko was described as having 'long specialised in writing vapid, contentless, vulgar pieces, in the advocacy of rotten unprincipledness, vulgarity and apoliticalness calculated to disorient our young people and poison their minds', while Akhmatova's poetry was condemned for its 'pessimism and decadence'. 'The Soviet order', stated the resolution,

> cannot allow youth to be educated in the spirit of indifference to Soviet policy. . . . The strength of Soviet literature . . . consists in the fact that it is a literature that does not and cannot have other interests besides the interest of the people, the interests of the state. The aim of Soviet literature is to help the state correctly educate young people.[42]

Both authors were expelled from the Writers' Union and publication of their poetry and prose prohibited. By the early 1950s, however, they were back in favour. In April 1952 Zoshchenko was wheeled out to meet a British writers' delegation that included the future Nobel laureate Doris Lessing, who was then still a communist. Asked by Arnold Kettle, another British communist, about the impact of the Zhdanovshchina on him personally, Zoshchenko replied:

> For me it was strange that my comic stories had made such a painful impression, and in the direction of telling me this, the criticism was useful. It was unpleasant. I felt bitter and offended, but I love literature more than anything in life, and that is why I will listen to anything for the sake of literature. If the criticism had offended me as a person, it would have been bad. But it was to me as a writer. And so it was very good.[43]

DOSTOEVSKY AND GOGOL

Fedor Dostoevsky was another writer Stalin believed was a bad influence on Soviet youth. He was a great reactionary as well as a great writer, Stalin told the Yugoslav communist Milovan Djilas in January 1948.[44] This was not the first time that Dostoevsky's name had come up in conversation between Stalin and Djilas. 'You have, of course, read Dostoevsky?' Stalin asked him in April 1945, in response to the Yugoslav's complaints about the behaviour of invading Red Army troops:

> Do you see what a complicated thing is man's soul, man's psyche? Well, then, imagine a man who has fought from Stalingrad to Belgrade – over thousands of kilometres of his own devastated land, across the dead bodies of his comrades and dearest ones! How can such a man react normally? And what is so awful in his having fun with a woman, after such horrors. You have imagined the Red Army to be ideal. . . . The Red Army is not ideal. The important thing is that it fights Germans.[45]

'My father did not care for poetical and deeply psychological art,' wrote Svetlana, who was herself a literature student. 'Yet about Dostoevsky he once said to me that he was a 'great psychologist'. Unfortunately, I did not ask him what he had in mind – the profound social psychology of *The Possessed* or the analysis of human behaviour in *Crime and Punishment*.'[46]

Zhdanov's deputy, Dmitry Shepilov, recalled that one day the boss called him into his office and told him Stalin was concerned that Soviet commentary was neglecting Dostoevsky's politics and social philosophy. 'As Dostoevsky saw it,' Zhdanov quoted Stalin saying,

> there is an element of the satanic and the perverse in each of us. If a man is a materialist, if he does not believe in God, if he – oh horror! – is a socialist, the satanic element wins out, and he becomes a criminal. What an abject philosophy. . . . No wonder Gorky called Dostoevsky the 'evil genius' of the Russian people. True, in his best work Dostoevsky described with stunning power the lot of the humiliated and injured, the savage behaviour of those in power. But for what? To call upon the humiliated and injured to struggle against evil, oppression, and tyranny? Far from it. Dostoevsky called for the renunciation of struggle; he called for humility, resignation, Christian virtue. Only that, according to him, could save Russia from the catastrophe of socialism.[47]

Like all memoirs, Shepilov's story should be treated with caution but politics was always to the fore in Stalin's judgements of great writers. The year 1952 was the centenary of Gogol's death, and his life and works were widely commemorated in the USSR. The principal speaker at a celebration meeting in the Bolshoi Theatre in March 1952 told his audience that Marx, Lenin and Stalin approved of Gogol because he was a 'great ally in the struggle to oppose with ruthless satire all the forces of darkness and hatred, all the forces hostile to peace on earth'. That same day a *Pravda* editorial declared, in words assumed to be Stalin's, that 'Soviet literature is the herald of a new communist morality. Its duty is to paint life in all its diversity and to unmask ruthlessly all that is stagnant, backward and hostile to the people. We need our Gogols and Shchedrins!' These words were echoed by Georgy Malenkov in his report to the 19th party congress in October 1952 – a speech heavily edited by Stalin: 'We need Soviet Gogols and Shchedrins who, with the fire of their satire, would burn everything which is undesirable, rotten and dying, everything which retards our progress.'[48]

STALIN'S PRIZES

Another source for Stalin's views on literature are the deliberations on the award of the state prizes that bore his name. Established in 1939 in honour of Stalin's sixtieth birthday, more than 11,000 Stalin prizes for scientific, technological and artistic works and achievements were awarded to individuals or groups between 1941 and 1955 (when the award was replaced by the Lenin Prize). Writers, poets and playwrights were the recipients of 264 of these awards. The prizes were prestigious, and lucrative: the top category of award earned the recipient a 100,000-rouble bonus. Most important, the award of a prize signalled that the work in question had the approval of the highest levels of the party and state. In theory, the prizes were awarded on the basis of recommendations by independent committees composed mainly of academics and practitioners. In practice, the awards process was subject to political interference by Stalin and the Politburo. This was particularly true of the work of the Committee on Literature and Art.[49]

Discussion of nominated works usually took place in Stalin's office: 'Stalin was probably better prepared for the meetings than anyone else,' recalled Shepilov. 'He was always a close reader of current literature, and found time to go over everything of any artistic, social or economic significance.' Confident as well as diligent, Stalin once asked a group of writers what they thought of this plot line: 'She's married, has a child, but falls in love with another man. Her lover does not understand her and she commits suicide.' Banal, replied the writers. 'With this banal plot,' Stalin retorted, 'Tolstoy wrote *Anna Karenina*.'

Stalin's views on works of art oscillated between stressing the importance of political considerations when making awards and insisting on high artistic standards. Among the writers he championed during these discussions were Konstantin Fedin, Alexander Korneichuk, Mikhail Bubennov, Vera Panova, Fedor Panferov, Nikolai Tikhonov, August Jakobson and Semen Babaevsky.[50]

Konstantin Simonov was another witness to Stalin's ruminations. A renowned poet, writer and journalist, he was deputy head of the Writers' Union as well as the chief editor of the 'thick' Soviet literary journal *Novyi Mir* (New World). According to Simonov, Stalin said of *Kruzhilikha*, Panova's novel about factory life during the Great Patriotic War: 'Everyone's criticising Panova for the fact that in the novel there's no unity between the personal and the social. . . . But surely in life things are not . . . so easily combined? It happens that they are not combined. . . . Her people are shown truthfully.'[51]

A novel by the Belorussian writer Yanka Bryl', *Light beyond the Marshes*, Stalin characterised as 'conflictless'.[52] 'We are so bad at drama,' said Stalin. 'It's as if we have no conflict, no bastards. It turns out that our dramatists think they are forbidden from writing about negative stuff. Critics demand of them ideals and the ideal life. If someone shows anything negative in their work they are immediately attacked . . . but we do have bad and nasty people. We have more than a few fakes and bad people and we need to combat them. Not to depict them is a sin against the truth. . . . We have conflict. There are conflicts in life. These conflicts have to be reflected in drama, otherwise it's not drama.'[53]

Stalin was particularly interested in historical dramas about events in which he had played a part. In the December 1949 issue of *Novyi Mir*, dedicated to him on his seventieth birthday, it was a play about 'The Unforgettable Year 1919' that caught Stalin's eye. He decided to edit it, striving mainly to improve playwright Vsevolod Vishnevsky's prose but also correcting historical inaccuracies such as characters referring to Lenin and Stalin by the patronymics rather than calling them comrade, and changing 'embassy' to 'diplomatic mission'.[54]

Stalin's dissatisfaction with the work of the Art and Literature Committee was evidenced by a critical central committee report of May 1952. Of the 133 works nominated for awards in 1951, fifty had been turned down by the government and nineteen other works given prizes had not even been considered by the committee. The committee had made serious mistakes in excluding from consideration novels such as Vilis Latsis's *Toward New Shores*, Orest Mal'tsev's *Yugoslav Tragedy*, and Dmitry Eremin's *Storm over Rome* – all highly political works. Members of the committee, including Simonov, were criticised for not attending meetings and for cavalier attitudes when assessing submitted works, for example, Wanda Wasilewska's novel *The Rivers Are Burning*. The committee was also accused of parochialism and cronyism when it came to selecting works for consideration. The report concluded that the committee's personnel should be changed and steps taken to ensure that new members were conversant with different artistic styles and familiar with all significant works of literature, including the theory and history of art and literature.[55]

That report had been preceded by one of Stalin's weirder interventions in the cultural arena: an anonymously published defence of Latsis's *Toward New Shores*, which was prompted by an article in *Literaturnaya Gazeta* that had reported criticisms of the novel in the writer's native Latvia.[56]

Latsis was chairman of Latvia's Council of People's Commissars, but that didn't protect him from the severe criticism of high-ranking officials in the country's cultural bureaucracy. Latsis's novel was about Latvia's path to socialism, said his critics, but its main hero was a peasant who was a kulak and, therefore, an enemy of the people.

Stalin's article, published anonymously in *Pravda* on 25 February 1952, expressed a different opinion: if the novel had an individual hero, it was an Old Bolshevik character. More importantly, the true hero of the book was the Latvian people and their epic struggle for socialism. 'We think that V. Latsis's *Toward a New Shore* is one of the great achievements of Soviet artistic literature, and is ideologically and politically mature from beginning to end,' concluded the unnamed 'group of writers' who had supposedly authored the article.[57]

As this episode shows, politics generally trumped all other considerations in Stalin's reading of literature. He preferred writing that captured complexity, conflict and contradiction and was reluctant to impose a party line on literature, but only fiction that depicted socialist progress did he consider to be really 'true to life'.

Stalin complained about the timidity of Soviet writers and critics, but in the authoritarian system he had done so much to create, the safest option was always to keep your head down and avoid saying anything that could be construed as overly critical. Those like Zoshchenko, who were deemed to have overstepped the mark, often found themselves facing official ire, not least from Stalin himself.

A prize for peace also bore Stalin's name. A rival to the Nobel Peace Prize, it was an international award and among its recipients were a good many writers, for example, the Chilean poet Pablo Neruda, the German playwright Bertolt Brecht, the American novelist Howard Fast, and the Soviet journalist Ilya Ehrenburg.

Neruda, who also served on the prize committee, was told by a Russian contact that when Stalin was presented with a list of possible winners, he exclaimed, 'And why isn't Neruda's among them?'[58]

Among the poems penned by Neruda, who won the Nobel Prize for Literature in 1971, was an 'Ode to Stalin':

Lenin left an inheritance
of a homeland free and wide.

Stalin populated it
with schools and flour,
printhouses and apples.
Stalin from the Volga
to the snow
of the inaccessible North
put his hand and in his hand a man
he started to build.
The cities were born.
The deserts sang
for the first time with the voice of water.[59]

Ehrenburg was another beneficiary of Stalin's patronage but not in relation to the peace prize award: as the Soviet Union's foremost international peace campaigner in the 1940s and 1950s, he was among the worthiest of its recipients. But Stalin was instrumental in awarding him a first-class literature prize for his 1948 novel *The Storm*, a story set in wartime France. Reviewers had criticised the novel for portraying the French resistance as more heroic than the Soviet people, so the literature prize committee recommended the award of only a second-class prize. When Stalin asked why, he was told the novel had no real heroes and that one of its main characters was a Soviet citizen who falls in love with a Frenchwoman, which was not a typical situation during the war. 'But I like this Frenchwoman, she's a nice girl. And besides, such things do happen in real life,' said Stalin. 'As regards heroes, I think that few people are born heroes, it's ordinary people who become heroes.'

Reflecting on this episode, Ehrenburg wrote in his memoirs: 'The more I think about Stalin the more it is fully borne in on me how little I understand.'[60] Around the same time, Stalin vetted a play by Simonov based on the Kliueva–Roskin affair. *Alien Shadow* concerned a Soviet microbiologist infatuated with the west who inadvertently betrays state secrets. At Stalin's insistence, Simonov changed the play's ending to one in which the government forgives the protagonist's sins. Some critics considered the play too weak and liberal. The play was awarded a Stalin Prize, but only a second-class one.[61]

CHAPTER 7

EDITOR-IN-CHIEF OF THE USSR

If there was anything Stalin loved as much as reading, it was editing. His red or blue pencil marks on documents were as familiar to Soviet officials as his face. The same is true for today's scholars of the Stalin era. How he processed the paperwork that crossed his desk is fundamental to understanding his thinking and decision-making. Rare were the draft documents that passed by his editorial eye unaltered.

Stalin's journalistic approach was the hallmark of his editorial style.[1] Filling in a party registration questionnaire in October 1921, he listed 'journalist' as one of his special skills.[2] His political life was founded on writing and editing agitational materials – leaflets, pamphlets, speeches, editorials, short articles – and it showed in the way that he cut, reorganised and sharpened texts he found unsatisfactory. The results were hardly scintillating but he was a highly competent editor and the texts that bore his name, or imprimatur, were invariably clear and accessible to their intended readers, whether party cadres, popular audiences, foreign officials or specialists. Supremely confident, Stalin was comfortable in his role as the Soviet Union's editor-in-chief.[3]

Mostly, Stalin edited for clarity and accuracy. But sometimes he felt the need to grapple with substance, particularly if the text was of major political importance. Such was the case with the five key texts considered in this chapter: the *Short Course History of the Communist Party of the Soviet Union* (1938); the interwar section of volume two of *Istoriya Diplomatii* (1941); the second edition of his short biography, *Joseph Stalin* (1947); the polemical booklet *Falsifiers of History* (1948); and a Soviet textbook on *Political Economy* (1954).

Stalin's first foray into full-length book-editing was his involvement in the early stages of the multi-part *History of the Civil War in the USSR*, the first two volumes of which dealt with pre-revolutionary history and the 1917 revolution.

The project was Maxim Gorky's idea and the aim was to produce a popular and accessible history that would highlight the feats and exploits of the ordinary people who fought for the Bolsheviks.[4] Stalin was a titular member of the editorial collective, which was headed by I. I. Mints, a specialist in civil war history. Mints later worked on the *History of Diplomacy* book (see below) and served on the government's Commission for the History of the Great Patriotic War. Mints was Jewish and in the late 1940s fell foul of the anti-cosmopolitan purge of suspected Zionists and lost all his academic posts. But he managed to avoid falling victim to more extreme measures.

Extensive consultations and discussions took place with Stalin on the first two volumes of the civil war history. In 1934 Gorky sent him the draft of volume one, which the dictator then edited in some detail, marking hundreds of corrections. Mints recalled that 'Stalin was pedantically interested in formal exactitude. He replaced "Piter" in one place with "Petrograd", "February in the Countryside" as a chapter title (he thought it suggested a landscape) with "The February Bourgeois-Democratic Revolution". . . . Grandiloquence was mandatory, too. "October Revolution" had to be replaced by "The Great October Revolution". There were dozens of such corrections.'[5]

Stalin the pedant was also a stickler for correct dates, accurate captions and informative subheadings, as well as making liberal use of adjectival qualifiers such as 'bourgeois' and 'proletarian'. He insisted the book's title should include the name of the country in which the civil war took place, i.e. the USSR.[6] Stalin was pleased with the result and in summer 1935 he wrote to congratulate Mints and his team: 'You've done your work well – the book reads like a novel.'[7] Elaine MacKinnon, the author of an in-depth study of the early years of the project, agrees:

> The first two volumes were definitely popular in form, with colourful illustrations, photographs, and a prose style that is more characteristic of fictional narratives than scientific treatises. The characterizations are simplistic and project in animated tone clear images of good and evil, positive and negative. The narratives read like fiction, with many short sentences and continual efforts to build up a sense of tension and drama in the unfolding of events. Enemies are clearly defined. The role of workers, soldiers, and peasants is highlighted, despite innumerable references to Stalin and other Bolshevik leaders.[8]

In a pre-publication puff piece for the first volume, Mints explained the editorial process to readers of the party journal *Bol'shevik*. He emphasised Stalin's personal involvement in the project but gave no details. He did, however, relate numerous examples of changes to the draft made by an unnamed 'Chief Editor', such as amending 'Russia – prison of the peoples' to 'Tsarist Russia – prison of the peoples' and changing 'October Revolution' to 'Great Proletarian Revolution'. The chief editor's changes, concluded Mints, merited close attention: 'All these corrections are a model of deep analysis, exceptional clarity and precise formulation.'[9]

KEEP IT SIMPLE: THE *SHORT COURSE HISTORY OF THE COMMUNIST PARTY OF THE SOVIET UNION*

The civil war book fulfilled Stalin's desire for heroic history to inspire the Soviet masses, but in the mid-1930s he was focused on a more important editing project – one aimed at key party members and activists: a new history of the party itself: a book that would explain clearly and credibly the complicated and tumultuous history of the party, its divisions and schisms, and its denouement in the Great Terror. How had the party succeeded in its historic mission while incubating clusters of high-level traitors, spies, assassins and saboteurs? The book also needed to educate members in matters theoretical, equip them with knowledge and understanding to shield them from malign influences and enable them to correctly implement the party line.[10]

The *Short History* arose from Stalin's dissatisfaction with extant textbook histories of the party which did not connect its history with that of the country or provide a Marxist explanation of internal factional struggles. Crucial was to depict the struggle against anti-Bolshevik tendencies as a principled struggle for Leninism and as a battle that stopped the party from degenerating into a reformist, social-democratic organisation.

Appended to this memorandum of Stalin's, which dates from spring 1937, was his schema for the periodisation of the new party history.[11] The writing task eventually fell to party propaganda chief Pyotr Pospelov and court historian Yemel'yan Yaroslavsky. Their final draft, presented to Stalin in spring 1938, cleaved closely to his preferred chapterisation but the boss was not happy with the results of their labour. As he later explained to his Politburo colleagues, eleven of the draft's twelve chapters required fundamental revision, principally to strengthen its treatment of the party's theoretical development – so necessary because of the 'weakness of our cadres in the sphere of theory'.[12]

When the *Short Course* was published in September 1938, initially in *Pravda* and then as a book, Stalin was identified as the author of the section on dialectical and historical materialism, while the rest was attributed to an anonymous commission of the central committee. After the Second World War, Stalin was credited as author of the whole book and it was earmarked for publication as volume 15 of his collected works. As the prime editor of Pospelov and Yaroslavsky's draft, he cut scores of pages, deleted hundreds of paragraphs and interpolated masses of his own text. He also made thousands of minor corrections. The *Short Course* was truly a history of the party as Stalin saw it and wanted it to be seen.

The end product of Stalin's efforts was a biased, distorted and simplistic account of the party's history, one manufactured by omission, elision and rhetorical tricks. Stalin was a past master at using such devices to present versions of events that were self-serving but credible. That doesn't mean he didn't believe in the essential truth of his version of the party's history.

Pospelov and Yaroslavsky wrote reams of invective directed against Trotsky and other opponents of Stalin, which he deleted, substituting a pithy narrative thread that conveyed a sustained critique of the opposition while at the same time dimming the spotlight on them. It told a story of how misguided opponents became a bunch of careerists and opportunists and then resorted to treachery. When the anti-party and anti-Soviet line of these oppositionists was roundly rejected by the great majority of party members, they allied themselves with foreign capitalists and imperialists and engaged in terrorism and sabotage. Only in the mid-1930s did the extent of their 'monstrous moral and political depravity', of their 'despicable villainy and treachery' become fully apparent.

Numerous laudatory accounts of his own role in the history of the party were deleted by Stalin. He disappeared almost entirely from the party's pre-revolutionary history, leaving Lenin as its one and only commanding figure. Stalin allowed himself to feature more heavily in the chapters dealing with the 1920s and 1930s, but given the centrality of his role in these years, it would have been difficult to do otherwise. Stalin also cut references to many other individuals, reducing Pospelov and Yaroslavsky's text to an essentially institutional history of the party, its policies, factions and major actions. For Stalin that was the whole edifying point: to engage readers with the history of the party as a collective body, as an institution. He wanted his people to love the party, not Big Brother.

To supplement his editorial efforts, Stalin held a series of meetings in his Kremlin office to review each segment of the book before it was published by *Pravda*. In attendance were Molotov, Zhdanov and *Pravda* editor I. Ya. Rovinsky, as well as Yaroslavsky and Pospelov.[13]

Following publication, Stalin explained to a conference of leading party propagandists that the book's main purpose was to educate cadres in matters of theory, specifically the laws of historical development. To illustrate the importance of theory, Stalin offered a rather dramatic example: 'When we talk about the saboteurs, about the Trotskyists, you have to keep in mind that . . . not all of them were spies . . . among them were our people who went crazy. Why? They weren't real Marxists, they were weak in theory.'[14]

The book was 'addressed to our cadres', said Stalin, 'not to ordinary workers on the shop floor, nor to ordinary employees in institutions, but to cadres who Lenin described as professional revolutionaries. This book is addressed to our administrative cadres. They most of all need to go and work on their theory; after that everyone else can.'[15]

Stalin defended the book's de-personalisation:

[Originally], this draft textbook was for the most part based on exemplary individuals – those who were the most heroic, those who escaped from exile and how many times they escaped, those who suffered in the name of the cause, etc., etc.

But should a textbook really be designed like that? Can we really use such a thing to train and educate our cadres? We ought to base our cadres' training on ideas, on theory. . . . If we possess such knowledge, then we'll have real cadres, but if people don't possess this knowledge, they won't be cadres – they'll be just empty spaces.

What do exemplary individuals really give us? I don't want to pit ideas and individuals against one another – sometimes it's necessary to refer to individuals, but we should refer to them only as much as is really necessary. It is ideas that really matter, not individuals – ideas in a theoretical context.[16]

At the end of the conference Stalin talked delegates through some of the book's historical content, making this general point about studying the past:

History should be truthful, it must be written as it was, without adding anything. What we have nowadays is history from 500 years ago being criticised from the point of view of the present. How can that be chronological? Religion had a positive significance in the time of Vladimir the Saint. At that time there was paganism, and Christianity was a step forward. Now our wise men say from the point of view of the new situation in the twentieth century that Vladimir was a scoundrel, the pagans were scoundrels and religion was vile i.e. they don't want to evaluate events dialectically so that everything has its time and place.[17]

The *Short Course* addressed fundamental theory in its section on dialectical and historical materialism. Written by Stalin, it was the culmination and synthesis of his studies of Marxist philosophy. It was inserted into chapter four of the book, which dealt with the party's history from 1908 to 1912, the pretext being that such a digression was necessary to understand the importance of Lenin's major theoretical work, *Materialism and Empirio-Criticism*.[18]

Stalin's active engagement with philosophical issues was sporadic.[19] His earliest major work, *Anarchism or Socialism?* (1906–7), was a fundamentalist defence of Marxist philosophy against criticisms levelled by various Russian anarchists. He didn't return to such discourse until the *Short Course*. In between he read a few philosophy texts, kept abreast of intra-Marxist theoretical disputes and, if the Jan Sten story is to be believed, took a few tutorials in Hegelian dialectics. In 1930 he intervened in a Soviet philosophy debate that pitted so-called 'mechanists' against 'dialecticians', essentially a dispute about how much credit should be given to Hegel as a dialectician. Stalin sided with the mechanists, who argued that Hegelian dialectics were too formal, too abstract and too detached from political practice.

Anarchism or Socialism? was based primarily on the writings of Marx and Engels. 'Marxism is not only the theory of socialism, it is an integral world outlook, a philosophical system, from which Marx's proletarian socialism logically flows,' wrote Stalin. 'This philosophical system is called dialectical materialism.'

Marxism's method was dialectical and its theory materialistic. Dialectics was based on the idea that in life change was constant. Marxist materialism asserted that when the material conditions of life changed so did people's consciousness, but only after a time lag. Adroit political intervention during that lag could speed up the changes necessary to achieve the revolutionary transformation of both material life and consciousness.

In Stalin's Marxist universe, history was inevitably moving in the direction of socialism because it was the only system in which the forces of economic development would be able to reach their full potential. Marxist struggles for socialism were not based on utopian aspirations but on knowledge of the objective dynamics of social development. 'Proletarian socialism', Stalin wrote, was a 'logical deduction from dialectical materialism'. It was a 'scientific socialism'.[20]

Stalin railed against anarchist accusations that Marxist dialectics were not a method but a metaphysics. But it is hard not to conclude that the anarchists were right: what Stalin proposed first and foremost was an ontology, a general theory of reality, a description and analysis of what the world was actually like.

The ontological foundations of dialectical and historical materialism were stressed even more by Stalin in the *Short Course*. Reality is material, knowable and subject to definite laws, argued Stalin. This is true of both nature and the social world. Dialectics revealed that reality – human and physical – was interconnected, integrated and holistic, and in a state of constant movement and change.

Stalin's ontology sought to make historical materialism a science of history based on the study of the laws of social development. Knowledge of these laws guided the party's practice: 'The prime task of historical science is to study and disclose the laws of production, the laws of development of the productive forces and of the relations of production, the laws of economic development of society.'

As he had in *Anarchism or Socialism?*, Stalin stepped back from the crude economic determinism implicit in his schema. Social ideas, theories, views and political institutions originated in the economic base of society but having arisen they acquired quite a lot of autonomy, including having a determining influence on material life. Indeed, Stalin's emphasis on the relative autonomy of the social superstructure vis-à-vis its economic base was his distinctive contribution to Marxist philosophy.

Many philosophical holes can be picked in dialectical and historical materialism, but its attractiveness as a mode of thinking should not be underestimated. As the eminent historian Eric Hobsbawm recalled in his memoirs:

> What made Marxism so irresistible was its comprehensiveness. 'Dialectical materialism' provided, if not a 'theory of everything', then at least a 'framework of everything', linking inorganic and organic nature with human affairs, collective and individual, and providing a guide to the nature of all interactions in a world of constant flux.[21]

Study of the *Short Course* was compulsory for virtually all educated Soviet citizens. Between 1938 and 1949 it went through 234 impressions, a total of 35.7 million copies, of which 27.5 million were in Russian, 6.4 million in the other languages of the Soviet Union and 1.8 million in foreign languages.[22] Not until after Khrushchev's 1956 denunciation of Stalin did the *Short Course* lose its official status as the definitive history of the party.

SHOW DON'T TELL: THE HISTORY OF DIPLOMACY

Stalin's favourite editing weapon was deletion, his prime targets being quotation-mongering and excessive rhetoric. The goal was to streamline and de-clutter text, avoid repetition, and not lose sight of the wood by focusing on the trees.

Istoriya Diplomatii was commissioned by the Politburo in spring 1940. Its first volume, on the history of diplomacy from ancient times up to the Franco-Prussian war, was sent to the printers at the end of December 1940. The second volume would deal with the late nineteenth century, the First World War, the

Russian Revolution and the origins of the Second World War. Stalin was sent the section on the politically tricky interwar years, the period when the Soviet Union became a central actor in the history of diplomacy.[23] The typescript was unsigned but the history's titular editor, V. P. Potemkin, had previously indicated to Stalin that its authors would be Mints and A. M. Pankratova (1897–1957).[24]

Stalin changed the title from 'Diplomacy after the First World War and the Socialist Revolution in Russia' to 'Diplomacy in Contemporary Times (1919–1940)'. He also indicated that Russia's exit from the First World War and the 1918 Brest-Litovsk peace treaty should be dealt with separately. Working through the text, he eliminated virtually all quotations from his and Lenin's writings, thereby turning a propagandistic tract into an approximation of professional history, albeit of the highly partisan variety.

In many of his own articles and speeches, Stalin spelled out his political messages. Such didacticism he deemed unnecessary in this instance. Hence his deletion of many passages in this text that cast the imperialists in a bad light or read like special pleading on behalf of the Soviet government. The story itself was allowed to tell its tale of imperialist predation, hypocrisy and double-dealing on the one hand, and Soviet virtue on the other.

It turned out that these detailed edits were mostly a waste of Stalin's time. Publication of volume two of *Istoriya Diplomatii* was disrupted by the outbreak of the Soviet–German war. When publication resumed in 1945, the project had metamorphosed into a much larger, three-volume work. Instead of one long chapter devoted to the interwar period, there were 700 pages in the third volume, mostly written by Mints and Pankratova, with Potemkin credited as the co-author of two chapters on 1938–9. The volume was subtitled 'Diplomacy in the Period of the Preparation of the Second World War (1919–1939)'. There is no evidence that Stalin had a hand in editing this volume. Presumably, he was far too busy waging war.

But in one important respect, Stalin's editing did endure: volume three contained hardly any Lenin or Stalin quotes. For the most part, it was a dry and dispassionate diplomatic history that only at the very end let rip a broadside against the 'methods of bourgeois diplomacy'. This was written by another historian favourite of Stalin's, E. V. Tarle (1874–1955), a specialist on Napoleon and the 1812 war. Among the aforesaid methods were aggression masquerading as defence; propaganda, disinformation and demagogy; threats and intimidation; and using the protection of weak states as a pretext for war. According to Tarle, Stalin asked him personally to write this chapter.[25]

British historian Max Beloff's highly critical review of volume three bemoaned its poor use of sources. Sources that suited the proffered interpretation were cited with no effort made to assess their accuracy and reliability, while the sources on Soviet foreign policy consisted entirely of official pronounce-ments.[26]

LESS IS MORE: THE *SHORT BIOGRAPHY*

Stalin's role during the Second World War was the culminating episode of his biography. Preparations for that 'inevitable war' drove his brutal push to modernise Russia. The Soviet victory over Nazi Germany was by far his greatest achievement. From near defeat in 1941 the USSR emerged as a mighty socialist state that controlled half of Europe and had the power to compete for global supremacy against the war's other great victor, the United States.

The momentous nature of the war made it imperative to revise Stalin's *Short Biography*, published by the Institute of Marx, Engels and Lenin (IMEL) in 1939. There was also a great deal of interest in his biography internationally. The Stalin cult had gone global. Stalin was *Time* Man of the Year in both 1939 and 1942. During the war, Stalin was inundated with questions and requests for interviews from foreign journalists. In January 1943 New York publishers Simon & Schuster wrote to Stalin suggesting that he write them a book about Soviet war and peace aims.[27] Soon after the war the Kremlin received enquiries from a British publisher wishing to issue a photographic biography of Stalin and from an American company that wanted to include him in its *Biographical Encyclopedia of the World*.[28]

A redraft of the *Short Biography* was sent to Stalin for approval in late 1946. Stalin had affected disinterest in the first edition but was greatly interested this time, perhaps because the new version dealt with his military leadership. The draft landed on his desk while he was still revelling in his feats as supreme commander and jostling to snatch the limelight of victory from generals such as his deputy, Marshal Georgy Zhukov, whom he had recently dismissed as commander-in-chief of Soviet ground forces.

Stalin was not satisfied with the new edition and at the end of December he called in the editorial team for what David Brandenberger rightly calls 'a collec-tive dressing-down'.[29]

The editorial team was headed by Agitprop chief Georgy Alexandrov, and included the historian Vasily Mochalov, who also played a key role in the production of Stalin's collected works. Twelve months previously, Mochalov had been summoned to Stalin's Kremlin office to discuss that project. As we learned in Chapter Two, he wrote a report of that memorable encounter, and he did the same for this meeting.

The need for a biography of Lenin that would teach people Marxism-Leninism was Stalin's first comment. As to his own biography, it was full of mistakes. 'I have all kinds of teachings,' said Stalin sarcastically – about the war, communism, industrialisation, collectivisation, etc. 'What are people supposed to do after reading this biography? Get down on their knees and pray to me?' The biography should instil in people a love of the party. It should feature other party cadres. The chapter on the Great Patriotic War wasn't bad, although it, too, needed to mention other prominent personalities.[30]

Mochalov's account tallies with that of *Pravda* editor P. N. Pospelov. 'There is some idiocy in the biography draft,' complained Stalin to Pospelov. 'And it is Alexandrov who is responsible for this idiocy.'[31] Pospelov took particular note of Stalin's demand that it should reference leading figures who had worked with him in Baku, name those who had also taken up Lenin's banner after his death, and mention the members of his Supreme Command during the war. Something should also be added about the role of women, said Stalin. The tone of the biography was 'SRish' i.e. too focused on him as a hero. To prove that point, he quoted the line, 'No one in the world ever led such broad masses.' And nowhere did the biography state what Stalin had told Emil Ludwig in 1931 – that he considered himself merely a pupil of Lenin's.[32]

Briefed by Stalin and armed with the boss's editorial corrections, Alexandrov's team quickly revised their draft text. The new edition of the biography was published by *Pravda* in February 1947 and then as a book with an initial print run of a million copies.

As was the case with the *Short Course*, Stalin toned down the adulation of himself. He inserted the names of many co-workers and made changes that emphasised his partnership with Lenin. He cut completely a section extolling his role as the leader of the international communist movement beloved by proletarians throughout the world. A substantial section was added on the role of women in the revolutionary movement and in building socialism. 'Working women are the most oppressed of all the oppressed,' Stalin is quoted as saying in one of his speeches.

One version of the draft ended with a stirring quote from Molotov: 'The names of Lenin and Stalin are a bright light of hope in all corners of the world and a thundering call to struggle for peace and happiness of all peoples, a struggle for complete liberation from capitalism.' This was deleted by Stalin, as were the concluding slogans: 'Long live our dear and great Stalin!'; 'Long live the great invincible banner of Marx, Engels, Lenin and Stalin!' In the final product, these were replaced by a more restrained quote from Molotov that the USSR had been fortunate to have at its disposal the great Stalin during the war, who would now lead it forward in peacetime.[33]

There were limits to Stalin's modesty and he left in many cultish statements, especially in the chapter on the Great Patriotic War. Like its predecessor, the new edition was more hagiography than biography, but not a ridiculous one. In the immediate aftermath of the Second World War, extravagant claims about Stalin's military genius had more than a modicum of credibility.[34]

Among his insertions was this one:

> Although he performed the task of leader of the party and the people with consummate skill and enjoyed the unreserved support of the entire Soviet people, Stalin never allowed his work to be marred by the slightest hint of vanity, conceit or self-adulation. When interviewed by the German writer, Emil Ludwig, Stalin paid glowing tribute to Lenin's genius in transforming Russia, but of himself he simply said: 'As for myself, I am merely a pupil of Lenin and my aim is to be a worthy pupil of his.'[35]

While there was some theory in the *Short Biography*, there was no equivalent to the section on dialectical and historical materialism in the *Short Course*. Perhaps that's what Alexandrov had in mind when he proposed a third edition in 1950 that would deal with Stalin's postwar activities but also summarise his major theoretical writings. Outlines were devised and dummies prepared by Alexandrov and his staff, but nothing came of the proposal.[36]

CONTROL THE NARRATIVE: *FALSIFIERS OF HISTORY*

Stalin's only public comment on the Nazi–Soviet pact came in his radio broadcast a few days after the German invasion of the USSR in June 1941:

> How could the Soviet Government have consented to conclude a non-aggression pact with such treacherous monsters as Hitler and Ribbentrop? Was this not a mistake on the part of the Soviet government? Of course not! A non-aggression pact is a pact of peace between two States. It was such a pact that Germany proposed to us in 1939. Could the Soviet Government have declined such a proposal? I think that not a single peace-loving state could decline a peace treaty with a neighbouring Power, even though the latter was headed by such monsters and cannibals as Hitler and Ribbentrop.[37]

In private, he spoke at length about the pact at a Kremlin dinner in honour of Lord Beaverbrook and Averell Harriman, who travelled to Moscow in September 1941 to discuss British and American supplies to the Soviet Union. Captain H. H. Balfour, a member of the British delegation, recorded in his diary:

> He explained plausibly how he had come to sign the Russo-German pact in 1939. . . . . He saw war coming, and Russia must know where she stood.

If he could not get an alliance with England, then he must not be left alone—isolated—only to be the victim of the victors when the war was over. Therefore, he had to make his pact with Germany.[38]

Churchill provided further insight into Stalin's calculations and thinking in his memoir-history of the Second World War:

At the Kremlin in August 1942 Stalin, in the early hours of the morning, gave me one aspect of the Soviet position. 'We formed the impression,' said Stalin, 'that the British and French Governments were not resolved to go to war if Poland were attacked,' but that they hoped the diplomatic line-up of Britain and France and Russia would deter Hitler. We were sure it would not. 'How many divisions,' Stalin had asked, 'will France send against Germany on mobilisation?' The answer was, 'About a hundred.' He then asked, 'How many will England send?' The answer was, 'Two, and two more later.' 'Ah, two and two more later,' Stalin had repeated. 'Do you know,' he asked, 'how many divisions we shall have to put on the Russian front if we go to war with Germany?' There was a pause. 'More than three hundred.'[39]

In its defence of the pact, the third volume of *Istoriya Diplomatii* highlighted the role of western anti-appeasement critics and their prewar campaign for an alliance with the Soviet Union. The most prominent of these critics had been Churchill, who advocated a 'grand alliance' of Britain, France and the Soviet Union against Hitler. It was the failure of Churchill's campaign and the collapse of the 1939 Anglo-Soviet-French triple alliance negotiations that had led to the Soviet–German non-aggression treaty.[40]

For decades the key Soviet text on the Nazi–Soviet pact was *Fal'sifikatory Istorii*, a brochure issued by the Soviet Information Buro in response to the documentary collection *Nazi–Soviet Relations, 1939–1941* (NSR), published by the US Department of State in January 1948.

NSR was a selection of diplomatic documents from captured German archives. It revealed the contacts between German and Soviet diplomats prior to the pact and the extensive co-operation between the two states after the agreement was signed. Most important, the book included the text of the non-aggression treaty's secret additional protocol that divided Poland and the Baltic States into Soviet and German spheres of influence. Implicit in the selection and arrangement of the NSR documents was a narrative that Soviet negotiations with Britain and France for an anti-German front were a sham; far from being a desperate, last-minute gamble, the origins of the pact lay in a carefully prepared secret rapprochement between Berlin and Moscow.

Stalin couldn't have been surprised by the Americans' weaponising of the secret protocol. It had cropped up at the Nuremburg Trial in 1946 when the Nazis' defence lawyers used it to show that if Germany was guilty of conspiracy to wage aggressive war then so, too, was the Soviet Union. Soviet jurists got the protocol excluded from evidence, but its text was discussed in open court by former German foreign minister Joachim von Ribbentrop, who had signed the pact in Moscow in August 1939. It was also leaked and published in the American press.[41]

The Soviet response to this American propaganda strike was remarkably speedy. *Nazi–Soviet Relations* was immediately translated into Russian by TASS and sent to Stalin.[42] By 3 February, Deputy Foreign Minister Andrei Vyshinsky (the former prosecutorial star of the Moscow show trials) sent Stalin a detailed draft rebuttal prepared by a group of historians.[43] The pamphlet's title was *Otvet Klevetnikam* (Reply to Slanderers), but Stalin changed this to *Fal'sifikatory Istorii* (Falsifiers of History), a phrase that he picked up from the Vyshinsky draft and decided to run with as a theme of the document. Stalin's chosen subtitle was *Istoricheskaya Spravka*, which can be variously translated as historical information, reference, enquiry or survey. He also changed the subtitles of sections two and three of the brochure to reflect the idea that western policy was aimed at *isolating* the USSR. By the late 1940s, Europe was dividing and the cold war heating up. In Fulton, Missouri in March 1946, Churchill claimed that 'from Stettin in the Baltic to Trieste in the Adriatic, an iron curtain has descended across the Continent'. To Stalin, however, it was the west once again striving to isolate the Soviet Union from the rest of Europe, as Hitler had done in the 1930s.

In modern parlance, the basic thrust of *Falsifiers of History* was that NSR was fake news, a selective spin on Nazi documents that did not correspond to the truth.

Falsifiers' four parts were published separately by *Pravda*, on 10, 12, 15 and 17 February. Stalin was in such a hurry that the first three parts appeared in the newspaper before he had even finished editing part four. All four parts were then republished and promoted by Soviet embassies across the world. Two million copies of the Russian-language brochure containing the complete text were printed, as were hundreds of thousands in English and other languages.[44]

Stalin edited the draft in detail and added about fifteen pages of his own text to the seventy-five pages of the Russian edition. Stalin's additions were either handwritten or dictated to a member of his staff and then hand-corrected by him.[45] Many of his additions were rhetorical in character:

> The slanderous claptrap that ... the USSR should not have agreed to conclude a pact with the Germans can only be regarded as ridiculous.

Why was it right for Poland . . . to conclude a non-aggression pact with the Germans in 1934, and not right for the Soviet Union. . . . Why was it right for Britain and France . . . to issue a joint declaration of non-aggression with the Germans in 1938, and not right for the Soviet Union. . . . Is it not a fact that of all the non-aggressive Great Powers in Europe, the Soviet Union was the last to conclude a pact with the Germans?[46]

Falsifiers of History promulgated Moscow's view of the Second World War's origins and of Soviet–German relations after the signature of the non-aggression treaty in August 1939. Western culpability for the outbreak of war was its major theme. Western states had aided and abetted Nazi rearmament, appeased and encouraged Hitlerite aggression, and attempted to direct German expansion eastward, in the Soviet direction. By contrast, the Soviet Union strove to negotiate a great-power collective security front against Hitler, only to be thwarted by double-dealing Anglo-French appeasers who had no intention of allying themselves with the Soviet Union and indeed were all the while secretly negotiating with Berlin. Hence Moscow found itself faced with the unenviable choice of a temporary non-aggression pact with Berlin or being manoeuvred by the western powers into waging a war with Germany that the British and French did not want to fight themselves.

The USSR's post-pact incorporation of Polish, Baltic, Finnish and Romanian territory was characterised as legitimate moves to build an 'Eastern Front' to defend against inevitable Nazi aggression against the Soviet Union – actions that pushed hundreds of miles to the west the line from which the Germans invaded Russia in summer 1941.

The booklet's relatively frank account of Soviet policy during the period of the pact with Hitler was all Stalin's doing. He wrote the first couple of pages of this section and framed Soviet policy in 1939–41 as the creation of an Eastern Front against German aggression – a narrative device he may well have derived from a speech of Churchill's in October 1939, quoted with approval – in which his comrade-in-arms during the Second World War had said the Soviets were right to create such a front by invading eastern Poland to keep the Nazis out.[47]

Later, in a passage that parodied Churchill's iron curtain speech, Stalin wrote of Soviet expansion into the Baltic States and Romania:

In this way the formation of an 'Eastern Front' against Hitler aggression from the Baltic to the Black Sea was complete. The British and French ruling circles, who continued to abuse the USSR and call it an aggressor for creating an 'Eastern Front', evidently did not realise that the appearance of an 'Eastern Front' signified a radical turn in the development of the war – to the disfavour of the Hitler tyranny and to the favour of the victory of democracy.[48]

Stalin's next interpolation concerned the Soviet Union's entry into what he called a 'war of liberation' against Hitler's Germany. Here he contrasted President Harry Truman's statement the day after the German invasion of the USSR with that of Churchill:

> If we see that Germany is winning we ought to help Russia and if Russia is winning we ought to help Germany and that way let them kill as many as possible. (Truman)

> The Russian danger is our danger, and the danger of the United States . . . the cause of free men and free peoples fighting in every quarter of the globe. (Churchill)[49]

Foreign Commissar Molotov's trip to Berlin in November 1940 was one of the most contentious episodes of Soviet–German relations during the period of the pact. Molotov's task was, if possible, to sign a new Nazi–Soviet pact with Hitler and Ribbentrop. In *Falsifiers*, Stalin presented it as a mission to 'sound out' and 'probe' Hitler's intentions, 'without having any intention of concluding an agreement of any kind with the Germans'.[50] This was only partly true. Stalin was willing to sign a new agreement if Soviet security could be guaranteed.[51]

The final words of the booklet were Stalin's, too:

> The falsifiers of history . . . have no respect for the facts – that is why they are dubbed falsifiers and slanderers. They prefer slander and calumny. But there is no reason to doubt that in the end these gentry will have to acknowledge a universally recognised truth – namely that slander and calumny perish, but the facts live on.[52]

Fal'sifikatory Istorii (1948) is the closest we get to a Stalin memoir about his pact with Hitler. It was designed to shift the conversation about the war's origins from the secret protocol to western appeasement of Hitler and to present a hard-headed defence of Soviet territorial expansion in 1939–1940. As a piece of propaganda, it had a glaring defect: it didn't even mention, let alone address, the issue of the secret protocol. At Nuremberg the Soviets had derided the protocol as a fabrication designed to deflect from the Nazi conspiracy to wage aggressive war. Having adopted that stance, there was no question of backing away from it. Stalin didn't do retractions.

TARGET THE AUDIENCE: THE TEXTBOOK ON
POLITICAL ECONOMY

Socialist economics was the lifeblood of the Soviet system. The success or failure of Soviet socialism rested on its economic performance. Stalin devoted a lot of time to studying and dealing with economics problems. Many of his seminal speeches were devoted wholly or in part to economic questions. In the 1920s and 1930s the Soviets developed from scratch a socialist, planned economy but they didn't theorise, generalise and codify their experience. As Ethan Pollock puts it, 'There were no acceptable Soviet textbooks on the socialist economy or the transition to communism.'[53]

This was a lacuna Stalin determined to fill, and in 1937 the central committee decreed the writing of a textbook on the political economy of both socialism and capitalism. In receipt of drafts from leading economists, Stalin summoned them to a meeting in the Kremlin in January 1941. The proposed textbook was impractical and overly theoretical, he told them. They had misconstrued the purpose of economic planning, which was, first, to ensure the independence of the economy under conditions of capitalist encirclement; second, to destroy the forces that could give rise to capitalism again; and, third, to deal with problems of disequilibrium in the economy. Stalin preferred practical observations of Soviet reality to abstract theories: 'If you search for an answer in Marx, you'll get off track. In the USSR you have a laboratory that has existed for more than twenty years. . . . You need to work with your own heads and not string together quotations.' The draft was too propagandistic and not scientific enough. Required was a textbook that would 'appeal to the mind'.[54]

Work on the textbook was disrupted by the war and postwar progress was slow, not least because the economists were afraid of political missteps: they preferred to be told by Stalin what they should write. Not until late 1949 did Stalin have a new draft to consider. At a meeting with his economists in April 1950, he said it required serious correction in both tone and substance. He wanted a textbook that was more historical, more geared to less educated people, a book that would be 'more approachable', wherein 'little by little the reader comes to understand the laws of economic development'. This was important because:

Our cadres need to know Marxist theory well. The first, older generation of Bolsheviks was well grounded. We memorised *Capital*, summarised, argued and tested one another. . . . The second generation was less prepared. People were busy with practical work and construction. They studied Marxism through brochures. The third generation has been raised on pamphlets and newspaper articles. They don't have a deep understanding of Marxism. They must be given food that is easily digestible.

There were too 'many babbling, empty and unnecessary words and many historical excursions', he said. 'I read 100 pages and crossed out 10 and could have crossed out even more. There shouldn't be a single extra word in a textbook. The descriptions should be like polished sculpture. . . . The literary side of the textbook is poorly developed.'

At yet another meeting a month or so later, Stalin instructed his economists to 'imagine the audience for whom you are writing. Don't imagine beginners. Instead keep in mind people who have finished eighth to tenth grade.' Further: 'The textbook is intended for millions of people. It will be read and studied not only here, but all over the world. It will be read by Americans and Chinese, and it will be studied in all countries. You need to keep in mind a more qualified audience.'[55]

Stalin did his usual detailed editing job and in January 1951 the economists presented him with another revised and rewritten draft. The saga continued with the circulation of nearly 250 copies of the draft textbook to economists and key party cadres. At a gathering to discuss this draft, some 110 speeches were made. Stalin pored over the hundreds of pages of the meeting's transcripts.[56] Like many of his library books, they are littered with his underlinings, margin lines, crossed-through paragraphs, question marks, NBs (scores of them), yes, no, so, not so, nonsense, stupid, ha ha and numerous other markings.[57]

In his first extended theoretical discourse on economic matters since the late 1920s, Stalin responded to what he read by composing some 'Remarks on Economic Questions Connected with the November 1951 Discussion'. Some 3,000 copies of these remarks were circulated within the party but he resisted wider publication, saying it would undermine the authority of the textbook. His remarks prompted many comments and queries, including three letters from economists to which he chose to reply. Those replies, together with his original 'Remarks', were published by *Pravda* under the collective title *Economic Problems of Socialism in the USSR*.[58]

Economic Problems was published in October 1952, on the eve of the 19th party congress. It was Stalin's first significant ideological outing since *Marxism and the Linguistic Question* in 1950 and was of more interest to the average Soviet citizen than his critique of the long-dead Marr's obscure theory of language. Like Stalin's linguistics intervention, *Economic Problems* was a model of clarity, sometimes tediously so in its more technical sections on commodity production, the law of value and the abolition of the antithesis between mental and physical labour. However, Stalin disregarded his own advice to the economists that they should stick to practical observations and stay away from abstract theorising.

While the ageing dictator retained considerable intellectual powers, his comments showed the stagnation of his thinking. His argument that there are objective laws of political economy which operate independently of human will was essentially no different from the position he had staked out in *Anarchism or Socialism?* and *Dialectical and Historical Materialism*. According to Stalin, social action could constrain economic laws but it couldn't change, override or abolish them, not even under socialism. Under capitalism the fundamental law of political economy was commodity production for profit; under socialism it was production for common welfare. The over-arching law of political economy was that the development of the forces of production determined history's direction towards socialism because that was the only system in which they could achieve their full potential.

Stalin's explanation for the continued existence of capitalism – a system whose private property relations were said to constrain the development of the productive forces – was that powerful interests blocked progress to socialism. That's why political action was required to change the status quo. The problem with this argument was that it highlighted the importance in human affairs of politics, not economics.

The knots into which Stalin tied himself to defend his position are best illustrated by the section on the 'Inevitability of War Between Capitalist Countries', provoked by Eugen Varga's contribution to the textbook discussion. Varga (1879–1964) was a Hungarian-born economist who for many years ran an influential Soviet think tank, the Institute of World Economy and World Politics.[59] He questioned the validity of 'Lenin's thesis on the inevitability of war between imperialist countries', suggesting it no longer applied because of the evident damage to capitalist interests caused by two world wars and because US domination of the imperialist order precluded the possibility of a major inter-capitalist war.[60]

Stalin did not name Varga but wrote vaguely of 'some comrades' who were wrong to question Lenin's thesis, because, he averred, 'profound forces' continued to operate and that meant war was inevitable. Particular wars could be averted by the struggle for peace but not war in general. So, according to Stalin's abstruse reasoning, war was inevitable but it might never happen. A more cogent hypothesis was that put forward in 1956 by his successor, Nikita Khrushchev: there was a *tendency* to war under capitalism but it was an eventuality that could be prevented by political struggle. Because of the strength of socialism and the forces for peace, said Khrushchev, war was no longer inevitable, which was a highly comforting thought in an age of nuclear weapons.

The statistician L. D. Yaroshenko (1896–1995) was another of Stalin's targets. Yaroshenko argued that the prime task of economists in a socialist society was the scientific and technical development of the productive forces through the rational organisation of the whole economy.[61] In *Economic Problems*, Stalin named and shamed Yaroshenko at length, insisting the political economy of socialism concerned the relations of production and their relationship to the productive forces. In other words, socialist political economy remained a science of the underlying laws of economic development, not a methodology for socialist planning.

For his 'unmarxian' sins, Yaroshenko was excluded from the party, arrested, imprisoned and then, after Stalin's death, released, rehabilitated and readmitted. The *Political Economy* textbook published in 1954 reflected Stalin's fundamentalist view, but post-Stalin Soviet economics was overwhelmingly focused on the task identified by Yaroshenko: how to improve planning to make socialism more economically productive and better able to meet the economic needs of state and society. Stalin's focus on scientific economic laws became increasingly irrelevant in Soviet economic discourse, and his last writings little more than a historical curiosity.[62]

Stalin's legacy for the economic study of capitalism was just as woeful, as Richard B. Day explained:

> He left behind a community of researchers whose thinking was frozen in analogies from the 1930s. The capitalist countries were entering one of the longest periods of economic growth in history; the Stalinist view held that they were languishing in a chronic depression. . . . Working class living standards would soon surpass anything imaginable in the 1930s; Stalinists predicted absolute impoverishment and unemployment for tens of millions. Capitalist countries were incorporating welfare-state measures into the fabric of modern life; Stalinist doctrine claimed that control of the state by the monopolies and their reactionary political agents inevitably produced a one-sided war economy.[63]

All these examples of Stalin as editor show that he was a Bolshevik first and an intellectual second. In theory, he stood for truth and intellectual rigour. In practice, his beliefs were politically driven dogma. He extolled the rigours of historical science but put them aside when it was expedient to do so. He thought Marxist philosophy was both rational and empirically verifiable but its ontological foundations were beyond questioning. Marxism-Leninism was, he claimed, a creative approach to understanding the world, a guide to practice and an instrument of progressive change, but unwavering was his fundamentalist belief that socialism was inevitable as well as desirable.

Stalin's unremitting pursuit of socialism and communism enabled his greatest achievements but at the cost of equally great misdeeds. Had he been more intellectual and less Bolshevik, he might have moderated his actions and achieved more at less cost to humanity.

CONCLUSION
The Dictator Who Loved Books

'I saw no less than five or six different Stalins,' recalled the dictator's loyal lieutenant, Lazar Kaganovich, in conversation with the Soviet writer Felix Chuev.
The postwar Stalin was different from the prewar person, said Kaganovich, and
before 1932 [the year Nadya committed suicide] he was somebody else entirely.
But he backtracked when Chuev asked him how Stalin was different. 'He was
different but he was one,' replied Kaganovich. He was tough, resolute and calm,
a self-controlled person who never said anything without first thinking things
over. 'Always I saw him thinking. He talked to you but he was always thinking,
always purposeful.'[1]

The idea that Stalin was a man of many parts and faces – what the Russians
call a *litsedei* – is a staple of his biography.[2] Revolutionary, state-builder, moderniser, monster, genius, genocidaire, warlord – these are just a few of his featured
lives.[3] Concluding his magnificent biography of the young Stalin, Ronald Suny
was at pains to distinguish the youthful idealist that populates most of his book's
many pages from the power-mad politician of the post-revolutionary years.[4] Yet
the story of Stalin's life as an intellectual is one of continuity. The young Stalin
and the mature man are recognisably the same person. Stalin read and marked
books in 1952 in much the same way he did in 1922 – actively, methodically and
with feeling. The same is true of Stalin the writer. 'In his first essays written for
the clandestine Georgian paper *Brdzola*', wrote Isaac Deutscher in 1947, 'one
finds already almost the same range of ideas, the same method of exposition,
the same style that would be characteristic for Stalin even thirty years later.'[5]

Books drew Stalin to the revolution and reading remained essential to his
autonomy as a political actor. As Suny showed so well, Stalin's intellectual and
political loyalty to Lenin was a matter of conviction, not faith. He read Lenin
and his critics and came to his own conclusions. His rationale for Bolshevik

CONCLUSION

violence, repression and authoritarianism was deeply flawed but it was his own, and it was rooted in reason. That's why he read Kautsky's critique of Bolshevism as well as Lenin's and Trotsky's defences of the new Soviet regime.

Stalin was a Marxist fundamentalist but some of his ideas did evolve in response to changing circumstances, new experiences and accumulated knowledge. The construction of the world's first socialist society was for him an intellectual as well as a practical project. Theorisation and strategisation were as important as policy detail. As party leader he was inundated with briefings and documentation, but more often than not it was extra-curricular reading that guided his responses to the challenges of building and defending Soviet socialism.

Stalin's adoption of the doctrine of socialism in one country in the mid-1920s is inexplicable without reference to his reading and interpretation of Lenin's writings, as well as his careful critique of the opposing views of Trotsky and Zinoviev. As consequential was his rereading of the lessons of Russian history. Defence of the Tsarist-created Russian state was a central task of Soviet communists by the mid-1930s. Stalin mobilised Russian cultural and historical traditions and embraced the concept of a Russocentric state based on 'the friendship of the Soviet peoples'. Popular history textbooks he helped to produce played a significant role in fostering Soviet patriotism.

During the Russian Civil War, Stalin shared Lenin's apocalyptic vision of a cataclysmic clash between socialism and capitalism. But when the civil war ended in Bolshevik victory, they both changed their minds about the possibilities of peaceful co-existence with the imperialists. The Soviets began to practise diplomacy and Stalin started to read about it. The Bolsheviks framed their diplomatic tactics as the 'exploitation of inter-imperialist contradictions', but Stalin was also attracted to the memoirs of that conservative master of realpolitik, Otto von Bismarck. At the same time, the threat of war continued to loom large and Stalin remained preoccupied by the danger of internal and external enemies forming an unholy alliance against him. The murderous mass repressions of the 1930s were driven by his perception of a dire existential threat to the Soviet state.

Stalin's interest in military affairs was a constant and he put his reading of military history and strategic theory to good use during the Second World War. Above all, it provided perspective and enabled him to take a bird's-eye view of the Soviet war effort. Stalin's generals marvelled at his strategic acumen and his deep understanding of modern warfare, the defeats and disasters of the early years of the Great Patriotic War notwithstanding.

Words were among Stalin's most potent weapons during the cold war and he personally rewrote the Soviet counterblast to western propagandising about his short-lived pact with Hitler.

Precisely because ideas were so important to him, he was reluctant to relinquish the doctrine of the inevitability of war under capitalism. But he did reduce it to a theory of little practical significance. Nor did this ideological orthodoxy prevent him from presiding over a massive communist-led peace movement whose *raison d'être* was that, in the nuclear age, war was not and could not be allowed to become inevitable.[6]

Stalin's views on roads to revolution underwent a fundamental transformation from the mid-1930s onwards when the Comintern prioritised anti-fascist unity and began to embrace the idea of a gradual, democratic transition to socialism. 'Today socialism is possible even under the English monarchy,' he told Yugoslavia's Marshal Tito in March 1945. 'Revolution in no longer necessary everywhere.' In May 1946 Poland's communist leaders were informed that 'Lenin never said there was no path to socialism other than the dictatorship of the proletariat,' he admitted that it was possible to arrive at the path to socialism utilising the foundations of the bourgeois democratic system such as Parliament'. Czechoslovakia's communist leader, Klement Gottwald, reported Stalin as saying in July 1946 that 'experience shows . . . there is not one path to the Soviet system and the dictatorship of the proletariat. . . . After the defeat of Hitler's Germany . . . there appeared many possibilities and paths open to the socialist movement.'[7]

Literature was another arena of patriotic mobilisation for Stalin, especially after the Second World War, when he became impatient of foreign influences on Soviet fiction. Promoting patriotism was also at the forefront of his various interventions in postwar scientific debates. Orchestrating discussion of the new *Political Economy* textbook proved to be his last effort to shape Soviet discourse on a matter of vital importance to the socialist system. It was a less than successful exercise but it showed how to the very end of his life he was grappling with the problems and challenges of the economics of socialism.

After his death the Soviet Union relaunched itself as far less violent, repressive and ideologically orthodox. Yet it remained recognisably Stalin's system – governed by ideas and led by people whose politics were framed by Marxist-Leninist theory. No post-Stalin Soviet leader was as intellectual as he was, but to one degree or another they all shared his love of reading, as did millions upon millions of their compatriots. The Bolsheviks failed to revolutionise people's consciousness, but their book culture continued to flourish. Its marks and traces linger on in contemporary Russia, not least in the archival remnants of Stalin's library.

NOTES

INTRODUCTION: THE KREMLIN SCHOLAR

1. D. Shepilov, *The Kremlin's Scholar*, Yale University Press: London & New Haven 2014 pp.2–3, 6; J. Rubenstein, *The Last Days of Stalin*, Yale University Press: London & New Haven 2016 chap.1.
2. The Russian title of Shepilov's memoir was *Neprimknyvshii*, literally: not-joined – a reference to his association with but non-membership of the Molotov-led group on the Presidium (Politburo) that tried to overthrow Khrushchev in 1957.
3. On Stalin's efforts at learning English, French and German, see M. Kun, *Stalin: An Unknown Portrait*, CEU Press: Budapest 2003 chap.8. In a party registration questionnaire dated October 1921, Stalin stated he could speak German as well as Georgian and Russian but this seems to have been an exaggeration. (Rossiiskii Gosudarstvennyi Arkhiv Sotsial'no-Politicheskoi Istorii (hereafter RGASPI), F.558, Op.4, D.333, L.1.)
4. D. Rayfield, *Stalin and His Hangmen*, Viking: London 2004 p.44.
5. S. Alliluyeva, *20 Letters to a Friend*, Penguin: Harmondsworth 1968 p.187.
6. S. Fitzpatrick, *The Commissariat of Enlightenment: Soviet Organisation of Education and the Arts under Lunacharsky*, Cambridge University Press: Cambridge 1970 pp.1–2.

CHAPTER 1: BLOODY TYRANT AND BOOKWORM

1. I. Deutscher, *Stalin: A Political Biography*, 2nd edn, Penguin: Harmondsworth 1966 p.44.
2. A. Alvarez, *Under Pressure: The Writer in Society: Eastern Europe and the USA*, Penguin: London 1965 p.11.
3. See D. Priestland, 'Stalin as Bolshevik Romantic: Ideology and Mobilisation, 1917–1939' in S. Davies & J. Harris (eds), *Stalin: A New History*, Cambridge University Press: Cambridge 2005.
4. E. van Ree, 'Heroes and Merchants: Stalin's Understanding of National Character', *Kritika*, 8/1 (Winter 2007) p.62.
5. Cited by P. Hollander, *Political Pilgrims: Western Intellectuals in Search of the Good Society*, Transaction Publishers: New Brunswick NJ 1998 p.xxxv.
6. J. Brent & V. P. Naumov, *Stalin's Last Crime: The Plot Against the Jewish Doctors, 1948–1953*, HarperCollins: New York 2003.
7. *Intelligent* – a member of the intelligentsia, the educated stratum of society engaged in intellectual, critical or creative work. The Bolsheviks believed that the role of the radical section of the intelligentsia should be to teach and lead the working class and its peasant allies towards its historic mission of overthrowing capitalism and replacing it with socialism. Stalin never referred to himself as an *intelligent* or an intellectual. His self-definition was

political: he was a Marxist and a revolutionary socialist. In Soviet times the concept of the intelligentsia was broadened to include administrative and technical cadres, the group as a whole being deemed an ally of the working class and the peasantry in the building of socialism. My use of the term 'intellectual' in this book is purely descriptive.

8. For a summary of reports of the fiction read by the young Stalin, see I. R. Makaryk, 'Stalin and Shakespeare' in N. Khomenko (ed.), *The Shakespeare International Yearbook*, vol. 18, Special Section on Soviet Shakespeare, Routledge: London July 2020 p.46. I am grateful to Professor Makaryk for a copy of her article.

9. Cited by E. van Ree, *The Political Thought of Joseph Stalin*, Routledge: London 2002 p.186.

10. A. Sergeev & E. Glushik, *Besedy o Staline*, Krymskii Most: Moscow 2006 pp.55–7. Sergeev was the son of an Old Bolshevik who died in a train accident in 1921. Adopted by Stalin, he was a companion and friend of Vasily's. His memoirs derive from conversations with the co-author of the book cited here.

11. Another Kipling fan, President Vladimir Putin referenced *The Jungle Book* in his annual address to the Russian Federation in April 2021 when he mentioned Tabaquis the jackal, and Shere Khan the tiger, warning other countries that they shouldn't treat Russia like these two treated other animals in Kipling's fairy tale, http://en.kremlin.ru/events/president/news/65418. Accessed 4 August 2021.

12. A. Sergeev & E. Glushik, *Kak Zhil, Rabotal i Vospityval Detei I. V. Stalin*, Krymskii Most: Moscow 2011 p.18. Stalin's inscription was drawn to my attention by Yuri Slezkine's *The House of Government: A Saga of the Russian Revolution*, Princeton University Press: Princeton 2019 p.611. Slezkine's book is the history of a building complex across the river from the Kremlin that housed government officials and other members of the Soviet elite. Artem Sergeev lived there with his mother when he wasn't staying with Stalin.

13. Rossiiskii Gosudarstvennyi Arkhiv Sotsial'no-Politicheskoi Istorii (hereafter RGASPI), F.558, Op.3, D.52.

14. Yu. G. Murin (ed.), *Iosif Stalin v Ob"yatiyakh Sem'i*, Rodina: Moscow 1993 doc.84.

15. D. Brandenberger & M. Zelenov (eds), *Stalin's Master Narrative: A Critical Edition of the History of the Communist Party of the Soviet Union (Bolsheviks): Short Course*, Yale University Press: London & New Haven 2019.

16. RGASPI, F.558, Op.3, D.76.The book was inscribed 'To Vasya from Stalin'.

17. Murin (ed.), *Iosif Stalin v Ob"yatiyakh Sem'i*, doc.94. Vasily joined the air force in 1940 and rose to the rank of general. After Stalin's death he was arrested for anti-Soviet slander and misappropriation of state funds and sentenced to eight years in prison. He spent the rest of his life in and out of gaol. Like his paternal grandfather Beso Dzhugashvili, he had a drink problem and died of causes related to alcohol abuse in 1962, a few days short of his forty-first birthday.

18. S. Alliluyeva, *Only One Year*, Penguin: London 1971 p.318.

19. Twenty or so of Svetlana's books may be found in Moscow's Gosudarstvennaya Obshchestvenno-Politicheskaya Biblioteka (State Socio-Political Library – hereafter SSPL) as part of a collection of books from Stalin's personal library, which the dictator himself did not mark. Many of her books contain *pometki* similar to her father's, including the interjections 'wrong', 'nonsense' and 'ha, ha, ha!', which she wrote in the margin of Lenin's hallowed text on materialist philosophy.

20. Quoted by R. Debray, 'Socialism: A Life-Cycle', *New Left Review*, 46 (July–August 2007).

21. K. Clark, *Moscow, The Fourth Rome: Stalinism, Cosmopolitanism, and the Evolution of Soviet Culture*, Harvard University Press: Cambridge MA 2011 p.13.

22. *Literaturnaya Gazeta*, 17 August 1934. My citation is from RGASPI, F.71, Op.10, D.170, L.162.

23. S. Lovell, *The Russian Reading Revolution: Print Culture in the Soviet and Post-Soviet Eras*, Palgrave Macmillan: London 2000 p.12.

24. M. David-Fox, *Revolution of the Mind: Higher Learning among the Bolsheviks, 1918–1929*, Cornell University Press: Ithaca NY & London 1997.

25. J. Pateman, 'Lenin on Library Organisation in Socialist Society', *Library & Information History*, 35/2 (2019). I am grateful to the author for a copy of his article. Statistics are

from E. Shishmareva and I. Malin, 'The Story of Soviet Libraries', *USSR* [information bulletin of the Soviet embassy in the USA], 6/53 (24 July 1946).

26. S. McMeekin, *Stalin's War*, Allen Lane: London 2021 p.625.
27. D. Fainberg, *Cold War Correspondents: Soviet and American Reporters on the Ideological Frontlines*, Johns Hopkins University Press: Baltimore 2020 p.50.
28. P. Kenez, *The Birth of the Propaganda State: Soviet Methods of Mass Mobilization, 1917–1929*, Cambridge University Press: Cambridge 1985 p.249.
29. P. Corrigan, 'Walking the Razor's Edge: The Origins of Soviet Censorship' in L. Douds, J. Harris & P. Whitewood (eds), *The Fate of the Bolshevik Revolution: Illiberal Liberation, 1917–41*, Bloomsbury Academic: London 2020 p.209.
30. A. Kemp-Welch, *Stalin and the Literary Intelligentsia, 1928–1939*, St Martin's Press: New York 1991 p.19.
31. H. Ermolaev, *Censorship in Soviet Literature, 1917–1991*, Rowman & Littlefield: Lanham MD 1997 p.57.
32. J. Arch Getty & O. V. Naumov, *The Road to Terror: Stalin and the Self-Destruction of the Bolsheviks, 1932–1939*, Yale University Press: London & New Haven 1999 docs16 & 44.
33. V. S. Astrakhanskii, 'Biblioteka G. K. Zhukova', *Arkhivno-Informatsionnyi Byulleten'*, 13 (1996); Alliluyeva, *Only One Year*, p.348.
34. S. Alliluyeva, *20 Letters to a Friend*, Penguin: Harmondsworth 1968 pp.150–1.
35. Molotov's grandson, Vyacheslav Nikonov, a prominent pro-Putin political commentator in post-Soviet Russia, wrote a two-volume biography of him: *Molotov*, Molodaya Gvardiya: Moscow 2016. A popular, abridged version has been published in French: *Molotov: notre cause est juste*, L'Harmattan: Paris 2020.
36. R. Polonsky, *Molotov's Magic Lantern*, Faber and Faber: London 2010 chap.2.
37. On Molotov: G. Roberts, *Molotov: Stalin's Cold Warrior*, Potomac Books: Washington DC 2012.
38. J. Brent, *Inside the Stalin Archives*, Atlas & Co.: New York 2008 pp.299–302.
39. Stalin's letters to his mother, wife and children may be found in Murin (ed.), *Iosif Stalin v Ob"yatiyakh Sem'i*.
40. S. Kotkin, *Stalin: Paradoxes of Power, 1878–1928*, Allen Lane: London 2014 p.597.
41. H. Kuromiya, *Stalin*, Pearson: Harlow 2005 p.137.
42. A. Werth, *Russia: The Post-War Years*, Robert Hale: London 1971 p.250.
43. RGASPI F.558, Op.3, D.46, L.15.

CHAPTER 2: THE SEARCH FOR THE STALIN BIOGRAPHERS' STONE

1. Stalin's staff kept a diary of visitors to his Kremlin office from 1924 to 1953 but not those to his apartment, dachas or elsewhere in the Kremlin: *Na Prieme u Stalina: Tetradi (Zhurnaly) Zapisei Lits, Prinyatykh I. V. Stalinym (1924–1953)*, Novyi Khronograf: Moscow 2008.
2. Cited by R. H. McNeal, *Stalin: Man and Ruler*, Macmillan: London 1989 p.9 (Papermac edition).
3. https://www.marxists.org/reference/archive/stalin/works/1931/dec/13a.htm. Accessed 4 August 2021. Not long after the interview, Stalin was asked about his impression of Ludwig. He replied: 'Nedalekii chelovek' (a dull man); *Mezhdu Molotom i Nakoval'nei: Soyuz Sovetskikh Pisatelei SSSR*, 1, Rosspen: Moscow 2010 p.156.
4. Recalled by Bulgakov's widow in a conversation with Edvard Radzinsky in the 1960s. E. Radzinsky, *Stalin*, Sceptre Books: London 1997 pp.9–11. Elena Bulgakova's recollection was recorded by Radzinsky in his diary.
5. G. Safarov, *Taktika Bol'shevizma: Osnovnye Etapy Razvitiya Taktiki R.K.P.*, Priboi: Petrograd 1923. Rossiiskii Gosudarstvennyi Arkhiv Sotsial'no-Politicheskoi Istorii (hereafter RGASPI), F.558. Op.3, D.309. Lenin volumes: Dd.115–18; Stalin volume: D.324. Safarov signed the resolution on the shooting of the Tsar and his family in July 1918. In the 1920s he was a member of the opposition to Stalin within the Bolshevik party and in the 1930s a victim of the purges. He was executed in the Gulag in 1942.
6. https://revolutionarydemocracy.org/rdv12n2/cpi2.htm. Accessed 4 August 2021.

7. Cited in M. Folly, G. Roberts & O. Rzheshevsky, *Churchill and Stalin: Comrades-in-Arms During the Second World War*, Pen & Sword Books: Barnsley 2019 pp.1–2.

8. R. G. Suny, *Stalin: Passage to Revolution*, Princeton University Press: Princeton 2020 p.2.

9. RGASPI, F.558, Op.1, D.4507. Stalin seems to have written 1879 and then changed the 9 to an 8, as if he wasn't sure himself. An article based on the questionnaire was published in the Swedish social democratic newspaper *Folkets Dagblad Politike* in August 1921.

10. Ibid., Op.4, D.333, L.1.

11. Ibid., Op.1, D.4343, Ll.1–3. See further: 'Kogda Rodilsya I. V. Stalin', *Izvestiya TsK KPSS*, 11 (1990) pp.132–4. 'Old-Style' and 'New-Style' refer to the change from the Julian to the Gregorian calendar after the Bolsheviks seized power, which meant that birth and other dates before January 1918 were twelve or thirteen days behind those of the new calendar.

12. On Tovstukha: N. E. Rosenfeldt, *The 'Special' World: Stalin's Power Apparatus and the Soviet System's Secret Structures of Communication*, Museum Tusculanum Press: Copenhagen 2009 passim; V. G. Mosolov, *IMEL: Tsitadel' Partiinoi Ortodoksii*, Novyi Khronograf: Moscow 2010 chap.3; V. A. Torchinov & A. M. Leontuk, *Vokrug Stalina: Istoriko-Biograficheskii Spravochnik*, Filologicheskii Fakul'tet Sankt-Peterburgskogo Gosudarstvennogo Universiteta: St Petersburg 2000 pp.481–3.

13. D. Brandenberger, *Propaganda State in Crisis: Soviet Ideology, Indoctrination and Terror under Stalin, 1927–1941*, Yale University Press: London & New Haven 2011 p.55. An English translation of Tovstukha's dictionary piece may found in G. Haupt & J-J. Marie (eds), *Makers of the Russian Revolution: Biographies of Bolshevik Leaders*, Allen & Unwin: London 1974 pp.65–75. This book also contains translations of the other *Granat* biographies of top Bolsheviks.

14. 'Reply to the Greetings of the Workers in the Chief Railway Workshops in Tiflis' in J. V. Stalin, *Works*, vol.8, Foreign Languages Publishing House: Moscow 1954 pp.182–4 (emphasis added). This speech and its religious connotations were brought to my attention by A. J. Rieber, 'Stalin: Man of the Borderlands', *American Historical Review* (December 2001) p.1673.

15. S. Alliluyeva, *20 Letters to a Friend*, Penguin: Harmondsworth 1968 p.35. My downplaying of the significance of Stalin's Georgian roots and identity would be contested by Alfred J. Rieber, Ronald Suny and many others.

16. Brandenberger, *Propaganda State in Crisis*, p.60.

17. J. Stalin, 'Some Questions Concerning the History of Bolshevism' in J. V. Stalin, *Works*, vol.13, Foreign Languages Publishing House: Moscow 1955 pp.86–104. On the letter and its background and broader consequences see J. Barber, *Soviet Historians in Crisis, 1928–1932*, Macmillan: London 1981 esp. chap.10.

18. Slutsky was arrested in 1937 and survived twenty years in the Gulag. He continued to work as a historian and published a book about Franz Mehring, Marx's first biographer. Employed in the 1960s by the Soviet Academy of Sciences' Institute for History, he died in 1979.

19. Stalin, *Works,* vol.13 p.99.

20. Ibid., pp.107–8.

21. See L. Yaresh, 'The Role of the Individual in History' in C. E. Black (ed.), *Rewriting Russian History*, Vintage: New York 1962.

22. J. Devlin, 'Beria and the Development of the Stalin Cult' in G. Roberts (ed.), *Stalin: His Times and Ours*, IAREES: Dublin 2005 pp.33–5. The copy of the book that Stalin marked may be viewed at RGASPI, F.558, Op.11, D.704. For an English translation of the 4th Russian edition of the book see L. Beria, *On the History of the Bolshevik Organizations in Transcaucasia*, Lawrence and Wishart: London n.d.

23. A. Sobanet, 'Henri Barbusse and Stalin's Official Biography' in his *Generation Stalin: French Writers, the Fatherland and the Cult of Personality*, Indiana University Press: Bloomington 2018 p.57.

24. *Bol'shaya Tsenzura: Pisateli i Zhurnalisty v Strane Sovetov, 1917–1956*, Demokratiya: Moscow 2005 doc.201.

25. Ibid., doc.200.

26. RGASPI, F.558, Op.11, D.699, doc.17. Also published in ibid., doc.256.

27. Sobanet, 'Henri Barbusse', pp.41, 83. At the time of his death Barbusse was working on a screenplay of Stalin's life.

28. Barbusse letter of February 1934. Cited by K. Morgan, 'Pseudo-Facts and Pseudo-Leaders: Henri Barbusse and the Dilemmas of Representing the Pre-War Stalin Cult' (forthcoming article).

29. H. Barbusse, *Stalin: A New World Seen Through One Man*, Macmillan: London 1935 pp.175–6.

30. Sobanet, 'Henri Barbusse', pp.86–7.

31. S. Davies & J. Harris, *Stalin's World: Dictating the Soviet Order*, Yale University Press: London & New Haven 2014 pp.149, 158–9.

32. Cited by D. Brandenberger, 'Stalin as Symbol: A Case Study of the Personality Cult and its Construction' in S. Davies & J. Harris (eds), *Stalin: A New History*, Cambridge University Press: Cambridge 2005 p.261.

33. The relevant documents may be found here: RGASPI, F.558, Op.11, D.1509. They are also published in *I. V. Stalin, Istoricheskaya Ideologiya v SSSR v 1920–1950-e gody*, Nauka-Piter: St Petersburg 2006 docs 226–9. This episode was brought to my attention by Davies & Harris, *Stalin's World*, pp.152–3.

34. The unfortunate Moskalev seems to have come to Stalin's notice again in 1942 as a result of a book he wrote about the dictator's period of exile in Siberia. Stalin apparently didn't like the book and it was withdrawn from publication. According to Simon Sebag Montefiore (*Young Stalin*, Weidenfeld & Nicolson: London 2007 p.241), Moskalev was commissioned to write the book by the then Krasnoyarsk party secretary, Konstantin Chernenko, who was destined to be the Soviet Union's penultimate leader. In the late 1940s Moskalev, who was Jewish, fell victim to the anti-cosmopolitan purge and was arrested. Rehabilitated after Stalin's death, he resumed work as a historian and published a number of books about early Bolshevik and Soviet history, including one about Lenin's exile in Siberia.

35. RGASPI, F558, Op.1, D.3226; Brandenberger, 'Stalin as Symbol', pp.262–3.

36. RGASPI, F558, Op.11, D.905, doc.4. This is the key file on the history of the publication of Stalin's *Works*. Many of the documents have been published in I. V. Stalin, *Trudy*, vol.1, Prometei Info: Moscow 2013.

37. Ibid., doc.6.

38. Many details may be found in S. Yu. Rychenkov, 'K Istorii Podgotovki Pervogo Izdaniya Sochinenii I. V. Stalina' in Stalin, *Trudy*, pp.274–302. On the purge of IMEL: Mosolov, *IMEL*, pp.312–41.

39. Stalin's selections and corrections may be viewed in RGASPI, F.558, Op.11, Dd.907 ff.

40. RGASPI, F.558, Op.11, D.941, doc.1. This twelve-page document, which IMEL sent to Stalin at the end of December 1945, concerned editorial changes to his writings for 1917–1920. It had three columns: in the left-hand column was the original text, in the middle column was the text proposed for publication, in the right-hand column there was space for explanation of the changes, though in the cited case no comment was deemed necessary. Most of the proposed changes were minor. The document was brought to my attention by Mosolov, *IMEL*, pp.442–3. The 1918 text as published may be found in J. Stalin, *Works*, vol.4, Foreign Languages Publishing House: Moscow 1953 pp.155–7.

41. Stalin, *Trudy*, pp.376–84.

42. Ibid., pp.385–406.

43. Ibid., pp.485–7.

44. Ibid., pp.506–11.

45. Stalin is referring to a strike and demonstration in Batumi in March 1902 that resulted in bloodshed when the authorities opened fire and killed thirteen protesters and wounded many more.

46. 'Na Priemu u I. V. Stalina: Zapis' V. D. Mochalova' in Stalin, *Trudy*, pp.512–22. It is not clear when Mochalov wrote up his report. The time, place and duration of the meeting recorded by Mochalov is confirmed by Stalin's appointments diary: *Na Prieme u Stalina* p.465. Post-IMEL, Mochalov, who died in 1970, had a distinguished academic career, including serving as chief editor of one the top Soviet history journals, *Istoriya SSSR*.

47. Konushaya's memoir may be found in I. V. Stalin, *Sochineniya*, vol.16, Pisatel': Moscow 1997 pp.231–6.
48. Cited by Mosolov, *IMEL*, p.439.
49. RGASPI, F.558 Op.11, D.906, Ll.7–8, 25ff.
50. J. Stalin, *Works*, vol. 1, Foreign Languages Publishing House: Moscow 1952 pp.xvii–xxi.
51. RGASPI, F.558, Op.11, Dd.1221–5; Brandenberger, *Propaganda State*, p.255.
52. Stalin's response to Ribbentrop was specifically listed for exclusion from his works: RGASPI, F.71, Op.10, D.170, L.162.
53. See G. Roberts, 'Stalin, the Pact with Nazi Germany and the Origins of Postwar Soviet Diplomatic Historiography: A Research Note', *Journal of Cold War Studies*, 4/4 (Fall 2002), and V. Pechatnov, 'How Soviet Cold Warriors Viewed World War II: The Inside Story of the 1957 Edition of the Big Three Correspondence', *Cold War History*, 14/1 (2014).
54. R. H. McNeal, *Stalin's Works: An Annotated Bibliography*, Hoover Institution: Stanford CA 1967 p.16.
55. See RGASPI, F.558, Op.11, Dd.1100 ff.
56. O. Edel'man, *Stalin, Koba i Soso: Molodoi Stalin v Istoricheskikh Istochnikakh*, Izdatel'skii Dom Vysshei Shkoly Ekonomiki: Moscow 2016 p.74.
57. McNeal's Introduction to J. F. Matlock, *An Index to the Collected Works of J. V. Stalin*, Johnson Reprint Corporation: New York 1971 p.v. Matlock was US ambassador to Moscow, 1987–91.

CHAPTER 3: READING, WRITING AND REVOLUTION

1. R. G. Suny, *Stalin: Passage to Revolution*, Princeton University Press: Princeton 2020 pp.26–7.
2. R. G. Suny, 'Beyond Psychohistory: The Young Stalin in Georgia', *Slavic Review*, 50/1 (Spring 1991) p.52.
3. R. Brackman, *The Secret File of Joseph Stalin: A Hidden Life*, Frank Cass: London 2001. For a summary: R. Brackman, 'Stalin's Greatest Secret', *Times Higher Education Supplement* (26 April 2001).
4. R. C. Tucker, 'A Stalin Biographer's Memoir' in S. Baron & C. Pletsch (eds), *Introspection in Biography*, Routledge: New York 1985.
5. 'Rech' Stalina I. V. na Soveshchanii Komandnogo Sostava', 22 March 1938, Rossiiskii Gosudarstvennyi Arkhiv Sotsial'no-Politicheskoi Istorii (hereafter RGASPI), F.558, Op.11, D.1121, Ll.49–50. Stalin told another version of his father's story in an early article as an illustration of how a former shoemaker fallen on hard times could acquire working-class consciousness (J. Stalin, *Works*, vol.1, Foreign Languages Publishing House: Moscow 1952 pp.317–18).
6. S. Kotkin, *Stalin: Paradoxes of Power, 1878–1928*, Allen Lane: London 2014 pp.21, 26.
7. *My Dear Son: The Memoirs of Stalin's Mother* (Kindle edition).
8. R. H. McNeal, *Stalin: Man and Ruler*, Macmillan: London 1988 p.4; I. Deutscher, *Stalin: A Political Biography*, Penguin: Harmondsworth 1966 p.36. The informant was G. Glurdzhidze, who was a teacher in Gori at the time he was interviewed about Stalin's childhood in 1939.
9. RGASPI, F.558, Op.4, D.5; O. Khlevniuk, *Stalin: New Biography of a Dictator*, Yale University Press: London & New Haven 2015 p.15.
10. R. Service, *Stalin: A Biography*, Macmillan: London 2004 p.35.
11. RGASPI, F.558, Op.4, D.600. The texts (in Russian) may also be found in I. Stalin, *Sochineniya*, vol.17, Severnaya Korona: Tver' 2004 pp.1–6. For translation of some extracts, including the one cited here, see Suny, *Stalin: Passage to Revolution*, pp.57–9.
12. Suny, ibid., pp.64–6.
13. Deutscher, *Stalin: A Political Biography*, p.37.
14. A. J. Rieber, 'Stalin as Georgian: The Formative Years' in S. Davies & J. Harris (eds), *Stalin: A New History*, Cambridge University Press: Cambridge 2005 p.36.
15. According to the 1922 chronology prepared by his staff, Stalin was excluded from the seminary for 'unreliability'.

16. RGASPI, F.558, Op.4, D.65; M. Kun, *Stalin: An Unknown Portrait*, CEU Press: Budapest 2003 p.31.
17. J. Stalin, *Works*, vol.2, Foreign Languages Publishing House: Moscow 1953, p.368.
18. Cited by R. Boer, 'Religion and Socialism: A. V. Lunacharsky and the God-Builders', *Political Theology*, 15/2 (March 2014) p.205. See also S. Fitzpatrick, *The Commissariat of Enlightenment: Soviet Organisation of Education and the Arts under Lunacharsky*, Cambridge University Press: Cambridge 1970 pp.4–5. For context and the relationship between the contemporaneous 'God-seeking' and 'God-building' movements see E. Clowes, 'From Beyond the Abyss: Nietzschean Myth in Zamiatin's "We" and Pasternak's "Doctor Zhivago"' in B. Glatzer Rosenthal (ed.), *Nietzsche and Soviet Culture*, Cambridge University Press: Cambridge 1994.
19. He may have read a review of the 1911 volume published in the January 1912 issue of the Bolshevik journal *Prosveshchenie* (Enlightenment) and underlined the reviewer's phrase that, for Lunacharsky, 'Marxism is a religion'. RGASPI, F.558, Op.3, D.274, p.86 of the journal. This copy of *Prosveshchenie* is one of nineteen in Stalin's library. Dating from 1911 to 1914, they contain quite a few scattered markings but, as Yevgeny Gromov pointed out, it is not certain that they all belong to Stalin (*Stalin: Iskusstvo i Vlast'*, Eksmo: Moscow 2003 p.59). The best bet is that the marking of several articles on Marxism and the National Question (including his own piece) are Stalin's. Certainly, these particular markings correspond to the arguments and points that Stalin subsequently made in discussions about this question. Boris Ilizarov (*Pochetnyi Akademik Stalin i Akademik Marr*, Veche: Moscow 2012 p.113) believes Stalin may have had these copies of the journal with him in Turukhansk and then brought them home with him, but more likely is that he obtained them soon after he returned to Petrograd from exile in 1917.
20. For detailed studies of Bolshevik policy on religion during the Stalin era, see I. A. Kurlyandskii, *Stalin, Vlast', Religiya*, Kuchkovo Pole: Moscow 2011, and A. Rokkuchchi, *Stalin i Patriarkh: Pravoslavnaya Tserkov' i Sovetskaya Vlast', 1917–1958*, Rosspen: Moscow 2016. Roccucci's (*sic*) book is also published in Italian: *Stalin e il Patriarca: La Chiesa Ortodossa e il Potere Sovietico*, Einaudi: Turin 2011.
21. See J. Ryan, 'Cleansing NEP Russia: State Violence Against the Russian Orthodox Church in 1922', *Europe-Asia Studies*, 65/9 (November 2013).
22. D. Peris, *Storming the Heavens: The Soviet League of the Militant Godless*, Cornell University Press: Ithaca NY 1998 p.39.
23. J. Stalin, *Works*, vol.10, Foreign Languages Publishing House: Moscow 1954 pp.138–9.
24. See L. H. Siegelbaum, *Soviet State and Society Between Revolutions, 1918–1929*, Cambridge University Press: Cambridge 1992.
25. V. Smolkin, *A Sacred Space Is Never Empty: A History of Soviet Atheism*, Princeton University Press: Princeton 2018 p.46.
26. Ibid., pp.47–9.
27. F. Corley (ed.), *Religion in the Soviet Union: An Archival Reader*, Macmillan: Basingstoke 1996 doc.89.
28. See Smolkin, *A Sacred Space is Never Empty*, chap.2.
29. R. Boer, 'Sergei and the "Divinely Appointed" Stalin', *Social Sciences* (April 2018) p.15.
30. Smolkin, *A Sacred Space is Never Empty*, p.53.
31. See S. Merritt Miner, *Stalin's Holy War: Religion, Nationalism and Alliance Politics, 1941–1945*, University of North Carolina Press: Chapel Hill 2003.
32. Ibid., p.6. See also Boer's *Stalin: From Theology to the Philosophy of Socialism in Power*, Springer: Singapore 2017.
33. J. Stalin, *Works*, vol.4, Foreign Languages Publishing House: Moscow 1953 p.406.
34. In relation to communism as a political religion I have followed closely the argument of Erik van Ree in his 'Stalinist Ritual and Belief System: Reflections on "Political Religion"', *Politics, Religion and Ideology*, 17/2–3 (June 2016).
35. I owe the Napoleon reference to Patrick Geoghegan's *Robert Emmet: A Life*, Four Courts Press: Dublin 2004. According to Donald Rayfield, Stalin wrote 'stupidity!' beside this remark in one of Konstantine Gamsakhurdia's historical novels: 'If brought up by the path of historical patriotism, we can make a Napoleon out of any bandit.' D. Rayfield, *Stalin and His Hangmen*, Viking: London 2004 p.16.

36. Stalin, *Works*, vol. 1, p.57.

37. See E. van Ree, 'The Stalinist Self: The Case of Ioseb Jughashvili (1898–1907)', *Kritika*, 11/2 (Spring 2010).

38. Suny, *Stalin: Passage to Revolution*, p.138. For the purposes of quotation, I have changed the order of this passage.

39. R. M. Slusser, *Stalin in October: The Man Who Missed the Revolution*, Johns Hopkins University Press: Baltimore 1987.

40. Stalin, *Works*, vol.1 pp.133–9.

41. S. Sebag Montefiore, *Young Stalin*, Weidenfeld & Nicolson: London 2007. For a more sober treatment of the Tbilisi robbery, see Suny, *Stalin: Passage to Revolution*, chap.17.

42. Cited by Suny in ibid., p.361.

43. L. Trotsky, *The Stalin School of Falsification*, Pioneer Publishers: New York 1962 p.181.

44. See J. Ryan, *Lenin's Terror: The Ideological Origins of Early Soviet State Violence*, Routledge: London 2012 chaps 1–2.

45. On the Malinovsky affair see I. Halfin, *Intimate Enemies: Demonizing the Bolshevik Opposition, 1918–1928*, University of Pittsburgh Press: Pittsburgh 2007 pp.1–17.

46. I. Deutscher, 'Writing a Biography of Stalin', *The Listener*, https://www.marxists.org /archive/deutscher/1947/writing-stalin.htm (25 December 1947).

47. See Suny, *Stalin: Passage to Revolution*, chap.23. Roy Medvedev suggests that later in life Stalin had trouble writing in Georgian and that this explains the paucity and brevity of his letters to his mother in the 1920s and 1930s. See his essay on 'Stalin's Mother' in R. & Z. Medvedev, *The Unknown Stalin: His Life, Death and Legacy*, Overlook Press: Woodstock NY 2004. At school and in the seminary Stalin studied ancient Greek but his command of that language is uncertain.

48. For a comprehensive collection of Stalin's writings on the national question, see J. Stalin, *Marxism and the National-Colonial Question*, Proletarian Publishers: San Francisco 1975.

49. For the view that Stalin's philosophical and political differences with Lenin were greater than suggested here see R. C. Williams, *The Other Bolsheviks: Lenin and His Critics, 1904–1914*, Indiana University Press: Bloomington 1986 pp.119–23.

50. Suny, *Stalin: Passage to Revolution*, pp.415–19.

51. For Onufrieva's testimony and the police reports on Stalin's library visits: RGASPI, F.558, Op.4, D.647, Ll.52–8. A copy of Stalin's dedication on the front page of the Kogan book may be found here: RGASPI, Op.1, D.32. I was drawn to this source by Y. Gromov, *Stalin: Iskusstvo i Vlast'*, Eksmo: Moscow 2003 pp.36–8. See also Suny, *Stalin: Passage to Revolution*, pp.465–7.

52. RGASPI, F.558, Op.4, D.138, Ll.3–5.

53. Stalin's letters may be found here: *Bol'shevistskoe Rukovodstvo: Perepiska, 1912–1927*, Rosspen: Moscow 1996. For many citations from these letters, see Suny, *Stalin: Passage to Revolution*, chap.24.

54. Stalin's marked copy of the 1938 edition may be found here: RGASPI, F.558, Op.3, D.251.

55. Service, *Stalin: A Biography*, p.128.

56. J. Stalin, *Works*, vol.3, Foreign Languages Publishing House: Moscow 1953 pp.199–200.

57. Suny, *Stalin: Passage to Revolution*, p.652.

58. The quote may be found in Trotsky's autobiography, *My Life*, https://www.marxists.org /archive/trotsky/1930/mylife/ch29.htm.

59. C. Read, *Stalin: From the Caucasus to the Kremlin*, Routledge: London 2017 p.40.

60. On the increasing authoritarianism of the Bolsheviks during their first year in power, see A. Rabinowitch, *The Bolsheviks in Power: The First Year of Soviet Rule in Petrograd*, Indiana University Press: Bloomington 2007.

61. McNeal, *Stalin: Man and Ruler*, p.63.

62. Read, *Stalin: From the Caucasus to the Kremlin*, p.71.

63. J. Stalin, *Works*, vol.4, Foreign Languages Publishing House: Moscow 1953 pp.351–2.

64. Khlevniuk, *Stalin: New Biography of a Dictator*, p.60.

65. Service, *Stalin: A Biography*, p.177.

66. I. Deutscher, *The Prophet Armed: Trotsky 1879–1921*, Oxford University Press: London 1970 p.467.

67. Stalin, *Sochineniya*, vol.17, pp.122–3.
68. Ibid., p.133. Budenny's memoirs of the civil war stopped short of this episode: S. Budyonny (*sic*), *The Path of Valour*, Progress Publishers: Moscow 1972.
69. W. J. Spahr, *Stalin's Lieutenants: A Study of Command under Duress*, Presidio Press: Novato CA 1997 p.145.
70. A. Seaton, *Stalin as Military Commander*, Combined Publishing: Conshohocken PA 1998 pp.76–7.
71. Stalin, *Works*, vol.4, pp.358–62.
72. Stalin, *Sochineniya*, vol.17, pp.135–6.
73. Kotkin, *Stalin: Paradoxes of Power*, pp.395–400.
74. The federation was dissolved into its constituent parts in 1936 as part of the reorganisation of the federal structure that accompanied the adoption of a new Soviet constitution.
75. Service, *Stalin: A Biography*, pp.186–90.
76. See L. Douds, *Inside Lenin's Government: Ideology, Power and Practice in the Early Soviet State*, Bloomsbury Academic: London 2018.
77. Ibid., pp.165–8.
78. For a sustained questioning of the assumption that Lenin was the author of the words attributed to him, see Kotkin, *Stalin: Paradoxes of Power*, chap.11. Kotkin's analysis is based mainly on the findings of the Russian historian Valentin Sakharov: *Politicheskoe Zaveshchanie Lenina: Real'nost' Istorii i Mify Politik*, Moskovskii Universitet 2003. For a completely different view, one which emphasises Stalin's manipulation of the text of the will and its presentation to the party, see Y. Buranov, *Lenin's Will: Falsified and Forbidden*, Prometheus Books: Amherst NY 1994.
79. https://www.marxists.org/history/etol/newspape/ni/vol02/no01/lenin.htm. Accessed 4 August 2021.
80. Cited by Read, *Stalin: From the Caucasus to the Kremlin*, p.102. The comment is said to have been occasioned by Stalin's rudeness to Lenin's wife.
81. Kotkin, *Stalin: Paradoxes of Power*, pp.528–9.
82. Buranov, *Lenin's Will*, p.201. Stalin repeated this point at the October 1927 plenum of the party but without quoting Lenin's Testament directly.
83. Stalin, *Works*, vol.10, p.53.
84. I. Banac (ed.), *The Diary of Georgi Dimitrov, 1933–1949*, Yale University Press: London & New Haven 2003 p.66.
85. J. Harris, 'Discipline versus Democracy: The 1923 Party Controversy' in L. Douds, J. Harris & P. Whitewood (eds), *The Fate of the Bolshevik Revolution: Illiberal Liberation, 1917–41*, Bloomsbury Academic: London 2020 p.111.
86. Interview with Barack Obama, *New York Times* (16 January 2017); rbth.com. Accessed 30 August 2021.

CHAPTER 4: THE LIFE AND FATE OF A DICTATOR'S LIBRARY

1. Rossiiskii Gosudarstvennyi Arkhiv Sotsial'no-Politicheskoi Istorii (hereafter RGASPI) F.558, Op.1, D.2510.
2. RGASPI, F.558, Op.3, Dd.273–4.
3. J. V. Stalin, *Concerning Marxism in Linguistics*, Soviet News Booklet: London 1950 pp.11–12, 20.
4. D. Volkogonov, *Triumf i Tragediya: Politicheskii Portret I. V. Stalina*, Book One, Part Two, Novosti: Moscow 1989 pp.118–20. In English: *Stalin: Triumph and Tragedy*, pb edition Phoenix Press: London 2000 pp.225–6.
5. Donald Rayfield states that Stalin's classification scheme was prompted by his wife Nadezhda Alliluyeva, who 'took the lead from Sergei Kirov, Stalin's satrap in Leningrad' and had a librarian classify and reshelve his books. 'Stalin was furious. He jotted down his own classification of books and had his secretary Alexander Poskrebyshev rearrange them accordingly.' (D. Rayfield, *Stalin and His Hangmen*, Viking: London 2004 p.21). Rayfield cites no source but it seems to derive from a memoir by the assassinated Kirov's widow, S. L. [Maria] Markus, who recalled that when she suggested to *her husband* that a librarian should tidy up *his books* he told her that when Stalin's wife had done the same

thing, he had not then been able to find anything! RGASPI, F.558, Op.4, D.649, L.213. This document was drawn to my attention by Y. Gromov, *Stalin: Iskusstvo i Vlast'*, Eksmo: Moscow 2003 p.59, which misprints the page number of the cited document as L.217.

6. RGASPI F.558, Op.1, D.2723. The existence of this note was drawn to my attention by M. Kun, *Stalin: An Unknown Portrait*, CEU Press: Budapest 2003 p.311 n.8.

7. RGASPI F.558, Op.1, D.2764.

8. *Ekslibrisy i Shtempeli Chastnykh Kollektsii v Fondakh Istoricheskoi Biblioteki*, GPIB: Moscow 2009 p.61. On the history of Russian bookplates and ex-libris stamps: W. E. Butler, 'The Ballard Collection of Russian Bookplates', *Yale University Library Gazette*, 60/3–4 (April 1986).

9. Sh. Manuchar'yants, *V Biblioteke Vladimira Il'icha*, 2nd edn, Politizdat: Moscow 1970 p.14.

10. B. Ilizarov, *Tainaya Zhizn' Stalina*, Veche: Moscow 2003 p.163. The source is a letter from Svetlana to the party leadership in 1955 in which she tried to claim ownership of her mother's books.

11. Cited by E. van Ree, *The Political Thought of Joseph Stalin*, Routledge: London 2002 p.120.

12. Cited by O. V. Khlevniuk, *Stalin: New Biography of a Dictator*, Yale University Press: London & New Haven 2015 p.96.

13. S. Kotkin, *Stalin: Paradoxes of Power, 1878–1928*, Allen Lane: London 2014 p.431.

14. Cited in R. Richardson, *The Long Shadow: Inside Stalin's Family*, Little, Brown & Co.: London 1993 p.85.

15. A. Sergeev & E. Glushik, *Besedy o Staline*, Krymskii Most: Moscow 2006 p.23.

16. 'Chuzhoi v Sem'e Stalina', *Rossiiskaya Gazeta* (12 June 2002). Morozov, who had a distinguished career as an academic specialising in international law, died in 2001.

17. A. H. Birse, *Memoirs of an Interpreter*, Michael Joseph: London 1967 p.103. Birse was with Churchill, and Stalin's bedroom was en route to a bathroom where the PM washed his hands.

18. D. Shepilov, *The Kremlin's Scholar*, Yale University Press: London & New Haven 2014 p.105.

19. S. Beria, *Beria, My Father*, Duckworth: London 2001 pp.142–3. This book, which is based on interviews Beria gave to the French historian Françoise Thom, is completely different to one with the same title that he published in Russian: S. Beria, *Moi Otets – Lavrentii Beriya*, Sovremennik: Moscow 1994.

20. A few of Stalin's books that he supposedly marked have no discernible markings. Could it be they had tags which have subsequently disintegrated or dropped out or were inadvertently removed by researchers?

21. Zh. & R. Medvedev, *Neizvestnyi Stalin*, 4th edn, Vremya: Moscow 2011 p.80. In English: R. & Z. Medvedev, *The Unknown Stalin*, Overlook Press: Woodstock NY 2004 p.97. The English translation states that the books were ordered from the 'Kremlin Library Service'. These words do not appear in any of the Russian editions of the book.

22. S. Lovell, *The Russian Reading Revolution: Print Culture in the Soviet and Post-Soviet Eras*, Palgrave Macmillan: Basingstoke 2000 p.27.

23. P. Kenez, *The Birth of the Propaganda State: Soviet Methods of Mass Mobilization, 1917–1929*, Cambridge University Press: Cambridge 1985 pp.239–47.

24. M. Viltsan, 'K Voprosu ob Intellekte Stalina', *Pravda-5 (Ezhenedel'naya Gazeta)* (27 September–4 October 1996).

25. W. J. Spahr, *Stalin's Lieutenants: A Study of Command under Duress*, Presidio Press: Novato CA 1997 pp.154–5. Spahr's reference is to a novel by the Soviet military journalist and writer Ivan Stadniuk, *Voina* (War), published in 1981. While the story rings true, there are no known copies of Shaposhnikov's book in Stalin's personal archive. Shaposhnikov's book was published in three volumes between 1927 and 1929 so the volume that we know Stalin received, presumably towards the end of 1926, must have been a pre-publication advance copy. Shaposhnikov met Stalin about what seems to have been a personal matter in June 1927 (RGASPI, F.558, Op.4, D.5853t, L.11). This out-of-sequence file may be found at the very end of *Opis' 4*.

26. N. Mandelstam, *Hope Against Hope: A Memoir*, Harvill Press: London 1999 p.26.

27. A. V. Ostrovskii, *Kto Stoyal za Spinoi Stalina?*, Olma-Press: St Petersburg 2002 p.155.

28. The archive document listing the seventy-two books was on display at an exhibition on the history of Stalin's *lichnyi fond* in the foyer of RGASPI in October 2018.

29. S. Alliluyeva, *20 Letters to a Friend*, Penguin: Harmondsworth 1968 pp.37–8.

30. R. Sullivan, *Stalin's Daughter*, Fourth Estate: London 2015 p.22.

31. Khlevniuk, *Stalin: New Biography of a Dictator*, p.252.

32. Their letters may be found in Yu. G. Murin (ed.), *Iosif Stalin v Ob"yatiyakh Sem'i*, Rodina: Moscow 1993 docs. 30–59.

33. On Polina: K. Schlögel, *The Scent of Empires: Chanel No.5 and Red Moscow*, Polity: London 2021 pp.96–125.

34. R. Lyuksemburg, *Vseobshchaya Zabastovka i Nemetskaya Sotsial-Demokratiya*, Kiev 1906. Stalin's copy: RGASPI, F.558, Op.3, D.196. Another book in Stalin's library, one that he marked in a few places, was this anti-Luxemburg tract: I. Narvskii, *K Istorii Bor'by Bol'shevizma s Luksemburgianstvom*, Partizdat: Moscow 1932 (D.227).

35. On gender relations at the top level of the party, see M. Delaloi (Delaloye), *Usy i Yubki: Gendernye Otnosheniya vnutri Kremlevskogo Kruga v Stalinskuyu Epokhu (1928–1953)*, Rosspen: Moscow 2018. A French variant of this book is the same author's *Une Histoire érotique du Kremlin*, Payot: Paris 2016. On Soviet policy on women: W. Z. Goldman, *Women, the State and Revolution: Soviet Family Policy and Social Life, 1917–1936*, Cambridge University Press: Cambridge 1993.

36. L. T. Lih et al. (eds), *Stalin's Letters to Molotov*, Yale University Press: New Haven & London 1995 p.232.

37. Cited by L. Vasilieva, *Kremlin Wives*, Weidenfeld & Nicolson: London 1994 p.68.

38. Cited by S. Kotkin, *Stalin: Waiting for Hitler, 1928–1941*, Penguin: London 2017 p.112.

39. S. Fitzpatrick, *On Stalin's Team*, Princeton University Press: Princeton 2015 p.80.

40. The material on the dacha is based on S. Devyatov, A. Shefov & Yu. Yur'ev, *Blizhnyaya Dacha Stalina*, Kremlin Multimedia: Moscow 2011. The book contains a chapter on the dacha's library room and a treatment of Stalin's library. The authors state (p.192) that Shushanika Manuchar'yants was Stalin's librarian in the 1930s but they cite no source.

41. F. Chuev, *Sto Sorok Besed s Molotovym*, Terra: Moscow 1991 p.296.

42. M. Djilas, *Conversations with Stalin*, Penguin: London 2014 pp.54, 105.

43. RGASPI, F558, Op.11 D.504–692. The maps have yet to be declassified but the type of map is described in Op.11 – which is the document that lists the contents of this subset of Stalin's *lichnyi fond*.

44. A. J. Rieber, 'Stalin: Man of the Borderlands', *American Historical Review* (December 2001).

45. A. J. Rieber, *Stalin and the Struggle for Supremacy in Eurasia*, Cambridge: Cambridge University Press, 2015.

46. A. Resis (ed.), *Molotov Remembers*, Ivan R. Dee: Chicago 1993 p.8. The anecdote is Felix Chuev's, the Soviet journalist whose conversations with Molotov are the subject of this book. Chuev's sources are Molotov and Akaki Mgeladze, who was leader of the Abkhazian communist party from 1943 to 1951 and the Georgian communist party from 1952 to 1953.

47. See M. Folly, G. Roberts & O. Rzheshevsky, *Churchill and Stalin: Comrades-in-Arms during the Second World War*, Pen & Sword Books: Barnsley 2019.

48. Stalin's extensive record collection disappeared after his death. According to Roy and Zhores Medvedev, Stalin was sent a copy of virtually every record produced in the USSR. After listening to records he would write on the sleeve 'good', 'so-so', 'bad' or 'rubbish'. The collection is known to have included recordings of opera, ballet and folk songs. Medvedev & Medvedev, *The Unknown Stalin*, p.100. Reports about dancing at the dacha may be found in various memoirs.

49. I. Deutscher, *Stalin: A Political Biography*, Penguin: Harmondsworth 1966 pp.456, 457.

50. G. Roberts, *Stalin's Wars: From World War to Cold War, 1939–1953*, Yale University Press: London & New Haven 2006.

51. On Stalin's death, see J. Rubenstein, *The Last Days of Stalin*, Yale University Press: London & New Haven 2016. Medical evidence relating to Stalin's death may be found in I. I. Chigirin, *Stalin: Bolezni i Smert': Dokumenty*, Dostoinstvo: Moscow 2016.

52. Medvedev & Medvedev, *The Unknown Stalin*, p.90.
53. Alliluyeva, *20 Letters to a Friend*, pp.13, 28–9.
54. *Bol'shaya Tsenzura: Pisateli i Zhurnalisty v Strane Sovetov, 1917–1956*, Demokratiya: Moscow 2005 doc.469.
55. Ibid., doc.467.
56. Murin, *Iosif Stalin v Ob"yatiyakh Sem'i*, doc.113.
57. Ilizarov, *Tainaya Zhizn' Stalina*, p.163.
58. S. Alliluyeva, *Only One Year*, Penguin: London 1971 p.348.
59. Among Stalin's Pushkin collection was a rare edition of *Yevgeny Onegin*, published in St Petersburg in 1837. This book was donated to the Lenin Library in the 1970s.
60. Gul fought for the 'Whites' during the Russian Civil War and then emigrated to Germany, France and the United States. In 1933 he published a book (in Russian) called *Red Marshals: Voroshilov, Budenny, Blyukher, Kotovskii*.
61. Cited by Medvedev & Medvedev, *The Unknown Stalin*, p.97.
62. Yu. Sharapov, 'Stalin's Personal Library: Meditations on Notes in the Margins', *Moscow News*, 38 (1988). In the Russian edition of the newspaper the article was headlined 'Pyat'sot Stranits v Den' (500 Pages a Day).
63. When the dissident poet Osip Mandelstam learned about Stalin's inscription from the Soviet press, he turned to his wife Nadezhda and said, 'We are finished!' (N. Mandelstam, *Hope against Hope: A Memoir*, p.339). When, in 1934, Stalin learned from Bukharin that Mandelstam had been exiled, Stalin wrote at the top of the letter: 'Who gave them the right to arrest Mandelstam? Disgraceful.' (RGASPI, F.558, Op.11, D.70, L.167). Subsequently, Mandelstam's situation improved, perhaps as a result of a telephone conversation between Stalin and Boris Pasternak, who was a friend of Mandelstam's. The poet was arrested again in 1938 and died in the Gulag that same year.
64. *Neizdannyi Shchedrin*, Leningrad 1931 (RGASPI, F.558, Op.3, D.231); Gromov, *Stalin: Iskusstvo i Vlast'*, p.161.
65. https://www.marxists.org/reference/archive/stalin/works/1936/11/25.htm. Accessed 4 August 2021.
66. 'Reshenie: Direktsii Instituta Marksizma Leninizma pri TsK KPSS ot 9 Yanvarya 1963'. This document was on display at the exhibition on the history of Stalin's *lichnyi fond* in the foyer of RGASPI in October 2018. The many letters and notes from publishers and authors may be found in RGASPI, F.558, Op.1, Dd.5754–5.
67. L. Spirin, 'Glazami Knig Lichnaya Biblioteka Stalina', *Nezavisimaya Gazeta* (25 May 1993). Spirin died in November 1993.
68. An electronic version of the SSPL catalogue is under construction by the library.
69. The document was on display at the exhibition on the history of Stalin's *lichnyi fond* in the foyer of RGASPI in October 2018.
70. The catalogue of the marked texts from Stalin's library is available on Yale's Stalin Digital Archive.
71. The first section of the SSPL catalogue – Books with the Library of J. V. Stalin stamp – may be viewed on Yale's Stalin Digital Archive. The catalogue was transcribed by Professor Yury Nikiforov in conjunction with the present author.
72. RGASPI, F.558, Op.3, Dd.301–3.
73. M. G. Leiteizen, *Nitsshe i Finansovyi Kapital*, Gosizdat: Moscow 1924.
74. Cited by M. Agursky, 'Nietzschean Roots of Stalinist Culture' in B. Glatzer Rosenthal (ed.), *Nietzsche and Soviet Culture*, Cambridge University Press: Cambridge 1994 p.272. Agursky (1933–1991), a Soviet-era dissident who emigrated to Israel in the mid-1970s, argued that many of Stalin's supporters were open or closet Nietzscheans who saw him as the embodiment of the 'will to power' of Nietzsche's 'superman'. Agursky claimed, without any direct evidence, that Nietzscheanism influenced Stalin, too. His weakest argument is that Stalin's Marxism had no real content; his strongest is that Stalin, like Nietzsche, supported the Lamarckian alternative to Darwinism (i.e. that acquired characteristics could be inherited).
75. E. van Ree, 'Stalin and Marxism: A Research Note', *Studies in East European Thought*, 49/1 (1997).

76. N. Lukin, *Iz Istorii Revolyutsionnykh Armii*, Gosizdat: Moscow 1923. RGASPI, F.558, Op.3, D.192 pp.33–4 of the book for the passage with Stalin's marginal comment.
77. https://www.marxists.org/reference/archive/stalin/works/1934/07/23.htm. Accessed 4 August 2021.
78. B. Ilizarov, *Stalin, Ivan Groznyi i Drugie*, Veche: Moscow 2019 pp.49–50, 56, 69–71.
79. J. Stalin, *Works*, vol.1, Foreign Languages Publishing House: Moscow 1952 pp.369–71.
80. See M. Perrie, 'The Tsar, the Emperor, the Leader: Ivan the Terrible, Peter the Great and Anatoli Rybakov's Stalin' in N. Lampert & G. T. Rittersporn (eds), *Stalinism: Its Nature and Aftermath*, Macmillan: London 1992 pp.80–1.
81. Cited by R. Service, *Stalin: A Biography*, Macmillan: London 2004 pp.273–4.
82. T. O'Conroy, *The Menace of Japan*, Hurst & Blackett: London 1933; T. O'Konroi, *Yaponskaya Ugroza*, Gossotsizdat: Moscow 1934. Stalin's copy of the book may be found here: RGASPI, F.558, Op.3, D.98. The book is marked but probably not by Stalin.
83. On O'Conroy's biography: P. O'Connor, 'Timothy or Taid or Taig Conroy or O'Conroy (1883–1935)' in H. Cortazzi (ed.), *Britain and Japan: Biographical Portraits*, vol.4, Routledge: London 2002.
84. O. Tanin & E. Iogan, *Voenno-Fashistskoe Dvizhenie v Yaponii*, Khabarovsk 1933; *Voenno-Morskie Sily Yaponii*, RKKA: Moscow 1933. The latter was a secret publication of Red Army Intelligence that was sent to Stalin in September 1933 (RGASPI, F.558. Op.1, D.5754, L.217). Stalin's copies of these books: ibid., Op.3, Dd.48–9.
85. Ibid., Op.11, D.206. I am grateful to Malcolm Spencer for pointing out the TASS bulletins, which he makes illuminating use of in his *Stalinism and the Soviet-Finnish War, 1939–40*, Palgrave: London 2018.
86. RGASPI, F.71, Op.10, Dd.327–8.
87. Volkogonov, *Stalin*, chap.23.
88. According to Boris Ilizarov, who sourced a copy in the archive of the Mikhail Kalinin, the Russian translation of *Mein Kampf* was quite good.
89. RGASPI, F.558, Op.11, Dd.301–2.
90. Ibid., D.207, doc.35.
91. Service, *Stalin*, pp.569–70.
92. Rayfield, *Stalin and His Hangmen*, p.20.
93. Khlevniuk, *Stalin: New Biography of a Dictator*, pp.93–8.
94. Kotkin, *Stalin: Paradoxes of Power*, p.10.
95. N. Simonov, 'Razmyshleniya o Pometkakh Stalina na Polyakh Marksistskoi Literatury', *Kommunist*, 18 (December 1990).
96. J. Stalin, *Leninism*, Allen & Unwin: London 1940 pp.656–63.
97. B. Slavin, 'Chelovek Absolyutnoi Vlasti: O Maloizvestnykh i Neizvestnykh Vystupleniyakh I. V. Stalina i Ego Zametkakh na Polyakh Knig', *Pravda* (21 December 1994). I am very grateful to Vladimir Nevezhin for obtaining a copy of this article for me.
98. Ree, *Political Thought*, esp. pp.14–17.
99. Ilizarov, *Stalin, Ivan Groznyi*, p.72.
100. In addition to the Ilizarov books already cited, there is *Pochetnyi Akademik Stalin i Akademik Marr*, Veche: Moscow 2012.
101. RGASPI, F.558, Op.3, D.53, L.123; Gromov, *Stalin: Iskusstvo i Vlast'*, pp.10–13. The translation of Gorky is taken from http://www.arvindguptatoys.com/arvindgupta/gorkymother.pdf p.399. Accessed 4 August 2021.
102. R. Medvedev, *Let History Judge: The Origins and Consequences of Stalinism*, Macmillan: London 1972 p.3.
103. Ibid., p.512.
104. Ibid., p.224.
105. RGASPI, F.558, Op.3, D.348.
106. Medvedev & Medvedev, *The Unknown Stalin*, p.8. The book was originally published in Russian in 2001.
107. I. R. Makaryk, 'Stalin and Shakespeare' in N. Khomenko (ed.), *The Shakespeare International Yearbook*, vol. 18, Special Section on Soviet Shakespeare, Routledge: London July 2020 p.45.

108. W. Benjamin, 'Unpacking My Library: A Talk About Book Collecting' in his *Illuminations*, Random House: New York 2002.

CHAPTER 5: BAH HUMBUG! STALIN'S *POMETKI*

1. E. van Ree, 'Stalin and Marxism: A Research Note', *Studies in East European Thought*, 49/1 (1996) p.25.
2. H. J. Jackson, *Marginalia: Readers Writing in Books*, Yale University Press: London & New Haven 2001 p.28.
3. Ibid., p.48.
4. M. J. Adler, 'How to Mark a Book', *Saturday Review of Literature* (6 July 1941).
5. While these bookmarks are real, they may have been placed there by archivists as a way of identifying the location of Stalin's *pometki*. However, not all the books have these strips of paper and those that do miss some of Stalin's markings. For many examples of Lenin's *pometki*, see the catalogue of the c.9,000 books in his personal library: *Biblioteka V. I. Lenina v Kremle*, Moscow 1961.
6. The absence of sex in the works of a Victorian novelist is not so surprising but it was brought to my attention by David Lodge's 'Dickens Our Contemporary' in his *Consciousness and the Novel*, Vintage: London 2018 p.128.
7. Rossiiskii Gosudarstvennyi Arkhiv Sotsial'no-Politicheskoi Istorii (hereafter RGASPI), F.558, Op.3, D.346.
8. RGASPI, F.558, Op.3, D.342. Mikhail Vaiskopf notes the similarities between Stalin's speeches at the 16th and 17th party congresses (*Pisatel' Stalin*, Novoe Literaturnoe Obozrenie: Moscow 2001 pp.36–7).
9. Ibid., D.62, pp.5, 7, 9–13, 16–20, 23–4, 30–3, 36–40 of the pamphlet for the markings.
10. Ibid., F.592, Op.1, Dd.6–9.
11. Y. Sharapov, 'Stalin's Personal Library', *Moscow News*, 38 (1988).
12. The relevant pages were on display at an exhibition on the history of Stalin's personal archive in Moscow in October 2018 and the handwriting was identified by the archivists as being Svetlana's.
13. Y. Gromov, *Stalin: Iskusstvo i Vlast'*, Eksmo: Moscow 2003 p.47.
14. RGASPI F.558, Op.3, D.350. As Svetlana Lokhova points out, Stalin doodled *Uchitel'* on a number of books. S. Lokhova, 'Stalin's Library' in L. F. Gearon (ed.), *The Routledge International Handbook of Universities, Security and Intelligence Studies*, Routledge: London 2020 p.428.
15. For example: E. Radzinsky, *Stalin*, Hodder & Stoughton: London 1997 p.454. See further the negative comments of Boris Ilizarov on Radzinsky's hypothesis in his *Stalin, Ivan Groznyi i Drugie*, Veche: Moscow 2019 p.28.
16. RGASPI, F.558, Op.3, D.11. p.33 of the book for the marking.
17. O. Volobuev & S. Kuleshov, *Ochishchenie: Istoriya i Perestroika*, Novosti: Moscow 1989 p.146.
18. RGASPI, F.558, Op.3, D.167. The first person to cite the quoted text seems to have been B. Slavin, 'Chelovek Absolyutnoi Vlasti: O Maloizvestnykh i Neizvestnykh Vystupleniyakh I. V. Stalina i Ego Zametkakh na Polyakh Knig', *Pravda* (21 December 1994).
19. D. Rayfield, *Stalin and His Hangmen*, Viking: London 2004 p.22. On the facing page is a photograph of the cited text.
20. R. Service, *Stalin: A Biography*, Macmillan: London 2004 p.342.
21. S. Žižek, *Less than Nothing: Hegel and the Shadow of Dialectical Materialism*, Verso Books: London 2013. Žižek quotes this text in a number of his publications.
22. J. Stalin, *Works*, vol.6, Foreign Languages Publishing House: Moscow 1953 pp.54–66.
23. See J. F. Matlock, *An Index to the Collected Works of J. V. Stalin*, Johnson Reprint Corporation: New York 1971 pp.145–6.
24. For example: *Put' k Leninu: Sobranie Vyderzhek iz Sochinenii V. I. Lenina*, vols 1–2, Voenizdat: Moscow 1924. RGASPI, F.558 Op.3, Dd.295–6.
25. *Leninskii Sbornik*, vols 2, 4, 13, Lenin Institute: Moscow-Leningrad 1924, 1925, 1930. RGASPI, F.558, Op.3, Dd.183–5.

26. I. Baz', *Pochemu My Pobedili v Grazhdanskoi Voine*, Moscow 1930. RGASPI, F.558, Op.3, D.10.

27. E. van Ree, *The Political Thought of Joseph Stalin: A Study in Twentieth-Century Patriotism*, Routledge: London 2002 p.258; Ree, 'Stalin and Marxism: A Research Note'.

28. https://www.marxists.org/reference/archive/stalin/works/1938/05/17.htm. I owe this reference to E. Dobrenko, *Late Stalinism: The Aesthetics of Politics*, Yale University Press: London & New Haven 2020 pp.362–3.

29. Ibid., p.267. Stalin lifted the quote from his copy of *The New Course*, which he read and marked in detail. The booklet was stamped as item 884 in his library. RGASPI, F.558, Op.11, D.1577. An English translation may be found here: https://www.marxists.org/archive/trotsky/1923/newcourse/index.htm. Accessed 4 August 2021.

30. On the socialism in one country debate see E. van Ree, *Boundaries of Utopia: Imagining Communism from Plato to Stalin*, Routledge: London 2015 chaps 14–15.

31. Cited by van Ree, *Political Thought*, n.64 pp.321–2.

32. An English translation may be found here: https://www.marxists.org/archive/trotsky/1924/lessons/1924-les.pdf.

33. J. Stalin, *Works*, vol.6, Foreign Languages Publishing House: Moscow 1953 pp.338–73.

34. https://www.marxists.org/archive/trotsky/1918/hrr/index.htm. Accessed 4 August 2021.

35. RGASPI, F558, Op.3, D.362.

36. Ibid., D.318. Dmitry Volkogonov's perception of Stalin's marking of Smolensky's book is completely different to mine: 'underlined in those places which criticise his arch-enemy: "Trotsky is prickly and impatient", he has "an imperious nature which loves to dominate", "he loves political power", "Trotsky is a political adventurist of genius".' (D. Volkogonov, *Stalin: Triumph and Tragedy*, Phoenix Press: London 2000 pp.226–7).

37. RGASPI, Op.3, D364. The book has Stalin's library stamp and is numbered 898. The English translations of Trotsky's text in what follows derive from https://www.marxists.org/archive/trotsky/1920/terrcomm/index.htm.

38. Stalin wrote the word without hyphenation.

39. RGASPI, F.558, Op.3, D.91.

40. Cited by Ree, *The Political Thought of Joseph Stalin* p.306, n.57.

41. Ibid., p.315 n.5.

42. See Stalin's marking of a 1923 edition of Kautsky's *The Agrarian Question*: RGASPI, F.558, Op.3, D.86. Other Kautsky works marked by Stalin may be found here: RGASPI, F.558, Op.3, Dd.87, 88, 89, 90, 92 and Op.1, D.1576.

43. Y. Buranov, *Lenin's Will: Falsified and Forbidden*, Prometheus Books: Amherst NY 1994 pp.150, 151.

44. RGASPI, F.558, Op.3 Dd.357, 359, 360, 361; Op.11, D.1577.

45. On the evolution of Trotsky's economic thinking in the 1920s, see Richard B. Day's classic *Leon Trotsky and the Politics of Economic Isolation*, Cambridge University Press: Cambridge 1973.

46. For a judicious overview of Trotsky's factional activities in the 1920s, see I. D. Thatcher, *Trotsky*, Routledge: London 2003 chaps 5–6.

47. See J. Harris, 'Discipline versus Democracy: The 1923 Party Controversy' in L. Douds, J. Harris & P. Whitewood (eds), *The Fate of the Bolshevik Revolution: Illiberal Liberation, 1917–41*, Bloomsbury Academic: London 2020. Many of the relevant documents may be found in V. Vilkova, *The Struggle for Power: Russia in 1923, from the Secret Archives of the Former Soviet Union*, Prometheus Books: Amherst NY 1996.

48. See S. F. Cohen, *Bukharin and the Bolshevik Revolution: A Political Biography, 1888–1938*, Oxford University Press: Oxford 1971.

49. I. Halfin, *Intimate Enemies: Demonizing the Bolshevik Opposition, 1918–1928*, University of Pittsburgh Press: Pittsburgh 2007.

50. Ibid., p.250.

51. M. David-Fox, *Revolution of the Mind: Higher Learning Among the Bolsheviks, 1918–1929*, Cornell University Press: Ithaca NY and London 1997 p.117. Stalin's copy of the text may be found among the collection of his library books in the State Socio-Political Library. Ironically, Kanatchikov himself became a member of the United Opposition.

He recanted and then held several responsible party posts but was arrested and executed in 1937.

52. Volkogonov, *Stalin*, p.260.
53. S. Kotkin, *Stalin: Waiting for Hitler, 1928–1941*, Penguin: London 2017 p.787.
54. Many relevant documents may be found in *Politburo i Lev Trotsky, 1922–1940gg: Sbornik Dokumentov*, IstLit: Moscow 2017.
55. J. Stalin, *Works*, vol.12, Foreign Languages Publishing House: Moscow 1955 p.358.
56. Ibid., vol.13 p.101.
57. Ibid., p.113.
58. Ibid., p.354.
59. J. Arch Getty & O. V. Naumov, *The Road to Terror: Stalin and the Self-Destruction of the Bolsheviks, 1932–1939*, Yale University Press: London & New Haven 1999 pp.140–1.
60. See J. Arch Getty, 'The Politics of Repression Revisited' in J. Arch Getty and R. T. Manning (eds), *Stalinist Terror: New Perspectives*, Cambridge University Press: Cambridge 1993. Also: M. E. Lenoe, *The Kirov Murder and Soviet History*, Yale University Press: London & New Haven 2010.
61. Thatcher, *Trotsky*, pp.190–1.
62. Cited by Y. Slezkine, *The House of Government: A Saga of the Russian Revolution*, Princeton University Press: Princeton 2019 p.716.
63. Getty & Naumov, *The Road to Terror*, doc.37.
64. M. Lenoe, 'Fear, Loathing, Conspiracy: The Kirov Murder as Impetus for Terror' in J. Harris (ed.), *The Anatomy of Terror*, Oxford University Press: Oxford 2013 p.208. Some of the interrogation documents may be found here: *Lubyanka: Stalin i VChK-GPU-OGPU-NKVD (Yanvar' 1922–Dekabr' 1936)*, Materik: Moscow 2003 docs.494, 505, 506–9, 511–14. English translations of these documents may be found in D. R. Shearer & V. Khaustov (eds), *Stalin and the Lubianka: A Documentary History of the Political Police and Security Organs in the Soviet Union, 1922–1953*, Yale University Press: London & New Haven 2015.
65. I have merged and separated by the ellipsis two quotations from Stalin's conversion with Rolland: from the archive document (RGASPI, F.558, Op.11, D.795, doc.1 Ll.10–11.) and from H. Kuromiya, *Stalin*, Pearson Longman: Harlow 2005 p.116. I am grateful to Michael David-Fox for the archival reference.
66. Ibid., L.12. Rolland wanted to publish the transcript of the interview but Stalin didn't respond to his requests. An English translation of the French version of the transcript may be found here: https://mltoday.com/from-the-archives-1935-interview-of-stalin-by-romain-rolland.
67. W. Z. Goldman, *Terror and Democracy in the Age of Stalin: The Social Dynamics of Repression*, Cambridge University Press: Cambridge 2007 p.72.
68. D. M. Crowe, 'Late Imperial and Soviet "Show" Trials, 1878–1938' in D. M. Crowe (ed.), *Stalin's Soviet Justice: 'Show' Trials, War Crimes Trials and Nuremberg*, Bloomsbury Academic: London 2019, and W. Chase, 'Stalin as Producer: The Moscow Show Trials and the Construction of Mortal Threats' in S. Davies & J. Harris (eds), *Stalin: A New History*, Cambridge: Cambridge 2005.
69. Ibid., pp.105–8.
70. Getty & Naumov, *The Road to Terror*, pp.565–6.
71. The full text (in Russian) of Stalin's speech to the plenum may be found in *Lubyanka: Stalin i Glavnoe Upravlenie Gosbezopastnosti NKVD, 1937–1938*, Demokratiya: Moscow 2004 doc.31. For a translated extract see https://www.marxists.org/reference/archive/stalin/works/1937/03/03.htm. Accessed 4 August 2021.
72. P. Whitewood, 'Stalin's Purge of the Red Army and the Misperception of Security Threats' in J. Ryan & S. Grant (eds), *Revisioning Stalin and Stalinism: Complexities, Contradictions and Controversies*, Bloomsbury Academic: London 2020 p.49. See also the same author's *The Red Army and the Great Terror: Stalin's Purge of the Soviet Military*, University Press of Kansas: Lawrence 2015.
73. *Lubyanka: Stalin i Glavnoe Upravlenie*, doc.92.
74. Shearer & Khaustov, *Stalin and the Lubianka*, doc.104.

75. Ibid., doc.109 and J. Harris, *The Great Fear: Stalin's Terror of the 1930s*, Oxford University Press: Oxford 2016 pp.176–7. For an analysis of what prompted these Politburo decisions, see also J. Arch Getty, 'Pre-Election Fever: The Origins of the 1937 Mass Operations' in Harris, *The Anatomy of Terror*. According to other figures, the plan was to repress 268,950 kulaks, including 75,950 executions. In the event, 767,397 people were repressed, of which 386,798 were executed.

76. On Stalin and Spain see O. Khlevniuk, *Stalin: New Biography of a Dictator*, Yale University Press: London & New Haven 2015 pp.153–6. Also: D. Kowalsky, 'Stalin and the Spanish Civil War, 1936–1939: The New Historiography' in Ryan & Grant (eds), *Revisioning Stalin and Stalinism*.

77. Khlevniuk, *Stalin: New Biography of a Dictator*, p.155.

78. I. Banac (ed.), *The Diary of Georgi Dimitrov, 1933–1949*, Yale University Press: London & New Haven 2003 p.67.

79. *Bol'shaya Tsenzura: Pisateli i Zhurnalisty v Strane Sovetov, 1917–1956*, doc.373. Stalin's handwritten corrections to the draft of the article may be viewed here: RGASPI, F.558, Op.11, D.1124, doc.6. The article was published in *Pravda* on 24 August, though not precisely in the form prescribed by Stalin.

80. See the documents in Getty & Naumov, *The Road to Terror*, chap.12.

81. Stalin's report to the 18th party congress in J. Stalin, *Leninism*, Allen & Unwin: London 1940, esp. pp.656–62.

82. The original of the document was on display at an exhibition in Moscow in 2016.

83. M. Folly, G. Roberts & O. Rzheshevsky, *Churchill and Stalin: Comrades-in-Arms during the Second World War*, Pen & Sword Books: Barnsley 2019 doc.38 p.145.

84. RGASPI, F558, Op.3, D.26 p.198 of the book for Stalin's underlining.

85. Ch. Rossel', *Razvedka i Kontr-Razvedka*, Moscow: Voenizdat 1937; RGASPI, F.558, Op.11, D.743.

86. Khlevniuk, *Stalin: New Biography of a Dictator*, p.155.

87. W. Bedell Smith, *Moscow Mission, 1946–1949*, Heinemann: London 1950 pp.176–7.

88. RGASPI, F.558, Op.1, D.5754, L.126. Cited by M. Lavrent'eva, *Osobennosti Tekhnologii i Metodov Informatsionno-Psikhologicheskikh Voin SSSR s Velikobritanniei i SShA v Period, 1939–1953 gg*, Candidate's Dissertation, Rossiiskii Universitet Druzhby Narodov, Moscow 2020 p.127.

89. Ibid., Op.11, D.1605.

90. It was initially published by *Pravda* in February–March 1948. It was published in English in a supplement to the journal *New Times* in March 1948.

91. For reasons that remain unclear, the film was not completed. Dovzhenko died in 1956 and there were rumours the project had been abandoned because Bucar had redefected to the west. That was not true. In the 1950s she started working for the English-language branch of Radio Moscow and remained there for the rest of her working life. Remembered with affection by her Soviet colleagues, she died in Moscow in 1998. *Stalin i Kosmopolitizm, 1945–1953: Dokumenty*, Demokratiya: Moscow 2005 docs.120 & 182; R. Magnúsdóttir, *Enemy Number One: The United States of America in Soviet Ideology and Propaganda, 1945–1959*, Oxford University Press: Oxford 2019 p.24; A. Kozovoi, ' "This Film Is Harmful": Resizing America for the Soviet Screen' in S. Autio-Saramo & B. Humphreys (eds), *Winter Kept Us Warm: Cold War Interactions Reconsidered*, Aleksanteri Cold War Series 1 (2010); https://history.state.gov/historicaldocuments/frus1949v05/d335; https://www.themoscowtimes.com/archive/moscow-mailbag-voice-of-russias-voices-that-came-from-afar. Dovzhenko's unfinished film may be viewed here: https://www.youtube.com/watch?v=pUpaqunbR9w.

92. RGASPI, F.558, Op.3, D.28. The cited text marked by Stalin may be found on pp.43–7 of the book.

93. G. Kennan, *Memoirs, 1925–1950*, Hutchinson: London 1968 pp.279–80.

94. See, for example, Kennan's Reith Lectures: *Russia, the Atom and the West*, Oxford University Press: London 1958.

95. I am grateful to Vladimir Nevezhin for pointing me in this direction and providing me with a copy of his article 'I. V. Stalin o Vneshnei Politike i Diplomatii: Po Materialam Lichnogo Arkhiva Vozhdya (1939–1941)', *Rossiiskaya Istoriya*, 6 (2019).

96. RGASPI, F.558, Op.11, D.200, L.13.

97. https://minimalistquotes.com/otto-von-bismarck-quote-45423/. Accessed 4 August 2021.

98. M. Ya. Gefter, 'Stalin Umer Vchera', *Rabochii Klass i Sovremennyi Mir*, no.1, 1988. I am grateful to Holly Case for this reference and to Vladimir Nevezhin for obtaining for me a copy of the Gefter interview. Yerusalimsky's introduction was subsequently published as a separate pamphlet under the title (in Russian) 'Bismarck as Diplomat'.

99. R. Medvedev, *Chto Chital Stalin?*, Prava Cheloveka: Moscow 2005 p.81.

100. RGASPI, F.558, Op.11.760 L.145.

101. A handwritten archive register listing these two volumes as having been marked by Stalin was on display at an exhibition on the history of Stalin's *lichnyi fond* in the foyer of RGASPI in October 2018.

102. N. Ryzhkov, *Perestroika: Istoriya Predatel'stv*, Novosti: Moscow 1992 pp.354–5. Stephen Cohen, who died in 2020, was an American historian who wrote a biography of the Bolshevik leader Nikolai Bukharin, which was translated into Russian and published in the USSR during the Gorbachev era.

103. R. G. Suny, *Stalin: Passage to Revolution*, Princeton University Press: Princeton 2020 p.584.

104. Kuromiya, *Stalin*, p.120. RGASPI, F.588, Op.3, D.84, p.51. Vyshinsky's remarks on Kamenev and Zinoviev may be found here: https://www.marxists.org/history/ussr/government/law/1936/moscow-trials/22/double-dealing.htm. Accessed 4 August 2021.

105. http://www.florentine-society.ru/Machiavelli_Nikitski_Club.htm. Accessed 4 August 2021. I am grateful to David Brandenberger for this reference.

106. RGASPI, F.558, Op.11, D.208, L.33.

107. Ibid., Op.1, D.5754, Ll.124–5.

108. Ibid., Op.3, D.18 pp.35–6 of the encyclopaedia.

109. *Stalin i Kaganovich: Perepiska, 1931–1936 gg.*, Rosspen: Moscow 2001 doc.621. I am grateful to Michael Carley for this reference. Stalin's remark about Anglo-German entente was prompted by the recent naval agreement between the two states.

110. RGASPI, F.558, Op.3, D.267, pp.32–3 of the book for Stalin's annotation.

111. Ibid., Op.1, D.5755, L.142.

112. Ibid., Op.3, D.232.

113. https://www.marxists.org/reference/archive/stalin/works/1934/07/19.htm. Accessed 4 August 2021.

114. Nevezhin, 'I. V. Stalin o Vneshnei Politike', p.71.

115. RGASPI F.558, Op.1, D.5754, Ll.98–100.

116. Nevezhin, 'I. V. Stalin o Vneshnei Politike', pp.72–3.

117. RGASPI, F.558, Op.1, D.5754, L.101.

118. Ibid., Op.3, D.79.

119. J. Stalin, *Works*, vol.2, Foreign Languages Publishing House: Moscow 1953 p.285.

120. *Dokumenty Vneshnei Politiki*, 1941, part two, Mezhdunarodnaya Otnosheniya: Moscow 1998 p.563.

121. Folly, Roberts & Rzheshevsky, *Churchill and Stalin*, p.88.

122. Ibid., pp.75–6.

123. *Ivan Mikhailovich Maiskii: Dnevnik Diplomata, London, 1934–1943*, book 1, Nauka: Moscow 2006 p.111. I am grateful to Michael Carley for this reference. Maisky's diary entry was based on a story he had heard about what was said at the Stalin–Laval meeting. There is no known official Soviet or French record of the conversation.

124. S. Alliluyeva, *20 Letters to a Friend*, Penguin: Harmondsworth 1968 p.161.

125. The third author of the book – Ivan Dzhavakhishvili – had died in 1940. Stalin's marked copy of this Georgian-language book may be found in RGASPI, F.558, Op.3, D.382. Donald Rayfield, who attributes authorship of the book to Dzhavakhishvili (Javakhishvili), reports that Stalin wrote in the margin: 'Why does the author fail to mention that Mithridates and the Pontic Empire were a Georgian ruler and a Georgian state?' D. Rayfield, *Stalin and His Hangmen*, p.16.

126. 'Novye Rechi Stalina o Gruzii, Istorii i Natsional'nostyakh (1945)', *Issledovaniya po Istorii Russkoi Mysli: Ezhegodnik 2019*, Modest Kolerov: Moscow 2019 pp. 491–525.

Berdzenishvili's recollection is dated December 1945 but the bulk of it seems to have been composed before that date. It was first published in 1998.

127. Ibid., p.504. Joseph Orbeli (1887–1961) was an Armenian orientalist who served as head of the Hermitage Museum from 1934 to 1951. Boris Turaev's (1868–1920) two-volume history of the 'Ancient East' was in Stalin's library, as was Nikolai Pavlov-Sil'vanskii's (1869–1908) book on feudalism in Ancient Rus'. Vasily Struve (1889–1965) was an Egyptologist and Assyriologist.

128. L. R. Tillett, The Great Friendship: Soviet Historians and the Non-Russian Nationalities, University of North Carolina Press: Chapel Hill 1969.

129. 'Novye Rechi Stalina', p.506.

130. Ibid., p.515. See further: E. van Ree, 'Heroes and Merchants: Stalin's Understanding of National Character', Kritika, 8/1 (Winter 2007).

131. J. Hellbeck, Stalingrad: The City that Defeated the Third Reich, paperback ed., PublicAffairs: New York 2016 p.437.

132. Alliluyeva, 20 Letters to a Friend, pp.140, 163.

133. Zh. Medvedev, Stalin i Evreiskaya Problema: Novyi Analiz, Prava Cheloveka: Moscow 2003.

134. F. Chuev, Tak Govoril Kaganovich: Ispoved' Stalinskogo Apostola, Otechestvo: Moscow 1992 p.89.

135. G. Kostyrchenko, Out of the Red Shadows: Anti-Semitism in Stalin's Russia, Prometheus Books: Amherst NY 1995.

136. 'Novye Rechi Stalina', p.494.

137. Apparently, Stalin marked these two books but they have disappeared from the archive.

138. RGASPI, F.558, Op.3, D.311.

139. Ibid., D.267, p.25 of the book. Stalin does not appear to have read the diary itself, only the introduction by Boris Shtein, a Soviet diplomat.

140. Stalin, Leninism, pp.479–80.

141. RGASPI, F.558, Op.3, D.37, p.5 of Vipper's book; D.97, p.3 of S. I. Kovalev et al., Istoriya Drevnego Mira: Drevnii Vostok i Gretsiya, Gosudarstvennoe Uchebno-Pedagogicheskoe Izdatel'stvo: Moscow 1937.

142. Ibid., D.36. Stalin's markings may be found in chap.4 of the book on pp.120–4, 126–7, 130–1, 133–7.

143. As Boris Ilizarov (Stalin, Ivan Groznyi, p.75) points out, the marginalia are written in the old Russian script, i.e. the one in use before the reform and rationalisation of the Cyrillic alphabet in 1917–18, so they won't have been made by Svetlana and are unlikely to belong to Stalin's young wife, Nadezhda.

144. RGASPI, F.558, Op.3, D.38, passim.

145. On Vipper: H. Graham, 'R. Iu. Vipper: A Russian Historian in Three Worlds', Canadian Slavonic Papers/Revue Canadienne des Slavistes, 28/1 (March 1986). Also the translation of the entry on Vipper in The Great Soviet Encyclopaedia: https://encyclopedia2. thefreedictionary.com/Robert+Iurevich+Vipper. Accessed 4 August 2021.

146. Cited by A. Dubrovsky, Vlast' i Istoricheskaya Mysl' v SSSR (1930–1950-e gg.), Rosspen: Moscow 2017 pp.150–1. See also D. Brandenberger, National Bolshevism: Stalinist Mass Culture and the Formation of Modern Russian National Identity, 1931–1956, Harvard University Press: Cambridge MA 2002 pp.32–3. Stalin's comments did not come out of the blue. Already in August 1932 the party central committee had issued a decree noting the poor state of the history curriculum (M. Pundeff (ed.), History in the USSR: Selected Readings, Chandler Publishing Co.: San Francisco 1967 doc.18).

147. Cited by D. Dorotich, 'A Turning Point in the Soviet School: The Seventeenth Party Congress and the Teaching of History', History of Education Quarterly (Fall 1967) p.299.

148. K. M. F. Platt, Terror and Greatness: Ivan and Peter as Russian Myths, Cornell University Press: Ithaca NY 2011 p.182.

149. Dubrovsky, Vlast' i Istoricheskaya Mysl', pp.157–9; Brandenberger, National Bolshevism, pp.34–5.

150. Ilizarov, Stalin, Ivan Groznyi, p.68.

151. *I.V. Stalin, Istoricheskaya Ideologiya v SSSR v 1920–1950-e gody*, Nauka-Piter: St Petersburg 2006 doc.79.
152. 'O Prepodavanii Grazhdanskoi Istorii v Shkolakh SSSR', *Pravda* (16 May 1934). The decree, which was published on the newspaper's front page, was hand-edited and corrected by Stalin. For an English text of the full decree: Pundeff, *History in the USSR*, doc.20.
153. 'Na Fronte Istoricheskoi Nauki', *Pravda* (27 January 1936); Tillett, *The Great Friendship*, pp.42–3. For the full English text of the *Pravda* editorial and the two notes of Stalin, Zhdanov and Kirov: Pundeff, *History in the USSR*, doc.21.
154. 'Postanovlenie Zhuri Pravitel'stvennoi Komissii po Konkursu na Luchshii Uchebnik dlya 3 i 4 Klassov Srednei Shkoly po Istorii SSSR', *Pravda* (22 August 1937).
155. The details of the process may be followed in the books by Brandenberger and Dubrovsky cited above. Much of the documentary basis of their research may be found in this publication of the Archive of the President of the Russian Federation: S. Kudryashov (ed.), *Istoriyu – v Shkolu: Sozdanie Pervykh Sovetskikh Uchebnikov*, APRF: Moscow 2008.
156. Svetlana's copy of the book is stored in the State Socio-Political Library in Moscow as part of its holdings of books from Stalin's personal library.
157. Tillett, *The Great Friendship*, p.50.
158. Dubrovsky, *Vlast' i Istoricheskaya Mysl'*, p.240.
159. The dummies may be found here: RGASPI, F.558, Op.3, Dd.374–5, Op.11, D.1584.
160. Dubrovsky, *Vlast' i Istoricheskaya Mysl'*, p.239.
161. Ibid., pp.235–6.
162. A. Shestakov (ed.), *Kratkii Kurs Istoriya SSSR*, Uchpedgiz: Moscow 1937 p.42. A detailed summary and analysis of the book may be found in Platt, *Terror and Greatness*, chap.5.
163. Ibid., p.37.
164. Ilizarov, *Stalin, Ivan Groznyi*, pp.100–1
165. Brandenberger, *National Bolshevism*, p.51.
166. Stalin, *Leninism*, p.5.
167. Dimitrov, *Diary*, p.65.
168. Both citations from I. Paperno, 'Nietzscheanism and the Return of Pushkin' in B. Glatzer Rosenthal (ed.), *Nietzsche and Soviet Culture*, Cambridge University Press: Cambridge 1994 pp.225–6. See further K. Petrone, *Life Has Become More Joyous, Comrades: Celebrations in the Time of Stalin*, Indiana University Press: Bloomington 2000 chap. 5 on the Pushkin centennial.
169. Petrone, *Life Has Become More Joyous, Comrades*, p.159.
170. R. Yu. Vipper, *Ivan Groznyi*, Del'fin: Moscow 1922. For an English-language text that makes a similar argument to Vipper's, see I. Grey, *Ivan the Terrible*, Hodder & Stoughton: London 1964. Ian Grey (1918–1996) was a New Zealand-born historian who served as a Royal Navy interpreter in Russia during the Second World War. After the war he worked in the Soviet section of the British Foreign Office and then for the Commonwealth Parliamentary Association. He published a number of books on Russian history, including a fine but neglected biography of Stalin: *Stalin: Man of History*, Weidenfeld & Nicolson: London 1979.
171. S. F. Platonov, *Ivan Groznyi*, Brokgauz-Efron: Peterburg 1923. This book is available on the internet: http://elib.shpl.ru/ru/nodes/4720-platonov-s-f-ivan-groznyy-pg-1923-obrazy-chelovechestva#mode/inspect/page/3/zoom/4. Accessed 4 August 2021.
172. S. F. Platonov, *Proshloe Russkogo Severa*, Obelisk: Berlin 1924. The book is in Stalin's library collection in the State Social-Political Library in Moscow.
173. RGASPI, F558, Op.1, D.3165 p.42 of the book. This reference was drawn to my attention by L. Maximenkov, 'Stalin's Meeting with a Delegation of Ukrainian Writers on 12 February 1929', *Harvard Ukrainian Studies*, 16/3–4 (December 1992), p.368.
174. *Soviet Writers' Congress 1934: The Debate on Socialist Realism and Modernism*, Lawrence & Wishart: London 1977 pp.43–4.
175. M. Perrie, 'R. Yu. Vipper and the Stalinisation of Ivan the Terrible', paper presented to the Soviet Industrialisation Project Series, University of Birmingham, December 1999 p.5.

176. Graham, 'R. Iu. Vipper: A Russian Historian in Three Worlds', pp.29–30.
177. Perrie, 'R. Yu. Vipper and the Stalinisation of Ivan the Terrible', p.10.
178. M. Perrie, 'The Tsar, the Emperor, the Leader: Ivan the Terrible, Peter the Great and Anatolii Rybakov's Stalin' in N. Lampert & G. T. Rittersporn (eds), *Stalinism: Its Nature and Aftermath*, Macmillan: Basingstoke 1992 pp.85–6.
179. *Vlast' i Khudozhestvennaya Intelligenstiya, 1917–1953*, Demokratiya: Moscow 2002 doc.3, p.478.
180. Platt, *Terror and Greatness*, p.210.
181. There does not appear to be a copy of Tolstoy's Peter book in Stalin's archive, but we know that the publishers sent him a copy of the postwar edition in November 1947: RGASPI, F.558, Op.3, D.5754, L.64.
182. Ibid., Op.11, D.717, Ll.99–100.
183. R. Wipper (*sic*), *Ivan Grozny*, Foreign Languages Publishing House: Moscow 1947.
184. Perrie, 'R. Yu. Vipper and the Stalinisation of Ivan the Terrible', p.13.
185. Ibid., p.11.
186. Cited by A. G. Mazour, *The Writing of History in the Soviet Union*, Stanford University: Stanford CA 1971 p.67.
187. '"Ivan Groznyi": Na Lektsii Doktora Istoricheskikh Nauk Professor R. Yu. Vippera', *Pravda* (19 September 1943).
188. *Mezhdu Molotom i Nakoval'nei: Soyuz Sovetskikh Pisatelei SSSR*, vol.1, Rosspen: Moscow 2010 doc.278, n.1.
189. RGASPI, F.558, Op.3, D.350. This was the same copy on which Stalin doodled 'Teacher' on the back cover.
190. *Vlast' i Khudozhestvennaya Intelligenstiya*, doc.3, p.478. For an English translation of this document, see K. Clark et al. (eds), *Soviet Culture and Power: A History in Documents, 1917–1953*, Yale University Press: London & New Haven 2007 doc.170.
191. A translation of this document, together with an explanation of its provenance, may be found in K. M. F. Platt & D. Brandenberger (eds), *Epic Revisionism: Russian History and Literature as Stalinist Propaganda*, University of Wisconsin Press: Madison 2006 pp.179–89. Additional clarification may be found in Ilizarov, *Stalin, Ivan Groznyi*, pp.270–9.
192. *Vlast' i Khudozhestvennaya Intelligenstiya*, docs 13 (pp.486–7), 16 (p.500) and 18 (p.501).
193. 'P'esa Al. Tolstogo "Ivan Groznyi" v Malom Teatre', *Pravda* (27 October 1944); 'Novaya Postanovka P'esy Al. Tolstogo na Stsene Malogo Teatra', *Pravda* (30 May 1945).
194. RGASPI, F.558, Op.3, D.351 p.57 of the play.
195. W. Averell Harriman, 'Stalin at War' in G. R. Urban (ed.), *Stalinism: Its Impact on Russia and the World*, Wildwood House: Aldershot 1985 pp.40–2.
196. Clark et al., *Soviet Culture and Power*, doc.172.
197. Eisenstein's background thinking about Ivan and his film is revealed in an article he published in *Literatura i Iskusstvo* (Literature and Art) in July 1942, summarised by Platt, *Terror and Greatness*, pp.212–13.
198. *Kremlevskii Kinoteatr, 1928–1953*, Rosspen: Moscow 2005 doc.257.
199. Clark et al., *Soviet Culture and Power*, doc.177. On this whole episode, see further M. Belodubrovskaya, *Not According to Plan: Filmmaking Under Stalin*, Cornell University Press: Ithaca NY 2017, and D. Brandenberger & K. M. F. Platt, 'Terribly Pragmatic: Rewriting the History of Ivan IV's Reign, 1937–1956' in Platt & Brandenberger, *Epic Revisionism*.
200. In May 1944 Cherkasov presented Zhdanov with a signed photograph of himself as Ivan the Terrible, which carried the inscription, 'We are standing at the edge of the sea and will continue to stand there.' This is a reference to Ivan's expansion of Russia to the Baltic. In 1944 Zhdanov was the head of the Leningrad communist party and the Red Army was in the process of recapturing the Baltic coastal lands from the Germans. See Platt, *Terror and Greatness*, p.214.
201. Clark et al., *Soviet Culture and Power*, pp.441–2.
202. *Vlast' i Khudozhestvennaya Intelligenstiya*, doc.34, pp.612–19. For an English translation of the entire discussion: Clark et al., *Soviet Culture and Power*, doc.175. Irena

Makaryk speculates that Stalin might have derived his view of Hamlet as a weak-willed character from Turgenev's essay 'Hamlet and Don Quixote' and his short story 'Hamlet of the Shchigrov District'. See her 'Stalin and Shakespeare' in N. Khomenko (ed.), *The Shakespeare International Yearbook*, vol. 18, Special Section on Soviet Shakespeare, Routledge: London July 2020 pp.46–7. The only other known Stalin reference to a specific work of Shakespeare is an ambiguous marginal comment on Pyotr Kogan's *Essays on the History of West European Literature* (1909) in which he appears to say the author has ignored *The Tempest*, a play which has a bearing on the Bard's character. However, it is not certain the crabbed handwriting is Stalin's (RGASPI, Op.1, D.32, p.158 of the book).

203. R. C. Tucker, *Stalin in Power: The Revolution from Above, 1928–1941*, paperback edn, Norton: New York 1992 pp.276–9; Perrie, 'The Tsar, the Emperor, the Leader', p.89.
204. Cited by Y. Gorlizki & O. Khlevniuk, *Cold Peace: Stalin and the Soviet Ruling Circle, 1945–1953*, Oxford University Press: Oxford 2004 pp.34–5.
205. Cited by Service, *Stalin: A Biography*, pp.561–2.
206. On the Alexandrov episode see chap.2 of E. Pollock, *Stalin and the Soviet Science Wars*, Princeton University Press: Princeton 2006.
207. G. Alexandrov, *Filosofskie Predshestvenniki Marksizma*, Politizdat: Moscow 1940. RGASPI, F.558, Op.3, D.1. The markings may possibly be Svetlana's.
208. RGASPI, F.558, Op.3, D.237, pp.76–7 of the book.
209. Dobrenko, *Late Stalinism*, pp.396–402; Gorlizki & Khlevniuk, *Cold Peace*, pp.36–8.
210. On the Lysenko affair, see chap.3 of Pollock, *Stalin and the Soviet Science Wars*.
211. Cited by J. Brooks, *Thank You, Comrade Stalin! Soviet Public Culture from Revolution to Cold War*, Princeton University Press: Princeton 2000 pp.213–14.
212. Platt, *Terror and Greatness*, p.177.
213. V. A. Nevezhin, *Zastol'nye Rechi Stalina*, AIRO: Moscow-St Petersburg 2003 doc.107.
214. On the Pushkin centenary: Petrone, *Life Has Become More Joyous, Comrades*, chap.5.
215. https://www.marxists.org/reference/archive/stalin/works/1947/09/08.htm. Accessed 4 August 2021.
216. J. Brunstedt, *The Soviet Myth of World War II: Patriotic Memory and the Russian Question in the USSR*, Cambridge University Press: Cambridge 2021 pp.37–8, 107–8.
217. *Rol' Russkoi Nauki v Razvetii Mirovoi Nauki i Kul'tury*, MGU: Moscow 1946; RGASPI, F.558, Op.3, D.368, pp.29–36 of the book for Stalin's markings.
218. A. Popovskii, 'Zametki o Russkoi Nauke', *Novyi Mir*, 3 (March 1948), RGASPI, F.558, Op.3, D.234, pp.174–85 for Stalin's markings.
219. Brooks, *Thank You, Comrade Stalin!*, pp.213–14.
220. Pollock, *Stalin and the Soviet Science Wars*, p.144. This section on Pavlov draws on chap.6 of Pollock's book.
221. I. P. Pavlov, *Dvadtsatiletnii Opyt Ob"ektivnogo Izucheniya Vysshei Nervnoi Deyatel'nosti Zhivotnykh*, LenMendizdat: Leningrad 1932. Copy in the Stalin collection in the SSPL.
222. RGASPI, F.558, Op.11, D.762, doc.9, l.27. The final two sentences were hand-inserted by Stalin into the draft of his letter to Zhdanov dated 6 October. This document was drawn to my attention by Pollock, *Stalin and the Soviet Science Wars*, p.146.
223. B. S. Ilizarov, *Pochetnyi Akademik Stalin i Akademik Marr*, Veche: Moscow 2012 pp.145–7.
224. On the Latinisation campaign, see chap.5 of Terry Martin's *The Affirmative Action Empire: Nations and Nationalism in the Soviet Union, 1923–1939*, Cornell University Press: Ithaca NY 2001.
225. R. Medvedev, 'Stalin and Linguistics' in R. & Z. Medvedev, *The Unknown Stalin: His Life, Death and Legacy*, Overlook Press: Woodstock NY 2004 p.211.
226. RGASPI, F.558, Op.11, D.773, docs 6–7.
227. On Marr and his ideas: Y. Slezkine, 'N. Ia. Marr and the National Origins of Soviet Ethnogenetics', *Slavic Review*, 55/4 (Winter 1996).
228. Ilizarov, *Pochetnyi Akademik Stalin* p.186. The book may be found in the Stalin collection in the SSPL. The book was inscribed by the author not to Stalin but to another fellow Georgian, Lavrenty Beria.

229. N. Marr (ed.), *Tristan i Izol'da: Ot Geroini Lyubvi Feodal'noi Evropy do Bogini Materiarkhal'noi Afrevrazii*, Akad.Nauk: Leningrad 1932; N. Marr, *Izvlechenie iz Svansko-Russkogo Slovarya*, Petrograd 1922 (RGASPI, F.558, Op.3, D.212); N. Marr, *O Yazyke i Istorii Abkhazov*, Moscow-Leningrad 1938 (RGASPI, F.558, Op.3, D.213). A copy of the first book may be found in the Stalin collection of the SSPL. Its presence there was brought to my attention by Ilizarov *Pochetnyi Akademik Stalin* p.184, which also contains (pp.185–7) a detailed analysis of Stalin's marks in the Abkhazia book.

230. RGASPI, F.558, Op.11, D.1250, doc.1. See also Pollock, *Stalin and the Soviet Science Wars*, p.112. I am generally indebted to Pollock's coverage of the linguistics controversy in chap.5 of his book.

231. The drafts of Chikobava's article, as edited by Stalin, may be found here: RGASPI, F558, Op.11, D.1251, doc.1. The cited additions by him may be seen on Ll.138–9, 162. See also Pollock, *Stalin and the Soviet Science Wars*, pp.112–14 and p.116, which contains a photocopy of the insertion by Stalin of the sentences about the withering away of national languages.

232. Translations of all the contributions published by *Pravda* may be found in *The Soviet Linguistics Controversy*, Columbia University Slavic Studies, King's Crown Press: New York 1951. This booklet may be found on the Internet.

233. Medvedev & Medvedev, *Unknown Stalin*, p.215. Among the books Stalin consulted was a 1912 introductory textbook on linguistics by D. N. Kudryavsky.

234. RGASPI, F.558, Op.3, D.19, p.378 of the book. It is not certain that Stalin read these entries at this time but it is highly likely that he did. Ilizarov (*Pochetnyi Akademik Stalin*, pp.202–10) provides a detailed analysis of these *pometki* but it does not add anything to Stalin's stated views on language and linguistics. As Ilizarov points out (p.203), Stalin did not mark the encyclopaedia entry on Japhetic languages.

235. My summary and quotations derive from J. V. Stalin, *Concerning Marxism in Linguistics*, Soviet News Booklet: London 1950.

236. G. B. Fedorov (ed.), *Po Sledam Drevnikh Kul'tur*, Gosizdat: Moscow 1951. RGASPI, F.558, Op.3, D.246, pp.8, 71–112 for Stalin's markings.

237. Dobrenko, *Late Stalinism*, p.385.

238. Kotkin, *Stalin: Waiting for Hitler*, p.544.

239. J. Stalin, *Works*, vol.2, Foreign Languages Publishing House: Moscow 1953 pp.28–32.

240. Kotkin, *Stalin: Waiting for Hitler*, p.753 n.88.

241. Ibid., pp.544–5; R. Medvedev, *Let History Judge: The Origins and Consequences of Stalinism*, Macmillan: London 1972, pp.509–10.

242. J. Stalin, *Works*, vol.9, Foreign Languages Publishing House: Moscow 1954 pp.156–8.

243. RGASPI, F.558, Op.3, D.105.

244. E. Dobrenko, *Late Stalinism*, p.358.

245. E. Fischer, *An Opposing Man*, Allen Lane: London 1974 p.261.

246. Some readings may be found here: H. F. Scott & W. F. Scott (eds), *The Soviet Art of War*, Westview Press: Boulder CO 1982. Tukhachevsky and Svechin perished in the purges.

247. RGASPI, F.558, Op.3, Dd.253–6, Op.11, Dd.494–9.

248. RGASPI, F.558, Op.3, Dd.9, 80. The photocopy may be found in the Stalin collection in SSPL.

249. *Artilleriya v Proshlom, Nastoyashchem i Budushchem*, Voenizdat: Moscow 1925. RGASPI, F.558, Op.3, D.380.

250. Urban, *Stalinism*, p.43.

251. On Leer: P. Von Wahlde, 'A Pioneer of Russian Strategic Thought: G. A. Leer, 1929–1904', *Military Affairs* (December 1971); D. A. Rich, *The Tsar's Colonels: Professionalism, Strategy, and Subversion in Late Imperial Russia*, Harvard University Press: Cambridge MA 1998 pp.55–6; J. W. Steinberg, *All The Tsar's Men: Russia's General Staff and the Fate of the Empire, 1898–1914*, Johns Hopkins University Press: Baltimore 2010 pp.47–52.

252. RGASPI, F.558, Op.3, Dd.108–11. Previously, the books belonged to Tsarist institutional libraries.

253. RGASPI, F.558, Op.3, D.224, for Stalin's markings of chapter one of Moltke's book, and D.195, pp.264–81 for his marking of Ludendorff's text.

254. Svechin's key work is available in an English translation: A. A. Svechin, *Strategy*, East View Press: Minneapolis 1992. Svechin's views were controversial, particularly his advocacy of preparations for a war of attrition that would wear the enemy down over time, as opposed to one of manoeuvre and the annihilation of enemy forces in decisive battles. In the 1920s and 1930s Svechin was criticised by a number of reviewers and discussants who advocated the latter strategy. Stalin's marked copy of the first edition of Svechin's history of military art may be found here: RGASPI, F.558, Op.3, Dd.311–12. His copy of Svechin's strategy book, together with a later edition of the military art history, is in the Stalin collection in SSPL.

255. Ibid., D.94, pp.v, vii, viii for Stalin's markings. Stalin had another, unmarked, copy of *On War*. This may be found in the SSPL Stalin collection.

256. Ibid., p.35 of the book.

257. G. Roberts, *Stalin's Wars: From World War to Cold War, 1939–1953*, Yale University Press: London & New Haven 2006 p.110.

258. O. Rzheshevsky, 'Shaposhnikov' in H. Shukman (ed.), *Stalin's Generals*, Phoenix Press: London 1997.

259. The general sections of the three volumes of *Mozg Armii* were republished in 1974 and reprinted in 1982: B. M. Shaposhnikov, *Vospominaniya [i] Voenno-Nauchnye Trudy*, Voenizdat: Moscow 1982. The volume also contains Shaposhnikov's memoir of his early life. Some extracts from *Mozg Armii* in English may be found in Scott & Scott, *The Soviet Art of War*, pp.46–50.

260. Shaposhnikov, *Vospominaniya*, p.507.

261. G. K. Zhukov, *Vospominaniya i Razmyshleniya*, vol.1, Novosti: Moscow 1990 p.367.

262. *Na Prieme Stalina*, Novyi Khronograf: Moscow 2008 pp.337–40.

263. M. Bragin, *Polkovodets Kutuzov*, Molodaya Gvardiya: Moscow 1941. An English translation called *Field Marshal Kutuzov* was published by the Foreign Languages Publishing House: Moscow 1944.

264. Talking to Stalin in August 1942, Churchill remarked that his ancestor the Duke of Marlborough had put an end to the menace to freedom posed by the War of the Spanish Succession (1701–14). In response, Stalin said that Wellington was the greater British general because he had defeated Napoleon. Churchill's interpreter, Major Birse, recalled that Stalin 'then proceeded to exhibit his knowledge of history by reference to Wellington's invasion of Spain . . . quoting chapter and verse with regard to some of the battles. I imagine that he had made a special study of the Napoleonic wars, which in many respects paralleled the one then in progress' (A. H. Birse, *Memoirs of an Interpreter*, Michael Joseph: London 1967 pp.103).

265. 'Zapis' Besedy I. V. Stalina s Otvetstvennymi Redaktorami Zhurnalov "Voennaya Mysl'" i "Voennyi Vestnik", 5 Marta 1945 goda', *Voenno-Istoricheskii Zhurnal*, 3 (2004) pp.3–4.

266. RGASPI, F.558, Op.3, D.25.

267. https://www.trumanlibrary.gov/library/oral-histories/harrima1. Accessed 4 August 2021.

268. K. Osipov, *Suvorov*, Gospolizdat: Moscow 1941. The book contains a note by Osipov dated 28 June 1941. It was also translated and published in English during the war: *Alexander Suvorov: A Biography*, Hutchinson & Co.: London n.d.

269. RGASPI F.558. Op.11, D.204, n.2.

270. RGASPI, F.558, op.11, D.1599. Osipov's second book on Suvorov, as corrected by Stalin, was published in various editions during the war. He also gave many public lectures on Suvorov.

271. Clark et al., *Soviet Culture and Power*, doc.130. Russian text: *I.V. Stalin: Istoricheskaya Ideologiya v SSSR v 1920–1950 e gody (Sbornik Dokumentov i Materialov)*, vol.1, Nauka-Piter: St Petersburg 2006 doc.221.

272. The stenograms of Stalin's speech may be found here: *Zimnyaya Voina, 1939–1940: I.V. Stalin i Finskaya Kampaniya*, Nauka: Moscow 1999 pp.272–82. In English: A. O. Chubaryan & H. Shukman (eds), *Stalin and the Soviet–Finnish War, 1939–1940*, Frank Cass: London 2001 pp.263–74. See further: M. L. G. Spencer, *Stalinism and the Soviet–Finnish War, 1939–40*, Palgrave: London 2018.

273. *Istoriya Russkoi Armii i Flota*, Obrazovanie: Moscow 1911. RGASPI, F.558, Op.3, F.80, pp.7–23 for Stalin's markings. He read the book in the mid-late 1930s.
274. 'Kratkaya Zapis' Vystupleniya na Vypuske Slushatelei Akademii Krasnoi Armii, 5 Maya 1941 goda', I. Stalin, *Sochineniya*, vol.18, Soyuz: Tver' 2006 pp.213–18.
275. Dimitrov, *Diary*, p.160.
276. E. Mawdsley, 'Explaining Military Failure: Stalin, the Red Army, and the First Period of the Patriotic War' in G. Roberts (ed.), *Stalin: His Times and Ours*, IAREES: Dublin 2005 p.138.
277. I. Stalin, *O Velikoi Otechestvennoi Voine Sovetskogo Soyuza*, Moscow 1950 p.205.
278. Ibid., pp.271–303.
279. https://digitalarchive.wilsoncenter.org/document/116179.pdf. Accessed 4 August 2021.
280. E. Mawdsley, 'Stalin: Victors Are Not Judged', *Journal of Slavic Military Studies* 19 (2006) p.715.
281. D. E. Davis & W. S. G. Kohn, 'Lenin's 'Notebook on Clausewitz', http://www.clausewitz.com/bibl/DavisKohn-LeninsNotebookOnClausewitz.pdf. Accessed 4 August 2021. Stalin's unmarked copy of the 1931 volume is located in the Stalin collection in the SSPL.
282. RGASPI, F.558, Op.3, D.47.
283. 'Zapis' Besedy', p.3.
284. https://www.marxists.org/reference/archive/stalin/works/1946/02/23.htm. Accessed 4 August 2021.
285. R. Medvedev, 'Generalissimo Stalin, General Clausewitz and Colonel Razin' in Medvedev & Medvedev, *Unknown Stalin*, p.188.
286. A. M. Ball, *Imagining America: Influence and Images in Twentieth-Century Russia*, Rowman & Littlefield: Lanham MD 2003 p.24.
287. J. Stalin, *Works*, vol.6, Foreign Languages Publishing House: Moscow 1953 pp.194–5.
288. Rayfield, *Stalin and His Hangmen*, p.43.
289. B. O'Keeffe, *Esperanto and Languages of Internationalism in Revolutionary Russia*, Bloomsbury Academic: London 2021 pp.148–51.
290. Yu. G. Murin (ed.), *Iosif Stalin v Ob"yatiyakh Sem'i*, Rodina: Moscow 1993 docs 46–7.
291. J. Stalin, *Works*, vol.13, Foreign Languages Publishing House: Moscow 1955 p.271.
292. Ibid., vol.3 (1953) pp.250–3.
293. K. Zubovich, *Moscow Monumental: Soviet Skyscrapers and Urban Life in Stalin's Capital*, Princeton University Press: Princeton 2021 chap.2; Belodubrovskaya, *Not According to Plan*, p.27.
294. S. Lomb, *Stalin's Constitution: Soviet Participatory Politics and the Discussion of the 1936 Draft*, Routledge: New York 2018.
295. https://www.marxists.org/reference/archive/stalin/works/1936/11/25.htm. Accessed 4 August 2021.
296. RGASPI, F.558, Op.11, D.143.
297. https://www.marxists.org/reference/archive/stalin/works/1937/12/11.htm.
298. RGASPI, F.558, Op.3, D.369.
299. Stalin, *Works*, vol.13, p.284.
300. https://www.marxists.org/reference/archive/stalin/works/1934/07/23.htm. Accessed 4 August 2021.
301. Cited by M. Edele, 'Better to Lose Australia', *Inside Story*, https://insidestory.org.au/better-to-lose-australia (25 May 2021).
302. Roberts, *Stalin's Wars*, p.267.
303. G. Roberts, 'Why Roosevelt Was Right about Stalin', *History News Network*, http://hnn.us/articles/36194.html (19 March 2007). For a radically different view of Stalin's attitude to Roosevelt: R. H. McNeal, 'Roosevelt through Stalin's Spectacles', *International Journal*, 18/2 (Spring 1963).
304. J. Stalin, *Works*, vol.10, Foreign Languages Publishing House: Moscow 1954 pp.141 ff.
305. RGASPI, F.558, Op.3, D.41, pp.82–4 of the article for the quotes marked by Stalin.
306. A. Girshfel'd, 'O Roli SShA v Organizatsii Antisovetskoi Interventsii v Sibiri i na Dal'nem Vostoke', *Voprosy Istorii*, 8 (August 1948) p.15 of the article for the Stalin notation.
307. Magnúsdóttir, *Enemy Number One*.

CHAPTER 6: REVERSE ENGINEERING: STALIN AND SOVIET LITERATURE

1. This chapter is focused on Stalin's general attitudes to fictional literature. On his relations with individual Soviet writers, see: A. Kemp-Welch, *Stalin and the Literary Intelligentsia, 1928–1939*, St Martin's Press: New York 1991; B. J. Boeck, *Stalin's Scribe: Literature, Ambition and Survival*, Pegasus Books: New York 2019; Y. Gromov, *Stalin: Iskusstvo i Vlast'*, Eksmo: Moscow 2003; B. Frezinskii, *Pisateli i Sovetskie Vozhdi*, Ellis Lak: Moscow 2008; and B. Sarnov, *Stalin i Pisateli*, 4 vols, Eksmo: Moscow 2010–11.

2. A. Gromyko, *Memories*, Hutchinson: London 1989 p.101.

3. K. Clark et al. (eds), *Soviet Culture and Power: A History in Documents, 1917–1953*, Yale University Press: London & New Haven 2007 doc.18.

4. Ibid., doc.19.

5. Ibid., doc.20.

6. *Vlast' i Khudozhestvennaya Intelligentsiya, 1917–1953*, Demokratiya: Moscow 2002 doc.46, p.40.

7. Clark et al., *Soviet Culture and Power*, doc.21.

8. J. Barber, 'The Establishment of Intellectual Orthodoxy in the U.S.S.R. 1928–1934', *Past & Present*, 83 (May, 1979) p.159.

9. L. Maximenkov & L. Heretz, 'Stalin's Meeting with a Delegation of Ukrainian Writers on 12 February 1929', *Harvard Ukrainian Studies*, 16/3–4 (December 1992). This publication contains the Russian transcript of the meeting, together with an English translation. A substantial extract from the transcript may be found in Clark et al., *Soviet Culture and Power*, doc.27. The archive typescript may be found here: Rossiiskii Gosudarstvennyi Arkhiv Sotsial'no-Politicheskoi Istorii (hereafter RGASPI), F.558, Op.1, D.4490.

10. Clark et al., *Soviet Culture and Power*, doc.33.

11. Stalin's reply was private at the time but published in his collected works after the war: J. Stalin, *Works*, vol.13, Foreign Languages Publishing House: Moscow 1955 pp.26–7.

12. N. Mandelstam, *Hope Against Hope: A Memoir*, Harvill Press: London 1999 p.26. Reputedly, Bedny was betrayed by his secretary, who copied this entry from his diary and sent it to Stalin.

13. R. V. Daniels, 'Soviet Thought in the 1930s: The Cultural Counterrevolution' in his *Trotsky, Stalin and Socialism*, Westview Press: Boulder CO 1991 p.143.

14. *Mezhdu Molotom i Nakoval'nei: Soyuz Sovetskikh Pisatelei SSSR*, vol.1, Rosspen: Moscow 2010 doc.29.

15. S. Kotkin, *Stalin: Waiting for Hitler, 1928–1941*, Penguin: London 2017 pp.151–2. See further Michael David-Fox's chapter 'Gorky's Gulag' in his *Showcasing the Great Experiment: Cultural Diplomacy & Western Visitors to the Soviet Union, 1921–1941*, Oxford University Press: Oxford 2012.

16. In making this point, Stalin doubtless had in mind what Lenin said in October 1920: 'Proletarian culture is not something that springs from nowhere, is not an invention of people who call themselves specialists in proletarian culture. This is complete nonsense. Proletarian culture must be a logical development of those funds of knowledge which humanity has worked out under the yoke of capitalist society' (R. K. Dasgupta, 'Lenin on Literature', *Indian Literature*, 13/3 (September 1970) p.21. See further: A. T. Rubinstein, 'Lenin on Literature, Language, and Censorship', *Science & Society*, 59/3 (Fall 1995). Stalin certainly read Lenin's speech because he marked it in vol.17 of the 1st edition of Lenin's collected works published in 1923 (RGASPI, Op.3, D.131, pp. 313–29). On Marx: S. S. Prawer, *Karl Marx and World Literature*, Verso: London 1976.

17. *Bol'shaya Tsenzura: Pisateli i Zhurnalisty v Strane Sovetov, 1917–1956*, Demokratiya: Moscow 2005 doc.196; S. Davies & J. Harris, *Stalin's World: Dictating the Soviet Order*, Yale University Press: London & New Haven 2014 pp.250–1.

18. Stalin's remarks are those recorded by the literary critic K. L. Zelinsky. RGASPI, F.558, Op.11, D.1116, doc.3, Ll.32–3; *Mezhdu Molotom i Nakoval'nei*, doc.38; C. A. Ruder, *Making History for Stalin: The Story of the Belomor Canal*, University Press of Florida: Gainesville 1998 p.44; Kemp-Welch, *Stalin and the Literary Intelligentsia*, pp.130–1. The authorship of the term 'socialist realism' is unclear. One possibility is that

it emerged in exchanges between Stalin and the journalist Ivan Gronsky in 1932–3. According to Gronsky, he suggested the term 'proletarian socialist realism' but Stalin thought it sounded better without the first adjective (Kemp-Welch p.132).

19. RGASPI, F.71, Op.10, D.170, L.162.
20. *Soviet Writers' Congress 1934: The Debate on Socialist Realism and Modernism*, Lawrence and Wishart: London 1977 pp.21–2. The quoted passage has been truncated and ellipses omitted.
21. Ibid., pp.252–5.
22. Clark et al., *Soviet Culture and Power*, doc.123.
23. *Bol'shaya Tsenzura*, doc.327.
24. RGASPI, F.558, Op.3, D.251. This connection was brought to my attention by ibid., p.455, n.11. The translation of Plekhanov derives from https://www.marxists.org/archive/plekhanov/1895/monist. Accessed 4 August 2021.
25. I. R. Makaryk, 'Stalin and Shakespeare' in N. Khomenko (ed.), *The Shakespeare International Yearbook*, vol. 18, Special Section on Soviet Shakespeare, Routledge: London 2020.
26. Clark et al., *Soviet Culture and Power*, doc.129.
27. Ibid., doc.131
28. On this whole episode, see M. Belodubrovskaya, *Not According to Plan: Filmmaking under Stalin*, Cornell University Press: Ithaca NY 2017 pp.41–2, 83–4, 192–3.
29. Davies & Harris, *Stalin's World*, pp.254–5.
30. The transcript of the meeting may be found in G. L. Bondareva (ed.), *Kremlevskii Kinoteatr, 1928–1953*, Rosspen: Moscow 2005 doc.214. This is the key documentary collection of Soviet film-making during the Stalin era. See further, J. Miller, *Soviet Cinema: Politics and Persuasion under Stalin*, I. B. Tauris: London 2010 especially pp.60–9.
31. Clark et al., *Soviet Culture and Power*, doc.132. The last three sentences added and translated by me from the Russian transcript.
32. S. Yekelchyk, *Stalin's Empire of Memory: Russian–Ukrainian Relations in the Soviet Historical Imagination*, Toronto University Press: Toronto 2004 pp.40, 54–5.
33. Clark et al., *Soviet Culture and Power*, doc.177.
34. Ibid., p.455. Stalin's comments took the form of an anonymous report on the film that was published in Soviet newspapers.
35. S. Alliluyeva, *20 Letters to a Friend*, Penguin: Harmondsworth 1968 p.129.
36. Cited by A. M. Ball, *Imagining America: Influence and Images in Twentieth-Century Russia*, Rowman & Littlefield: Lanham MD 2003 p.87.
37. A. Mikoyan, *Tak Bylo*, Moscow: Vagrius 1999 pp.533–4.
38. Clark et al., *Soviet Culture and Power*, doc.163.
39. *Bol'shaya Tsenzura*, doc.414.
40. Clark et al., *Soviet Culture and Power*, docs 153–5.
41. *Vlast' i Khudozhestvennaya Intelligentsiya*, docs 14, 22 pp.565, 598.
42. Clark et al., *Soviet Culture and Power*, doc.162.
43. N. Mitchison, 'AWPA Writers Visit to the USSR', Authors World Peace Appeal, Bulletin no.7 (1952) p.9. The AWPA was a 1950s non-aligned peace movement.
44. M. Djilas, *Conversations with Stalin*, Penguin: London 2014 p.111.
45. Ibid., pp.77–8.
46. S. Alliluyeva, *Only One Year*, Penguin: London 1971 p.336.
47. D. Shepilov, *The Kremlin's Scholar*, Yale University Press: London & New Haven 2014 p.92. Only two volumes of Dostoevsky's collected writing and his diary for 1873–6 survived the dispersal of Stalin's library. These books may be found in the SSPL's collection of Stalin's books. According to Boris Ilizarov, Stalin marked parts of Dostoevsky's novel *The Brothers Karamazov*. However, upon inspection of the book in the library it is practically certain that these are *not* Stalin's markings.
48. R. L. Strong, 'The Soviet Interpretation of Gogol', *American Slavic and East European Review*, 14/4 (December 1955) pp.528–9, 533.

49. O. Johnson, 'The Stalin Prize and the Soviet Artist: Status Symbol or Stigma?', *Slavic Review*, 70/4 (Winter 2011) p.826. See further: P. Akhmanaev, *Stalinskie Premii*, Russkie Vityazi: Moscow 2016. Details of all the awards made, together with other documentation, may be found in V. F. Svin'in & K. A. Oseev (eds), *Stalinskie Premii*, Svin'in i Synov'ya: Novosibirsk 2007.

50. Shepilov, *The Kremlin's Scholar*, pp.104–9.

51. Davies & Harris, *Stalin's World*, pp.270–1.

52. Ibid., p.271.

53. K. Simonov, *Glazami Cheloveka Moego Pokoleniya: Razmyshleniya o I. V. Staline*, Novosti: Moscow 1989 p.233.

54. RGASPI, F.558, Op.3, D.233, pp.41–101 for Stalin's editing of the play.

55. *Vlast' i Khudozhestvennaya Intelligentsiya*, doc.104 pp.675–81. The author of the report was Vladimir Kruzhkov, the former head of IMEL.

56. M. Zorin, 'Obsuzhdenie Romana V. Latisa "K Novomu Beregu"', *Literaturnaya Gazeta* (15 December 1952).

57. *Vlast' i Khudozhestvennaya Intelligentsiya*, doc.101. The handwritten draft and typescript of the letter may be found in RGASPI, F.558, Op.11, D.205, Ll.1929–136. These documents were brought to my attention by Davies & Harris, *Stalin's World*, p.263. It seems that Stalin's original intention was to publish the letter as coming from a group of high-ranking party officials, including himself.

58. P. Neruda, *Memoirs*, Penguin: London 1977 p.317.

59. https://redcaucasus.wordpress.com/2018/09/18/ode-to-stalin-by-pablo-neruda. Accessed 4 August 2021.

60. I. Ehrenburg, *Post-War Years, 1945–1954*, MacGibbon & Kee: London 1966 p.46. The story about Stalin and his novel was told to him by Alexander Fadeev, the head of the Soviet Writers' Union, who worked closely with Ehrenburg in the international peace movement.

61. N. Krementsov, *The Cure: A Story of Cancer and Politics from the Annals of the Cold War*, University of Chicago Press: Chicago 2004 pp.136–43.

CHAPTER 7: EDITOR-IN-CHIEF OF THE USSR

1. A point made by Holly Case's thought-provoking piece 'The Tyrant as Editor', *Chronicle of Higher Education* (7 October 2013).

2. Rossiiskii Gosudarstvennyi Arkhiv Sotsial'no-Politicheskoi Istorii (hereafter RGASPI), F.558, Op.4, D.333, L.1.

3. E. Pollock, *Conversations with Stalin on Questions of Political Economy*, Cold War International History Project Working Paper No.33 (July 2001) p.9.

4. On the writer's relationship with Stalin, see L. Spiridonova, 'Gorky and Stalin (According to New Materials from A. M. Gorky's Archive)', *Russian Review*, 54/3 (July 1995).

5. Mints's memoir is summarised by R. C. Tucker, *Stalin in Power: The Revolution from Above, 1928–1941*, Norton: New York 1992 pp.531–2.

6. Stalin's editing of this first volume may be found in RGASPI, F.558, Op.1, D.3165. It bears out Mints's recollection.

7. D. Brandenberger, *Propaganda State in Crisis: Soviet Ideology, Indoctrination and Terror under Stalin, 1927–1941*, Yale University Press: London & New Haven 2011 p.80.

8. E. MacKinnon, 'Writing History for Stalin: Isaak Izrailevich Mints and the *Istoriia grazhdanskoi voiny*', *Kritika*, 6/1 (2005) p.22.

9. I. Mints, 'Podgotovka Velikoi Proletarskoi Revolyutsii: K Vykhodu v Svet Pervogo Toma "Istoriya Grazhdanskoi Voiny v SSSR", *Bol'shevik*, 12/15 (November 1935) p.30 for the quote.

10. This section on the *Short Course* leans heavily on the work of David Brandenberger: 'The Fate of Interwar Soviet Internationalism: A Case Study of the Editing of Stalin's 1938 *Short Course on the History of the ACP(B)*', *Revolutionary Russia*, 29/1 (2016); 'Stalin and the Muse of History: The Dictator and His Critics on the Editing of the 1938 Short

Course' in V. Tismaneanu & B. C. Iacob (eds), *Ideological Storms: Intellectuals, Dictators and the Totalitarian Temptation*, CEU Press: Budapest 2019; *Stalin's Master Narrative: A Critical Edition of the History of the Communist Party of the Soviet Union (Bolsheviks): Short Course*, Yale University Press: London & New Haven 2019 (co-edited with M. Zelenov); and *'Kratkii Kurs Istorii VKP (b)': Tekst i Ego Istoriya v 2 Chastyakh: Chast' 1*, Rosspen: Moscow 2014 (co-edited with M. Zelenov). The former edited volume reproduces the official English-language translation of the *Short Course* together with the details of Stalin's editing, while the latter contains the archive documents appertaining to the process of producing the book.

11. Brandenberger & Zelenov, *'Kratkii Kurs Istorii VKP (b)'*, doc.112.
12. Ibid., doc.165.
13. Brandenberger & Zelenov, *Stalin's Master Narrative*, pp.17–18.
14. Brandenberger & Zelenov, *Kratkii Kurs Istorii VKP (b)'*, doc.231 p.429. The conference took place from 27 September to 1 October 1938.
15. Brandenberger & Zelenov, *Stalin's Master Narrative*, p.20.
16. Ibid., p.21.
17. Brandenberger & Zelenov, *Kratkii Kurs Istorii VKP (b)'*, doc.231 p.457.
18. The text of the section may be found in Brandenberger & Zelenov, *Stalin's Master Narrative*, pp.48–73.
19. For an overview, see E. van Ree, 'Stalin as a Marxist Philosopher', *Studies in East European Thought*, 52/4 (December 2000). See further G. V. Wetter, *Dialectical Materialism: A Historical and Systematic Survey of Philosophy in the Soviet Union*, Routledge & Kegan Paul: London 1958 chap.10, and Z. A. Jordan, *The Evolution of Dialectical Materialism*, Macmillan: London 1967 chap.8.
20. J. Stalin, 'Anarchism or Socialism?' in *Works*, vol.1, Foreign Languages Publishing House: Moscow 1952 pp.297–372.
21. Cited by A. Bonfanti, 'Eric Hobsbawm's Dialectical Materialism in the Postwar Period 1946–56', *Twentieth Century Communism*, 19 (November 2020).
22. Wetter, *Dialectical Materialism*, p.212. Brandenberger quotes a figure of 40 million copies during Stalin's time.
23. RGASPI, Op.558, Dd.1602–4. In the archive the typescript is misidentified as being that of a separate book but the pagination indicates that it is part of a larger MS, i.e. *Istoriya Diplomatii*. Only the chapters dealing with the 1920s are preserved in these files.
24. RGASPI F.558, Op.1, D.5754, L.98. On Pankratova, see R. E. Zelnik, *Perils of Pankratova: Some Stories from the Annals of Soviet Historiography*, University of Washington Press: Seattle 2005.
25. V. P. Potemkin (ed.), *Istoriya Diplomatii*, vol.3, Ogiz: Moscow-Leningrad 1945 pp.701–64. See further V. V. Aspaturian, 'Diplomacy in the Mirror of Soviet Scholarship' in J. Keep & L. Brisby (eds), *Contemporary History in the Soviet Mirror*, Praeger: New York 1964. Tarle made the claim about Stalin in a letter to the party leader, G. M. Malenkov, in September 1945, to whom he had written complaining about a critical review of his book on the Crimean War that had just appeared in the party's journal *Bol'shevik*: I. A. Sheina, 'Akademik E. V. Tarle i Vlast': Pis'ma Istorika I. V. Stalinu i G. M. Malenkovu, 1937–1950gg', *Istoricheskii Arkhiv*, 3 (2001). Unbeknown to Tarle, but not to Stalin, he had recently come under attack within the party for advocating a soft line on the iniquities of nineteenth-century Tsarist foreign policy. The review reflected that criticism of Tarle, even though it had not and did not become public knowledge. It's possible that Stalin asked Tarle to write the piece on the methods of bourgeois diplomacy when he met him and Potemkin on 3 June 1941, a meeting that lasted an hour and a half, at which the three men presumably discussed the follow-up to the recently published first volume of *Istoriya Diplomatii*.
26. M. Beloff, 'A Soviet History of Diplomacy', *Soviet Studies*, 1/2 (October 1949). In a 1941 book on the history of Soviet foreign policy by A. A. Troyanovskii & B. E. Shtein, Stalin deleted a reference that attributed the direction of diplomacy to him and Lenin and substituted the party. RGASPI, F.558, Op.3, D.390, p.6 of the book.

27. Ibid., Op.11, Dd.221–2. The Simon & Schuster letter may be found in D.221, doc.19. The letter was translated into Russian and its salient points marked by either Stalin or his staff. Stalin did not reply. The letter was brought to my attention by S. McMeekin, *Stalin's War*, Allen Lane: London 2021 p.455. McMeekin mischaracterises the letter as a proposal that Stalin should write an autobiography.

28. Ibid., D.1280, Ll.4–9.

29. D. Brandenberger, 'Stalin as Symbol: A Case Study of the Personality Cult and Its Construction', in S. Davies & J. Harris (eds), *Stalin: A New History*, Cambridge University Press: Cambridge 2005 p.265.

30. I. Stalin, *Sochineniya*, vol.17, Severnaya Korona: Tver 2004 pp.630–3. The meeting took place during the evening of 23 December 1946 and lasted for an hour and a quarter.

31. Brandenberger, 'Stalin as Symbol'.

32. *Bol'shaya Tsenzura: Pisateli i Zhurnalisty v Strane Sovetov, 1917–1956*, Demokratiya: Moscow 2005 doc.416.

33. My summary of Stalin's editing of the *Short Biography* is based on S. Davies & J. Harris, *Stalin's World: Dictating the Soviet Order*, Yale University Press: London & New Haven 2014 pp.155–6; V. A. Belyanov, 'I. V. Stalin Sam o Sebe: Redaktsionnaya Pravka Sobstvennoi Biografii', *Izvestiya TsK KPSS*, 9 (1990); and RGASPI, F.558, Op.11, D.1280. The latter file contains one of the dummies of the *Short Biography* corrected by Stalin. There are other *makety* in Dd.1281–2, not seen by me.

34. During the war, Stalin was more modest about his contribution. Upon receipt of a 1943 General Staff history of the battle for Moscow, he deleted a reference to the 'leadership of comrade Stalin'. RGASPI, F.558, Op.3, D.300, p.4 of the book. This was one of a number of internal studies of the battles and campaigns of the Great Patriotic War that were not published until post-Soviet times.

35. *Joseph Stalin: A Short Biography*, Foreign Languages Publishing House: Moscow 1949 p.89.

36. RGASPI, F.558, Op.11, D.1284.

37. J. Degras (ed.), *Soviet Documents on Foreign Policy*, vol.3 (1933–1941), Oxford University Press: London 1953 p.492.

38. 'Captain H. H. Balfour Moscow Diary 1941', Harriman Papers, Library of Congress Manuscript Division, container 64.

39. W. S. Churchill, *The Second World War*, vol.1, Cassell: London 1948 p.344.

40. *Istoriya Diplomatii*, vol.3 pp.668–9, 672, 680, 682.

41. See F. Hirsch, *Soviet Judgment at Nuremberg: A New History of the International Military Tribunal after World War II*, Oxford University Press: New York 2020 passim.

42. RGASPI F.558, Op.11, Dd.239–42. Stalin did not mark the translation.

43. Ibid., D.243, doc.1, L.1. Reportedly, the historians group consisted of V. M. Khvostov (1905–1972), G. A. Deborin (1907–1987) and B. E. Shtein (1892–1961).

44. *Fal'sifikatory Istorii (Istoricheskaya Spravka)*, Ogiz: Moscow 1948. In English: *Falsifiers of History (Historical Survey)*, Foreign Languages Publishing House: Moscow 1948.

45. RGASPI, F.558, Op.11, D.243, docs.1, 5, 5a.

46. *Falsifiers of History (Historical Survey)*, p.41.

47. Ibid., p.43.

48. Ibid., pp.47–8.

49. Ibid., p.51. Stalin was being a little unfair to Truman. In that same speech he said that on no account did he want Hitler to win. During the war he was a highly effective overseer of Roosevelt's Lend-Lease aid to Britain and the Soviet Union.

50. Ibid., p.52.

51. See G. Roberts, *Molotov: Stalin's Cold Warrior*, Potomac Books: Washington DC 2012 chap.2.

52. *Falsifiers of History*, p.59.

53. E. Pollock, *Stalin and the Soviet Science Wars*, Princeton University Press: Princeton 2006 p.169. In this section I follow in the footsteps of chap.7 of Pollock's book: ' "Everyone Is Waiting": Stalin and the Economic Problems of Communism'. See also the memoirs of

Dmitry Shepilov, who was heavily involved in the textbook discussion and production: *The Kremlin's Scholar*, Yale University Press: London & New Haven 2014.

54. An English translation of the record of Stalin's January 1941 meeting with the economists may be found in Pollock, *Conversations with Stalin*.

55. English translation of Stalin's February, April and May conversations with economists may be found in ibid.

56. They are published in *Stalinskoe Ekonomicheskoe Nasledstvo: Plany i Diskussii, 1947–1955gg*, Rosspen: Moscow 2017.

57. RGASPI, F.558, Op.11, Dd.1242–6.

58. J. Stalin, *Economic Problems of Socialism in the USSR*, Foreign Languages Publishing House: Moscow 1952. For a nit-picking scholastic critique, see N. Leites, 'Stalin as Intellectual', *World Politics*, 6/1 (October 1953).

59. See K. D. Roh, *Stalin's Economic Advisors: The Varga Institute and the Making of Soviet Foreign Policy*, I. B. Tauris: London 2018.

60. Pollock, *Stalin and the Soviet Science Wars*, p.192.

61. Ibid., p.207.

62. An English translation of the textbook may be found here: https://www.marxists.org /subject/economy/authors/pe/index.htm. Accessed 4 August 2021.

63. R. B. Day, *Cold War Capitalism: The View from Moscow, 1945–1975*, M. E. Sharpe: Armonk NY 1995 pp.83–4.

CONCLUSION: THE DICTATOR WHO LOVED BOOKS

1. F. Chuev, *Tak Govoril Kaganovich: Ispoved' Stalinskogo Apostola*, Otechestvo: Moscow 1992 pp.154, 190. The conversation took place in 1991.

2. *Litsedei*: Russian for an actor. I owe this reference to S. Sebag Montefiore, *Stalin: The Court of the Red Tsar*, Weidenfeld & Nicolson: London 2003 p.3, who, in turn, derived it from V. Zubok & C. Pleshakov, *Inside the Kremlin's Cold War: From Stalin to Khrushchev*, Harvard University Press: Cambridge MA 1996 p.21.

3. C. Read, 'The Many Lives of Joseph Stalin: Writing the Biography of a "Monster" ' in J. Ryan & S. Grant (eds), *Revisioning Stalin and Stalinism: Complexities, Contradictions and Controversies*, Bloomsbury Academic: London 2021.

4. R. G. Suny, *Stalin: Passage to Revolution*, Princeton University Press: Princeton 2020 pp.668–95.

5. I. Deutscher, 'Writing a Biography of Stalin', *The Listener*, https://www.marxists.org/ archive/deutscher/1947/writing-stalin.htm (25 December 1947).

6. G. Roberts, 'Working Towards the *Vozhd*? Stalin and the Peace Movement' in Grant & Ryan, *Revisioning Stalin and Stalinism*.

7. G. Roberts, *Stalin's Wars: From World War to Cold War, 1939–1953*, Yale University Press: London & New Haven 2006 pp.247–8.

FURTHER READING

The primary source for this book has been the many thousands of files in Stalin's *lichnyi fond*, or personal file series. A good deal of this archive has been digitised and documents may be viewed online at Yale's Stalin Digital Archive (stalindigitalarchive.com) or its Russian government equivalent (sovdoc.rusarchives.ru) – a facility that proved to be priceless during the last phase of my research. Unfortunately, only a third of Stalin's marked library books (those containing his *pometki*) are available online. The rest may be viewed in Moscow's Russian State Archive of Social-Political History (RGASPI is its Russian acronym). There are another hundred or so marked books in other sections of Stalin's archive, mostly undigitised. Several thousand unmarked books from Stalin's collection may be found in the special collections section of the Centre for Social-Political History of the Russian State Historical Library (formerly the State Socio-Political Library) in Moscow. I had a look at a few of these but mostly studied the handwritten card catalogues of their titles.

Throughout the book, I have allowed Stalin to speak with his own voice so that readers may judge for themselves his qualities as an intellectual. Fifty years ago, when I began to amass my own personal library, I bought a second-hand set of the thirteen volumes of the English edition of Stalin's collected works. I can't say I paid them much attention in the ensuing decades but it proved a prescient purchase. These works, together with many other writings by Stalin, are now available on www.marxists.org.

It will be evident from my endnotes that I have benefited enormously from the researches of other scholars. The quality of work on Stalin and his era is truly astounding. It has been a great pleasure to read and make copious use of this research. Below is a list of English-language books focused on Stalin that I have found the most useful and reliable. I have excluded books by authors who published before the collapse of the USSR and didn't have the opportunity to work in the Russian archives. But older works by Isaac Deutscher, Robert McNeal, Ian Grey, Robert Tucker and many others can still be read with great profit.

Brandenberger, D., & M. Zelenov (eds), *Stalin's Master Narrative: A Critical Edition of the History of the Communist Party of the Soviet Union (Bolsheviks): Short Course*, Yale University Press: London & New Haven 2019

Davies, S., & J. Harris, *Stalin's World: Dictating the Soviet Order*, Yale University Press: London & New Haven 2014

Fitzpatrick, S., *On Stalin's Team: The Years of Living Dangerously in Soviet Politics*, Princeton University Press: Princeton 2015

Getty, J. Arch, & O. V. Naumov, *The Road to Terror: Stalin and the Self-Destruction of the Bolsheviks, 1932–1939*, Yale University Press: London & New Haven 1999

Kemp-Welch, A., *Stalin and the Literary Intelligentsia, 1928–1939*, St Martin's Press: New York 1991

FURTHER READING

Khlevniuk, O., *Stalin: New Biography of a Dictator*, Yale University Press: London & New Haven 2015

Kotkin, S., *Stalin: Paradoxes of Power, 1878–1928*, Allen Lane: London 2014

—, *Stalin: Waiting for Hitler, 1928–1941*, Penguin: London 2017

Kun, M., *Stalin: An Unknown Portrait*, CEU Press: Budapest 2003

Kuromiya, H., *Stalin*, Pearson: Harlow 2005

Medvedev, R., and Z. Medvedev, *The Unknown Stalin: His Life, Death and Legacy*, Overlook Press: Woodstock NY 2004

Pollock, E., *Stalin and the Soviet Science Wars*, Princeton University Press: Princeton 2006

Rayfield, D., *Stalin and His Hangmen*, Viking: London 2004.

Read, C., *Stalin: From the Caucasus to the Kremlin*, Routledge: London 2017

Ree, E. van, *The Political Thought of Joseph Stalin*, Routledge: London 2002

Rieber, A. J., *Stalin and the Struggle for Supremacy in Eurasia*, Cambridge: Cambridge University Press 2015

Roberts, G., *Stalin's Wars: From World War to Cold War, 1939–1953*, Yale University Press: London & New Haven 2006

Rubenstein, J., *The Last Days of Stalin*, Yale University Press: London & New Haven 2016

Service, R., *Stalin: A Biography*, Macmillan: London 2004

Suny, R. G., *Stalin: Passage to Revolution*, Princeton University Press: Princeton 2020

ACKNOWLEDGEMENTS

Never have I felt so pleased to express my heartfelt gratitude to the many people who have helped me to complete a book. First and foremost, there is my partner and editor *extraordinaire*, Celia Weston. Celia's approach to editing is similar to Stalin's: books should be finely sculpted so they contain no superfluous words. But even more important than the editing has been her intellectual companionship. She has interrogated and supported me during every phase of this exploration into the inner intellectual life of a learned dictator.

My biggest technical challenge was deciphering Stalin's handwriting. In that regard, the help of Alexander Pozdeyev was indispensable. And both he and Alexandra Urakova were always on hand to discuss translation issues.

Sasha and Alexandra are among the Moscow friends to whom this book is dedicated. Another is Sergey Listikov, who has been helping me to access Russian archives for a quarter of a century. The late Oleg Rzheshevsky was also a welcoming and helpful host in Moscow.

Supportive from beginning to end was Erik van Ree. It was his pathbreaking book on Stalin's political thought that encouraged me to take Stalin seriously as an intellectual. His own research on Stalin's library has been invaluable, as has his advice and his answers to my many questions.

During the pandemic, when I was actually writing the book, David Brandenberger was amazingly generous with his time and resources. His writings on Soviet politics, culture and society in the 1930s and 1940s have been hugely influential in shaping my own views.

Jim Cornelius, Judith Devlin, Alfred J. Rieber and James Ryan read the book's draft and their astute and expert feedback was gratefully received. The same is true of the three publishers' reviews, who saved me from untold errors and prompted me to revamp the book's structure. Be it on my own head that I

ACKNOWLEDGEMENTS

took most but not all of the advice of these friends and colleagues and any remaining errors are, of course, mine.

A number of people responded to my various pleas for help: Michael Carley, Holly Case, Michael David-Fox, Susan Grant, Francis King, Mark Kramer, Irene Makaryk, Evan Mawdsley, Bruce Menning, Kevin Morgan, Vladimir Nevezhin, Pamela Neville-Sington, Joe Patman, Ethan Pollock, Malcolm Spencer, Dmitry Surzhik, John Turner, David C. Wojhan and Alexey Zadorozhny. A special thanks to Ronald Suny for sharing the manuscript of his definitive biography of the young Stalin.

While most of the Russian-language texts in my personal book collection were bought in Moscow and then shipped back home to Ireland, in recent times I relied heavily on the highly efficient services of Leonid Mejibovski of Esterum Books. I have him to thank for the prized acquisition of the memoirs of Lenin's librarian, Shushanika Manuchar'yants, who served Stalin in the same capacity.

Over the years I received much assistance from Russian librarians and archivists but particular thanks are due to Dr Irina Novichenko, head of special collections at the Russian Historical Library's Centre for Socio-Political History (formerly the State Socio-Political Library). On the very last day of my research for this book – in Moscow in September 2021 – she was instrumental in helping me to answer some nagging questions about Stalin's library.

I was fortunate in being able to present my ideas about Stalin's library to a number of probing audiences, the first being at the Dublin History Festival in 2016. This was followed by talks at the University of Tampere, University College Cork, the Helsinki Collegium for Advanced Studies, the Central European University's Institute for Advanced Study in Budapest and the Polish Institute of Advanced Studies. A scheduled appearance at New York University's Jordan Center for the Advanced Study of Russia in March 2018 was thwarted by an emergency tooth extraction!

My earliest published pieces on the library were commissioned by Vadim Staklo for Yale's Stalin Digital Archive. He was also instrumental in commissioning a Russian colleague, Yury Nikiforov, to transcribe the major part of the catalogue of Stalin's surviving library books. The UK's Society for Cooperation in Russian and Soviet Studies (formerly the Society for Cultural Relations with the USSR) published an article by me on the library in their Bulletin. Another piece was published on the *Irish Times* website under the headline 'Bloody Tyrant and Bookworm'.

Facundo Garcia, interviewed me about the project in 2019 and published an article about Stalin's library in the Argentinian newspaper *Página/12*. I was also interviewed on the radio in Ireland, a country fortunate to have outstanding programmes such as Newstalk's *Talking History*, and *The History Show* produced by its public broadcaster, RTÉ.

ACKNOWLEDGEMENTS

Researching the book required a lot of trips to Moscow, which would not have been possible without generous financial support from the School of History and the College of Arts, Celtic Studies and Social Sciences at University College Cork.

The book was commissioned by Heather McCallum. Her dedication to publishing books that are both accessible and scholarly never ceases to amaze me. Many thanks to Heather and her colleagues at Yale London.

Like Heather, my agent Andrew Lownie displayed super-human patience during the years it took me to produce this book.

Finally, thank you Susan Certo for compiling such an excellent index, and Svetlana Frolova for double-checking my transliterations from Russian to English.

INDEX

Abakumov, Victor, 120
Abyssinia, 124
Adler, Mortimer J., 98
Admiral Nakhimov (Pudovkin), 182
'Adventures of a Monkey' (Zoshchenko), 183–4
'Against Federalism' (Stalin), 167
Agursky, M., 224n74
Air War 1936 (Helders), 10
Akhmatova, Anna, 183, 184
Alexander Nevsky (Eisenstein), 137
Alexandrov, Georgy, 33, 143, 198–9, 200
Alien Shadow (Simonov), 189
Alliluyeva, Nadezhda 'Nadya', 70, 75–7, 221n5
Alliluyeva, Svetlana *see* Stalina, Svetlana
All-Russian Communist Party, 57
All-Union Congress of Soviet Writers, 136, 177–8
'American Billions' (Stalin), 166
Anarchism or Socialism? (Stalin), 53, 89, 152–3, 195
Ancient Europe and the East (Vipper), 130
Antaeus, 115
anti-cosmopolitan campaign, 129, 191
anti-religious propaganda, 44
anti-Semitism, question of Stalin and, 128–9
Anti-Soviet Parallel Trotskyist Centre trial, 114
anti-western cultural campaign, 142–4
'Armed Insurrection and Our Tactics' (Stalin), 50
Armenia, 61, 79
Arnould, Arthur, 56
Around the Union of Soviets (Gorky), 176
Art and Literature Committee, 186, 187

atheism, Soviet, 44
atheist, Stalin as an, 42–3
Avdeenko, Alexander, 180–1
Azerbaijan, 61, 79

backwardness of Russia, 89
Bakhrushin, S. V., 137, 138
Baku Commune, 174–5
Balashov, A. P., 71
Balfour, H. H., 200–1
Barber, John, 173
Barbusse, Henri, 24–7, 217n27
Battle for Our Soviet Ukraine (Dovzhenko), 181
Batumi shootings, 32, 217n45
Bedny, Demyan, 73, 141, 175, 238n12
Before Sunrise (Zoshchenko), 184
Beloff, Max, 197
Benjamin, Walter, 96
Berdzenishvili, Nikolai, 127–8, 231n126
Beria, Lavrenty, 24, 80–1, 118
Beria, Sergo, 72
Bernstein, Eduard, 86, 105
Bible, the, 3, 42
biographies on Stalin: background and overview of, 18–20, 215n1; absence of, 23; Barbusse and, 24–7; Beria and, 24; biographical questionnaire and, 20–1, 216n9; childhood and youth and, 28, 50; by Medvedev, 94; in memoirs, 49, 55; by Moskalev, 28–9; reimagining Stalin in, 91–3; *Short Biography*, 4, 27, 29, 37, 41, 198–200; *Stalin and His Hangmen*, 91; *Stalin: A Political Biography*, 80; *Stalin's Mind*, 90–1; Tovstukha and, 21–2; *Triumph and Tragedy*, 68–9

Birse, A. H., 72, 222n17
Bismarck, Otto von, 2, 121–4, 126
Bismarck and the European Great Powers
(Windelband), 123–4
Black Sea straits, 79, 80
Bliokh, Yakov, 182
Blizhnyaya, 77, 80–1, 82, 83, 159
'Bloc of Rightists and Trotskyites' trial, 114
Bloody Sunday, 50
Boer, Roland, 46
Bogatyrs, The (Bedny), 141
Bol'shevik, 24, 125, 191–2
Bolsheviks: book culture and, 10–13;
Brest-Litovsk peace treaty and, 56–8;
Dickens and, 98; in the Duma, 51; gender
and, 76; nationalism and, 51; national
self-determination and, 51–2; Petrograd
coup of, 55; Provisional Government
and, 54; religion and, 43–4, 219n19;
RSDLP split and, 48; self-effacement of,
22; socialism and, 110; Stalin and, 5, 49
bookmarks, Stalin's, 72, 98, 226n5
bookplate of Stalin, 1, 13, 69, 85–6
borderlands, 78–9
bourgeois military specialists, 58
Brackman, Roman, 36–7
Bragin, Mikhail, 159–60
Brandenberger, David, 134, 198
Brdzola, 32, 210
Brent, Jonathan, 15
Brest-Litovsk peace treaty, 56–7, 105
Brik, Lilya, 178
Brunstedt, Jonathan, 146
Bryl, Yanka, 187
Bubnov, Andrei, 131
Bucar, Annabelle, 89, 120–1, 181, 229n91
Budenny, Semen, 59, 60
Bukharin, Nikolai: All-Union Congress of
Soviet Writers and, 178; opposition of,
56, 95, 109, 110, 114–15, 116, 172; in
Stalin's library, 85–6
Bulgakov, Mikhail, 18–19, 173–4
Burdzhalov, E. N., 160
Burlatsky, Fedor, 123

Caesar, Julius, 130
capitalism, 92, 94–5, 98, 144, 207–8
censorship, 12–13, 31
Chapaev, 180
Charkviani, Kandid, 129, 149
Chavchavadze, Ilia, 40
'Cheap Library', 40–1
Cheka, the, 58, 61
Cherkasov, Nikolai, 141, 161, 233n200
Chernenko, Konstantin, 217n34
Chernyshevsky, Nikolai, 123

Chikobava, Arnold, 149–50
Chizhikov, Petr, 52
Christianity, 43, 46, 47, 141; *see also* Russian
Orthodox Church
Chuev, Felix, 210
Churchill, Winston: *History of the Second
World War*, 14; 'iron curtain' speech, 142,
202; Stalin and, 2, 19–20, 34; treaty of
alliance with USSR and, 125, 126, 201,
204; *The World Crisis*, 86
Clark, Katerina, 11
class and language, 148, 151
class and political parties, 168
Clausewitz, Carl von, 155–6, 163–4
'Clausewitz and German Military Ideology'
(Meshcheryakov), 164
cold war, 100, 119–20, 202
Collected Works (Lenin), 90–1
collected works of Stalin, 29–35, 217n40
collectivisation, forced, 78, 109, 116
communism, 11, 17, 45–6, 142
Communist International (Comintern), 9,
25, 117
Comrade Stalin with Mother (Kutateladze),
38
conflict, Stalin on, 187
Constituent Assembly, 54, 56, 106
Constitution, US, 167, 168
constitution of 1936, Soviet, 44, 83, 167,
221n74
Constitutions of the Bourgeois Countries, 167
Contemporary Literature, 135
Corbett, Julian Stafford, 79
Council of People's Commissars
(Sovnarkom), 62
counter-intelligence, 119
counter-offensives, 164
counter-revolution, US backed, 166
Crime and Punishment (Dostoevsky), 185
Cromwell, Oliver, 88
Curzon Line, 58–9
Cyrillic alphabet, 148

D'Abernon, Viscount, 124, 129
dachas of Stalin, 1, 74, 77, 80–1
daily reading by Stalin, 72
Davis, Jerome, 18
Davrishev, Soso, 36
Day, Richard B., 208
Days of the Turbins (Bulgakov), 173–4
Dead Souls (Gogol), 179
Death and the Maiden (Gorky), 83
Decline of the West (Spengler), 14
Defoe, Daniel, 9–10
*Democracy and the Organization of Political
Parties* (Ostrogorsky), 86

INDEX

democratic centralism, 55
demonisation of dissent, 110
Denikin, Anton, 73
destalinisation, 94
Deutscher, Isaac, 6, 51, 80, 210
Devdariani, Seit, 40
Development of the Monist View of History, The (Plekhanov), 179
Devlin, Judith, 24
Dialectical and Historical Materialism (Stalin), 30
dialectical materialism, 148, 177, 194–6
Dickens, Charles, 98–9
dictatorship of the party, 107
dictatorship of the proletariat, 92, 106, 108, 212
Dimitrov, Georgi, 117, 162
diplomacy, 124–6, 196–7, 211
Diplomacy (Nicolson), 124–5
'disunite in order to unite', 174
Djilas, Milovan, 77–8
Dobrenko, Evgeny, 152, 153
'Doctors' Plot', 7
Doller, Mikhail, 161
Dostoevsky, Fedor, 184–5, 239n47
Dovzhenko, Alexander, 120, 181, 229n91
Dubrovsky, Alexander, 133
Duma elections, 51
Dzerzhinsky, Felix, 58
Dzhanshiya, Simon, 127–8
Dzhavakhishvili, Ivan, 230n125
Dzhugashvili, Vissarion 'Beso', 25, 36, 38

Eastern Front, 56, 203–4
Eastern Orthodox Church, 47
Economic Problems of Socialism in the USSR, 206–8
economics, socialist, 205–8
Edel'man, Olga, 35
Eden, Anthony, 126
'Editor-in-Chief', Stalin as, 190–209; background and overview of, 4–5, 190–2, 208–9; *Falsifiers of History* and, 200–4; *Istoriya Diplomatii* and, 196–8; political economy textbook and, 205–8; *Short Biography* and, 198–200; *Short Course History of the Communist Party in the Soviet Union* and, 192–6
Ehrenburg, Ilya, 188, 189
8 Years: Results and Perspectives (Trotsky), 108
Eisenstein, Sergei, 137, 140–1, 142, 182
elections, 51, 56, 167–8
election speech of 1946, Stalin's, 33, 99, 146, 163
émigré literature, 83, 91

emotionally charged mobilisation, 7
Engels, Friedrich, 68, 86, 102, 125
English history, Stalin's knowledge of, 88
Enlightenment (*Prosveshenie*), 51, 68, 219n19
Erasmus, 98
'Eremin letter', 37
Ermler, Fridrikh, 180
Essays on the History of the Roman Empire (Vipper), 130
Essays on the History of West European Literature (Kogan), 52
ex-libris stamps, 1, 13, 69, 85–6

Falsifiers of History, 200–4
Farberov, N. P., 168
Farewell, America!, 120, 229n91
Fedoseev, Pyotr, 33
Feuchtwanger, Lion, 179
fiction: Bolsheviks and, 12–13; Stalin and, 4, 8, 65, 83, 85, 171; *see also specific fiction books*
Field Service Regulations of the Red Army, 154
films, 137, 140–2, 161, 166, 180–3; *see also specific films*
Finland, 162
First World War, 53–4, 119, 125, 157
Fischer, Ernst, 153
Fishermen of the Caspian (Bliokh), 182
Fitzpatrick, Sheila, 77
Flaubert, Gustave, 86
Flight (Bulgakov), 173
Foreign Affairs, 120–1
'Foreign Languages to the Masses' campaign, 165–6
foreign policy, 124–5
'Foreign Policy of Russian Tsardom, The' (Engels) 125
Foundations of Leninism (Stalin), 30, 134; lectures 153, 165
France, Anatole, 100
Franco, Francisco, 116–17
'Friendship of the Peoples', 127–8
Frolov, E. P., 94, 95
frontiers, question of, 126
Frunze, Mikhail, 154

Gefter, Mikhail, 122
Geladze, Keke, 38–9
general-secretary of the communist party, Stalin as, 62–5
Genghis Khan, 101
Georgia: about, 47, 48, 79, 127, 230n125; Lenin and, 61; Stalin museum at, 81;

INDEX

Stalin's background and disassociation with, 22, 216n15
Germany, 56–8, 91, 118, 122, 124–6, 158, 162–3
Getty, J. Arch, 114
Gibbon, Edward, 129
gifting books, 9–10
Glavlit, 12
Gogol, Nikolai, 179, 181, 185–6
Goldman, Wendy, 113
Gorbachev, Mikhail, 12
Gorky, Maxim, 13, 83, 93, 136, 175–6, 180, 191
Gosudarstvennaya Obshchestvenno-Politicheskaya Biblioteka, 84
Gottwald, Klement, 212
Granat, 21–2
Grand Life, A (Lukov), 182
Great Citizen, The (Ermler), 180
Great Patriotic War: Nazi-Soviet Pact and, 34, 126, 158, 200–4; *Short Biography* and, 198, 242n34; spies and, 118; Stalin and, 80, 99, 158–63, 169
Great Soviet Encyclopaedia, 14, 124, 136–7, 151
'Great Stalinist Plan to Transform Nature, The', 144
Great Terror, 7, 30, 37, 45, 78, 111–18, 119, 142
Greece in the Classical Epoch (Vipper), 130
Greek history, 130
Gromov, Yevgeny, 93, 100
Gromyko, Andrei, 171
Gudok, 28
Gul, Raymond, 83, 224n60

Halfin, Igal, 110
Harriman, Averell, 140, 154, 160, 169, 200
Hegel, Georg Wilhelm Friedrich, 95, 164, 179, 195
Heraclius II, 127
Herodotus, 74, 129
heroes, 24, 181, 189
Herr, Frédéric-Georges, 154
historical materialism, 194–6
Histories (Herodotus), 74, 129
History of One Deviation (Kanatchikov), 110–11, 227–8n51
History of the Civil War in the USSR, 136, 190–2
History of the Middle Ages (Vipper), 137
History of the Russian Revolution to Brest-Litovsk (Trotsky), 105
History of the Second World War (Churchill), 14

history teaching in Soviet schools, 131–4, 231n146, 232n152
Hitler, Adolf, 19–20, 91, 159, 203–4
Hobsbawm, Eric, 196
homes of Stalin, 1, 74, 77, 80–1
homosexuality, 129
honour courts, 143–4
Horney, Karen, 37
Hugo, Victor, 10, 40–1
human souls, 177–8

Ilizarov, Boris, 88, 93, 219n19
imperialism, 100, 134
industrialisation, 46, 78, 108–9
Industrial Party trial, 113–14
Institute of Marx, Engels, and Lenin (IMEL), 29, 30, 32, 70, 74, 198
Institute of Marxism-Leninism (IM-L), 83, 84, 87
intelligence, 116, 118–19
Intelligence and Counter-Intelligence (Rossel), 119
intelligentsia, 8, 143, 213–14n7
Iran, 79
Iremashvili, Joseph, 36, 61
Israel, 128
Istoriya Diplomatii, 125–6, 196–8, 201
Italo-Abyssinian Crisis, 124
Ivan Grozny (Tolstoy), 100–1, 138–9
Ivan Grozny (Vipper), 135–6, 138
Ivan I, 134
Ivan the Terrible, 2, 89, 100–1, 133–4, 135–42, 233n200
Ivan the Terrible (Eisenstein), 140–1
Ivan the Terrible Part Two (Eisenstein), 182
Iveria, 40

Jackson, H. J., 97–8
Japan, 90, 119
Japhetic theory, 151
July Days, 55, 105
Jungle Book, The (Kipling), 9, 214n11
'J. V. Stalin at the Head of Baku Bolsheviks and Workers' (Moskalev), 28–9

Kaganovich, Lazar, 69, 129, 210
Kamenev, Lev, 54, 85–6, 104, 109–10, 112–14, 123
Kanatchikov, Semen, 110–11, 227–8n51
Kaplan, Fanny, 57
Karl Marx and World Literature (Prawer), 238n16
Karpov, Georgy, 45
Kautsky, Karl, 68, 86, 103, 105–6, 107, 108, 110

Kenez, Peter, 12
Kennan, George F., 120–1
Ketskhoveli, Lado, 42, 47
Kettle, Arnold, 184
Khlevniuk, Oleg, 91
Khrushchev, Nikita: films and, 182–3; Stalin denunciation by, 1, 4, 14, 34, 37, 78, 158; Stalin's death and, 80; on war and capitalism, 207
'Kind of Monologue, A' (Akhmatova), 183, 184
Kipling, Rudyard, 9, 214n11
Kirov, Sergei, 27, 112–13, 132, 180, 221n5
Kirshon, V. M., 175
Kliueva, Nina, 144, 189
Knauss, Robert, 10
Kogan, P. S., 52
Kommunist, 91–2
Komsomol'skaya Pravda, 146
Konushaya, Raisa, 32–3
Kotkin, Stephen, 16, 38, 63, 91, 111, 152–3
Kovalev, I. V., 71
Kremlin Affair, 70–1, 112, 113
Kremlin's Scholar, The (Shepilov), 1
Krupskaya, Nadezhda, 3, 12, 62, 73, 76
Kruzhilikha (Panova), 187
Kruzhkov, Vladimir, 31–2
Ksenofontov, F. A., 153
Kuibyshev, 13–14
kulaks, 108, 116, 229n75
Kuntsevo mansion, 77, 80–1, 82, 83
Kursk, battle of, 163
Kutateladze, Apollon, 38
Kutuzov, Mikhail, 2, 9, 156, 159–60

Labriola, Antonio, 86
Lafargue, Paul, 13, 68, 106
land distribution, 54
Language and Revolution (Lafargue), 68
languages, 51, 148–52, 165–6, 220n47
Lapshin, Konstantin, 120
Latinisation, 148, 149
Latsis, Vilis, 187, 188
Laval, Pierre, 126
League of the Godless, 44
Leer, Genrikh, 87, 155–6
Left Socialist Revolutionaries, 55, 56
Leiteizen, Moris G., 86–7
Lenin, Vladimir, 2; Brest-Litovsk peace treaty and, 56; collected works of, 29, 90–1; ex-libris stamp of, 69; First World War and, 53; 'Lenin's Testament', 3, 62–4; on Marxism and communism, 11, 46; Materialism and Empirio-Criticism, 10, 101, 195; note taking by, 98; personal library of, 69–70, 98, 226n5; Poland and,

59, 60; Provisional Government and, 54; public libraries and, 12; religion and, 43; revolution and, 55, 104; RSDLP and, 47–8; Stalin and, 2, 16, 48, 49, 63, 101–3; Stalin differences with, 52, 54, 61; Stalin's library books by, 85; trade unions and, 62
Leningrad, 183–4
Lenin Institute, 21, 70
Leninism, 103, 153
Lenin Library, 12, 73–4, 84, 121
Lenin's Doctrine of Revolution (Ksenofontov), 153
'Lenin's Testament', 3, 62–4
Lermontov, Mikhail, 64
Lessing, Doris, 184
Lessons of October, The (Trotsky), 103, 104–5
Let History Judge (Medvedev), 94
Levitsky, Nikolai, 159
libraries, private, 11
libraries, public, 11–13
library of Stalin, 66–71; background and overview of, 1–5, 8, 13–15, 16, 74, 96; about the books of, 85–90; Alexandrov writings of, 143; at Blizhnyaya, 80–1; classification of, 66–7, 68–9, 71, 84–5, 103, 221–2n5; collecting and borrowing books for, 71–4; discovering, 82–5, 90; female authors of, 76; foreign language books of, 87; foreign translations of, 86; language books of, 149; Lenin and, 102, 163; letters and notes of, 84; librarians of, 68–9, 70; maps of, 77–9, 223n43; marked books in (see marked books in Stalin's library); memoirs and diaries of, 89–90, 121–3; military writings of, 154–8, 159; non-fiction book acquisition for, 84, 85; pamphlets of, 85, 94, 99–100, 105; philosophy books of, 86–7; poetry of, 178; record collection of, 80, 223n48; re-imaging Stalin and, 90–5; reports of congresses, conferences and organisations of, 86; science books in, 147; stamped books of, 85
library purges, 12–13
lichnyi fond of Stalin, 15, 72, 78
Life magazine, 37
Light beyond the Marshes (Bryl), 187
Lissagaray, Olivier, 89
literacy, 11
literary journals, 183–4; see also specific journals
Literature and Art Committee, 186, 187
literature and Stalin, Soviet see Soviet literature and Stalin
Literaturnaya Gazeta, 177, 188

INDEX

litsedei, Stalin as a, 210
Litvinov, Maxim, 119
Livonian War, 138
Lockhart, R. H. Bruce, 118–19
Lozovsky, Solomon, 86, 122
Ludendorff, Erich, 89, 155
Ludwig, Emil, 18, 23–4, 50, 165, 215n3
Lukin, Nikolai, 88
Lukov, Leonid, 182
Lunacharsky, Anatoly, 5, 43, 87, 135, 148
Luther, Martin, 46
Luxemburg, Rosa, 76, 86
Lysenko, Trofim, 9, 144
Lysenko affair, 144

Machiavelli, Niccolò, 123
MacKinnon, Elaine, 191
Malenkov, Georgy, 80, 100, 186
Malinovsky, Roman, 51
Malory, Thomas, 14
Mandelstam, Osip, 224n63
Manuchar'yants, Shushanika, 69–71
Mao Tse Tung, 165
maps, 77–9, 223n43
marginalia, 97–8
marked books in Stalin's library:
    background and overview of, 4, 97–101;
    ancient history books and, 129–31;
    Bismarck writings and, 122–3; diplomacy
    writings and, 125–6; expressions used in,
    99; *Great Soviet Encyclopaedia*, 124;
    historical works and, 87–90; Kautsky
    writings and, 108; Ksenofontov writings
    and, 153; Lenin writings and, 102,
    238n16; Machiavelli writings and, 123;
    Marxism and, 16–17; military writings
    and, 154, 155–6, 160; pre-1917 writings
    and, 87; question of, 72, 222n20;
    reimagining Stalin and, 91–4; of Shtein
    intro to D'Abernon, 124; Trotsky
    writings and, 103–6
Marr, Nikolai, 68, 148–52
Martov, Julius, 47
Marx, Karl, 85, 102
Marx-Engels-Lenin-Stalin Institute, 82
Marxism: individual and, 23–4; language
    and, 149, 150, 151; Lenin versus Trotsky
    and, 105; materialism and, 52; science
    and, 144; Stalin and, 3, 53, 92, 153, 195,
    205–6, 208; working class and, 47
*Marxism and the National and Colonial
    Question* (Stalin), 30
Marxism and the National Question (Stalin),
    21, 49, 51, 53, 78, 89, 152
materialism, 52; dialectical, 148, 177, 194–6;
    historical, 194–6

Materialism and Empirio-Criticism (Lenin),
    10, 101, 195
Maximenkov, Leonid, 173
Mayakovsky, Vladimir, 178
McNeal, Robert H., 34, 35, 57
Medvedev, Roy, 72, 94, 95, 122, 153, 220n47
Medvedev, Zhores, 72, 94, 128
Mein Kampf (Hitler), 91
Memoirs of a British Agent (Lockhart), 119
Menace of Japan (O'Conroy), 89–90
Mensheviks, 36, 47–8, 50, 51, 61, 114
Meshcheryakov, G., 164
Meskovsky, A. A., 166
Metro-Vickers, 114
Mikoyan, Anastas, 166, 183
military knowledge of Stalin, 154–5
military purge, 115–16
Military-Revolutionary Committee, 31,
    55
military science versus military art, 163
Military Thought, 164
Mints, I. I., 191–2, 197
Mishulin, A. V., 137
Mitin, M. B., 31–2
mobilisation, 7, 157–8
Mochalov, Vasily, 31–3, 198–9, 217n46
Molotov, Vyacheslav: about, 14, 34, 120,
    215n35; books in Stalin's library by, 86;
    library of, 14; radio address of, 159; *Short
    Biography* and, 199; on Stalin, 77; trips of,
    126, 204
Moltke, Helmuth von, 155
Monist View of History, The (Plekhanov),
    53
Montefiore, Simon Sebag, 50, 217n34
Morozov, Grigory, 71–2, 128, 222n16
Morte D'Arthur (Malory), 14
Moscow, 145–6, 156
Moscow News, 90
Moskalev, Mikhail, 28–9, 217n34
Mother (Gorky), 93
movie-making, 166
Mozg Armii (Shaposhnikov), 73, 157–8,
    222n25, 236n259
Münzenberg, Willi, 25
'Myth of the Beloved Leader, The'
    exhibition, 81

Napoleon, 46, 156, 159–60
national anthem, 144–5
national Bolshevism, 134
nationalism, 51, 61, 78, 128, 134
national self-determination, 51–2, 78
Naumov, Oleg, 114
Nazis, 11, 117, 129
Nazi-Soviet pact, 34, 126, 158, 200–4

INDEX

Nazi-Soviet Relations, 1939–1941 (NSR), 201–2
Nechkina, M. V., 136
Neruda, Pablo, 188–9
nervous collapse myth of Stalin, 158–9
New Course, The (Trotsky), 103, 227n29
New Economic Policy (NEP): publishing and, 73; Stalin and, 95, 108–9, 153; Trotsky and, 108
New Model Army, 88
New Times, 21
Nicholas II, 14, 51, 53
Nicolson, Harold, 124–5
Nietzsche, Friedrich, 86–7, 224n74
Nietzsche and Finance Capital (Leiteizen), 86–87
Nikolaev, Leonid, 112
Nikolaevsky, Boris, 123
Nikonov, Vyacheslav, 215n35
Nin, Andreas, 117
Ninety-Three (Hugo), 41
NKVD, 116, 117–18, 119
Nobel Prize, 147, 188
non-party versus party writers, 176
'Not a step back!' phrase, 161

Obama, Barack, 65
O'Conroy, Taid, 89–90
'Ode to Stalin' (Neruda), 188–9
Okhrana, 37, 47, 51
Oktyabr', 139
Oktyabr'skaya Revolutsiya (Trotsky), 105
'On Party Policy in the Sphere of Literature' resolution, 172
On the Great Patriotic War of the Soviet Union (Stalin), 30
On the History of the Bolshevik Organisations in Transcaucasia (Beria), 24
On the Ideological and Tactical Foundations of Bolshevism (Ksenofontov), 153
On the Vistula: Towards a History of the 1920 Campaign (Shaposhnikov), 60
ontology, 195–6
Onufrieva, Polina, 52
On War (Clausewitz), 155–6
Oprichnina, 136, 137, 140, 141
Orbeli, Joseph, 127, 231n127
Orlov, Alexander, 37
Osip, K., 160–1, 236n268, 236n270
Osnovy Inostrannogo Gosudarstvennogo Prava (Farberov), 168
Ostrogorsky, Moisey, 86
Our New Tasks (Trotsky), 108
owl of Minerva metaphor, 179

Palace of the Soviets, 166–7
pamphlets, 21, 85, 94, 99–100, 105
Pankratova, A. M., 197
Panova, Vera, 186–7
paranoia, Stalin's, 15–17
party versus non-party writers, 176
pathological theories of Stalin's personality, 36–8
patriotism, 134, 211
Pavlov, G. D., 159
Pavlov, Ivan, 146–7
Pavlov, Nikolai, 127, 231n127
Pavlov Institute of Physiology, 147
'People's Library', 12–13
Perrie, Maureen, 142
personal file series *(lichnyi fond),* 15, 72, 78
personality cult of Stalin, 16, 37–8
Peter the Great, 2, 89, 132, 135, 162
Pilsudski, Józef, 58
Piotrovsky, Boris, 152
plagiariser, Stalin as a, 152–3
Platonov, S. F., 136, 137
Platt, Kevin, 137
play-writing, encouragement of, 176–7
Plekhanov, Georgy, 53, 86, 103, 179
Podorozhnyi, Nikolai, 161
poetry, 40, 65, 171, 184, 188–9
Pokrovsky, Mikhail, 131–2, 136
Poland, 58–60, 158, 201, 203
Poletaev, A. A., 169–70
political economy textbook, 205–8
political violence, 50–1
Polkovodets Kutuzov (Bragin), 159–60
Pollock, Ethan, 205
Polonsky, Rachel, 14
pometki, Stalin's *see* marked books in Stalin's library
Pope, the, 126
Poskrebyshev, Alexander, 7, 123, 221n5
Pospelov, Pyotr, 192–3, 199
Possessed, The (Dostoevsky), 185
Potemkin, Vladimir, 125–6, 197
POUM (Workers Party of Marxist Unification), 117
praktik, 8, 26
Pravda: 'Against Federalism', 167; on Alliluyeva's death, 76–7; biographies of Stalin and, 22, 28, 29; *Falsifiers of History* and, 202; films and, 180; Kennan and, 121; language and, 150–2; literature and, 188; *The New Course* and, 109; 'Notebook on Clausewitz' and, 163; science and, 144, 146; *Short Biography* and, 199; on spies, 119; Stalin and, 33, 58–9, 92, 105,

255

186; textbooks and, 132; Trotsky and, 117, 181; Vipper and, 138

Prawar, S. S., 238n16

Prince, The (Machiavelli), 123

prizes, Stalin's, 127, 137, 140, 143, 161, 182, 186–9

Problems of Leninism (Stalin), 10, 69

'Proletarian Class and the Proletarian Party' (Stalin), 19

Proletarian culture, 172, 238n16

Proletarian Revolution and its Program, The (Kautsky), 108

Proletarian socialism, 195

Proletarskaya Revolutsiya, 23

propaganda, anti-religious, 44

Provisional Government, 53–4, 55

Provisional Polish Revolutionary Committee, 59

public libraries, 11–13

publishing industry, 11, 29, 72–3

Pudovkin, Vsevolod, 161, 182

purges of libraries, 12–13

Pushkin, Alexander, 82, 135, 145, 224n59

Putin, Vladimir, 214n11

Pyatakov, Georgy, 114

Qazbegi, Alexander, 41

'Question of the Stabilisation of Capitalism, The' (Sten), 94–5

Questions of History, 169–70

Radek, Karl, 86, 114

RAPP (Russian Association of Proletarian Writers), 173, 175

Rayfield, Donald, 91, 101, 219n35, 221n5, 230n125

Razin, Yevgeny, 164–5

Read, Chris, 56

reading for the revolution, 8–9

record collection of Stalin, 80, 223n48

Red Army: as a contemporary army, 162; Georgia and, 61; interwar years and, 154; medals of, 160; Poland campaign and, 58–60; purge of, 115–16; Russian Civil War and, 57; Shaposhnikov and, 157; size of, 157; Winter War and, 162

Red Terror, 58, 106–7

'Reflections on Stalin's Markings in the Margins of Marxist Literature' (Simonov), 91–2

Religion and Socialism (Lunacharsky), 43

religion and Stalin, 3, 42–6

Repin, Ilya, 134

revivication of Stalin, 95–6

revolutionary patriotism, 93, 134

Revolution Betrayed, The (Trotsky), 111

Ribbentrop, Joachim von, 34, 129, 202

Rieber, Alfred J., 41, 78

Right Opposition, 109, 114, 172

Right to be Lazy, The (Lafargue), 68

Robins, Raymond, 166

Robinson Crusoe (Defoe), 9–10

Rolland, Romain, 112–13, 228n66

Roman history, 129–30

romanticism, 176, 177

Roosevelt, Franklin Delano, 2, 34, 168–9

Rosenthal, Richard S., 166

Roskin, Grigory, 144, 189

Rossel, Charles, 119

ROSTA questionnaire, 20–1

Rozenberg, David, 86

Rozenfel'd, Nina, 70

RSDLP (Russian Social-Democratic Labour Party), 19, 20, 41, 47–8, 50

Rubinstein, Nikolai, 119

Russia, about, 46–7

Russian Association of Proletarian Writers (RAPP), 173, 175

Russian Civil War, 57–8, 60, 166

Russian Orthodox Church, 3, 39, 43, 45

Russian Revolution, 50, 54, 104

Russian Social-Democratic Labour Party (RSDLP), 19, 20, 41, 47–8, 50

Russian Tsarist Empire, 47

Russocentrism, 144–6

Rykov, Alexei, 86, 114, 116

Ryzhkov, Nikolai, 123

Saakadze, Giorgi, 180

Safarov, Georgy, 19, 215n5

Salammbô (Flaubert), 86

Saltykov-Shchedrin, Mikhail, 83–4

science, 44, 143–4, 146–7

Science Council, 147

Scientific Session on Physiological Teachings of Academician I. P. Pavlov, 147

scientific socialism, 48, 195

scientific writers, 179

Scopes trial, 44

Seaton, Albert, 60

Second World War *see* Great Patriotic War

secret protocol, 158, 202, 204

secret speech of Khrushchev, 14, 158

Sedov, Lev, 113

self-determination, national, 51–2, 78

Sergeev, Artem, 9–10, 71, 214n10, 214n12

Service, Robert, 39, 91, 101

Shakespeare, William, 176, 180, 181

Shakhty trial, 113

Shaposhnikov, Boris, 60, 73, 90, 154, 157–8, 222n25, 236n259

Sharapov, Yury, 83, 90, 100

INDEX

Shariya, Pyotr, 32–3
Shcherbakov, Alexander, 139
Shepilov, Dmitry, 1, 185, 213n2
Shestakov, Andrei, 133–4
Short Biography, 4, 27, 29, 37, 41, 198–200
Short Course History of the Communist Party of the Soviet Union, 4, 10, 14, 23, 33–4, 46, 133, 192–6
Short Course History of the USSR, 133
show trials, 113–15, 123
Shtein, Boris, 124, 242n43
Simonov, Konstantin, 187, 189
Simonov, Nikolai, 91–2
Simon & Schuster, 198
Singh, Brajesh, 82
Slavin, Boris, 92
Slutsky, Anatoly, 23, 216n18
Smirnov, I. I., 138
Smirnova, V., 28
Smith, Adam, 86
Smith, Walter Bedell, 120
Smolensky, M., 105, 227n36
Smolkin, Victoria, 45
Sobanet, Andrew, 27
Sochineniya, 29–35, 217n40
socialisation of agriculture, 54
socialism: Dostoevsky and, 185; Lunacharsky and, 43; RSDLP split and, 48; scientific, 48, 195; Stalin and, 6, 7, 11, 92, 109, 195, 212; Trotsky and, 103–4, 106, 109
socialism in one country, 64, 104, 109, 211
socialist economics, 205–8
socialist realism, 176–9, 238–9n18
'Society for the Development of Russian Culture', 172
Society of Old Bolsheviks, 27
Sokolnikov, Grigory, 114
Some Principles of Maritime Strategy (Corbett), 79
'Some Problems of Soviet Linguistics' (Chikobava), 150
'Some Questions Concerning the History of Bolshevism' (Stalin), 23
'Sources of Soviet Conduct, The', 120–1
Soviet Jewish Anti-Fascist Committee, 119, 128
Soviet Jews, 119–20, 128–9
Soviet literature and Stalin, 171–89; background and overview of, 171–6; Dostoevsky and Gogol and, 184–6; films and, 180–3; literary journals and, 183–4; socialist realism and, 176–9, 238–9n18; Stalin's prizes and, 127, 137, 140, 143, 161, 182, 186–9
Soviet patriotism, 134, 211

Soviets, the, 54, 56
Soviet-Turkish treaty, 79
Sovnarkom (Council of People's Commissars), 62
Spanish Civil War, 116–17
Spengler, Oswald, 14
spies, 118–21
Spirin, Leonid, 84, 85, 224n67
Stalin, Joseph: background and overview of, 6–8; 'Against Federalism', 167; 'American Billions', 166; as an activist, 47–8, 49–50, 55; *Anarchism or Socialism?,* 53, 89, 152–3, 195; as an intellectual, 2, 3, 5, 7, 48, 90, 213–14n7; 'Armed Insurrection and Our Tactics', 50; birth date of, 21; childhood of, 18–19, 28, 36, 38–9, 218n5; death of, 80–1; *Dialectical and Historical Materialism,* 30; in exile, 52–3; family of, 74–7; *Foundations of Leninism,* 30, 134; *Foundations of Leninism* lectures, 153, 165; *On the Great Patriotic War of the Soviet Union,* 30; *Marxism and the National and Colonial Question,* 30; *Marxism and the National Question,* 21, 49, 51, 53, 78, 89, 152; *Problems of Leninism,* 10, 69; 'Proletarian Class and the Proletarian Party', 19; 'Some Questions Concerning the History of Bolshevism', 23; 'To the Moon', 40; youth of, 3, 18–19, 47, 48–50
Stalin, Vasily, 9–10, 75, 214n17
Stalin, Yakov, 75
Stalina, Svetlana: about, 75, 82, 128; book markings by, 100; films and, 182; on Stalin, 22, 36, 71, 185; Stalin's death and, 81; Stalin's library and, 14, 81–2, 214n18; studies of, 10, 127; textbook and, 133; on Zubalovo dacha, 74
Stalin and His Hangmen (Rayfield), 91
Stalin: A Political Biography (Deutscher), 80
Stalin Digital Archive (SDA), 15
Stalingrad, battle of, 163
Stalin museum at Gori, 81
Stalin Museum project, 81, 82
Stalin Prizes, 127, 137, 140, 143, 161, 182, 186–9
Stalin's Mind (Volkogonov), 90–1
Star, The, 21, 183–4
State Socio-Political Library (SSPL), 84
Sten, Jan, 94–5
stereotyping, Stalin's, 128
Stetsky, Alexei, 25–6, 29, 30, 131
Storm, The (Ehrenburg), 189
Strategiya (Leer), 156
strikes, labour, 47, 76
Strong, Anna Louise, 120

INDEX

Struve, Vasily, 127, 231n127
Sukhanov, Nikolai, 55
Sulla, 129, 130
Sullivan, Rosemary, 75
Suny, Ronald, 20, 49, 52, 210
Suvorov, Alexander, 2, 9, 156, 160–1, 236n270
Svanidze, Ekaterina, 75
Svechin, Alexander, 129, 154, 155, 235n246, 236n254

Tales of Stalin's Childhood (Smirnova), 28
Talmud, 12
Tanin, M., 167
Tarle, E. V., 197, 241n25
Tasks in the East (Trotsky), 104
TASS bulletins, 90, 91, 123–4
Tbilisi coach robbery, 50
Tbilisi Meteorological Observatory, 42
Tbilisi Spiritual Seminary, 39–42, 218n15
teaching history in Soviet schools, 131–4, 231n146, 232n152
Teliya, Giorgi, 152–3
terror and Stalin, 57, 70–1, 106–7
Terrorism and Communism (Kautsky), 108
Terrorism and Communism (Trotsky), 92, 105–6, 227n37
textbooks, 131–4, 137, 194, 205–8, 232n152; see also specific textbooks
Time Man of the Year, 198
Timoshenko, Semen, 158
Tito, Josip Broz, 34
Toilers of the Sea (Hugo), 40
Tolstoy, Alexei, 100–1, 135, 137–40
Tomsky, Mikhail, 114
'To the Moon' (Stalin), 40
Tovstukha, Ivan P., 21–2, 23, 25, 29, 68
Toward New Shores (Latsis), 187, 188
Towards Socialism or Capitalism? (Trotsky), 108
trade unions, 47, 62
Transcaucasian Socialist Federation, 61, 221n74
Treaty of Riga, 59–60
Triandafillov, Vladimir, 154
Triumph and Tragedy (Volkogonov), 68–9
triumvirate of Stalin, Zinoviev, and Kamenev, 109
Trotsky, Leon: books on, 26–7, 51, 110–11; Brest-Litovsk peace treaty and, 56; collected works of, 29; death of, 117; *8 Years: Results and Perspectives*, 108; expulsion and exile of, 109–11, 113; Kirov and, 112; Lenin and, 63; *The Lessons of October*, 103, 104–5; military-political conspiracy and, 116; *The New Course*, 103, 227n29; *Oktyabr'skaya Revolutsiya*, 105; opposition of, 106–9; *Our New Tasks*, 108; Poland and, 60; Red Army and, 57; *The Revolution Betrayed*, 111; Russian Civil War and, 58; Soviet's Executive Committee and, 55; Stalin and, 4, 46, 50, 64, 104, 109, 181; Stalin's library and, 86, 103–5; *Tasks in the East*, 104; *Terrorism and Communism*, 92, 105–6, 227n37; *Towards Socialism or Capitalism?*, 108; trade unions and, 62; Trotsky-Zinoviev United Opposition and, 94–5; young writers and, 172
Trotskyism, 103, 110, 111, 117
Trotskyist-Zinovievite Centre, 114
Trotsky-Zinoviev United Opposition, 94–5, 109–10
Troyanovsky, A. A., 125
Truman, Harry, 142, 204, 242n49
Truth about American Diplomats, The (Bucar), 120, 181, 229n90
Tsarist Russia, 72, 79, 125, 134
Tucker, Robert, 37, 142
Tukhachevsky, Mikhail N., 115–16, 154, 235n246
Turaev, Boris, 127, 231n127
Turkey, 79
20 Letters to a Friend (Alliluyeva), 82
Twenty Years of Experience of the Objective Study of the Higher Nervous Activities of Animals (Pavlov), 147

Ukraine in Flames (Dovzhenko), 181
underground labour movement, 47
Under the Rose (France), 100
'Unforgettable Year 1919, The' (Vishnevsky), 187
Union of Soviet Socialist Republics (USSR) creation, 61
United Opposition, 94–5, 109–10, 227n51
United States, 100, 142, 165–70
United Trotskyite-Zinovievite Centre, 113
unreturned books of Stalin, 74, 121, 129, 132

van Ree, Erik, 87, 93, 97, 102, 134
Varga, Eugen, 207
Vasnetsov, Victor, 134
Victory in Right-Bank Ukraine (Dovzhenko), 181
'V. I. Lenin and the American Workers Movement' (Poletaev), 169–70
Vinogradov, Victor, 86, 149, 152
Vipper, Robert, 87, 130, 135–8
Vishnevsky, Vsevolod, 187
Vladimir Ilyich Lenin (Mayakovsky), 178

INDEX

Vlasik, Nikolai, 7
Voitolovsky, L. N., 86
Volkogonov, Dmitry, 68–9, 90–1, 111
Voroshilov, Kliment, 13, 116
Vyshinsky, Andrei, 113, 120, 123, 202

war inevitability, 207, 212
Wealth of Nations (Smith), 86
Wells, H. G., 88, 169
western culture, 142–4, 147
What Did Stalin Read? (Medvedev), 94
White Armies, 57, 58
Whitman, Walt, 165
Wilson, Woodrow, 166
Windelband, Wolfgang, 123–4
Winter War, 162
women, 76, 199
Woolf, Virginia, 98
Worker-Peasant Inspectorate, 61
Workers Opposition, 62
Workers Party of Marxist Unification
    (POUM), 117
Worker's Way, The, 21
working class, 47, 48, 107, 169–70
work style, 165, 166
World Crisis, The (Churchill), 86
world revolution, 54, 64, 104, 109, 173
World War II *see* Great Patriotic War
Writers' Union, 143, 184

Yakovlev, Ya. A., 172
Yaroshenko, L. D., 208
Yaroslavsky, Yemel'yan, 23, 28, 29, 44,
    192–3
Yegorov, Alexander, 27
Yerusalimsky, Arkady, 122
Yezhov, Nikolai, 112, 113, 114–15, 118, 119
Young Stalin (Montefiore), 50
Yugoslavia, 34

Zakon Zhizni (Avdeenko), 180–1
Zhdanov, Andrei: All-Union Congress of
    Soviet Writers and, 177–8; anti-western
    campaign and, 119, 143; history textbook
    and, 132, 134, 233n200; literary journals
    and, 183; 'On the International Situation',
    100
Zhdanov, Yury, 144, 147
Zhdanovshchina, 119, 142–4
Zhemchuzhina, Polina, 76, 120
Zhordania, Noe, 61
Zhukov, Georgy, 13, 158, 198
Zinoviev, Grigory, 29, 54, 85–6, 94–5, 104,
    109–10, 112–14
Žižek, Slavo, 101
Zola, Émile, 25
Zolotukhina, Yevgenia, 82, 94
Zoshchenko, Mikhail, 183–4
Zubalovo dacha, 74, 77, 85